W9-CIN-104

RHETORIC & DEMOCRACY

RHETORIC AND PUBLIC AFFAIRS SERIES

RHETORIC & DEMOCRACY

PEDAGOGICAL AND POLITICAL PRACTICES

Edited by Todd F. McDorman and David M. Timmerman

Michigan State University Press • *East Lansing*

Michigan State University Press
East Lansing, Michigan 48823-5245

Printed and bound in the United States of America.

14 13 12 11 10 09 08   1 2 3 4 5 6 7 8 9 10

LIBRARY OF CONGRESS CATALOGING-IN-PUBLICATION DATA
Rhetoric and democracy : pedagogical and political practices / edited by Todd F. McDorman and David M. Timmerman.
p. cm.—(Rhetoric and public affairs series)
Includes bibliographical references and index.
ISBN 978-0-87013-835-5 (hardcover : alk. paper) 1. Democracy. 2. Democracy—Study and teaching. 3. Rhetoric—Political aspects. I. McDorman, Todd F. II. Timmerman, David M.
JC423.R458 2008
321.801'4—dc22
2008017054

Cover and book design by Sharp Des!gns, Inc., Lansing, Michigan

g green press initiative   Michigan State University Press is a member of the Green Press Initiative and is committed to developing and encouraging ecologically responsible publishing practices. For more information about the Green Press Initiative and the use of recycled paper in book publishing, please visit *www.greenpressinitiative.org*.

Visit Michigan State University Press on the World Wide Web at
www.msupress.msu.edu

Contents

Acknowledgments

The essays in this volume began their public life as working papers designed to stimulate discussion. That is to say that they were first presentations on the theme of rhetoric and democratic citizenship at a conference held at Wabash College in April of 2005. That conference, the Brigance Colloquy, was also held in honor of W. Norwood Brigance, a Wabash professor from 1922 until 1960, a leader in the early history of the contemporary field of rhetorical studies in the United States, and a fierce proponent of the role of rhetoric in the formation and maintenance of democracies. This colloquy was hosted and funded by the Center of Inquiry in the Liberal Arts (CILA), an enterprise supported by the Lilly Endowment. CILA supports the good work of scholars and teachers through initiatives and studies undertaken to strengthen and enhance liberal arts education. The Brigance Colloquy and this volume are appropriately and happily part of this larger project.

From our first contacts with our disciplinary colleagues about the colloquy, it was clear that both W. Norwood Brigance and the connections between rhetoric and democracy remain foundational and enduring for scholars in the field. In addition, the beginnings of the liberal arts tradition, founded as it was in the schools of Isocrates, Plato, and Aristotle, locates its origin within this same intellectual and material space created by the interplay of rhetoric and democracy.

There are many to recognize for their contributions to this project and we are thankful to have the opportunity and space to do so. We thank Roger Billings, Wabash College Trustee and student of Brigance, for encouraging us to pursue the Brigance Colloquy. We also thank Mauri Ditzler, former Dean of Wabash College and current President of Monmouth College, for his enthusiastic response in our earliest conversations with him. Charlie Blaich, the Director of Inquires for CILA, provided helpful guidance and suggestions that improved our plans each step of the way. The Center staff, most especially Bill Doemel and Christina Gilbert, helped execute a flawless meeting of sixteen Colloquy scholars over three days including several campus events and multiple audiences. Jeana Rogers and her staff in the Wabash Media Center handled a range of media needs from the individuals involved, both on and off campus, and did so with professionalism and ease.

As the colloquy honored W. Norwood Brigance, we were greatly and significantly aided by our colleagues Vic Powell and Joe O'Rourke, emerti professors in our department. They contributed from their libraries, files, and, most importantly, from their memories. They were able to do much that none of us currently in the department, all born after Brigance's passing, could ever do. Joe also made available materials concerning the Speakers Bureau that Brigance founded to Denise Bostdorff for her chapter on the pedagogical legacy of Brigance. We were similarly aided by Brigance's daughter, Shirley Oest, and his grandson, Jack Oest. Their continued support of the annual Brigance Forum Lecture, as well as their contribution of pictures and memories to the colloquy, were also indispensable. Wabash alumnus David Burns wrote the only known PhD dissertation on Brigance, and we were aided by that work and his special donation of a copy of it to the department, given at the time of the colloquy. Beth Swift, Wabash College archivist, also contributed significantly as we worked to trace Brigance's career, particularly as it related to his work on rhetoric and democracy. A student research intern, Aaron Flagg, Wabash class of 2005, helped to track down nearly every work published by Brigance and to construct a time line we utilized in several ways during the colloquy and continue to use in our classes. Additional help came from Debbie Polley in the Lilly Library at Wabash and Eileen Bowen, administrative assistant for the Rhetoric Department.

The colloquy in April 2005 included a larger collection of scholars than is represented in this volume. In addition to the contributors of these essays, the colloquy included Jennifer Abbott (Wabash College), Cara Finnegan (University of Illinois), Thomas Goodnight (University of Southern California), Robert Hariman (Northwestern University), and John Lucaites (Indiana University). The colloquy conversations and discussions, to which these scholars contributed, became the fuel that kept this project going and resulted in this volume. We are obviously in a better position than most to see this, but it is clear to us the many ways in which those discussions, the common recognition of the value of democracy and the potential of rhetoric, came together to produce the fine set of essays here included.

We greatly appreciate the generosity of time and intellectual fellowship provided by the scholars who contributed chapters to this volume. In particular, we appreciate their humility and good humor in responding to our guidance and feedback, and their patience in seeing this project through to completion. For us it was a particularly interesting experience given the pedigree of the contributors to the volume, as well as our relationships with them (which in some cases include former professors and dissertation committee members). As for the work of the volume editors, the effort put into this project, from conceptualizing and planning the colloquy, to the writing and editing, was shared equally. The order of our names on the final product is nothing more—or less—than the result of a coin flip. This has been an enriching experience and one that allowed us to further grow from genial colleagues to good friends.

We also owe a good deal to the professional staff at Michigan State University Press for overseeing the production of this work. The two anonymous reviewers of the volume played a significant role in improving its quality through their close reading and critiques. Finally, series editor Marty Medhurst, while also contributing to the volume, helped these two first time editors see a productive, if difficult, path forward; when left to themselves, they saw only obstacles and barriers.

We dedicate this volume to W. Norwood Brigance for his contributions to the field of Speech and the legacy he established at Wabash College.

We, along with our colleague Jennifer Abbott, have sought to preserve the legacy that he, Vic Powell, and Joe O'Rourke have left to us while seeking to extend and strengthen it in our own unique ways.

Rhetoric and Democracy

David M. Timmerman and Todd F. McDorman

Not only is history written with words. It is made with words. Most of the mighty movements affecting the destiny of the American nation have gathered strength in obscure places from the talk of nameless men, and gained final momentum from leaders who could state in common words the needs and hopes of common people. Great movements, in fact, are usually led by men of action who are also men of words, who use words as instruments of power, who voice their aims in words of historic simplicity.

—William Norwood Brigance, "Preface" to *A History and Criticism of American Public Address*, vol. 1, 1943

From the Declaration of Independence to the Constitution, from the Gettysburg Address to Martin Luther King Jr.'s "I Have a Dream," it is no exaggeration to suggest that the American democratic revolution has been nourished and accompanied by a rhetorical revolution of similar magnitude. Perhaps this is what W. Norwood Brigance sought to convey in the above quotation found in the preface to the first volume of *A History and Criticism of American Public Address*.[1] Brigance's perspective may have given too much credence to the notion that "great men" [*sic*] make history, and certainly the study of rhetoric has developed and matured since his time. But his idea that American nationhood, history, democracy, and social movements are driven by the power of rhetoric is one that rhetorical scholars continue to embrace and explore.

This volume offers perspectives on the relationship of rhetoric and democracy. Each chapter, in varied ways, examines the relationship of these entities. In some cases this is achieved by considering the importance and potential of rhetorical education; in others this is done by offering rhetorical critique of democratic practice. In some chapters the focus is on democratic citizenship, and in others it is on democratic deliberation. Regardless of orientation, however, each offers insights into the commonalities of rhetoric and democracy and their mutually interdependent and complex relationship.

The essays in this volume were originally working papers developed by scholars who gathered at Wabash College for the Brigance Colloquy in the spring of 2005 to discuss the relationship of rhetoric and democracy. By starting with the work of Brigance, the volume provides an opportunity to consider the beginnings of the rhetoric-democracy relationship; encourages the examination of the development of that relationship via the emergence of rhetoric, or speech, as a discipline of study and focus in modern academic departments; and prompts reflection on what the tools of rhetoric can bring to the study of democracy as we move forward as a discipline, society, and world. Put differently, the volume is intended to be a resource for students and scholars of rhetoric in making the best use of the past of the discipline, setting forth some of the best work and thinking on rhetoric and democracy in the present, and challenging rhetorical studies in terms of what it can become and contribute in the future. In doing so, we hope this volume can be of great use to students of rhetoric in thinking about the birth, growth, and future of the discipline, as well as of value and benefit to those outside the discipline who have interests in democracy, its operation, and its potential betterment.

This examination of the foundational relationship between rhetoric and democracy demonstrates their symbiosis, as well as how each is critical to and challenging of the other. It is clear that rhetoric and democracy feed off of one another in complex ways. We find their relationship to be a fascinating one, and the essays in this volume serve to heighten our appreciation. In introducing the volume, we begin with a brief reflection on the classical history of the rhetoric-democracy relationship, consider the reemergence of that relationship in the American birth of academic rhetoric and the work of Brigance, and frame the volume's essays as reflections and responses not only to the present state of the rhetoric-democracy relationship, but as commentaries on what each might become in conjunction with the other.

Rhetoric and Democracy in Classical Athens

Democracy, the power of the people, was constituted in and through rhetoric. We take the relationship between the two to be a necessary one, in the sense that democracy is impossible without the practice of public discourse and dialogue among citizens. We find it difficult to imagine a society in which the power to rule is shared among those ruled without the presence of rhetoric through which to do the sharing. Indeed, at the most basic level we see that the power of the people was founded in and exercised through rhetoric. This occurred initially, we know, in a particular place and time, fifth and fourth century BCE Athens. It was there and then that tyranny was overthrown—but not only that. As Josiah Ober notes, with the invention of the term and the practice of *demokratia*, classical Athens "achieved and maintained the 'negative freedom' from subjection not by a doctrine of inalienable constitutional or legal rights, but by the 'positive freedom' of citizens to participate directly in politics—to deploy power and to establish public meanings."[2]

Perhaps the central characteristic of classical Athenian democracy was the prominence of the citizen as the chief political agent. Harvey Yunis captures this aspect of Athenian democratic culture by noting the absence of many other political agents we might imagine, and that often dominate contemporary democracies in ways they did not in Athens.

> *Demokratia* was meant literally: the *demos*—the adult male citizen body in its entirety—held power (*kratos*), and they did so unconditionally. Traditional social and economic divisions within the citizen body did not disappear; but full and equal political and legal privileges—that is,

citizenship—were held by all Athenian men regardless of family background or wealth. The demos delegated no authority or power to any person or group of persons to decide matters independently on their behalf.
There was no legislature or parliament. There were no political offices.
There were no political parties. The polis employed clerks and scribes
and possessed slaves for numerous tasks, but there was no professional
state bureaucracy. There were no professional politicians, professional
lawyers, or professional judges. Neither any religious office nor status of
wealth, birth, or education entailed legitimate political authority. Within
the citizen body, there was no ruling elite of any kind.[3]

While rhetoric was central to the operation of the democratic polis, at the
same time we must be careful not to idealize what took place in ancient
Athens, which, much like early America, included the complete exclusion of women, the foreign-born, and slaves. However, even with these
and other qualifications, the shift to democracy in classical Athens was
stunning. Before turning to the emergence of rhetoric as an academic
discipline, as well as the work of Brigance, we wish to highlight the synergistic and at times contentious relationship between classical rhetoric and
democracy—a relationship that remains relevant and likewise previews
some of the themes of the essays in this volume.

The political structure of Athenian democracy essentially established
the mutual interplay of democracy and rhetoric. The sharing of power
took place, principally, through the sharing of discourse, and the sharing
of discourse among citizens was the chief means for constituting democratic governance and society, and at a foundational level, power itself.
For example, citizens were both enabled and encouraged to participate in
the assembly and juries through pay, all citizens were enabled to serve as
magistrates of various types through the use of the lot in choosing those
who filled the office, and all matters of the state were brought for public
discussion and deliberation. Of course, these patterns of operation put
great responsibility on the shoulders of average citizens. As Ober explains,
"The practice of democracy assumed that citizens had a capacity to reason
together, in public (as well as in private), via frank speech, and that the
results of those deliberations would (in general and over time) conduce
to the common good. Deliberating meant listening as well as speaking;
accepting good arguments as well as making them."[4] These democratic
practices, drawing in a relatively high percentage of the citizenry, naturally

highlight the prominence and importance of rhetoric for democracy. In our own day, what public communication we do have is typically one way: from media source to our televisions, computer screens, radios, or iPods. Perhaps it is easy for us to forget the day in ancient Greece when the exchange of information was largely two-way: where citizens met in a live setting and exchanged discourse via the human voice in the various levels of governmental structure from the deme to the polis.

One of the persistent claims that is made about this live, unmediated public communication is that the decisions that the assembly and the juries made were enhanced, beyond those that would be made by individuals themselves or even smaller groups of individuals. As Manville notes, "The citizens, through debate and common discussion as a multitude, were able to reach sounder, more sensible decisions than could individuals or any elite."[5] We will see this theme reiterated in this volume as several essays lament that the presence of in-person, face-to-face rhetorical exchange has receded dramatically in the modern context. To the extent that groups, on the basis of such exchange, do in fact make better decisions than individuals, our democracy is harmed by this reality. Sadly, at every level of American governance we seem to see this same pattern, a move away from open, rational, and engaged debate. The results may include less effective decision making, but in what amounts to a downward spiral, it is clear that it also leads to decreased unity and public identity.

At the same time, the relationship between rhetoric and democracy is also one of both challenge and critique. The rhetorical practices of a community must continuously adapt, grow, and develop if they are to serve the community well. The citizens of these communities must themselves take up these practices and engage in rhetorical exchange. This gives rise to the ongoing need for education generally in a democracy, and to rhetorical education in particular.

At a number of levels, however, we must acknowledge that the empowerment of the public through the use of public discourse was not seen as a pure good. The citizen, individually and corporately, was seen to have significant limitations. These weaknesses are chronicled well in the writings of elite critics such as Plato, Isocrates, Thucydides, and Aristophanes, to name a few.[6] Their works paint a reasonably consistent picture of a demos that at times was easy to manipulate, gullible, distracted, and lacking in motivation for the task of self-governance. In addition, their characterizations of assembly meetings leave the impression that those meetings were, to a certain extent, chaotic and disorganized. Moreover, the great fear that individual political speakers would seek their own personal gain or welfare over that of the city-state was also a persistent concern.

In a related matter, in the dialogues of Plato, we find the intelligence of political speakers repeatedly questioned. Plato feared that those who did not know were leading the assembled citizens into error. Many have noted, and it is not too hard for us to imagine, the motivated characterizations of the demos by these elite classical authors, but even still, we must resist the urge to imagine either the demos themselves, or the public meetings at which they operated as a demos as ideal users or receivers of rhetoric. As Yunis argues, "Political rhetoric was meant to persuade the demos while overcoming their natural and inherent resistance to prudence and understanding."[7] Better is recognition that, particularly in the writings of Isocrates and Aristotle on political rhetoric, there was the call to improve the quality of political speaking and deliberation in the face of such limitations.[8]

We can infer from a number of Athenian practices and laws that the potentially negative factors involved in the pairing of rhetoric and democracy were held in check. These would include the oath magistrates took not to arbitrarily redistribute private property, the law forbidding hubris, the law against passing restrictions designed to apply to a single individual, and "the procedures of *graphē paranomōn* and *graphē nomōn mē epitēdeiōn theinai*, whereby the proposer of a decree in the Assembly or a law to the *nomothetai* could be indicted for having proposed a measure inimicable to the established values of the Athenians."[9] Two-and-a-half millennia later, many of these same fears persist in our own day. There is still concern in our country that the majority of the citizenry lack the ability, either intellectually or practically, to stay well-enough informed to engage fully in the political process. The enormous size of the American democracy also poses tremendous difficulties for participation that classical Athens did not face.

Finally, the challenge and critique operates in the other direction as well, as rhetorical practice serves to challenge both individuals and communities in their democratic engagement. Included in this is the absolute necessity of dissenting voices. Such voices pull back on the reins of a citizenry that might otherwise charge ahead without adequate thoughtfulness and reflection. This is because, as Ober contends, "A vibrant democracy depends on the efforts, not only of citizen advocates dedicated to promoting its continued existence, but also of citizen dissidents who advocate its revision or even its replacement."[10] Thus, in this way, rhetoric and democracy, even in the process of challenge and critique, work hand in hand with one another.

Rhetoric and Democracy in the American Context

When we advance to the American context, we find reverberations from the same dynamics and concerns generated by the classical relationship of rhetoric and democracy. Although the American democratic revolution relied upon and created space for expanded rhetorical practice, here rhetorical education was of a vastly different sort than in classical Athens. This is not to deny that the revolution relied upon the power of rhetoric in the unity- and identity-building functions of its founding documents. Nor does it discount the rich rhetorical tradition of iconic episodes of American nationhood—from the oratory of Webster, Clay, and Calhoun, to the Lincoln-Douglas debates, to the abolitionist and women's rights movements—but principled rhetorical study was of a different character The rich, overt connections of rhetoric and democracy so essential to the practice of both during the classical era were largely absent at the birth of American democracy. In fact, Warren Guthrie notes the "almost complete lack of the classical influence in early rhetorical teaching in America." According to Guthrie, "it seems clear that Aristotle, Cicero, and Quintillian exerted little influence on the beginnings of American rhetorical theory."[11] Instead, the writings of Peter Ramus, who reduced rhetoric to ornamentation of style and delivery and gave all elements of invention and substance to logic, were the most influential in the American colonies, much to the detriment of the development and practice of a substantive rhetoric.[12]

Early interest in rhetoric was limited to the teaching of speechmaking. Students were trained to demonstrate their "oral prowess" in the context of literary and debating societies.[13] Almost from their founding, colleges such as Harvard and Yale required student training in syllogistic disputation and orations, while in 1744, Benjamin Franklin advocated more extensive training in speaking in his *Proposals Relating to the Education of Youth in Pennsilvania (sic)*.[14] In the decades after the American

Revolution, the study of rhetoric was dominated by the work of Hugh Blair, which was widely adopted at colleges beginning in the 1780s. Blair's work was supplemented by treatises by George Campbell and Richard Whately. All of this is to say that a distinctively American rhetoric had little influence. Nonetheless, the study of rhetoric and oratory, as the two were frequently linked, was a predominant component in American education, with a mixing of the principles of elocutionists and the influence of Blair's *belles-lettres*.[15] To be sure, American rhetorics developed—notable among them the lectures of Princeton president John Witherspoon and the lectures of John Quincy Adams, first Boylston Professor of Rhetoric and Oratory at Harvard College. Still, these and subsequent rhetorics developed after 1850 were almost purely functional, with an emphasis on rhetoric as exclusively a practical art rather than a discipline with tools of critique.[16]

However, the state of democracy and rhetorical education began to change—in ways of benefit to both—between 1880 and 1920. Politically, this time frame included the rise of populism and the Progressive Era, while at the same time, the democratic ideals of the nation were tested by ongoing social inequalities and divisions related to race, gender, and class. The meaning of democracy and the power of the people to advocate for substantial change were at issue. Platform speaking, the organization of lyceums, and the Chautauqua thrived, with Henry Ward Beecher, Wendell Phillips, and Susan B. Anthony among the most popular and prolific speakers.[17] At the same time, it was an era of growth and development in American speech education, with the foundations of professional association being established. During this time, the National Association of Elocutionists (1892–1916), the Eastern Public Speaking Conference (1910), and the National Association of Academic Teachers of Public Speaking (1914), the forerunner to today's National Communication Association, were formed.[18] Split from English departments over disagreements regarding how speech should be taught and regarded, as well as what should be its content, the founders of the NAATPS laid the groundwork for later discussion of the relevance of rhetoric to democracy. NAATPS founders "believed that public speaking, debate, and discussion were indispensable to the operation and success of a political and economic society founded on freedom of enterprise and freedom of debate."[19] The basis for the optimism, voiced as early as an editorial in volume 2 of the *Public Speaking Review* in 1912, was located in the tenor of orations and intercollegiate debates—debates that "directly reflected the political, social, and reform movements" of the times.[20]

By 1920, few colleges and universities lacked at least some instruction in speech or rhetoric, with academic departments being common. With the assistance of intercollegiate debate and oratory contests, speech course work in argumentation and public speaking bloomed, while elocution instruction declined. Infused with "new vigor from the modern sciences, particularly psychology, from which it derived material for the study of audience behavior," and buoyed by the growth of curricular specialization, "Speech departments, accordingly, came into being as an expression of the great forces which were changing the American educational scene, as these forces converged with the interest and energies of men who made the teaching of speech their profession."[21] Moreover, post-1920 rhetoric courses began to focus more on the study of the "history and criticism of rhetoric" rather than on "rhetoric as practical instruction in composition."[22]

During this time, and through the conclusion of World War II, early work in the field was frequently "motivated by the perception that speech was an important characteristic of democracy." As Herman Cohen explains in his history of the discipline, "The profession viewed the teaching of speech as a means of providing students with tools of democracy. The commitment to speech in the interest of a democratic society was most marked in the late 1930s and 1940s."[23] For instance, scholars such as A. Craig Baird, Alan H. Monroe, James M. O'Neill, and Herbert Wichelns reflected on the relationship of speech, citizenship, and democracy. Baird, a 1907 graduate of Wabash College and a teacher of Brigance at the University of Iowa, argued that speech scholars must "see that the participants in debate and discussion . . . present the varied points of view. We assume that the best democracy results from free discussion."[24]

It was in this context and era, as Medhurst explores in chapter 1, that W. Norwood Brigance not only established a well-known legacy as a teacher-scholar and as a president of the Speech Association of America, but was among these early scholars in engaging the relationship of rhetoric—or speech, as he called it—and democracy in a sustained fashion. For Brigance and his contemporaries, rhetoric was the foundational element that made democratic citizenship possible. And although Brigance did not fail to see rhetoric's potential for harm, he argued that this too was a necessity. In short, this potential for harm was a necessary condition for its presence in democratic societies, for "People in democracies believe that the greatest freedom of speech gives the greatest safety. They believe it is just as important to have the right to be wrong as the right to be right; for where you cannot utter a wrong opinion, you will not long have the right to utter the right opinion. They believe that even if a man is a quack or a fool, the best safeguard is to let him advertise his state of mind by speaking."[25] The close connection that Brigance made between rhetorical practice and a free, democratic society was a central feature of his life and work. His Wabash colleague Victor M. Powell praised Professor Brigance in a eulogy published in the *Quarterly Journal of Speech*: "For forty years by precept and example he taught the highest ideals of responsible citizenship in a free society."[26]

Evidence of Brigance's concern for the relationship between rhetoric and democratic citizenship can be located in some of his earliest works, such as "The Debate as Training for Citizenship" in 1926. Though the forms that speechmaking take have expanded dramatically since 1926, Brigance's words continue to ring true: "We are still a nation of speechmakers and so long as we continue as a republic we shall in all probability remain one. We demand of our public citizens that they be effective speakers. Let us then not cast aside this valuable training for citizenship."[27] Similarly, in the inaugural 1935 issue of the *Southern Speech Bulletin* (known today as the *Southern Communication Journal*), Brigance praised the influence of speech in a changing society. Not only did he claim that "it is almost literally true that good speech has replaced the gun and the axe as an instrument of survival on fittest terms," but that teachers of speech were obligated to heed the "coming age." To this end, he prophesied and forewarned that "The undetected undercurrent for good speech is becoming a visible wave. If we teachers of speech fail to recognize it we are blind to the facts and negligent to our responsibility. Now is the time to take measure of the facts, to take stock of our ability to meet the needs, and to press forward."[28]

The relationship of rhetoric and democracy became a more prominent, almost constant, feature of Brigance's work during and subsequent to World War II. In his second editorial upon assuming the editorship of the *Quarterly Journal of Speech* (*QJS*) in 1942, Brigance praised speech as "the chief tool with which civilization was developed and it remains the chief tool by which men work and live together. It transcends the epochs of war and peace. Our mission is to see that it is used effectively and, if possible, wisely."[29] And, under Brigance's editorship, in 1943 *QJS* began to run a section entitled "The Nation at War," which published scholarly reflections on the connections of teaching speech to the preservation of freedom and democracy during wartime.[30]

Over the next ten years, Brigance's scholarship reflected his concern for democracy, public deliberation, citizenship, and the connection of speech to these concepts. This included essays such as "Effectiveness of the Public Platform" for the *Annals of the American Academy of Political and Social Science* in 1947, and his Speech Association of America presidential address, "Year of Decision," which was subsequently reprinted in the *Quarterly Journal of Speech, Vital Speeches of the Day,* and the *Congressional Record.*[31] In "Effectiveness of the Public Platform," Brigance provides an explanation of the relationship of speech and democracy that is particularly relevant to the debate over the role of rhetoric in democratic decision making:

> Democracy, in truth, is not maintained by developing identical convictions among its citizens. . . . Democracy is rather maintained by developing common sentiments and enthusiasms; and these sentiments and enthusiasms are acquired by *contagion,* by the assembling of groups in the quiet of the schoolroom, in the calm of the church, in the boisterousness of the meeting place, by people meeting together, listening together, thinking together, applauding together.
>
> This, then, is the basic purpose of public address: to water and cultivate ideas, convictions, hopes, sentiments, and enthusiasms in a way and to a degree that cannot be reached while people are separated as individuals.[32]

Brigance's words have as much meaning today as they did sixty years ago—and they serve as a powerful reminder of rhetoric's centrality to the practice of reasoned deliberation. The type of public address, speech, and rhetoric referred to by Brigance is eminently respectful ("common sentiment," "listening together"), entirely inclusive, and met with focused reflection ("quiet," "calm," "thinking"). It is the type of discourse that enables a community to prosper.

If the nature of the rhetorical practice advocated by Brigance was in any doubt, that doubt is resolved in his other works on the topic. In underscoring the importance of developing nations peopled by "those who have learned to *talk* it out," as opposed to those who "want to *shoot* it out," in "Year of Decision" Brigance puts the onus of democratic civilization's survival on the effectiveness of education. Furthermore, this education is based on the type of rationality most highly prized in a democracy: "I submit further that every educated person ought to know when a thing is proved and when it is not proved, should know how to investigate and to analyze a proposition that confronts him, and how to search for a solution, how to talk about it effectively before others, and how to contribute to a discussion on problems of joint interest."[33] Similarly, in his April 1952 *QJS* essay, "General Education in an Industrial and Free Society," Brigance argued that the survival of democracy was dependent on speech instruction—a point he reiterated in a September 1952 essay in *The Speech Teacher.* There he argued that "From the beginning of civilization speech-making has been inherent in human society, and a free society cannot exist without it."[34] From the vantage point of his own day, a time when the cold war threatened to develop into something even more devastating, the inherent and deeply rooted relationship between rhetoric and democracy clearly necessitated practical instruction in speechmaking.

Arguably, with the transition of several former Soviet-bloc countries to more democratic forms of governance, and with more democratically oriented governments arising in other parts of the world, Brigance's focus is just as timely today. In his own day, Brigance saw democracy on the rise around the world, and this clearly fueled his passion for rhetorical pedagogy. He referred to this as "the rise of the little man" and believed that it placed a great responsibility upon colleges and universities to train for citizenship:

Now, in the mid-twentieth century, we are faced by a world revolution which colleges ought to enable students to understand. This revolution is not Communism. The Communists are in fact only surf riders on the crest. The real revolution is the rise of the little man all over the world; 2,000 years ago he was a slave; 500 years ago he was a serf; 200 years ago he was a political eunuch; 100 years ago he was inarticulate and unorganized. . . . Two centuries ago this little man could live in hunger—while college students were taught Plato and were excluded by the curriculum from the study of social justice in the age of machines. Today if he lives in hunger he will destroy nations."[35]

For his part, Brigance's embrace of the potentialities of rhetorical education and the threat posed by a failure to meet these potentialities culminated in his 1952 textbook, *Speech: Its Techniques and Disciplines in a Free Society*, through which he influenced generations of students concerning the relationship of rhetoric to democracy.[36]

Rhetoric and Democracy: Present Challenges and Future Possibilities

As noted, the essays in this volume began as contributions to a colloquy held at Wabash College in honor of W. Norwood Brigance. The enthusiastic response we received from the rhetorical scholars interested in discussing rhetoric and democracy was a testament to the continuing significance of this most important relationship for human societies. Following the example of Brigance and his commitment to the absolutely necessary relationship between rhetoric and democracy, the colloquy, the work of the scholars, and this volume are all dedicated to the examination of this relationship. But this volume is more than an effort to establish the constitutive nature of rhetorical practice for democracy. It is a broad analysis and critique spanning a range of theoretical positions and contexts.

While, as Cohen notes, the field's concern for the relationship of speech to a democratic society seemingly dissipated after the conclusion of World War II, which also corresponded with the conclusion of Brigance's *QJS* editorship, more recently rhetorical scholarship of both theoretical and practical import addressing the implications of rhetoric for the practice of democracy has reemerged.[37] One avenue for this work has been to focus on fostering improved rhetorical praxis in American democracy.[38] Another major area of focus is the study of presidential rhetoric, including campaign rhetoric, the use of crisis rhetoric, and presidential debates.[39] Furthermore, scholars have traced a dramatic shift in the manner in which American presidents have utilized the powers of the office to short-circuit the democratic process under the rubric of the "rhetorical presidency."[40] Other work in the field of rhetorical studies has returned to a focus on pedagogy, and in doing so underscores that a critical component of healthy democracy is citizenship.[41] Such scholarship envisions democracy as inherently rhetorical and best sustained by those with training in rhetoric. The idea, one that is developed in this volume, is one of both promoting civic participation, and using the tools of rhetorical studies to produce citizens who can assess the complex dimensions of democratic decision making. And yet other scholars have engaged the issue of deliberative democracy—as do some authors in this volume—and rhetoric's role in that discussion.[42]

This book seeks to bring together some of these threads in the study of rhetoric and democracy, to offer an examination of rhetoric and democracy in an age where both have grown in stature and complexity. What is the relationship of rhetoric and democracy? How can rhetorical theory help us understand the democratic experiment? How can rhetorical pedagogy improve it? Questions such as these motivate this project and are addressed in various ways by the authors. On the whole, their answers demonstrate that rhetoric and rhetorical training support the creation of useful discourse by citizen-actors, as well as provide the tools and perspectives that enable democratic audiences to evaluate, and critique, the discourses they encounter. Rhetoric can meet the challenges of democracy; it can enhance our skills of deliberation, our power of interpretation, and significantly contribute to the production of democratic citizenship. Ultimately, the volume seeks to serve as a substantive work that brings into focus the role of rhetoric in democracy in producing productive citizens with deliberative prowess.

In addressing the relationship of rhetoric and democracy, the essays in this volume are divided into two parts. The essays constituting part 1 are dedicated to the relationship of rhetoric, rhetorical education, and democracy. Each chapter recalls the importance of speech education to democracy while extending the relationship in new ways and in new places. Each suggests that without the commitment of educators, the role of rhetoric in contemporary democracies may return to an earlier, less powerful role. The essays are also based on another important assumption of rhetorical pedagogy: engaging in public discussion and debate, reason-giving and reason-receiving, is a skill and practice that individuals must learn through the educational process and through engagement in the civic realm.

Chapter 1 is a discussion of Brigance and the development of rhetorical studies into a mature discipline with tools well suited to the consideration of complex issues and questions such as those posed by democracy. Martin J. Medhurst's "William Norwood Brigance and the Democracy of the Dead: Toward a Genealogy of the Rhetorical Renaissance" demonstrates not only the importance of Brigance to rhetorical studies during its infancy but also his contributions in establishing the connection between rhetorical training, rhetorical scholarship, and democracy. Of equal importance is the manner in which Medhurst demonstrates the growth of rhetorical studies—via the foundations established by Brigance and others of his era—into a discipline that offers important contributions to pragmatic and theoretical understandings of the nature of democratic citizenship and deliberation. That is, in the context of a study of Brigance, Medhurst makes the case for how scholars of rhetoric can both enhance our understanding of democratic practice and contribute to robust discussions of citizenship.

Chapter 2, "Preparing Undergraduates for Democratic Citizenship: Upholding the Legacy of William Norwood Brigance through Rhetorical Education," by Denise M. Bostdorff, continues the line of argument developed by Medhurst by further utilizing Brigance in advocating our devotion to the rhetorical training of undergraduate students. Bostdorff demonstrates the importance and influence of a rhetorical education for our students, and the potential impact of this training on their interest in, and capacity for, participation in American democratic practice. Bostdorff's chapter reminds scholars that our most lasting contribution to society is through our students—students who can transform democracy through their intelligent participation. As such, Bostdorff encourages teacher-scholars of rhetoric to foster civic engagement both through the forum of the classroom and beyond it in the form of extracurricular efforts, experiential learning, faculty modeling, and, perhaps most importantly, by promoting undergraduate research.

Chapter 3, "Rhetorical Pedagogy and Democratic Citizenship: Reviving the Traditions of Civic Engagement and Public Deliberation," by J. Michael Hogan, also speaks to the importance of rhetorical education while, simultaneously, encouraging the production of civic-minded scholarship. After detailing problems within the democratic public that have revitalized scholarly interest in civic engagement and democratic deliberation, Hogan challenges scholars to engage in teaching and research grounded in the rhetorical tradition that can assist discourse communities in prosperous deliberation. Specifically, Hogan encourages a re-embrace of the classical and neoclassical traditions of rhetorical theory in teaching citizens how to participate in civic life and to engage in responsible public advocacy. Scholars can assist in this endeavor not only through their teaching, but in the performance of rhetorical criticism whereby they can monitor events in the "marketplace of ideas." Finally, scholars of rhetoric are well armed with the lessons of history—a history steeped in the Progressive Era's success at fostering citizen engagement and deliberation, pointing toward traditions that those trained in rhetoric can pass on to society through renewed efforts to sustain and revitalize the democratic republic.

In chapter 4, James A. Herrick examines the potential of rhetorical pedagogy in a non-Western culture. "Democracy and Rhetorical Education in Lithuania" draws from Herrick's personal experience as a visiting scholar in that country to give an account of the importance rhetorical education might have in burgeoning democracies. Herrick explains that the well-established traditions of Western rhetorical education are often not the shared assumptions of Eastern Europe, where Greek and Roman traditions have little weight, and the individualistic display of rhetorical performance can be regarded with scorn and contempt. As a result, Herrick advocates the culturally sensitive promotion of what he terms the "rhetorical worldview." Such a view, transmitted through rhetorical education, promotes the ethical values of rhetorical practice that are fundamental to nurturing vibrant public discourse. Steeped in a belief that we are all givers and hearers of reason, and with a commitment to skill in rhetoric, standards of evidence, and tested methods of public rationality, it is a perspective that seeks to promote citizenship through the teaching of rhetorical values. Herrick closes with a hopeful example of the enactment of the rhetorical worldview as seen through the 2004 public impeachment of Lithuania's president, Rolandas Paksas.

Collectively, the chapters in part 1 focus on how rhetoric scholars, committed to civic education, may most powerfully shape student ownership of and empowerment in democratic participation through classroom work, assignments, and the modeling teachers do through their own civic engagement. Furthermore, each of these authors brings something new to the understanding of rhetoric and democracy by suggesting new ways to achieve long-held objectives as well as, interestingly, by suggesting the use of tested methods of thinking to renew engagement with democratic practices.

The essays that make up part 2 share an interest in the relationship of rhetoric and democracy, as well as a concern over the challenges confronting continued adherence and dedication to democratic principles. These essays come from different theoretical perspectives in confronting contemporary political situations and practices. Moreover, they show the tremendous need and value in having the public rhetoric that is shared in a democracy analyzed and critiqued on an ongoing basis. Each chapter uses rhetorical critique and theory to consider the challenges and possibilities facing democracy, and demonstrates how an understanding of rhetoric can enhance an understanding of democracy. The authors show that rhetorical scholars in particular can provide a deep level of political and social understanding as well as the best historical and theoretical connections that are most likely to aid rhetoric and democracy.

Part 2 opens with David Zarefsky's chapter, "Two Faces of Democratic Rhetoric." Zarefsky's contribution examines the divide often found between the practice and potential of political rhetoric. In setting forth warnings about, as well as standards for, the production of political rhetoric, Zarefsky sets a path for citizens to engage in productive deliberation, while calling into question the rhetorical performances of public officials. The chapter is an intriguing reflection on the potential rhetorical studies has for serving as a corrective for the powerful tensions inherent in rhetoric and democracy's coexistence.

Remaining in the realm of national politics, in chapter 6, Shawn J. Parry-Giles offers an analysis of campaign discourse from the 2004 presidential election. In "Constituting Presidentiality and U.S. Citizenship in Campaign 2004: NASCAR Dads, Security Moms, and Single Women Voters," Parry-Giles argues that the presidential campaign rhetoric of 2004 constituted a white, gendered citizenry with little deliberative role in the democracy of the United States. Parry-Giles's analysis allows us to see how citizens were constituted in the political campaign, with this constitution offering an extremely narrow perspective on political engagement— essentially reducing it to the act of voting. In so doing, political discourse constitutes citizen participation in such a way as to limit political agency and reduce our deliberative role. According to Parry-Giles, campaign 2004 cast the undecided electorate as almost exclusively white, with males primarily constituted as citizen-spectators defined by sports, married women constituted as citizen-mothers driven to select a candidate based upon limited assessments of security, and single women sexualized and cast as citizen-ingenues. Parry-Giles's conclusion is worth remembering, as she problematizes the reduction of voting to the status of the quintessential act of civic participation. But voting is an act that portends disappointment and post-election alienation unless a more meaningful rhetoric of citizenship, one that moves beyond campaign discourse, emerges to offer citizens continued meaningful avenues for civic action.

Stephen John Hartnett and Greg Goodale offer an analysis of the means by which institutions may surreptitiously erode democratic deliberation within the republic. Thus chapter 7, "Debating 'The Means of Apocalypse': The Defense Science Board, the Military-Industrial Complex, and the Production of Imperial Propaganda," challenges rhetorical critics to attend to institutional actors, particularly those that have encroached upon the deliberative realm. Specifically, Hartnett and Goodale examine the operations of the Defense Science Board, a government-created institution involved in military and weapons planning, and foreign- and domestic-policy analysis. In examining the rise of the organization, from its Eisenhower-era founding, to its role in shaping Reagan-era defense policy, to its influence on policies related to the Global War on Terror, Hartnett and Goodale argue that elite-populated, nonelected institutional entities have vast influence over political decisions. These institutional contexts of rhetorical production, cloaked in invisibility, provide the frameworks for supporting the creation of presidential speeches and policy decisions—the result being that rather than seeing speakers, including the president, as the "seats of origin" for policy decisions, they are more accurately conceived of as nodal points through which decisions are advanced.

Part 2 closes with Gerard A. Hauser's examination of rhetoric, deliberation, and citizenship in political contexts in his chapter, "Rethinking Deliberative Democracy: Rhetoric, Power, and Civil Society." Hauser's chapter, an interesting parallel to Herrick's chapter from part 1 in that they both address rhetoric in emerging democracies, advances a theoretical perspective on a rhetorically influenced model of deliberation in civil society. Hauser's point is that to understand politics as it is experienced in society necessitates using a rhetorical perspective. The claim is borne out through the protest rhetoric of the Solidarity movement in Poland, with their demands weighted toward conditions that enhance communication, and which, in the process, illustrate citizen performance of democracy. Proceeding from his representative anecdote, Hauser sets out a vision for the role of rhetoric as an inventional resource in civil society—a practice that enables social changes. Such changes, which challenge convention, occur most noticeably at the informal level of bottom-up relations that emphasize an inclusion model of participation, rather than models that insert idealized rational norms existing apart from the actual practices of citizen deliberation. Most importantly, the fostering of these relations is dependent on the development of trust among the participants in order to be fully effective in minimizing the impact of power differentials.

The conclusion, "Speaking Democratically in the Backwash of War: Lessons from Brigance on Rhetoric and Human Relations," by Robert L. Ivie, intertextualizes Brigance's scholarly legacy with his own well-known interest in the rhetoric of war. The result is a personal reflection on the prospects and promise of rhetoric for citizenship in a future that ideally will be dedicated much more to solving international problems through *talking* it out rather than *shooting* it out. In returning to W. Norwood Brigance and the meaning of his work on democracy, Ivie sees not only a source of inspiration for a generation of already productive scholars, but the possibility for yet another generation to benefit from his political critique. Ivie offers a glimpse into the politics of Brigance, his view on the future of democracy and rhetoric's role in it, and demonstrates Brigance's foresight into the rise of mass communication and the need and responsibility of leaders to learn the effective practice of ethical rhetoric, as well as his placement of rhetoric as a substantive liberal art charged with the enhancement of human relations. In considering the chapters making up this volume in the context of Brigance's project on democracy, Ivie argues that the contributors have recovered the spirit of Brigance's work, while in the process they have complicated his conception of democracy and revitalized the study of democratic relations. At the same time, Ivie poses new challenges—questioning our ability to interact peaceably and effectively with the democratic Other—for citizens, leaders, and critics as we move into the future.

The contributors to this volume offer a rich set of perspectives regarding how rhetoric, through our teaching, research, and actions, is vital to democracy. Likewise, the scholars offer what we think are engaging commentaries on not only the kinds of political discourse we currently have, but the kinds of discourse—by our leaders, in our campaigns, in our institutions, and in democratic movements—that will allow democratic community to prosper. The relationship between rhetoric and democracy is rich, complex, and synergistic. Appreciation and attention to the implications arising out of their interaction is an important way that we as scholars and citizens can seek to benefit our society, even as political, social, and material contexts shift in dramatic ways.

NOTES

1. The most appropriate way to refer to Brigance is a matter of some debate. His name appears in print in a variety of fashions, including "William Norwood Brigance," "W. Norwood Brigance," and "W. N. Brigance." Adding to the confusion is that his colleagues typically called him "Norwood," some of his friends outside the academy knew him as "Bill," and his students referred to him as "Briggie," at least when he was out of earshot. Commenting on his own preference, Brigance indicates that it is "W. Norwood." Thus that is the manner in which he is primarily referred to when called upon in this volume. David George Burns, "The Contributions of William Norwood Brigance to the Field of Speech" (Ph.D. diss., Indiana University, 1970); Roger Billings, "Briggie," *Wabash Magazine* (Summer/Fall 2005): 58–59.

2. Josiah Ober, *Political Dissent in Democratic Athens: Intellectual Critics of Popular Rule* (Princeton, N.J.: Princeton University Press, 1998), 6.

3. Harvey Yunis, *Taming Democracy: Models of Political Rhetoric in Classical Athens* (Ithaca, N.Y.: Cornell University Press, 1996), 4.

4. Josiah Ober, *Athenian Legacies: Essays on the Politics of Going On Together* (Princeton, N.J.: Princeton University Press, 2005), 130.

5. Philip Brooke Manville, "Ancient Greek Democracy and the Modern Knowledge-Based Organization: Reflections on the Ideology of two Revolutions," in *Demokratia: A Conversation on Democracies, Ancient and Modern*, ed. Josiah Ober and Charles Hedric (Princeton, N.J.: Princeton University Press, 1996), 381–82. See also Aristotle's *Politics 1281a*.

6. *Republic 492b, 493d; Phaedrus 237b; Theaetetus 172b; Nicocles 19; On the Peace 52; History of the Peloponnesian War 3:38, 42.*

7. Yunis, *Taming Democracy*, 280.

8. *Gorgias 456a, 502d, 559d; Phaedrus 259e, 261d; Republic 473d; On the Peace 5; Antidosis 271.2; History of the Peloponnesian War 3.40.*

9. Ober, *Athenian Legacies*, 136.

10. Ibid., 132.

11. Warren Guthrie, "Rhetorical Theory in Colonial America," in *A History of Speech Education: Background Studies*, ed. Karl Richards Wallace (New York: Appleton-Century-Crofts, 1954), 53; Warren Guthrie, "The Development of Rhetorical Theory in America," *Speech Monographs* 13 (1946): 14–15.

12. Guthrie, "The Development of Rhetorical Theory in America," 16.

13. George V. Bohman, "Rhetorical Practice in Colonial America," in *A History of Speech Education in America: Background Studies*, ed. Karl Richards Wallace (New York: Appleton-Century-Crofts, 1954), 61.

14. Bohman, "Rhetorical Practice," 66–67; Guthrie, "The Development of Rhetorical Theory in America," 21; George V. Bohman, "The Colonial Period," in *A History and Criticism of American Public Address*, vol. 1, ed. William Norwood Brigance (New York: McGraw-Hill, 1943), 18–19.

15. Warren Guthrie, "The Development of Rhetorical Theory in America, 1635–1850," *Speech Monographs* 15 (1948): 61–71. For further discussion of elocution in early America, see chapter 1 of Herman Cohen, *The History of Speech Communication: The Emergence of a Discipline, 1914–1945* (Annandale, Va.: Speech Communication Association, 1994), 1–12.

16. Warren Guthrie, "The Development of Rhetorical Theory in America: 1635–1850," *Speech Monographs* 16 (1949): 98–113; Ota Thomas, "The Teaching of Rhetoric in the United States during the Classical Period of Education," in *A History and Criticism of American Public Address*, vol. 1, ed. William Norwood Brigance (New York: McGraw-Hill), 193–209.

17. Kenneth G. Hance, H. O. Hendrickson, and Edwin W. Schoenberger, "The Later National Period, 1860–1930," in *A History and Criticism of American Public Address*, vol. 1, ed. William Norwood Brigance (New York: McGraw-Hill), 120–27, 130–35.

18. Giles Wilkeson Gray, "Some Teachers and the Transition to Twentieth-Century Speech Education," in *A History of Speech Education in America: Background Studies*, ed. Karl Richards Wallace (New York: Appleton-Century-Crofts, 1954), 422–23. As Cohen notes, the Eastern Public Speaking Conference later became the Eastern Communication Association (p. 29). For more on the details of the founding of the NAATPS and its split from the National Council of Teachers of English, as well as the early years of the NAATPS, see chapter 3 of Cohen, *The History of Speech Communication*, 29–84.

19. Frank M. Rarig and Halbert S. Greaves, "National Speech Organizations and Speech Education," in *A History of Speech Education in America: Background Studies*, ed. Karl Richards Wallace (New York: Appleton-Century-Crofts, 1954), 500.

20. Rarig and Greaves, "National Speech Organizations," 502. The editorial referred to is from *Public Speaking Review* 2 (1912): 56.

21. Donald K. Smith, "Origin and Development of Departments of Speech," in *A History of Speech Education in America: Background Studies*, ed. Karl Richards Wallace (New York: Appleton-Century-Crofts, 1954), 456, 459.

22. Smith, "Origin and Development of Departments of Speech," 465. Cohen also discusses the early disciplinary study of rhetoric (*The History of Speech Communication*, 109–18).

23. Cohen, *The History of Speech Communication*, xi. However, none of this is to suggest that the field possessed an egalitarian philosophy superior to that of the rest of the nation. Just as the United States struggled with the internal contradiction of a society that championed democracy while practicing race- and gender-based discrimination, the literature of the emerging field also reflected and confronted such issues (Cohen, xi–xii).

24. Quoted in Cohen, *The History of Speech Communication*, 146. For a more extensive discussion of the relationship of scholarship on speech pedagogy with issues of democracy and freedom, see Cohen, 144–57.

25. Wilhelmina G. Hedde, William Norwood Brigance, and Victor M. Powell, *The New American Speech*, rev. ed. (Philadelphia: J. B. Lippincott Co., 1963), 6.

26. Victor M. Powell, "W. Norwood Brigance, 1896–1960," *Quarterly Journal of Speech* 46 (1960): 236.

27. William Norwood Brigance, "The Debate as Training for Citizenship," *Educational Review* (Nov. 1926): 222–25, at 225.

28. William Norwood Brigance, "American Speech in this Changing Age," *Southern Speech Bulletin* 1 (1935): 15–18, at 16 and 18.

29. W. N. B., "Editorial," *Quarterly Journal of Speech* 28 (1942): 240.

30. Cohen, *The History of Speech Communication*, 152–56.

31. W. Norwood Brigance, "Effectiveness of the Public Platform," *Annals of the American Academy of Political Science* 1 (1947): 70–75; W. Norwood Brigance, "1946: Year of Decision," *Quarterly Journal of Speech* 33 (1947): 127–33.

32. Brigance, "Effectiveness of the Public Platform," 70–71, emphasis in original.

33. Brigance, "1946: Year of Decision," 133.

34. William Norwood Brigance, "General Education in an Industrial Free Society," *Quarterly Journal of Speech* 38 (1952): 177–83; William Norwood Brigance, "Demagogues, 'Good' People, and Teachers of Speech," *Speech Teacher* 1 (1952): 157–62.

35. Brigance, "General Education," 179.

36. William Norwood Brigance, *Speech: Its Techniques and Disciplines in a Free Society* (New York: Appleton-Century-Crofts, 1952). Other rhetorical scholars of the era expressed interest in the rhetoric-democracy relationship as well, though none appear to have pursued it with as much consistency and depth as Brigance. See, for example, Earl W. Wiley, "The Rhetoric of the American Democracy," *Quarterly Journal of Speech* 29 (1943): 157–63. Even more to the point is Virgil L.

Baker and Ralph T. Eubanks, "Democracy: Challenge to Rhetorical Education," *Quarterly Journal of Speech* 46 (1960): 72–78. Echoing Brigance, Baker and Eubanks contended that "The overriding aim of rhetorical education should be the development of men and women with the power to give impulse to the humane values of the democratic ideal" (p. 74). Moreover, they saw speech, speech making, and rhetorical education as having a "special mission" in "reaffirming the ideals of democracy. Democracy will live universally only as its principles and spirit are made articulate through daily speech" (p. 75). See additional examples in Cohen, *The History of Speech Communication*, chapter 6.

37. Cohen, *The History of Speech Communication*, 146, 157. Cohen perhaps overstates the case for the disappearance of discussions of speech and democracy in the discipline's scholarship, given Brigance's continued interest in the issue throughout the 1950s as well as, as Cohen himself notes, the continued publication of Brigance's textbook *Speech: Its Techniques and Disciplines in a Free Society*, even following his death.

38. For example, Professor Shawn Parry-Giles is the director of the Center for Political Communication and Civic Leadership at the University of Maryland. The CPCCL "unites research, education, and public engagement to foster democratic communication by a diverse people" (available online: http://www.comm.center.umd.edu/home.htm, accessed January 31, 2006). Likewise, Professor Roderick P. Hart directs the Annette Strauss Institute for Civic Participation at the University of Texas at Austin. The institute seeks "(1) to conduct cutting-edge research on the ways in which civic participation and community understanding are undermined or sustained, and (2) to develop new programs for increasing democratic understanding among citizens" (available online: http://communication.utexas.edu/strauss/, accessed January 31, 2006). Professor Kathleen Hall Jamieson is the director of the Annenberg Public Policy Center of the University of Pennsylvania. The center conducts "an ongoing evaluation of the quality of contemporary political discourse, including political campaigns, advertising, and speeches" (available online: http://www.annenbergpublicpolicycenter.org/, accessed January 31, 2006). The center also maintains *FactCheck.org*, which evaluates the claims made by presidential candidates (available online: http://www.factcheck.org/, accessed January 31, 2006). Finally, the Voices of Democracy Project, an interdisciplinary collaboration of scholars from Baylor University, Pennsylvania State University, and the University of Maryland, "promotes the study of great speeches and public debates in the humanities in the undergraduate classroom" (available online: http://www.voicesofdemocracy.com/, accessed January 31, 2006).

39. John M. Murphy, "Knowing the President: The Dialogic Evolution of the Campaign History," *Quarterly Journal of Speech* 84 (1998): 23–40; Robert E. Denton Jr., ed., *The 2004 Presidential Campaign: A Communication Perspective* (Lanham: Rowman and Littlefield, 2005); Karlyn Kohrs Campbell and Kathleen Hall Jamieson, *Deeds Done in Words: Presidential Rhetoric and the Genres of Governance* (Chicago: University of Chicago Press, 1990); Leroy G. Dorsey, *The Presidency and Rhetorical Leadership* (College Station: Texas A&M University Press, 2002); Roderick P. Hart, *Verbal Style and the Presidency: A Computer Based Analysis* (Orlando: Academic Press, 1984); Denise Bostdorff, *The Presidency and the Rhetoric of Foreign Crisis* (Columbia: University of South Carolina, 1993); Jim A. Kuypers, *Presidential Crisis Rhetoric and the Press in the Post–Cold War World* (Westport, Conn.: Praeger, 1997); Robert V. Friedenberg, ed., *Rhetorical Studies of National Political Debates–1996* (Westport, Conn.: Praeger, 1997).

40. James W. Caeser, Glen E. Thurow, Jeffrey Tulis, and Joseph M. Bessette, "The Rise of the Rhetorical Presidency," *Presidential Studies Quarterly* 11 (1981): 158–71; Jeffrey K. Tulis, *The Rhetorical Presidency* (Princeton, N.J.: Princeton University Press, 1987); Richard J. Ellis, ed., *Speaking to the People: The Rhetorical Presidency in Historical Perspective* (Amherst: University of Massachusetts Press, 1998); Martin Medhurst, ed., *Beyond the Rhetorical Presidency* (College Station: Texas A&M University Press, 1996); Shawn J. Parry-Giles, *The Rhetorical Presidency, Propaganda, and the Cold War, 1945–1955* (Westport, Conn.: Praeger, 2001).

41. Troy A. Murphy, "Deliberative Civic Education and Civil Society: A Consideration of Ideals and Actualities in Democracy and Communication Education," *Communication Education* 53 (2004): 74–91. Pedagogically significant works noted by Murphy include J. Gastil and J. P. Dillard, "The Aims, Methods, and Effects of Deliberative Civic Education through the National Issues Forums," *Communication Education* 48 (1999): 179–92; J. J. McMillan and J. Harriger, "College Students and Deliberation: A Benchmark Study," *Communication Education* 51 (2002): 237–53; Gordon R. Mitchell, "Pedagogical Possibilities for Argumentative Agency in Academic Debate," *Argumentation and Advocacy* 35 (1998): 41–61; S. P. Morreale and P. M. Backlund, "Communication Curricula: History, Recommendations, Resources," *Communication Education* 51 (2002): 2–18; D. Droge and B. O. Murphy, eds., *Voices of Strong Democracy: Concepts and Models for Service-Learning in Communication Studies* (Washington, D.C.: American Association for Higher Education, 1999); Robert Asen, "A Discourse Theory of Citizenship," *Quarterly Journal of Speech* 90 (2004): 189–211.

42. In 2002, the journal *Rhetoric and Public Affairs* devoted volume 5, issue 2 to deliberative democracy. Particularly pertinent articles for the current discussion

include Gerard A. Hauser and Chantal Benoit-Barné, "Reflections on Rhetoric, Deliberative Democracy, Civil Society, and Trust," 261–76; Robert L. Ivie, "Rhetorical Deliberation and Democratic Politics in the Here and Now," 277–86; and J. Michael Sproule, "Oratory, Democracy, and the Culture of Participation," 301–10.

PART 1

Rhetoric, Rhetorical Education, and Democracy

1

William Norwood Brigance and the Democracy of the Dead: Toward a Genealogy of the Rhetorical Renaissance

Martin J. Medhurst

Rhetoric, as a formal area of study, is an interdisciplinary field. It stretches back to such early Sophists as Protagoras, Gorgias, and Isocrates, rising and falling with peoples and empires over the course of more than 2,500 years, and being reborn only yesterday, in 1914, with the founding of the National Association of Academic Teachers of Public Speaking. Today, rhetoric is taught, in one form or another, in every university in the United States and throughout most of the world. But it was not always so. At the beginning of the twentieth century the study of rhetoric, to the extent that it existed at all, was confined to the netherworld of the elocutionist, or the practiced disregard of the English department. And it was from these two sources—one enthusiastic but nonacademic, and the other academic but unenthusiastic—that the modern study of rhetoric was reconstituted in departments of public speaking and speech. From those humble beginnings, the formal study of rhetoric has now spread to many other disciplines, including classics, language and literature, English, and even certain sectors of political science, government, and sociology. The study of rhetoric, under one label or another, is now ubiquitous.

During the midst of a new rhetorical renaissance, it is appropriate to pause and reflect on where we have been and how we have arrived at our current place of abode. Today's rhetorical scholars, in whatever department of the university they may be housed, are the living embodiment of a rich intellectual tradition. Such scholars represent not only a contemporary presence on the academic scene, but also a living tradition, a corporate embodiment of generations of scholars now long removed from the scene. There is, as G. K. Chesterton put it, a "democracy of the dead," whereby traditions and ideas live on in those who come after. We do not, despite what we might think, invent the world *ex nihilo*. If we are to understand fully our present moment, we must embrace our past, seek to understand it, and celebrate those parts of it that have contributed significantly to who and what we are today.

In this spirit of historical understanding, I begin with a periodization of the field formerly known as "speech," and now called communication, by dividing the field into six eras. I then use this division into eras to discuss the contributions of William Norwood Brigance. My argument is straightforward: the contemporary state of rhetorical studies owes as much to W. Norwood Brigance as to any other single scholar of the founding. To understand why this is so, we need to specify the characteristics of what has come to be called the rhetorical renaissance, trace the pathway by which that renaissance developed, and demonstrate that it was Brigance, perhaps more than any other single scholar, who planted and watered the ground upon which the renaissance has been erected. If we are to understand why the current renaissance has seen a renewed interest in the interface of rhetoric and democratic governance, including studies of judicial, legislative, and presidential rhetoric, we must return to our roots in the early years of the twentieth century.

The Periodization of Rhetorical Research in the Twentieth Century

For analytical purposes, it is useful to divide the rebirth of rhetorical scholarship in the twentieth and early twenty-first centuries into six eras of fifteen years each. Starting with the publication of the first issue of the

CHART 1. SIX ERAS OF RHETORICAL SCHOLARSHIP

Era 1	1915–1930	Era 4	1960–1975
Era 2	1930–1945	Era 5	1975–1990
Era 3	1945–1960	Era 6	1990–2005

Quarterly Journal of Public Speaking in April 1915, our eras break out as set forth in chart 1.

The driving force behind Era 6 is what I and others have labeled the rhetorical renaissance.[1] This renaissance, I shall argue, is characterized by ten markers. These markers will serve as our touchstone for examining the life and scholarship of W. Norwood Brigance, so it behooves me to lay them out in enough detail so that we can clearly discern their chromosomal imprints when we encounter them. These ten markers are listed in chart 2. There may well be other dimensions of the current renaissance, but these ten seem clearly to be present.

The emphasis on texts in context and the study of textuality can be traced to the early and mid-1970s in the work of Newman, Campbell, Hill, Stelzner, Andrews, Lucas, Leff, and Mohrmann in oratory, and in the later 1970s and early 1980s to the work of Benson and Medhurst in film.[2] One of the characteristics of this move toward texts was to open up all sorts of works for rhetorical examination. Not just speeches and films, but novels, letters, songs, prayers, and many other forms of

CHART 2. TEN MARKERS OF THE RHETORICAL RENAISSANCE

1. Recovery of the text in context, and the practice of textual criticism
2. Reemergence of rhetorical history and rhetorical biography
3. Primary focus on making a significant difference in the world of scholarship
4. Contribution to historical revisionism
5. Exploitation of primary sources
6. Establishment of new publishing venues for both books and articles
7. Greatly increased production of scholarly books
8. Engagement with cross-disciplinary audiences
9. Emergence of narrower specialization leading to expert status
10. Expansion and reconceptualization of the public sphere

CHART 3. BOOKS ON RHETORICAL HISTORY, THEORY, CRITICISM, OR BIOGRAPHY, 2000–04

2000	Zelizer	*Remembering to Forget*
2000	Zelizer	*Visual Culture and the Holocaust*
2000	Jamieson	*Everything You Think You Know*
2000	Hasian	*Legal Memories and Amnesias*
2000	Houck	*Rhetoric as Currency*
2000	Eberly	*Citizen Critics*
2000	Mitchell	*Strategic Deception*
2000	Smith	*Quest for Charisma*
2001	Pauley	*Modern Presidency and Civil Rights*
2001	Parry-Giles	*Rhetorical Presidency, Propaganda, and the Cold War*
2001	Hollihan	*Uncivil Wars*
2001	Warnick	*Critical Literacy in a Digital Era*
2001	Ceccarelli	*Shaping Science with Rhetoric*
2001	Benoit	*The Primary Decision*
2001	Hyde	*The Call of Conscience*
2001	Blaney/Benoit	*The Clinton Scandals*
2002	Aune	*Selling the Free Market*
2002	Hasian	*Colonial Legacies*
2002	Bruner	*Strategies of Remembrance*
2002	Branham/Hartnett	*Sweet Freedom's Song*
2002	Wiethoff	*The Insolent Slave*

symbolic inducement were subjected to rhetorical analysis.[3] Given theoretical explication by Leff in 1980, 1986, and 1990,[4] what has come to be known as close reading, in its several varieties, both benefits from and motivates other aspects of the renaissance, including the marker that may, at first glance, seem furthest removed from close reading—the writing of rhetorical history.

Rhetorical history and rhetorical biography have long been claimed as fields of expertise in rhetorical studies. Yet the plain fact is that prior to 1960, prior to the onset of Era 4, our field had produced only seventeen scholarly books on rhetorical/literary history, criticism, theory, or biography, and that includes edited books. Insofar as I can tell, none of these

2002	Hart	*Campaign Talk*
2002	Houck	*FDR and Fear Itself*
2002	Wilson	*The Reconstruction Desegregation Debate*
2002	Hartnett	*Democratic Dissent*
2002	Rowland/Frank	*Shared Land/Conflicting Identity*
2002	Asen	*Visions of Poverty*
2003	Zaeske	*Signatures of Citizenship*
2003	Finnegan	*Picturing Poverty*
2003	Sloop	*Disciplining Gender*
2003	Brummett	*The World and How We Describe It*
2003	Schiappa	*Defining Reality*
2003	Browne	*Jefferson's Call for Nationhood*
2003	Houck/Kiewe	*FDR's Body Politics*
2003	Schultze	*Christianity and the Mass Media*
2003	Haiman	*Religious Expression and the American Constitution*
2004	Kraig	*Woodrow Wilson*
2004	Olson	*Franklin's Vision of Community*
2004	Beasley	*You, the People*
2004	Benson	*Writing JFK*
2004	Stuckey	*Defining Americans*
2004	Terrill	*Malcolm X*
2004	Bytwerk	*Bending Spines*
2004	Hart et al.	*Political Keywords*
2004	Phillips	*Testing Controversy*

book-length treatments led to close examination of individual texts. Yet in the current renaissance, close textual examination has already led to numerous rhetorical histories, criticisms, and biographies of book length. As chart 3 illustrates, in just one five-year period, from 2000–2004, we have produced no fewer than forty-five works.[5]

It is a demonstrable fact that most of these works—and many others—have flowed from close examination of texts. The practice of engaging texts, whether through close reading or some other approach, has led to full-length rhetorical histories, criticisms, and biographies.

The exciting news about all of these new works is that they are making a difference in the scholarly world at large. Not only are they being

noticed by scholars outside of rhetoric proper, but they are being lauded as
significant contributions to scholarship. Recently, the *Journal of American
History* and the *American Historical Review* published reviews of the Browne
and Wilson books. They say, "This is one of the best books on Thomas
Jefferson ever written: sophisticated and clear, persuasive and insightful.
. . . Professor Stephen Howard Browne reveals the depth of Jefferson's
political thought through the medium of his rhetoric. This book is highly
recommended for those interested in American political history, Jeffer-
sonian democracy, political rhetoric, and nineteenth-century political
parties in the United States";[6] and "Kirt H. Wilson has written a very fine
book on one aspect of late nineteenth-century racial rhetoric. His study
centers on the 1875 Civil Rights Act. . . . Wilson has written a careful,
inventive book. He adds complexity and detail to this moment that is not
there in more broadly reaching works such as Eric Foner's *Reconstruction:
America's Unfinished Revolution, 1863–1877* (1988) or Rogers Smith's *Civic
Ideals: Conflicting Visions of Citizenship in U.S. History* (1997). Scholars interested in the history of American political thought will do well to consult
this excellent study."[7]

One reason that many historians are finding our work of such
significance is that we are contributing to historical revisionism. We are
revising the received views of people, products, and processes. We are
advancing our own, often original, interpretations and adducing evidence
to support those claims. And we are doing all this in language and ter-
minology that is both sophisticated and accessible. We are participating
in conceptual and theoretical debates, from the nature of the rhetorical
presidency to Robert Ivie's latest works on the relationship of rhetoric,
war, and democracy.[8] Political scientists, too, are starting to take note, as
the works of Mel Laracey, Francis A. Beer, and Colleen Shogan attest.[9]

Driving all of this remarkable scholarship is the realization that the
days of the armchair philosopher/rhetorician are gone. Research in
primary sources is now the engine that powers most of the rhetorical
renaissance. Whether it is James Kimble's award-winning dissertation on
the war-bond drives of World War II, or Cara Finnegan's research in the
visual archives of the Farm Security Administration, or Davis Houck and
David Dixon's mining of speeches and sermons from the early civil rights
movement, all are based on primary-source documentation.[10] Without
continuing recourse to research in primary sources, the rhetorical renaissance could not—and cannot—be sustained.

It is precisely this renewed commitment to primary sources that has led to and sustained the founding and operation of new book series and journals over the course of the last two eras, from 1975–2005. It is hard to say which was cause and which effect—whether research called forth the book series, or whether the establishment of the book series called forth the research. I suspect it was a little of both. In any event, the reinvigoration of the one and only pre-1975 scholarly book series at Southern Illinois University Press, combined with the founding of new series at University of South Carolina Press (1984), University of Alabama Press (1989), Michigan State University Press (1994), and Texas A&M University Press (1996), has resulted in the publication of scores of books that might not otherwise exist. These university presses, combined with the early commitment of Praeger/Greenwood to series in "Political Communication" and "Great American Orators," has allowed rhetorical studies to make the move from an almost exclusively article-based field in 1975 to a field where books are now expected for tenure and promotion.

This transition from an article-based field to a book-based discipline has happened entirely in Eras 5 and 6. That is not to claim that no one published a book before 1975. It is to claim that prior to the mid-1980s, sole-authored books were such a rarity as to occasion as much comment about the form (book) as the content. While Marie Hochmuth Nichols (1963), Edwin Black (1965), and Anthony Hillbruner (1966) had all produced book-length works on critical method in the 1960s, it fell to Stephen E. Lucas (1976), Roderick P. Hart (1977), Robert Underhill (1981), Ronald L. Hatzenbuehler and Robert L. Ivie (1983), and Kathleen Hall Jamieson (1984) to inaugurate the scholarly-book era in the discipline by producing substantive rhetorical studies, all of which were published by university presses.[11] Era 6 alone has produced more books than all other previous eras combined. And that is precisely why book publication is a mark of the rhetorical renaissance.

Another mark of the renaissance is the active engagement with cross-disciplinary audiences. This engagement takes several forms: (1) publication of books that include scholars from multiple disciplines; (2) sponsorship of conferences that feature scholars from multiple disciplines; (3) publication in journals outside of rhetorical studies, including such venues as *Presidential Studies Quarterly, Armed Forces & Society, Pacific Historical Review, Journal of the History of Ideas, Journal of Church and State, Journal of Popular Film and Television*, and many more; (4) utilization of scholars from other disciplines as reviewers for manuscripts and grant applications; (5) presentation of research at disciplinary and interdisciplinary conferences outside of rhetoric or communication proper; and (6) engagement of public audiences through lectures, debates, letters to the editor, guest columns, and articles in popular magazines. In the current rhetorical renaissance, we have continually striven to reach audiences other than ourselves.

One way in which we may be able to reach those other audiences is by becoming acknowledged experts in something specific—a person, an era, a type of discourse, an issue, an ur-text such as the Declaration of Independence, the Federalist Papers, or the Lincoln-Douglas debates. The days of Eras 1–3, when the speech professor was supposed to know a little bit about a lot of different topics, is long past. Audiences, whether scholarly or popular, want to hear acknowledged experts. The only way I know to become such an expert is to study, teach, and publish, preferably in that order. The best test I can think of as to whether someone is an expert in the field is whether that person can publish his or her work not only in our own journals but also in specialized journals and with respected university presses. For example, if one is an expert on Abraham Lincoln, it would be natural to publish in the *Journal of the Abraham Lincoln Association*, as our colleague David Zarefsky has done. All scholars of the rhetorical renaissance are striving to become expert in something.[12]

Finally, our renaissance is marked by the expansion and reconceptualization of the public sphere. The expansion should be clear to all. The public sphere is no longer confined only to the powerful white male, nor is our scholarship. In Era 6, we have produced book-length works on Angelina Grimké, women who signed suffrage petitions, Lady Astor, Margaret Chase Smith, the governing codes of female candidates for political office, and Sojourner Truth; we have written books on Frederick Douglass, Malcolm X, the ideograph of <equality>, Cesar Chavez, the Israeli-Palestinian conflict; we have produced entire issues of journals devoted to the rhetoric of civil rights, to Martin Luther King Jr.'s "Letter from Birmingham Jail," and to the rhetorical dimensions of the murder of Emmett Till.[13] We have also advanced our renaissance by reconceptualizing what it is we mean by the public sphere, with books like Gerard Hauser's *Vernacular Voices* and Robert Ivie's *Democracy and the War on Terror*, as well as a special issue of *Rhetoric & Public Affairs* on deliberative democracy, and a national task-force report on that same topic.[14]

These are the ten markers that constitute a broad, though certainly not exhaustive, outline of the rhetorical renaissance that has character-ized Eras 5 and 6. It is a snapshot of who we are in the first decade of the twenty-first century. But what does all of this have to do with W. Nor-wood Brigance? After all, Brigance was born in the nineteenth century—in 1896, to be precise—and died in 1960. So his active career spanned the last half of Era 1 and all of Eras 2 and 3. I have argued, and still maintain, that the current renaissance was begun, nurtured, and established by what I have called the "greatest generation" of rhetoric scholars—those who received their Ph.D.'s in Era 4, from 1960–1975.[15] Brigance was dead before many in the greatest generation had finished even their bachelor's degrees. So why do I insist that the field today owes as much to Brigance as to any other single scholar of the founding?

Please note my carefully worded proposition. By "the field," I mean rhetorical studies only, not the much larger field of communication studies generally. By "owes," I mean has an intellectual debt to—that rhetorical studies is intellectually indebted to Brigance in ways that relate directly to the rhetorical renaissance. By "as much . . . as to any other single scholar," I mean that Brigance is one of perhaps seven or eight people without whom the field as we know it today would not have developed as it did. And by "the founding," I mean Era 1, the period from 1915–1930. For purposes of my analysis, however, I am going to extend the founding by five years—until 1935—and begin by analyzing the publication patterns of those first twenty years. Since Brigance is now our focus, it is important to note that he published his first article in the *Quarterly Journal of Speech Education* in 1925. By extending ten years before—to the founding of the national journal in 1915—and ten years after—to 1935, we find that thirty-one scholars, arrayed in alphabetical order in chart 4, published their first scholarly article during this twenty-year span.[16]

Of those who began publishing between 1915 and 1935, only these thirty-one rhetoric scholars ended up with five or more articles in com-munication journals over the course of their careers. Hence, the scholarly base upon which the field was erected was extremely narrow. These were the thirty-one scholars whose works sustained the association as a scholarly enterprise through Era 1 and most of Era 2. This listing includes scholars whose interests ranged from classical rhetoric (Smith, Hunt), to literary rhetoric (Hudson, Howes), to argumentation (Utterback, Baird), to interpretive reading (Parrish), to American oratory (Crocker, Wiley),

**CHART 4. RHETORIC SCHOLARS PUBLISHED
IN *QJS* BETWEEN 1915 AND 1935**

SCHOLAR	DATE OF FIRST ARTICLE	TOTAL NUMBER OF ARTICLES
A. Craig Baird	1923	13
Mildred Freburg Berry	1928	11
Gladys L. Borchers	1930	10
W. Norwood Brigance	1925	16
Donald C. Bryant	1929	23
H. Philip Constans	1934	6
Lionel Crocker	1924	54
John Dolman Jr.	1921	8
Louis M. Eich	1925	8
Henry Lee Ewbank	1931	12
Charles Andrew Fritz	1920	5
Raymond Howes	1925	9
Hoyt H. Hudson	1921	5
Everett Lee Hunt	1915	23
Charles F. Lindsley	1919	6
Drayton D. McKean	1930	5
Elwood Murray	1928	23
Robert T. Oliver	1932	36
James M. O'Neill	1915	14
Wayland Maxfield Parrish	1923	13
Horace G. Rahskopf	1932	10
Edward Z. Rowell	1930	7
Bromley Smith	1917	15
Lester W. Thonssen	1930	6
William E. Utterback	1924	17
Andrew T. Weaver	1916	12
Herbert A. Wichelns	1923	9
Earl W. Wiley	1932	10
James A. Winans	1915	6
Claude M. Wise	1932	17
Charles H. Woolbert	1915	15

to speech education (O'Neill), to British oratory (Bryant, Oliver), to language and persuasion (Woolbert, Winans, Brigance). Prior to 1935, the only people on this list that even came close to practicing something that we might today recognize as rhetorical criticism were Lindsley, Wiley, Wichelns, Crocker, and Brigance.

In point of fact, there was very little rhetorical history or rhetorical criticism prior to 1935. There was no textual criticism whatsoever. Neither Brigance nor anyone else was practicing textual criticism, as we now understand that term, prior to 1935. I have grouped Brigance with Winans and Woolbert as being primarily interested in language and persuasion because much of his research between 1925 and 1935 was devoted to understanding the bases of persuasion in order to better teach public speaking, advanced public speaking, and debate. Indeed, one could make the case that between Brigance's books of 1927 (*The Spoken Word*) and 1928 (*Classified Speech Models of Eighteen Forms of Public Address*), and his *QJS* articles on persuasion of 1931 ("A Genetic Approach to Persuasion") and 1935 ("Can We Redefine the James-Winans Theory of Persuasion?"), that he was one of the top three or four persuasion theorists in the field by the end of 1935.[17] I think I could make that case, but that is not the case I want to make. Instead, I want to look at four different items that seem to me to speak directly to today's rhetorical renaissance: Brigance's *QJS* articles of 1925 ("What Is a Successful Speech?") and 1933 ("Whither Research?"), his article in the *Mississippi Valley Historical Review* in 1932 ("Jeremiah Black and Andrew Johnson"), and the publication of his university-press book, based on his 1930 dissertation on Jeremiah Sullivan Black and published in 1934 as *Jeremiah Sullivan Black: A Defender of the Constitution and the Ten Commandments*.[18] What we will find is that the taproot of our current renaissance lies largely in this body of work. And it is precisely in this body of work that the seedbed of Brigance's lifelong interest in the relationship between rhetoric and democracy is to be found.

After earning his master's degree in American History in 1920 from the University of Nebraska, Brigance joined the emerging speech discipline in 1922. He published his first article in the field in 1925. To realize the importance of Brigance's 1925 article on "What Is a Successful Speech?" one need do nothing more than read George Edwards's recent book *On Deaf Ears* (2003), in which he makes the claim that presidential speech is of only marginal effect in moving public opinion. For Edwards, any speech that does not have an immediate, measurable effect is a failure.[19]

But what Brigance teaches us are three important truths: First, that there is a difference between success understood as the achieving of one's immediate goals, and success understood as a process of moving an audience toward an ultimate goal. Second, that there is a difference between a successful speech, in the narrow sense of that term, and a great speech. That in point of fact, successful speeches can be rhetorically (artistically) poor, and unsuccessful speeches can be rhetorically (artistically) praiseworthy. And third, that context must always be considered, including the difficulty of the immediate goal, its worth both to the speaker and the society, and the type or genre of the speech. As Brigance says, "In short, the success of any speech depends upon the speaker's purpose, the obstacles to be overcome, and the progress it makes toward overcoming those obstacles."[20]

One of the marks of the rhetorical renaissance has been the insistence on studying texts in context. Part of that process of contextualization has been the realization that correctly understanding a speaker's purpose is central to the interpretive process. Understanding, for example, that Eisenhower's immediate purpose in delivering his "Atoms for Peace" speech was primarily psychological warfare and not nuclear disarmament profoundly changes our evaluation of that effort.[21] Likewise, locating Lincoln's Cooper Union address within the genre of campaign oratory throws a whole new light on what Lincoln was trying to do and why he was trying to do it.[22] Brigance not only understands the complexities of rhetorical discourse, but he specifically identifies purpose and genre as mediating factors, and explicitly recognizes the processual nature of persuasion by emphasizing movement toward the goal rather than a linear cause-effect model.

Five years later, in 1930, Brigance completed his Ph.D. at the University of Iowa. He did this in one nine-month period from September 1929 to June 1930. During this time, he not only took a full course load, but he also researched, wrote, and defended his 661-page dissertation. If this feat has ever been duplicated in the field of rhetorical studies, I am unaware of it. In so doing, he became the first person to earn the Ph.D. at Iowa while emphasizing rhetorical studies. But this is where the story gets really interesting. The normative pattern for scholars in rhetorical studies from 1930 until at least 1975 was to complete the dissertation and then publish one article drawn from the dissertation in either *QJS* or *Speech Monographs*. By the time Brigance earned the Ph.D., he had already published seventeen articles—some in scholarly journals, some in literary magazines, and some in mass-circulation magazines. He had also published two textbooks. This established a pattern that Brigance would follow for the rest of his life—devising ways and means by which to share his ideas with multiple audiences, both lay and professional. Long before the contemporary outcry for scholars to become public intellectuals, Brigance *was* a public intellectual. His work appeared in *The Christian Century*, in *Century Magazine*, in *The Independent*, in *The North American Review*, and in *The American Mercury*—all by 1930. Later in his career, he would publish in such mass-circulation magazines as *Woman's Home Companion*, *Ladies' Home Journal*, and *Popular Photography*. His views on issues of the day appeared in *Vital Speeches* and were reproduced in numerous venues, including, on one occasion, *The Congressional Record*.[23] However, Brigance did not limit his outreach to lay audiences alone. In the spirit of the rhetorical renaissance, he published his first article based on the dissertation in the *Mississippi Valley Historical Review* in 1932. We need to linger for a moment on this article, because it teaches us not only about Brigance but also about ourselves as we were collectively incarnated at the end of the founding era.

The *MVHR* article is titled "Jeremiah Black and Andrew Johnson" and runs for thirteen pages in print. I mention the length because most articles in *QJS* in the early 1930s ran between seven and ten pages in print. Some were considerably shorter, only four or five pages. There were a few as long as fifteen pages, but they were the exceptions. If length did not preclude publication of Brigance's article in *QJS*, subject matter and approach probably did. This is unfortunate, inasmuch as many of the lessons that were fully learned only with the emergence of the rhetorical renaissance could have been taught through careful study of this article. But of course since it was published outside the field, few people ever read or referenced it. The article is a systematic refutation of claims set forth by the popular historians Claude G. Bowers, Paul L. Stryker, and George F. Milton to the effect that Jeremiah Sullivan Black—former chief justice of the Supreme Court of Pennsylvania, former attorney general of the United States, and secretary of state in the Buchanan administration—had, in 1868, withdrawn from the team of lawyers defending President Andrew Johnson against impeachment charges because the president had refused to give special treatment to one of Black's clients. In effect, these historians had charged Black with trying to blackmail the president, and then resigning from his defense team when the attempted blackmail failed. At issue was not only Black's historical reputation, but also an accurate understanding of what happened during Johnson's impeachment.

Like a surgeon wielding his scalpel, Brigance sets about to examine systematically—and to destroy—the case set forth by these historians. He begins by tracing the origins of the story back to its source—an eighty-eight-year-old man who was trying to recall events that had happened fifty-nine years earlier and to which he had not been an eyewitness. This man, Brigance discovered, was the one and only source for the interpretation offered by these historians. In a manner that only a master teacher and practitioner of argument could orchestrate, Brigance systematically shows that the evidence upon which the historians based their case is discredited, that even if it were not discredited it could not prove their case, that more and better evidence exists that proves their claims to be "unfounded" and "inaccurate," and that there are significant omissions in the evidence adduced. Brigance then calls for the application of "tests of historical accuracy."[24] By systematically applying these tests, Brigance is able to show:

1. That Black never had an attorney-client relationship with the man for whom he was supposedly trying to get preferential treatment.
2. That it was not Black but an entirely different person who conspired with members of the impeachment committee to make this deal with Johnson.
3. That Johnson could not have discussed Black's supposed offer with William Seward on March 18, as alleged, because Seward was gone from Washington, D.C., from March 12 through March 24.
4. That the letter supposedly sent by Black to Johnson on March 19, trying to rescind his decision to resign from the president's defense team, was nowhere to be found among Johnson's papers, even though every other letter from Black to Johnson was present and accounted for. Since such a letter, had it existed, would have shown Johnson in a highly positive light (as one who had resisted the attempted blackmail), then there is every reason to believe that Johnson, as one of the most careful record-keepers ever to occupy the White House, would have kept it. But no such letter was found, because it never existed in the first place.

Brigance then goes on to explain what had actually motivated Black to resign from Johnson's defense team. Between his destruction of the historians' arguments and his own constructive case for Black's actions, Brigance offers a textbook study in how to do and employ historical research. Of course, in 1932 rhetoricians had no such textbook, so Brigance could have served an extremely useful function in the development of what would soon come to be called the "history and criticism" approach to rhetorical analysis. That Brigance clearly saw danger signs on the horizon when it came to rhetorical research is evident in his 1933 *QJS* article "Whither Research?"

There is so much wisdom in "Whither Research?" that were I to be forced to select just one Brigance article as his all-time best, this one would get my vote. Coming, as it does, in 1933, after eighteen years of struggle to try to determine what research in the field of speech should be like, this article sets forth an agenda the complete fulfillment of which has not been accomplished to this day. Indeed, I will contend that most of what Brigance sets forth in "Whither Research?" does not even come into clear focus until the onset of the rhetorical renaissance, more than forty years later. Specifically, this article foreshadows the treatment of speeches as a form of rhetorical literature, an understanding of the audience—and particularly of rhetorical constraints—that foreshadows Bitzer's explication in 1968, a concern with textual authenticity, an insistence on primary-source research, and an understanding of speech content as ideas that have force in history and through time. Not all of these ideas are developed in great depth, but they are all present in this one article.

Brigance begins by stating that he is "writing this article in an attempt to hasten the coming out [from our intellectual wilderness] and to suggest one of several possible directions which research should next take." He then wrote, "I think we ought to recognize that there is a great body of rhetorical or oratorical literature almost untouched by scholars in our field. Of it, I think we might safely say that this literature can do without our scholarship, but that our scholarship cannot do without that literature. Sooner or later we shall be called to the bar to answer for our neglect."[25]

More than forty years later, at the dawn of the rhetorical renaissance, Michael Leff and G. P. Mohrmann issued the indictment: "We used to study speeches, right? Wrong! How about Clay, Calhoun, and Webster for openers? A total of seventeen articles in national and regional journals, but no writer has seen fit to deal with the entire text of one of their speeches. Emerson? Eight articles, none on a particular speech. Jonathan Edwards? Not one article. Acres of Diamonds? No article. The New South? One, a Hegelian analysis."[26] Ten years after this indictment, in 1987, Stephen E. Lucas writing in *QJS* could still exclaim: "Indeed, our persistent neglect of major texts in the history of American oratory is nothing short of astonishing. How can it be that we are in our seventh decade as a discipline and have yet to produce a body of rich critical literature . . . ?"[27] The reason it could be was that we did not heed Brigance's counsel.

Long before there was any systematic explication of the rhetorical situation, Brigance wrote, "The statesman who must dominate a crisis, or the advocate who must mold the mind of a court or jury . . . must seize the hour, strike the iron at white heat, adapt himself to the mind, mood, and temperature of the audience and occasion. It is impossible ever to read the speech apart from the hopes, fears, prejudices, and passions that beset the hearers at the moment of delivery."[28] Even more clearly than Wichelns, Brigance locates rhetoric as the contingent art of adapting discourse to audiences in the immediate situation. Today this may strike us as old hat, but it was not so considered in 1933. And while many would subsequently repeat Brigance's ideas, none would put them into practice for many, many years. In extending his analysis of the research situation of 1933, Brigance goes on to note that a recent biographer of Daniel Webster "ignores comparisons between Webster's actual speeches and the revised literary manuscripts which pass today as Webster's speeches."[29] Already the issue of textual authenticity was percolating in Brigance's brain, but no one pursued that line of analysis either.

Having already completed a dissertation using historical methods, and having just published an article in a professional history journal, Brigance closed by noting, "Commonly we are content to edit what other biographers and essayists have said. But this is mere rewriting. We must, if we expect recognition of our scholarship, go to the records themselves. We must examine first-hand the manuscripts, letters, documents, and read again the newspapers, periodicals, and memoirs of that period."[30] Here it was in black and white: do primary-source research. Brigance had done it, and would do it again. But few followed his lead. What seems so clear to us today, in the midst of a great revival of all things rhetorical, was strangely obscure to Brigance's generation—and the one following. Indeed, as chart 5 illustrates, a survey of the books produced throughout

CHART 5. RHETORIC BOOKS PUBLISHED IN THE FIELD
OF SPEECH, 1930–1960

YEAR	AUTHOR	TITLE	PUBLISHER
1934	Brigance	*Jeremiah Sullivan Black*	U. of Pennsylvania
1934	Crocker	*Beecher's Art of Preaching*	U. of Chicago
1934	Greene/Hudson	*Religion within the Limits*	Open Court
1939	Bryant	*Edmund Burke*	Washington U. Press
1940	Armour/Howes	*Coleridge the Talker*	Cornell U. Press
1941	Howell	*Rhet. of Alcuin/Charlemagne*	Princeton U. Press
1941	Robb	*Oral Interp. of Literature*	H.W. Wilson Co.
1941	Hudson	*In Praise of Folly*	Princeton U. Press
1941	Aly	*Rhet. of Alexander Hamilton*	Columbia U. Press
1943	Brigance	*Hist. & Crit. Amer. Public Ad.*	McGraw-Hill
1943	Wallace	*Francis Bacon on Comm./Rhet.*	U. of North Carolina
1944	Oliver	*Korea: Forgotten Nation*	Public Affairs Press
1944	Hudson	*Studies in Speech & Drama*	Cornell U. Press
1946	Oliver	*Four Who Spoke Out*	Syracuse U. Press
1947	Hudson	*Epigram in Eng. Renaissance*	Princeton U. Press
1949	O'Neill	*Religion and Education*	Harper
1950	Roach	*History of Sp. Ed. at Columbia*	Columbia U. Press
1952	O'Neill	*Catholicism and Am. Freedom*	Harper & Brothers
1954	Wallace	*History of Speech Education*	Appleton-Century
1955	Hochmuth	*Hist. & Crit. Amer. Public Ad.*	McGraw-Hill
1957	Gunderson	*Log Cabin Campaign*	U. of Kentucky
1957	Aly	*Alexander Hamilton: Selections*	Liberal Arts Press
1958	Bryant	*The Rhetorical Idiom*	Cornell U. Press
1959	Oliver/Bauer	*Re-Establishing the Sp. Profession*	Eastern States Sp. Assoc.

Eras 2 and 3 yields only twenty-four titles, which include monographs, edited books, and translations.

One of the more amazing aspects of this list, aside from its brevity, is the fact that of the twenty-four titles produced, seventeen of them were written by the same people who were the leading producers of articles between 1915 and 1935. Only seven new names appear—Howell, Robb, Wallace, Roach, Hochmuth, Gunderson, and Aly—and this in a thirty-year span! Clearly, research in primary sources was not a high priority during Eras 1, 2, and 3. Those who did conduct such research were a small minority whose example did not transfer to the larger body of scholars. But if anyone tried to encourage that larger body to do significant research, that person was W. Norwood Brigance. As he noted in 1933, "These facts suggest one direction, at least, in which our scholarship ought to move next, namely to undertake a *combined historical* and *critical* study of orators and oratorical literature, and to produce thereby a body of oratorical studies and criticisms worthy of the orators and oratory which induced it."[31]

The next year, in 1934, Brigance would be appointed by the president of the national association to chair the "Committee on Joint Research in the History of American Oratory." Over the course of the next nine years, Brigance and his committee would strive to give form to many of the ideas he had expressed in "Whither Research?" The result, both for better and worse, would be the first two volumes of *A History and Criticism of American Public Address*, published in 1943. At the time of his appointment, Brigance was thirty-eight years old, making him one of the youngest members of the editorial committee. But his appointment was more than justified, for not only had he set forth the agenda in his 1933 article, but he had also published, in 1934, one of the first—perhaps the first—scholarly book by a member of the speech profession.[32] I turn now to that book.

In his history of the discipline, Herman Cohen says of Brigance's book on Jeremiah Sullivan Black: "Without detracting from the book's quality, which was considerable, we can note that history, not rhetoric, dominated it."[33] That statement is true as far as it goes, but it does not really get at the nature of the contribution Brigance made. His was the first rhetorical biography produced by a member of the speech field. I describe it as such because it (a) was motivated by the fact that Black was a renowned barrister, (b) focused on the nature and quality of the arguments that Black made, and (c) set those arguments in their historical, constitutional, and situational contexts. The book does, in fact, put a stronger accent on the biographical rather than the rhetorical, but the latter is present, even if not thoroughly articulated. Like others of his era, Brigance saw oratory primarily as a "force in history." Black's courtroom speaking was important, therefore, because it was one of the causes of historical change. Brigance accepted this view as a given and proceeded to treat Black's speaking accordingly. It is a masterful biography that takes the reader from Black's youth through his apprenticeship as a lawyer, his appointment as a judge, his service as chief justice of the Supreme Court of Pennsylvania, his appointment by President Buchanan first as attorney general of the United States and then as secretary of state, his return to private practice, and his central role in some of the most important cases of the mid-nineteenth century—including, most centrally, *Ex Parte Milligan*, a case involving the constitutionality of secret military tribunals during times of peace.[34] Along the way, we learn about Black's relations with a cast of characters, including James Buchanan, Edwin Stanton, William Seward, James Garfield, and Andrew Johnson.

Brigance was an elegant writer whose rhetorical insights were there for the reader to discern, but often were not underscored or emphasized. Consider the following quotation from his analysis of the *Milligan* case: "They were transient things and petty. He lifted the case to higher ground, made Freedom his client, made the great cause of Constitutional Liberty hang by the slender thread of Milligan's life."[35] Clearly this is rhetorical criticism of a sort, but it is not the sort typically practiced today. Brigance gives no close readings of Black's oratory, though he does, from time to time, quote small portions of the barrister's rhetoric, which, he tells us, was delivered extemporaneously, for Black never once used a note or outline in his entire life.

As a rhetorical biography from 1934, Brigance's book is without peer. Is it the way we might write a rhetorical biography today? Probably not. Could it be more rhetorical and less biographical? Doubtless. But those really are not the crucial questions. The real questions are the ones raised by Brigance in "Whither Research?" Does he work from primary-source documents? Yes, he does. He not only uses the Black Papers, the Buchanan Papers, and the Johnson Papers in the Library of Congress, he also uses private collections then in the hands of Black's relatives. He uses official court transcripts as well as the archives of the Department of State. He draws on first-hand testimony and memoirs of the period. In short, he practices exactly what he preached in his 1933 article. Does he use the tests of history? Yes, he does. On numerous occasions he corrects the historical record, takes note of documents that are misplaced or misfiled in archives, and adds to historical revisionism by adducing evidence or making observations that had never been made before. When discussing the impeachment of Johnson, for example, Brigance writes in a footnote: "Milton assumes that Shaffer was a member of the Black law firm. This is an error. Except for about five years Black had neither law partner nor office."[36] Brigance also discovers documents that had been suppressed during Johnson's impeachment trial. All in all, this is a book that could have been—and should have been—a model for how to conduct historical research. But it was not. The role of model fell to a different Brigance project, one over which he had only limited control. I turn now to the project for which Brigance is most remembered today, the two-volume *A History and Criticism of American Public Address*, published in 1943.

A History and Criticism of American Public Address

Much has been written about *A History and Criticism of American Public Address*. It was the first big, coordinated project executed under the auspices of the national association. I use the term "executed" intentionally, for in many ways the sheer execution of the project—the conceptualization, planning, editing, and publishing—was an achievement unto itself, quite apart from the content of the volumes. That execution was under the direction of W. Norwood Brigance. Although scholars who came of age in the post–Edwin Black era have found much to criticize in the volumes— and I explicitly acknowledge that I am one of those who has been critical[37] —we must always keep in mind several facts:

1. That this was an association project that carried both the strengths and weaknesses of a product produced by a group.
2. That there not only was no model of how to do a "history and criticism" project in public address, there were only a handful of scholars actually trying to do such studies in the 1930s—the decade in which the project was conceived and all of the decisions made.
3. That there was almost no theory of criticism to draw on beyond that articulated by Wichelns in 1925 or that borrowed from literary scholars of the 1920s and 1930s—the very group public-address scholars conceived themselves to be fighting against.
4. That when the project was launched in 1934, there had been a grand total of three scholarly books published in the speech field—the Drummond collection in which the Wichelns essay had appeared, and the books by Brigance and Crocker.[38]

It is important to put these two volumes in the context of Era 2, for they were wholly products of the period from 1930–1945. When compared to the scholarship that appeared in *QJS* during Era 1 and the early part of Era 2, the essays in *A History and Criticism* were far superior to anything that had been produced in public address until that point in time. They were so largely because of the persistence of W. Norwood Brigance.

Because Brigance kept meticulous records, we have a pretty full picture of what happened in the nine years between 1934 and 1943. Furthermore, Brigance gave a sort of interim report in his *QJS* article of 1938 titled "The Twenty-Eight Foremost American Orators."[39] In that article, he reported on the procedures being used and listed the twenty-eight orators whom the editorial committee's methods of selection had yielded. In the end, it was those twenty-eight figures plus the six synthetic essays that formed the content of the two volumes. That Brigance had all the problems normally associated with big projects was evidenced in a letter he wrote in 1950 to J. Jeffrey Auer. Speaking of his efforts to get the project moving, he wrote:

Once I tried having each contributor present [at an SAA convention] tell briefly, in 30 to 60 seconds, what interesting new sources he had uncovered. At another and later time, I asked each of them to tell exactly how far along he was, how much more work there was left to be done, and when the project was expected to be completed. That was the time when half a dozen boys who had not done anything to speak of, or perhaps anything at all, found out that the project actually was going to be done. And when I asked them publicly, but not speaking personally to any one of them, that if they wanted to withdraw, would they do so at that meeting because I had at hand the names of seven or eight more persons who would like to do those studies, they all vowed to dig in, which they did.[40]

David George Burns, in his 1970 dissertation titled "The Contributions of William Norwood Brigance to the Field of Speech," reports that during this nine-year process, Brigance "had written over 3500 letters, had averaged more than ten hours a week in editing manuscripts, and had secured the approval of four out of five associate editors for each manuscript, a process which saw the thirty-four manuscripts pass in and out of his office a total of 419 times."[41]

CHART 6. CONTRIBUTORS TO VOLUMES 1 AND 2
OF *A HISTORY AND CRITICISM*

CONTRIBUTOR	YEAR OF FIRST PUBLICATION	NUMBER OF PUBS BY 1943
Bower Aly	1936	1
Marvin G. Bauer	1925	2
Mildred Freburg Berry	1928	6
John W. Black	1937	3
George H. Bohman	1937	1
William Norwood Brigance	1925	6
Lionel G. Crocker	1924	15
Herbert L. Curry	——	0
Carl Dallinger	——	0
Louis M. Eich	1925	5
Walter B. Emery	——	0
Charles A. Fritz	1920	5
Kenneth Hance	1939	1
H. O. Hendrickson	——	0
Orville Hitchcock	——	0
Marie Hochmuth	1941	1
Wilbur Samuel Howell	——	0
Hoyt Hopewell Hudson	1921	5
Alfred Dwight Huston	——	0
Carroll P. Lahman	1927	3

Such close attention was necessary because Brigance was working with a group of authors who ranged widely in their talent and experience. Anyone who has edited a scholarly volume, much less two, will testify that the single biggest obstacle is the selection of the contributors. The more experienced and widely published the contributors are, the easier it is to make the volume come together. But Brigance did not have the luxury of a deep roster of scholars from which to choose; of the forty-one individuals who contributed to these two volumes, fourteen had never published a scholarly article in their lives, and another eleven had published but one. So twenty-five of the forty-one were basically novices when it came to published research. Chart 6 tells the story.

CONTRIBUTOR	YEAR OF FIRST PUBLICATION	NUMBER OF PUBS BY 1943
Louis A. Mallory	1936	1
Norman Mattis	1929	2
Roy C. McCall	——	0
Dayton David McKean	1930	15
Rexford S. Mitchell	——	0
R. Elaine Pagel	1940	1
Wayland Maxfield Parrish	1923	5
Myron G. Phillips	——	0
Henry G. Roberts	——	0
Herold Truslow Ross	1932	1
Edwin W. Schoenberger	——	0
Grafton Tanquary	——	0
Ota Thomas	——	0
Lester Thonssen	1930	4
Karl R. Wallace	1936	1
Forest L. Whan	1939	1
Herbert A. Wichelns	1923	4
Earl W. Wiley	1932	4
Ernest J. Wrage	——	0
Willard Hayes Yeager	1929	1
Doris G. Yoakam	1937	1

The contributors to the Brigance volumes fell roughly into three categories—those who had never published before, those who had published one or two articles, and those who were regular contributors to the journal. It is true that several of those who had zero or one publication in 1943 later went on to substantial careers as publishing scholars—Karl Wallace, Walter Emery, and Ernest Wrage, among others. But this was early in their careers, and they needed a strong editorial hand. Brigance provided that hand and produced an important work despite having to superintend many contributors who had little idea of what they were trying to do.

While there were no book series specializing in rhetorical studies during the 1930s or 1940s, Brigance became the model of the consummate editor who through his time, energy, editing pen, and sheer force of will caused something to happen that had never happened before and would not happen again for more than a decade. He synthesized the best that the field had to offer and presented it in a form, the edited multivolume set, that would not be rivaled in the speech field for almost half a century. If our current renaissance is characterized by book series, multivolume projects, and cooperative ventures, such projects have their genesis in Brigance's original project of 1943. For both good and ill, those two volumes became the model for historical-critical scholarship during all of Era 3 and well into Era 4.

Brigance himself was aware of the many shortcomings of the project. Shortly after the volumes appeared in 1943, he wrote to Auer: "I am keenly aware of its limitations and shortcomings. Many of its studies are not so good as I wanted them to be, but I am fairly well convinced that I had each author rewrite again and again until he was unable to improve . . . by further rewriting. If I were doing the job over again, I would even plan it differently."[42] The plan, as it had evolved, featured speakers rather than speeches or genres. Trying to cover any important speaker's entire career in only 15,000 words was a near-impossible task, and many of the essays suffer more from lack of depth than anything else.

Brigance was a meticulous editor. No sooner had he sent the two-volume *History and Criticism* to press than he assumed the editorship of *QJS*. From 1942–1944, during the midst of World War II, Brigance guided the field's flagship journal through one of the toughest periods in its history, brought on not just by the war that snatched away many a prospective scholar, but also by the rationing that accompanied the war and that resulted in shortages of paper. Brigance juggled the format, the typeface, and finally the type of paper itself in an effort to keep the journal afloat. Not only did he succeed in publishing all twelve issues, he filled those issues with some of the most important content ever published in *QJS* to that point in time, including Bower Aly's "The History of Public Address as a Research Field," Kenneth Hance's "Public Address in a Democracy at War," and Loren Reid's "The Perils of Rhetorical Criticism."[43] Over his three years as editor, Brigance published such scholars as Douglas Ehninger, Marie Hochmuth, Irving J. Lee, Richard Murphy, Lionel Crocker, Halbert Gulley, Thomas Sebeok, Everett Lee Hunt, Robert T. Oliver, Earnest Brandenburg, Wayne Thompson, Dallas Dickey, A. Craig Baird, J. Jeffrey Auer, Harold F. Harding, Elwood Murray, Donald C. Bryant, Wendell Johnson, and Karl R. Wallace. By his own testimony, Brigance was a hands-on editor. In a 1943 letter to Rupert Cortright, Brigance wrote: "At least four articles out of five are pretty thoroughly redrafted by me before they ever get to press, and one out of five is so thoroughly rewritten that I must type it over myself, even rearranging the order and structure and putting in a few ideas of my own that the author forgot to put in but that seemed to me ought to be there."[44]

There are no awards for editors. But should one ever be established, no name should be attached to it other than that of William Norwood Brigance. As Brigance completed his editorial duties, he turned once again to the question of civic discourse in a democracy.

Democracy, Speech, and the Vocation of a Teacher

Throughout his thirty-eight-year career in higher education, Brigance often wrote about the role of speech in a democracy, even titling his 1952 textbook *Speech: Its Techniques and Disciplines in a Free Society.* To appreciate Brigance's views about the relationship of speech to democracy, we must begin by seeking to understand both his political and educational philosophies. Politically, Brigance was a realist. He had served in World War I with the 33rd Army Division in France. In two years of service, approximately 50 percent of the men in the 33rd Division were killed. Brigance himself was a forward observer and locator, one of the most dangerous positions on the battlefield. He did not glorify war; neither did he shrink from it. Throughout the rest of his life, he credited the battlefield with instilling in him a certain fearlessness, not of the *que sera sera* variety, but of the now-having-looked-death-in-the-face-what-more-is-there-to-fear? variety. He accepted the world as it was and worked to make it better. His educational philosophy was that of Isocrates—rhetorical training for leadership in public contexts. Examination of his earliest textbooks shows that he adopted the Isocratean method of instruction. As he wrote in *The Spoken Word* (1927): "The plan of the course is built on a triangle. The study of the text forms one leg; a study of speech models forms the second leg; and the preparation and delivery of speeches forms the third."[45] Even his publications followed this pattern. *The Spoken Word* (1927) was the theory, *Classified Speech Models of Eighteen Forms of Public Address* (1928) presented the models, and *Wabash College Orations: 1879–1923* (1932) was a record of the practice. To Isocrates' method, he added Quintilian's goal: the production of "the good man speaking well." For Brigance, there was always an ethical component to both the teaching and practice of public address. We start, then, with a political realist who deeply believed in "the basic, liberal, educational aspect of speech which springs from a comprehensive study of the whole field."[46]

For Brigance, a reciprocal relationship existed between speech and democracy. Without the political context of democratic governance, speech could not be free—would, in fact, be stifled, coerced, and dictated. Likewise, without free speech, democracy could not function, could not conduct its business in an open, rational, public way. Hence, free speech and democracy reinforced one another; neither could survive in the absence of the other. He saw *"free public discussion"* as *"an imperative form of force among free people."*[47] Free public discussion meant that society must tolerate a wide range of views, especially those with which the majority might disagree. Applying that philosophy to his own practices as editor of *QJS*, Brigance wrote: "I have not and do not propose ever to intrude my personal prejudices into the editorial policies of this magazine. So long as America remains a democracy, I know of no other way of conducting a magazine for intellectuals except by allowing freedom of thought to all contributors."[48] His was a classical liberal or libertarian orientation—maximum freedom consistent with order and the moral norms of civilization.

Echoing Isocrates, Brigance held that speech is "the chief tool with which civilization was developed and it remains the chief tool by which men live and work together."[49] "Intelligent discussion," he held, "is the life of democracy." Speech, whether in the form of discussion, debate, or oratory, was central because it *"arouses interest in public questions. It stirs the indifferent into thinking. It sheds light on both sides of a public question."*[50] Brigance refused to separate men of words from men of action. To him, a public leader was one who could both speak and act—one who could persuade, influence, move men's minds and hearts in line with the dictates of conscience, truth, liberty, and justice. "Great movements," he held, "are usually led by men of action who are also men of words, who use words as instruments of power, who voice their aims in words of historic simplicity."[51]

Brigance understood that the American form of democracy was not perfect. As early as October 1945, he gave a speech in which he warned about the danger of allowing our democratic practices to mimic those of our adversaries. This was four months before George Kennan sent his Long Telegram from Moscow, a message that contained a similar warning.[52] Long before most people had even heard the term *cold war*, Brigance was taking its measure: "1946 is Year One of a power struggle between two political philosophies, communism and democracy—or what passes for communism and democracy. . . . [W]hat we have done in this year [1946], and shall do during the first half of 1947, is likely to determine for a long time to come the course of history, not for America alone but for the world."[53] Seldom has any member of our profession been so prescient.

As the Cold War took shape and form in the first half of 1947, with the Truman Doctrine and the Marshall Plan as rhetorical anchors, Brigance sensed the change in the political atmosphere. He insisted that every generation, especially the postwar generation, be taught *"that democracy rests on discussion and persuasion, that its people shall discuss their problems and reach an intelligent consensus, that they shall not goosestep to military commands, nor yield to mob law."*[54] Noting the tendency toward group-think and conformity, Brigance wrote: "A democracy is not maintained by developing identical convictions among its citizens but is rather maintained by developing common sentiments and common enthusiasms."[55]

As the Cold War mentality became more entrenched, Brigance identified "respect for human dignity" as the chief characteristic of democratic regimes. He noted that the true revolutionary force in the world was "not communism," but what he called *"the rise of the little man"*—the empowerment of the masses of humanity around the globe who have the *"power to destroy us, or tax us to death, or merely socialize us."* To Brigance, the real danger lay not in Moscow, but in Washington, D.C.; not in the power of communism, but in the lack of faith in democracy. Based on his study of history, Brigance held that "the Communists may enforce the rule-from-Moscow for 25 years, or 30 or 40 years, but not longer. Time is on our side." The Cold War, he believed, was really "a *struggle for the minds of men! . . . you can shoot men, but you cannot shoot an idea. . . . You can destroy it only with the power of a better idea."*[56]

Suppression of ideas in the name of national security clearly bothered Brigance. "We must not suppress freedom of thought," he wrote. "Yet we are going to face that danger, for in our fear for national security, there will be some people in government and out who will trample on the edges of the constitution [*sic*] and attempt to set up a system of thought

control. In fact, we have already done it." Brigance fully realized that
the world was *"full of dangerous ideas,"* but he insisted that *"in a free society
you allow free trade in ideas, and produce a nation of tough-minded realists."* He
specifically warned about the "danger in purges and loyalty oaths."[57]

To Brigance, the primary answer to these problems was better education, one based on the science of "human relations" and a commitment to
identification with the Other. "Persuasion begins," he wrote, "only when
you understand the hopes, wants, ideals, and aspirations of other people.
And the white, Christian people of Western democracies, with their arrogant sense of racial superiority, have never wanted to understand the
hopes and wants of other people."[58] Brigance was particularly biting in
his criticism of elite educators who would "rearrange the old curriculum
of the powermakers" by subordinating "psychology and anthropology to
philosophy, sociology to history, and instruction in writing and speaking
to 'the historical development of Modern English' and 'the position of
English in the Indo-European family of languages.'"[59] Long before mul-
ticulturalism became an educational concern, Brigance was advocating
a university education sensitive to the needs and wants of non-Western
and non-English-speaking audiences.

Though a strong advocate of free speech and democratic governance,
Brigance clearly understood that absent a set of ethics encapsulated by
Quintilian's notion of the "good man," even speech itself could be sub-
verted. "Speech is a form of power that may also be used as an instrument
of *tyranny*," he wrote in his 1952 textbook. "Speech, even free speech,
may be used as an instrument of *double-talk and deception*. Speech, and
especially free speech, may be used as an anesthesia for *self-complacency*.
. . . A free society survives only when speech is used in the main as an
instrument of *enlightenment*."[60] Almost certainly the contemporary situation was on his mind as he wrote these words, for in that same year he
also criticized the "demagogue technique of shooting-it-out with a war
of words" and noted: "Some go even further, and resort to the Big Lie
Repetition of the Communists. We have them today even in the United
States Senate and you know who they are."[61]

Brigance was no political theorist, but he knew what he believed.
The title he applied to Jeremiah Sullivan Black might just as easily have
applied to himself: defender of the Constitution and the Ten Commandments. Like Black, he had a radical commitment to constitutional liberty.
Also like Black, he did not flaunt his moral code, but he lived by it and

it permeates his writing, especially his 1934 biography of Judge Black. In that work, Brigance uses a long list of descriptors to characterize his subject. After completing this study, however, I have come to believe that those very same descriptors apply equally well to William Norwood Brigance: "severe discipline," "precision of language," "an intense man," "loved a fight," "a character," "hated fraud," "assured authority," "consistent logic," "freshness of style," "forcible sentences," "not easily awed," and "fearlessness in manner."[62] Whether Brigance selected a man like himself to study, or whether he became the man he studied, I cannot say; but the multiple similarities are too many and too profound to be merely accidental.

Brigance was a man of his time. He helped to define the end of Era 1, totally dominated Era 2, and lived to the end of Era 3, defending the ethos of democracy and championing a fully orbed university curriculum that faced toward the modern world, not away—a curriculum that would allow students to learn how to identify with the rising masses of the world, not just the white Christian West. In the end, it was all about human relations and the central role that the process of communication played in developing those relations.[63] Brigance died in 1960. The world as we know it changed shortly thereafter.

Era 4 would produce the greatest generation, led by Edwin Black. The scholars of that era would rewrite forever the rules and modes of rhetorical scholarship, and the era of Brigance would slowly fade from memory. But the spirit of Brigance lives among us still. It lives in the commitment to primary-source research. It lives in multivolume projects and cross-disciplinary scholarship. It lives in rhetorical history and rhetorical biography. It lives in studies of deliberative democracy, of democratic governance in times of war, and in concerns over the ethics of rhetoric in democratic societies. It lives in the production of university-press books and articles published in interdisciplinary outlets. It lives in the ideal of the public intellectual, and in every contribution to historical revisionism. Every time we celebrate the significant differences our current scholarship is making, and point with pride to our latest books and journals, the spirit of Brigance lives among us. We need not be nostalgic for our youth, or lament the passing of time. For we all live, and work, and compete in the world we inherited from our predecessors. And one day we, too, shall pass—our era and works consigned to the sands of time, but our spirits still hovering near, ever reminding those who remain of days gone by, and waiting to cast ballots, if only by proxy, through the democracy of the dead.

NOTES

1. On the idea of a rhetorical renaissance, see Stephen E. Lucas, "The Renaissance of American Public Address: Text and Context in Rhetorical Criticism," *Quarterly Journal of Speech* 74 (1988): 241–60; Martin J. Medhurst, "Public Address and Significant Scholarship: Four Challenges to the Rhetorical Renaissance," in *Texts in Context*, ed. Michael C. Leff and Fred J. Kauffeld (Davis, Calif.: Hermagoras Press, 1989), 29–42; Martin J. Medhurst, "The Academic Study of Public Address: A Tradition in Transition," in *Landmark Essays on American Public Address*, ed. Martin J. Medhurst (Davis, Calif.: Hermagoras Press, 1993), xi–xliii; Martin J. Medhurst, "The Rhetorical Renaissance: A Battlefield Report," *Southern Communication Journal* 63 (1998): 309–14; Martin J. Medhurst, "The Contemporary Study of Public Address: Renewal, Recovery, and Reconfiguration," *Rhetoric & Public Affairs* 4 (2001): 495–511.

2. See, for example, the four different analyses of Nixon's November 3, 1969, speech on "Vietnamization" by Robert P. Newman, Karlyn Kohrs Campbell, Forbes I. Hill, and Hermann G. Stelzner, produced between 1970 and 1972, and reprinted in James R. Andrews, *The Practice of Rhetorical Criticism*, 2nd ed. (New York: Longmans, 1990), 91–150; James R. Andrews, "The Rhetoric of Coercion and Persuasion: The Reform Bill of 1832," *Quarterly Journal of Speech* 52 (1970): 187–95; Stephen E. Lucas, "The Man with a Muck Rake: A Reinterpretation," *Quarterly Journal of Speech* 59 (1973): 452–62; Michael C. Leff and G. P. Mohrmann, "Lincoln at Cooper Union: A Rhetorical Analysis of the Text," *Quarterly Journal of Speech* 60 (1974): 346–58; Thomas W. Benson, "*Joe:* An Essay on the Rhetoric of Film," *Journal of Popular Culture* 8 (Winter 1974): 610–18; Martin J. Medhurst, "Image and Ambiguity: A Rhetorical Approach to *The Exorcist*," *Southern Speech Communication Journal* 44 (1978): 73–92; Thomas W. Benson, "The Rhetorical Structure of Frederick Wiseman's *High School*," *Communication Monographs* 47 (1980): 233–61; Martin J. Medhurst and Thomas W. Benson, "*The City*: The Rhetoric of Rhythm," *Communication Monographs* 48 (1981): 54–72.

3. For an overview of various rhetorical genres of discourse, see Martin J. Medhurst and Thomas W. Benson, eds., *Rhetorical Dimensions in Media: A Critical Casebook* (Dubuque, Iowa: Kendall/Hunt, 1984, 1991). For an overview of the expansion in rhetorical studies at the midpoint of Era 6, see Richard B. Gregg,

"The Criticism of Symbolic Inducement: A Critical-Theoretical Connection," in *Speech Communication in the 20th Century*, ed. Thomas W. Benson (Carbondale: Southern Illinois University Press, 1985), 41–62.

4. Michael Leff, "Interpretation and the Art of the Rhetorical Critic," *Western Journal of Speech Communication* 44 (1980): 337–49; Michael Leff, "Textual Criticism: The Legacy of G. P. Mohrmann," *Quarterly Journal of Speech* 72 (1986): 377–89; Michael Leff and Andrew Sachs, "Words the Most Like Things: Iconicity and the Rhetorical Text," *Western Journal of Speech Communication* 54 (1990): 252–73. For challenges to Leff's views and his reaction to those challenges, see "Forum: Text, Theory, and the Rhetorical Critic," *Quarterly Journal of Speech* 78 (1992): 219–37.

5. I have doubtless missed some titles, but these forty-five illustrate my point.

6. Garrett Ward Sheldon, Review of *Jefferson's Call to Nationhood*, in *Journal of American History* 91 (2004): 610–11.

7. Kenneth Cmiel, review of *The Reconstruction Desegregation Debate*, in *American Historical Review* 109 (2004): 920.

8. See, for example, Martin J. Medhurst, ed., *Beyond the Rhetorical Presidency* (College Station: Texas A&M University Press, 1996); Leroy G. Dorsey, ed., *The Presidency and Rhetorical Leadership* (College Station: Texas A&M University Press, 2002); Robert L. Ivie, *Democracy and the War on Terror* (Tuscaloosa: University of Alabama Press, 2005). Also articles by Robert E. Denton Jr., Mary E. Stuckey, Robert L. Ivie, David Zarefsky, and John M. Murphy in "Forum on the Future of the Presidency," *Rhetoric & Public Affairs* 3 (2000): 445–70.

9. Mel Laracey, *The President and the People* (College Station: Texas A&M University Press, 2002); Francis A. Beer, *Meanings of War and Peace* (College Station: Texas A&M University Press, 2002); Colleen Shogan, *The Moral Rhetoric of American Presidents* (College Station: Texas A&M University Press, 2006).

10. See James Kimble, *Mobilizing the Home Front: The War Bonds Campaign* (College Station: Texas A&M University Press, 2006); Cara A. Finnegan, *Picturing Poverty: Print Culture and FSA Photographs* (Washington, D.C.: Smithsonian Institute Press, 2004); Davis W. Houck and David E. Dixon, eds., *Rhetoric, Religion, and the Civil Rights Movement, 1954–1965* (Waco, Tex.: Baylor University Press, 2006).

11. See Stephen E. Lucas, *Portents of Rebellion* (Philadelphia: Temple University Press, 1976); Roderick P. Hart, *The Political Pulpit* (West Lafayette, Ind.: Purdue University Press, 1977); Robert Underhill, *The Truman Persuasions* (Ames: Iowa State University Press, 1981); Ronald L. Hatzenbuehler and Robert L. Ivie, *Congress Declares War* (Kent, Ohio: Kent State University Press, 1983); and Kathleen Hall Jamieson, *Packaging the Presidency* (New York: Oxford University Press, 1984).

12. For an expansion of the ideas in this paragraph, see Martin J. Medhurst, "The Contemporary Study of Public Address: Renewal, Recovery, and Reconfiguration," 495–511.

13. See Stephen Howard Browne, *Angelina Grimke: Rhetoric, Identity, and the Radical Imagination* (East Lansing: Michigan State University Press, 1999); Susan Zaeske, *Signatures of Citizenship* (Chapel Hill: University of North Carolina Press, 2003); Karen J. Musolf, *From Plymouth to Parliament: A Rhetorical History of Nancy Astor's 1919 Campaign* (New York: St. Martin's Press, 1998); Patricia L. Schmidt, *Margaret Chase Smith: Beyond Convention* (Orono: University of Maine Press, 1996); Karrin Vasby Anderson and Kristine Sheeler, *Governing Codes* (Lanham, Md.: Rowman and Littlefield, 2005); Suzanne Pullon Fitch and Roseann Mandziuk, *Sojourner Truth as Orator: Wit, Story, and Song* (Westport, Conn.: Greenwood Press, 1997); Gregory P. Lampe, *Frederick Douglass: Freedom's Voice, 1818–1845* (East Lansing: Michigan State University Press, 1998); Robert E. Terrill, *Malcolm X: Inventing Radical Judgment* (East Lansing: Michigan State University Press, 2004); Celeste Michelle Condit and John Louis Lucaites, *Crafting Equality: America's Anglo-African Word* (Chicago: University of Chicago Press, 1993); John C. Hammerback and Richard J. Jensen, *The Rhetorical Career of Cesar Chavez* (College Station: Texas A&M University Press, 1998); Robert C. Rowland and David A. Frank, *Shared Land/Conflicting Identities: Trajectories of Israeli and Palestinian Symbol Use* (East Lansing: Michigan State University Press, 2002); Special issue on civil rights, *Rhetoric & Public Affairs* 2 (1999): 171–365; Special issue on King's "Letter from Birmingham Jail," *Rhetoric & Public Affairs* 7 (2004): 1–114; Special issue on the American civil rights movement in 1955, including the murder of Emmett Till, *Rhetoric & Public Affairs* 8 (2005): 175–354.

14. Gerard A. Hauser, *Vernacular Voices: The Rhetoric of Publics and Public Spheres* (Columbia: University of South Carolina Press, 1999); Robert L. Ivie, *Democracy and the War on Terror*; Special issue on deliberative democracy, *Rhetoric & Public Affairs* 5 (2002): 219–391; Vanessa B. Beasley et al., "Report of the National Task Force on Deliberative Democracy," in *The Prospect of Presidential Rhetoric*, ed. James Arnt Aune and Martin J. Medhurst (College Station: Texas A&M University Press, 2008), 251–71.

15. For my argument as to why the scholars of Era 4 constitute the "greatest generation," see Medhurst, "The Contemporary Study of Public Address," 497–98, 509n.

16. The information in chart 4 is derived from Ronald J. Matlon, ed., *Index to Journals in Communication Studies through 1985* (Annandale, Va.: Speech Communication Association, 1987).

17. Winans and Woolbert had set the pace in this area, but Woolbert died in 1929. Brigance had been close to Woolbert, citing him extensively in his 1927 book *The Spoken Word* (New York: F. S. Crofts and Company) and dedicating his 1928 book *Classified Speech Models of Eighteen Forms of Public Address* (New York: F. S. Crofts) to him.

18. William Norwood Brigance, "What Is a Successful Speech?" *Quarterly Journal of Speech Education* 11 (1925): 372–77; William Norwood Brigance, "Whither Research?" *Quarterly Journal of Speech* 19 (1933): 552–61; William Norwood Brigance, "Jeremiah Black and Andrew Johnson," *The Mississippi Valley Historical Review* 19 (1932): 205–18; William Norwood Brigance, *Jeremiah Sullivan Black: A Defender of the Constitution and the Ten Commandments* (Philadelphia: University of Pennsylvania Press, 1934).

19. See George C. Edwards III, *On Deaf Ears: The Limits of the Bully Pulpit* (New Haven: Yale University Press, 2003); George C. Edwards III, "Presidential Rhetoric: What Difference Does It Make?" in *Beyond the Rhetorical Presidency*, 199–217.

20. Brigance, "What Is a Successful Speech?" 376–77.

21. See Martin J. Medhurst, "Eisenhower's 'Atoms for Peace' Speech: A Case Study in the Strategic Use of Language," *Communication Monographs* 54 (1987): 204–20; Martin J. Medhurst, "Atoms for Peace and Nuclear Hegemony: The Rhetorical Structure of a Cold War Campaign," *Armed Forces & Society* 23 (1997): 571–93.

22. See G. P. Mohrmann and Michael C. Leff, "Lincoln at Cooper Union: A Rationale for Neo-Classical Criticism," *Quarterly Journal of Speech* 40 (1974): 459–67.

23. William Norwood Brigance, "What's in Our Schoolbooks?" *The Christian Century*, March 25, 1926, 382–84; William Norwood Brigance, "Ye Ancient Game of Foote Ball," *Century Magazine*, November 1926, 32–42; William Norwood Brigance, "The Bible of the Isolationists: Washington's Farewell Address as Twentieth Century Document," *The Independent*, February 19, 1927, 213–15; William Norwood Brigance, "Life for a Life," *The Independent*, August 27, 1927, 200–202; William Norwood Brigance, "War Graves," *The Independent*, July 14, 1928, 39–40; William Norwood Brigance, "The Invading Goth of Literature," *North American Review* (September 1928): 316–20; William Norwood Brigance, "Wisdom While You Wait," *North American Review* (December 1928): 751–57; William Norwood Brigance, "The Foreign Language Grindstone," *American Mercury* (April 1930): 438–45; William Norwood Brigance, "How Good Is Your Speech?" *Woman's Home Companion*, January 1935, 20ff.; William Norwood Brigance, "Why Children Stutter," *Ladies' Home Journal*, October 1935, 132–33; William Norwood Brigance, "Has Your Child Defective Speech?" *Woman's Home Companion*, May 1936, 49–50; William Norwood Brigance, "Aloha—In Color," *Popular*

Photography, July 1941, 27ff.; W. Norwood Brigance, "The Backwash of War," *Vital Speeches*, December 1, 1945, 105–8; W. Norwood Brigance, "1946: Year of Decision," *Vital Speeches*, February 1, 1947, 246–49; W. Norwood Brigance, "Security Is an Illusion," *Vital Speeches*, July 15, 1951, 593–96.

24. Brigance, "Jeremiah Black and Andrew Johnson," 205, 208.

25. Brigance, "Whither Research?" 556.

26. Michael C. Leff and G. P. Mohrmann, "Old Paths and New: A Fable for Critics," paper presented at the Speech Communication Association annual convention, Washington, D.C., 1977. Cited in G. P. Mohrmann, "Elegy in a Critical Graveyard," *Western Journal of Speech Communication* 44 (1980): 265–74.

27. Lucas, "The Renaissance of American Public Address," 247.

28. Brigance, "Whither Research?" 556–57.

29. Brigance, "Whither Research?" 557. For a recent work that does at least recognize this problem, see Craig R. Smith, *Daniel Webster and the Oratory of Civil Religion* (Columbia: University of Missouri Press, 2005).

30. Brigance, "Whither Research?" 558–59.

31. Brigance, "Whither Research?" 557.

32. The issue of who was the first person to publish a sole-authored scholarly book in the speech field seems to come down to whether Brigance's book on *Jeremiah Sullivan Black* or Lionel G. Crocker's book *Henry Ward Beecher's Art of Preaching* (Chicago: University of Chicago Press, 1934) appeared first. Both bear 1934 copyright dates.

33. Herman Cohen, *The History of Speech Communication: The Emergence of a Discipline, 1914–1945* (Annandale, Va.: Speech Communication Association, 1994), 170.

34. On the relevance of *Ex Parte Milligan* to contemporary criticism, see Marouf A. Hasian Jr., "Franklin D. Roosevelt, Wartime Anxieties, and the Saboteurs' Case," *Rhetoric & Public Affairs* 6 (2003): 233–60.

35. Brigance, *Jeremiah Sullivan Black*, 150–51

36. Brigance, *Jeremiah Sullivan Black*, 192n.

37. See Medhurst, "The Academic Study of Public Address: A Tradition in Transition," xx–xxx.

38. A. M. Drummond, ed., *Studies in Rhetoric and Public Speaking in Honor of James Albert Winans* (New York: Century Publishing Company, 1925); Brigance, *Jeremiah Sullivan Black*; Crocker, *Henry Ward Beecher's Art of Preaching*. There was also a volume on *Poetry of the English Renaissance, 1509–1660* (New York: F. S. Crofts, 1929), coedited by Hoyt H. Hudson; and a translation of Kant's *Religion within the Limits of Reason Alone* (Chicago: Open Court Publishing Company, 1934) by

Theodore M. Greene and Hoyt H. Hudson. Though Hudson was a founder of the field, neither of these works speaks directly to rhetoric.

39. William Norwood Brigance, "The Twenty-Eight Foremost American Orators," *Quarterly Journal of Speech* 24 (1938): 376–80.

40. Letter from William Norwood Brigance to J. Jeffrey Auer, April 25, 1950. Cited in David George Burns, "The Contributions of William Norwood Brigance to the Field of Speech," Ph.D. diss., Indiana University, 1970, 311–12.

41. Burns, "The Contributions of William Norwood Brigance to the Field of Speech," 311.

42. Letter from Brigance to J. Jeffrey Auer, September 20, 1943, cited in Burns, "The Contributions of William Norwood Brigance," 314.

43. Bower Aly, "The History of Public Address as a Research Field," *Quarterly Journal of Speech* 29 (1943): 308–14; Kenneth G. Hance, "Public Address in a Democracy at War," *Quarterly Journal of Speech* 30 (1944): 158–64; Loren D. Reid, "The Perils of Rhetorical Criticism," *Quarterly Journal of Speech* 30 (1944): 416–22.

44. Letter from Brigance to Rupert Cortright, August 3, 1943, cited in Burns, "The Contributions of William Norwood Brigance," 321.

45. Brigance, *The Spoken Word*, xii.

46. W. N. Brigance, "More about Business Speaking," *Quarterly Journal of Speech* 16 (1930): 219.

47. Brigance, "The Twenty-Eight Foremost American Orators," 376.

48. Letter from Brigance to Professor Hogdon, March 2, 1942, cited in Burns, "The Contributions of William Norwood Brigance," 330.

49. W.N.B., "The Contribution of Speech to National Defense," editorial, *Quarterly Journal of Speech* 28 (1942): 240.

50. Wilhelmina G. Hedde and William Norwood Brigance, *American Speech*, 3rd ed. (Chicago: J. B. Lippincott, 1951), 231.

51. William Norwood Brigance, "Preface," *A History and Criticism of American Public Address*, vol. 1 (New York: McGraw-Hill, 1943), vii.

52. See Brigance, "The Backwash of War," 107. For Kennan's Long Telegram, see Kenneth M. Jensen, ed., *Origins of the Cold War: The Novikov, Kennan, and Roberts 'Long Telegrams' of 1946* (Washington, D.C.: United States Institute of Peace Press, 1993), 17–31.

53. W. Norwood Brigance, "1946: Year of Decision," 246. Also reprinted in the *Quarterly Journal of Speech* 33 (1947): 127–33. Quote on page 131 of *QJS* version.

54. Brigance, "1946: Year of Decision," on page 131 of the *QJS* version.

55. W. Norwood Brigance, "Public Address," *Southern Speech Journal* 12 (1947): 42.

56. Brigance, "Security Is an Illusion," 593–95.

57. Brigance, "Security Is an Illusion," 596.

58. Brigance, "Security Is an Illusion," 595–96.

59. William Norwood Brigance, "General Education in an Industrial Free Society," *Quarterly Journal of Speech* 38 (1952): 177.

60. W. Norwood Brigance, *Speech: Its Techniques and Disciplines in a Free Society* (New York: Appleton-Century-Crofts, Inc., 1952), ix.

61. William Norwood Brigance, "Demagogues, 'Good' People, and Teachers of Speech," *The Speech Teacher* 1 (1952): 161.

62. These descriptors are found on pages 48–49, 72, and 258 of Brigance, *Jeremiah Sullivan Black.*

63. Brigance, "General Education in an Industrial Free Society"; W. Norwood Brigance, "On Talking a New Language," *Quarterly Journal of Speech* 44 (1958): 299–302.

2

Preparing Undergraduates for Democratic Citizenship: Upholding the Legacy of William Norwood Brigance through Rhetorical Education

Denise M. Bostdorff

In *Speech: Its Techniques and Disciplines in a Free Society*, W. Norwood Brigance declared, "There are two kinds of nations and two kinds of people in the world: Those who in disagreements and crises want to *shoot* it out, and those who have learned to *talk* it out. To shoot it out is the way of the concentration camp, machine gun, and the bomb. To talk it out is the way of mediation, parliamentary discussion, and political campaigns settled by the ballot."[1] Brigance's views were undoubtedly shaped by his generation's experience with the two World Wars, but they also reflected his firm belief, rooted in classical rhetoric, that speech was essential to democracy. In his text, Brigance warned, "A free society survives only when speech is used in the main as an instrument of *enlightenment*." Rhetoric was, therefore *"a dangerous form of power requiring a sense of high responsibility by those who use it,"* which made public-speaking courses particularly important.[2]

As Medhurst has detailed so beautifully, Brigance was a giant whose leadership in research broke new ground and helped the fledgling discipline of speech communication gain legitimacy. What today's communication scholars also should remember, however, is that Brigance was, first and foremost, not a researcher but a teacher of undergraduates. Despite the efforts of a number of graduate programs to recruit him, and a brief visiting stint at the University of Hawaii, Brigance chose to spend his thirty-eight-year professorial career at Wabash, a small liberal-arts college for men in Indiana. While David Burns has explained a number of factors that led to that decision—summers free from teaching duties so Brigance could write, financial remuneration, and his family's desire to remain in Crawfordsville, for example—his own interest in civic engagement seemed to play a very large role. Brigance saw his instruction in public speaking at Wabash as critical to a democratic society, and he was highly involved with the campus and larger community. Moreover, Brigance spoke often before groups himself and established the nation's first collegiate speakers bureau at Wabash, which by the time of his death in 1960 had delivered 2,654 programs to audiences appraised at over 150,000 people.[3]

If we wish to fulfill our own civic responsibility as a discipline, we should look to Brigance's example by paying much more attention to our undergraduate teaching than we have in recent years. Brigance, not unlike Isocrates, believed that a rhetorical education was essential for wise citizenship and "a democratic way of life."[4] By rediscovering our undergraduate students and using rhetorical pedagogy to prepare them for citizenship, we can strengthen democratic practices. A rhetorical education can help students grow into substantive, compelling, and responsible rhetors; likewise, it can aid them in becoming discerning listeners and offer them experiential learning in deliberation and in civic affairs where rhetoric and politics intersect.

In the past few decades, both rhetorical studies and our larger discipline of communication—like many other disciplines—have tended to concentrate on professionalization through academic research and graduate education. These activities are important, but they have caused us to lose sight of our most important constituency: undergraduate students. For most of us, undergraduates make up the largest segment of our student audience and have the potential to shape our polity for good or ill as they leave us to work in business, medicine, law, science, education, religion, the media, the nonprofit sector, and even politics. To be blunt, how will we have our greatest impact on society: through the articles we publish in scholarly journals, or through the rhetorical education we provide to prepare college students for citizenship?

Let me be clear that I do not intend this essay as an attack on research institutions, nor as an encomium for small liberal-arts colleges. For many years, I taught at a research university, reaped benefits that the institution had to offer, earned tenure and promotion there, and then left for Ohio to begin my teaching career anew at a liberal-arts college of 1,800 students, where I have remained for more than a decade. Indeed, I have affection and respect for both kinds of institutions, at the same time that I have experienced firsthand the frustrations of each. Good teaching takes place at both types of institutions, as does good research, and obviously, graduate training and research—at their best—lead to outstanding scholar-teachers. Nonetheless, if we as rhetorical scholars do not refocus our attention on our undergraduates, then we are missing the opportunity to exert much-needed positive influence on a civic society that currently is ailing.

To make my case, I first examine the issue of decreased civic engagement, particularly in regard to young people; how colleges and universities have contributed to this problem; and how they can be part of the solution. I then explore the legacy of W. Norwood Brigance and how scholar-teachers of rhetoric might uphold it by making our classrooms into forums for civic engagement, by using service learning and modeling civic engagement ourselves, and by sharing our research with the public and promoting undergraduate research. Finally, I look at some additional steps we need to take to place the focus back on undergraduates and civic engagement both at our institutions and within our discipline.

Decreased Civic Engagement and the Role of Higher Education

Scholars in a number of disciplines have, in recent years, warned of a crisis in civic engagement. In 2000, Robert Putnam's *Bowling Alone* drew on data about Americans' behavior and attitudes over the past quarter century to reveal that with each subsequent generation, community and social capital were dwindling. Americans were participating less in politics, civic and work-related organizations, and religion; interacting less with one another socially; and experiencing lower levels of social trust.[5] Although Putnam's voice may have received the most attention, he certainly was not alone in his concerns. Political economist Robert Reich argued that the changes of the new economy had led to widening economic and social stratification and to more harried lives with less time for family and community, while communication scholar Joe Turow pointed to the ways in which advertisers had used target marketing—a tool that reaches specific groups of consumers, but that also has the effect of creating a sense of division among diverse groups by creating "image tribes" based on their characteristics as consumers.[6] For his part, political scientist John Freie lamented the ways in which planned communities, shopping malls, employers, politicians, church marketers, and cyberspace have exploited Americans' desire for a sense of connectedness by offering counterfeit community instead.[7] Scholars argued that the crisis in civic engagement had been further exacerbated by the growth, increased commercialism, and changing coverage patterns of the mass media.[8] The result, as David Zarefsky noted, was that "At the very time that media and communication technology permit *greater* access to politics, we find instead *declining* rates of political participation, a declining belief in the efficacy of political action, a declining belief that it makes any difference who is elected, and a vastly diminished belief in the nobility of politics as a profession."[9] Putnam and others also warned that the crisis in civic engagement was especially acute among young people, where rates of cynicism about politics appear to run particularly high and political involvement appears to be particularly low.[10]

Other scholars, however, have claimed that calls to crisis are off the mark. According to Bennett, the nature of civic engagement is changing, but that does not mean that citizens are not involved in political life.[11] Even Putnam's research found that one exception to the generational downward spiral of civic engagement was the fact that young people had substantially increased their volunteer work and community service during the most recent decade studied.[12] Youniss et al. argued that scholars should recognize "a continuum between formal political acts such as voting, political actions such as protesting for a moral cause, and performing a service such as working in a rural literacy campaign." While research confirms that young people are uninvolved in "traditional politics" such as voting or volunteering for political organizations, their rates of volunteering for other types of causes and organizations actually exceed those of older age groups.[13] In addition, the Higher Education Research Institute's annual survey of incoming first-year students in 2004 reported that 34 percent of students said that "keeping up to date with political affairs" was one of their "very important" or "essential" life goals, which continued a four-year rise from 28.1 percent in 2000.[14] And in the 2004 presidential election, 51.6 percent of young people ages 18 to 29 voted, compared to 42.3 percent in 2000. In battleground states, the rate was even higher at a phenomenal 64 percent.[15]

If the civic involvement of young people is more nuanced than some research would lead us to believe, however, the state of their political engagement raises concerns nonetheless. The annual survey of incoming first-year students, for instance, also found that only 19.7 percent rated "influencing the political structure" as a very important or essential goal, a finding that may reflect students' self-perceptions of inefficacy in the political realm.[16] The decision of many young people not to participate in traditional politics may well be "a clear rejection" of a system that is "perceived to be broken," but it is a decision that also functions to disenfranchise them.[17] While volunteering in other areas of the civic realm is certainly commendable, the potential danger of an exclusive focus on such volunteer work—for example, at the local food bank—is that it may prevent students from seeing the larger political structures that function to create inequality in the first place, and from acting to change those structures.

In addition, young people are remarkably uninformed both about how civic institutions work and about current events. Galston explained that "Today's college graduates know no more about politics than high school graduates did fifty years ago, and today's high school graduates are no more knowledgeable than were the high school dropouts of the past."[18] In regard to current events, Mindich found that young people are following the news at much lower rates than earlier generations. Individuals in the age group of 18–24 are far less interested in the news, far less interested in politics, and far less likely to pay attention to news coverage from newspapers, news magazines, radio, or television than previous generations. For example, young women are more apt to read *Cosmopolitan* and young men to read *Maxim* than they are to read *Newsweek* or *Time*. Nor are young people turning to the Internet for news. According to Mindich, a 2002 survey that asked respondents ages 18–24 about their preferred news source found that only 11 percent picked the Internet.[19] In sum, then, young people are less participative in, attentive to, and knowledgeable about political life than previous generations.

While the huge turnout among young people for the 2004 presidential election is heartening, it is too early to know whether it represents a new trend or is simply a blip in typical youth patterns of nonvoting. This age group was the only one to prefer John Kerry (55 percent) over George W. Bush (44 percent),[20] and their preference was not upheld by the electorate as a whole. Given young people's past patterns, the resilience of their engagement in electoral politics is uncertain. Even if young people do continue to vote, their lack of knowledge about and interest in traditional politics will continue to deter their wise and fruitful participation in democracy.

While I do not have time to go into all of the elements that have led us to this point, I do want to discuss one relevant factor that has undermined civic engagement, and that is the retreat of colleges and universities from the public realm. Schneider points out that higher education distanced itself, in part, as a way to protect funding and scholarship from politically motivated attacks in the anticommunist furor after World War II.[21] However, Zlotkowski argues that research institutions were also interested in attracting government funds during the Cold War arms race, which led them to detach from the world of politics in order to enhance their credibility through the appearance of objectivity.[22]

This same period saw the culmination of a conflict that first emerged in American higher education in the nineteenth century between those who adopted a traditionally American model that made clear connections between education and citizenship, and those who began to adopt a German educational model of research and expertise.[23] According to Mathews, higher education began to devalue the public further as "a new philosophy, supposedly nonpolitical, which I would call 'professionalism,' was taking hold. It accompanied the professionalization of most vocations and institutions. In higher education, it not only gave rise to professional schools but also to the professionalization of disciplines within the liberal arts. A new generation of academics began talking more to each other than to their fellow citizens, who could not understand their expert language."[24] Eventually, he says, academics who chose to talk to the public were viewed with suspicion by their peers.[25]

In recent years, critics of and from higher education have called upon their colleagues to involve themselves once more in educating citizens. However, Zlotkowski maintains that because academics from research universities continue to dominate the governing bodies of most national disciplinary associations, disciplines, and in turn, the institutions that house them, have been slow to answer the call.[26] Some academics are reluctant to bolster citizenship because they remember the demands for "judgment-free patriotism" during the Vietnam War.[27] Others, no doubt, are troubled by the fact that higher education's attempts to bolster civic engagement in the past tended to presume a universally Western, white, male point of view.

Today, colleges also increasingly find themselves in competitive situations where they are vying with other schools for students and with state legislatures for funding, and relying upon grants, many of which come from corporations with clear self-interests that may be at odds with the public good. At the 2004 Central States Communication Association Conference panel on commercialism in higher education, faculty members in the audience from a large university not far from Wooster, Ohio, told those of us on the panel how they had organized a teach-in after the start of the Iraq war, only to have their institution bring in police to force them off school property over fears of the "bad publicity" such a political event would draw. Decisions such as this one to detach from the public realm do, of course, have political implications of their own, for they permit powerful political forces outside academe to exert their influence unchallenged and do little to prepare students to analyze dominant societal values and principles thoughtfully—or, if they choose to do so, to oppose them effectively.

According to Boyte and Kari, the retreat of higher education has also altered the culture of civic engagement on campus. Many faculty members report that the institutional culture at their colleges and universities has come to focus on market values and individual self-interests.[28] Given the current state of civic engagement among youth and the withdrawal of academe from civic life, Newman's words from a 1985 Carnegie Foundation report seem as pertinent today as they were then: "If there is a crisis in education in the United States today, it is less that test scores have declined than it is that we have failed to provide the education for citizenship that is still the most significant responsibility of the nation's schools and colleges."[29]

Just as young people's extensive volunteer work and their turnout in the 2004 election provide signs of hope, however, the state of higher education's willingness to tend to the civic education of its students indicates positive points of development as well. The Carnegie Foundation for the Advancement of Teaching and the American Association for Higher Education have focused time, attention, and resources on this issue, as the plethora of recent publications on civic engagement and pedagogy in higher education attests.[30] With this greater interest have come discussions of what it means to be a citizen. Barber notes that the messages people most often receive today equate citizenship with voting or with consuming, rather than with participation in self-governance.[31] If we define citizenship as the hard work of joining together to solve community problems, this conception has clear implications for civic education. We need to teach students how politics deals not just with our relationships with the government (voting for a candidate or paying taxes, for example), but with our relationships with one another,[32] and we must help students attain the knowledge and skills they need to be effective citizens.

Scholar-teachers of rhetoric are especially well poised to fulfill this pressing need. After all, from the time of ancient Greece, rhetoric has concerned itself with preparing students for citizenship, a goal that our discipline as a whole historically has held as well.[33] Moreover, Zlotkowski pointed to our discipline in 2000 as a "notable" exception to disciplines' typical indifference to the call for civic education because our leadership, under the tutelage of then National Communication Association (NCA) president Jim Applegate, had "demonstrated a strong commitment to service and social engagement—a commitment that has already had a significant effect" on national programming.[34] The time, then, is ripe for scholar-teachers of rhetoric to reexamine Brigance's legacy in regard to civic education and how we might uphold it through efforts to reinvigorate our undergraduate teaching.

Brigance's Legacy of Rhetorical Education for Citizenship

In so much of what he did, Brigance concentrated on civic education, particularly on rhetorical pedagogy, to prepare undergraduates for citizenship. We need to uphold his legacy by making our classrooms into forums for civic engagement, by using service learning and modeling civic engagement ourselves, and by sharing our research with the public and promoting undergraduate research.

BRIGANCE AND THE CLASSROOM AS
A FORUM FOR CIVIC ENGAGEMENT

In *Speech: Its Techniques and Disciplines in a Free Society*, Brigance harkened back to ancient Greece when he wrote that speechmaking arose out of humans' initial efforts at self-government.[35] Brigance, like Dewey, saw democracy as working itself out in association with other people. According to Brigance, students must learn to speak for several reasons: "To keep a free society free. To settle differences by talk instead of force. To alter and promote thought. To water and cultivate ideas, hopes, sentiments, and enthusiasms in a way and to a degree that cannot be done while we are separated from one another." He emphasized the importance of speech and of audience members sitting "together elbow to elbow . . . stimulated by the presence of others."[36]

Brigance fulfilled his devotion to civic engagement, in large part, through the public-speaking classroom. In fact, he insisted on always teaching at least one section of the basic course because, he said, "I am making [this student] not merely able to give a little classroom speech, but a better citizen and a better man."[37] Learning how to think, research, outline, write, and rewrite was an important part of the Brigance regimen in public speaking. In his text *Speech: Its Techniques and Disciplines in a Free Society*, he entitled a chapter on thinking about and researching the subject matter of a speech "Earning the Right to Speak."[38] A copy of one of Brigance's speaking assignments shows that he was especially concerned that students learn how to analyze critically the information they gleaned from the mass media; his assignment sheet reveals that the good professor was covering such topics as how to read newspapers, how to make sense of public-opinion polls, and how to detect propaganda.[39] Wrote Brigance: "Giving a good speech is the equivalent of testifying that, 'Here is a subject I have thought about, and have investigated.'"[40] In addition to instruction on structure, support, language, delivery, and ethics, Brigance emphasized what he called "the rights of listeners." He mused that in an ideal world, speakers would be required to take a version of the Hippocratic oath, in which they would promise, among other things, to keep the audience's welfare in mind, to deliver their address clearly, and never to speak *"unless I have prepared myself with substance worth saying."*[41] In the civic world, as in the public-speaking classroom, Brigance wanted speakers to choose their subject matter carefully, research thoroughly, and decide upon their goal and rhetorical strategy with the good of the larger community in mind. Akin to physicians, rhetors were to avoid advocating any action that would deliberately harm listeners in order to benefit someone else.

Brigance also thought it important that students examine speeches given outside the classroom, as well as exemplary texts, because of what students could learn from them.[42] In 1928, Brigance published *Classified Speech Models of Eighteen Forms of Public Address*, which organized exemplary speeches by their occasion. In his acknowledgments, he thanked a long list of noteworthy individuals who gave him permission to include particular speeches. Among those mentioned were Mr. Clarence Darrow, President Calvin Coolidge, Mrs. William Jennings Bryan, Justice Oliver Wendell Holmes Jr., and Mrs. Woodrow Wilson.[43]

Indeed, Brigance seemed to be in perpetual motion when it came to teaching his undergraduates. Belying the myths of leisure often associated with teaching at a small liberal-arts college, Brigance said he rarely worked fewer than fifty-five hours each week during the academic year and often worked closer to seventy hours, all of it spent on his classes, students, and other college duties.[44] His efforts did not go unrewarded, for he became a figure of veneration among students and on campus as a whole. In 1956, the school newspaper expressed such sentiments well when it used the following analogy to define "Brigance" for new students: "Brigance—what is to Wabash as God is to the rest of the world."[45]

Given Brigance's legacy of classroom teaching, what can we do in our classrooms to provide students with the education they need to be civically engaged? First, we must revitalize our commitment to teaching undergraduates how to speak and how to deliberate. This is a feature of our undergraduate curriculum that has received short shrift in recent years as more specialized courses push out public speaking as a common educational experience. Courses on argumentation and debate have, if anything, fared even worse. One recurrent criticism of public deliberation has been that not everyone in society gets to participate, and not everyone has the resources and skills to be equal participants.[46] Yet it is in our public-speaking and debate courses where we have the chance to equalize the playing field somewhat. We cannot control the curricula that all students encounter in their primary and secondary schooling, nor the families and communities where they grow up, but we can offer those students who do reach us a rhetorical education, which is not an insignificant act. As Rod Hart put it, "Freedom goes to the articulate," and "Teachers of communication . . . peddle freedom."[47]

In this context, classrooms become community forums, or what Eberly refers to as "protopublic spaces," where students "encounter each other as deliberating bodies, something that large lecture classes that focus only on rhetoric as analytical do not allow." The classroom is not the same as a naturally occurring community, but Campbell argues that the inequalities between the teacher and student "faithfully mirror the conditions of post-modern life and the challenges to democratic practice that it poses." The "pedagogic *polis*" of the public-speaking classroom demands that students use critical reasoning to construct their speeches for an actual audience, to make judgments about the subjects of others' addresses, and to critique others' presentations in terms of their support, strategy, delivery, audience adaptation, and so on.[48] In addition, students learn to reflect upon the judgments they themselves make in constructing their speeches. The classroom also provides a safe community in which to learn and, yes, in which to make mistakes. In my own experience, the give-and-take of speeches and responses in the public-speaking or debate classroom fosters an environment in which people come to know each other well, learn to disagree respectfully, and tend to support one another in both failure and success, despite their differences. Students also learn what it means to become a community *through* deliberation. In the public-speaking and debate classroom, then, students have a chance to practice deliberation, and such practice, as Ivie noted, is essential to the health of democracy.[49]

Beyond revitalizing our commitment to courses in public speaking and debate, we must provide more assignments in both those courses and others that not only teach such skills, but also establish the relationship between rhetorical ways of knowing and doing and civic participation. This can be done through varied means. For instance, instructors may emphasize the importance of speaking skills to students' roles as citizens, in terms of their relationship both to the government and to other people. This is the essence of what it means to participate in civil society, defined by Hauser and Benoit-Barné as *"a network of associations independent of the state whose members, through discursive exchanges that balance conflict and consensus, seek to regulate themselves in ways consistent with a valuation of difference."*[50] I require that my own public-speaking students subscribe to *Washington Post Weekly*, and I draw on articles from the publication, as well as the student newspaper, for frequent in-class exercises and homework assignments. Not surprisingly, our class discussion regularly revolves around issues of international, national, and local import, often exposing students to questions they previously had not considered. Speech assignments themselves demand extensive research from a variety of different sources. For the final assignment, students must present their views on a controversial issue and then engage in discussion with the class about it, after which they must modify their prepared conclusion in light of the discussion.[51] Students usually prepare for this last assignment with trepidation, but it clearly is an empowering experience for them. As a result of the course, students not only learn about public speaking, but they also frequently report being more informed, more confident about articulating their views in public, and—as students often put it—"more political."

Other methods also abound. In their courses, for example, McMillan and Harriger taught deliberative skills using National Issues Forum booklets, moderating the early class efforts more stringently as students learned how to speak, how to listen, and how to consider whose voices were not represented—and then attempting "to 'speak' for them."[52] Campbell recommends an assignment in which both a team in favor of a policy and a team opposed to a policy must argue for their own position, but from the perspective of the values and ideals of the other team. "The idea," Campbell writes, "is not to show the other side up, but to win them over."[53] Through cross-arguing in this way, each side—even those who might be ideologically opposed—becomes adept at employing the arguments of the other side, thereby opening up the possibility of identification such that opponents are perceived as adversaries, rather than as enemies.[54] Instructors can use simulations in their courses—for example, assigning each student a role in a constructed community to demonstrate how issues develop through discourse and how differential power affects the outcome—to great effect, as well. In her classroom, Eberly prepares students and then assigns them to enter public deliberation by writing a well-supported letter or op-ed piece for the local paper, or by calling a local talk-radio show with a well-supported argument and capturing their call on audiotape.[55]

In all of these teaching methods, we must show students that issues are not just a given, but rather that issues are defined, often strategically, so that some problems receive attention while others do not, and so that particular issue definitions will lead to particular policy resolutions.

Students must learn that public deliberation is, in Welsh's words, "inherently competitive and cooperative as political actors struggle over common vocabularies and prevailing meanings."[56] Even more traditional teaching methods, such as providing exemplary texts, can serve this purpose. Students who study both Lincoln's Gettysburg Address and Martin Luther King Jr.'s "I Have a Dream" can learn how Lincoln used his speech to redefine the Declaration of Independence as the nation's founding document, and how King then used that premise to redefine the United States' treatment of African Americans. Afterward, instructors can follow up such study with explanations of how Ronald Reagan, in his turn, used strategic excerpts of King's rhetoric to argue that King was opposed to affirmative action, in order to bolster support for his own conservative policies.[57] Similar points can be made by having students examine controversies on campus and the differing ways in which various parties define them.

Yet another way in which we can establish the relationship between rhetoric and civic participation is by bringing in guests, when appropriate, who can demonstrate such ideas. In my argumentation-and-debate course, students have gleaned insights from both a public defender and a former federal judge. Students in my leadership class have had the opportunity to ask questions of a businessman, a social-justice activist, a city-council representative, a school superintendent, and a doctor who started the free clinic in our community. Through such interactions, students learn more about rhetoric in practice (even if the guests would not always identify what they do in those terms), more about public issues, and, often, the intersection between the two.

Through hands-on activities—what scholars in the area of civic engagement call "experiential education"[58]—and through careful analysis of exemplary texts and interaction with relevant classroom guests, students not only gain a rhetorical education but also prepare themselves for meaningful civic engagement. As Eberly argues, rhetorical practices in the classroom "can form collective habits, these habits can be experienced as pleasurable, and these shared rhetorical practices can sustain publics and counterpublics—on campus and beyond campus."[59]

A third way in which we can live up to Brigance's legacy of civic engagement in the classroom is by teaching students to be rhetorical analysts who have both a healthy skepticism in regard to rhetoric and an appreciation of its artistry and potential. Most scholar-teachers of rhetoric do a good job of helping students learn how to examine messages more critically. In their classrooms, they expose students to a wide range of texts—from Jane Addams to George W. Bush, from the medical reports of the Tuskegee Syphilis Project to the sales pitch of the *Vermont Country Store Catalogue*, for example—and teach them how messages use *"language to help people narrow their choices among specifiable, if not specified, policy options."*[60] This type of analysis is, of course, also present in responses to student performances in public-speaking and debate classes. Given how reliant students—and all citizens for that matter—are on media coverage for their news information, we should be especially attentive to teaching students to analyze media rhetoric more carefully: to note how leaks are used in newspaper accounts to shape perceptions of issues, to examine the visual backdrops of messages, and to analyze the seductive rhetorical form of particular media, such as *Fox News*'s use of typical news formats that cast partisanship as objectivity, for instance. Young people's increased dependence on TV comedy shows for current-events information indicates that this media venue should particularly draw our pedagogical attention.[61]

Furthermore, we must think carefully about the ways in which we discuss rhetoric. I have been somewhat astonished at conferences in recent years, for example, at the number of scholars who have talked about rhetoric in disparaging ways without making a distinction between the particular political message that they were critiquing and political rhetoric in general. While the current political scene has frequently generated discourse that justifies our criticism, if we convey—explicitly or implicitly—that all political rhetoric is inauthentic speech, then we should hardly be surprised when students feel no compulsion to participate in civic life. I am not suggesting that we eliminate criticism, but I am arguing that cynicism in our discourse about rhetoric will only feed the cynicism that our students already feel, and deter the potential for renewed civic engagement. Instead, we should foster a healthy skepticism about rhetoric, along with an appreciation of its potential for transformation. That is, we should encourage our students to value the artistry of political rhetoric while simultaneously questioning it, instead of viewing politics and political discourse with debilitating cynicism or contempt. Some—perhaps many—of our fellow rhetorical critics would argue that students are perfectly justified in opting out of our political system, but this argument holds no weight for me. Instead, the choices seem more stark: we can retreat and hand over all control to individuals in power whose views we may disdain, we can use violence to bring about change, or—if we wish to work democratically for change—then we must work, ultimately, within the existing political structure.[62] The way in which we talk about rhetoric with our undergraduates has the potential to enhance or deter their willingness to undertake such difficult democratic work.

BRIGANCE AND THE EXTENSION OF PEDAGOGY
BEYOND THE CLASSROOM

Brigance believed that pedagogy should not be contained merely within the classroom walls, but rather extended beyond the classroom in the form of intercollegiate debating and speaking contests.[63] Although he coached debate at Wabash for two years in the 1920s, Brigance's true love was oratorical contests of various kinds, particularly the Interstate Oratorical Association contest. He prepared students for such competitions for over two decades, always insisting that they gain a clear sense of audience by giving their speeches before civic organizations and other actual audiences prior to delivering their addresses in competition. From 1922 to 1943, Wabash dominated the field, taking four national championships, five second places, two third places, and one fourth place. No other school was as successful as Wabash was under Brigance's leadership. Indeed, the prestige of these competitions gave public speakers at Wabash a degree of status akin to college athletes today. In Burns's words, "The orator was the 'big man on campus.'"[64]

Brigance's keen interest in civic education, however, led him in 1927 to move beyond oratorical competitions alone to begin the nation's first collegiate speakers bureau.[65] According to Brigance, oratorical contests were a wonderful educational experience for the students who participated, but he wanted more young men to be able to benefit, and the Wabash College Speakers Bureau provided such a venue.[66] Brigance had the civic education of the populace in mind as well, for the bureau provided its speakers to civic organizations, schools, churches, and other groups free of charge; the only required remuneration was the speaker's travel expenses. In the 1928 announcement of the speakers bureau's formation, the department's flyer stated that its purpose was to "offer public discussion of affairs having current interest and importance."[67]

This was a goal that the bureau clearly fulfilled. From 1928 to 1960, the bureau presented an average of eighty-three programs each year—an astonishingly high mean when one considers that the war years limited the department's ability to furnish speakers, since so many of its students had been drafted. The bureau sponsored only four programs in 1943 and just eleven in 1944, and it had to close down entirely in 1945.[68] In examining the promotional flyers for the bureau, one can see that some of the speeches were primarily inspirational (e.g., a Christian sermon), entertaining (e.g., a student's tale of working his way through college as a boxer), or informative (e.g., the birds of Indiana) in nature. The majority of speeches, however, dealt with current events: U.S. policy in the Caribbean and Nicaragua, deception in advertising, farm relief, racketeering, lack of state funding for education, the 1940 presidential election, Japan's Far East policy, and coal strikes, for example.[69] Nor did students shy away from taking controversial stands. One John M. Kitchen, for instance, examined the fallacies of "the American Gospel of 'sweat success,'" while Terence Anderson defended Castro's Cuba before an audience of Jaycees.[70] Through the speakers bureau, Brigance not only provided his students with an excellent education in speaking and civic engagement but also enriched the communities in which they spoke, thereby contributing to thoughtful public deliberation. His example also inspired similar programs at other schools, including a speakers bureau at Oberlin College, begun by a former Brigance student, J. Jeffery Auer.[71]

Brigance did not leave such efforts at community outreach solely to his students, however; he also modeled civic engagement himself in two primary ways. First, he spoke to local groups such as high school assemblies and service clubs, and through the National Lecture Bureau, he spoke to audiences throughout the United States. Second, Brigance was actively involved in groups like Kiwanis, the Methodist Church, the American Legion, the Crawfordsville Planning Commission, and what Burns describes as "a small band of Democrats."[72] Brigance believed it was his duty to reach out to the community, but what is also important to realize here is that he often took students with him to observe his local speeches, and that he frequently drew on examples from his experiences with community organizations in class.[73] In this manner, Brigance taught his students about speechmaking and persuasion, while simultaneously providing them with a role model for what a citizen should be.

From the standpoint of the present day, Brigance's extension of pedagogy beyond the classroom through competitions and the speakers bureau seems an easier task than it might be for us. Brigance spent a great deal of time outside of class assisting students as they prepared, but exten-sive public-speaking coursework also helped immeasurably. During the Brigance era at Wabash, students took a one-year fundamentals course in public speaking, and if they wished, they enrolled in two additional one-year courses—a fact that explains Brigance's insistence that it took contest speakers three years to prepare.[74] By contrast, students today might be lucky to take a single-semester course in public speaking, let alone advanced courses. This curricular change is a natural result of the development and corresponding specialization of courses in the discipline, but also—as noted earlier—an outcome of our unfortunate neglect of the art of public speaking in our own curricula. As a result, if one were to ensure quality speeches, the time commitment of forensics or a speakers bureau would be far greater now than it was then, and might, even with the requirement of a course in public speaking, be out of the question for many faculty members already carrying heavy loads.

How, then, can we fulfill Brigance's legacy of civic education outside the classroom? Certainly, schools with the funding and staffing to support a forensics program should be encouraged to do so, but I argue that such competitions need to put the audience back into the picture. National De-bate Tournament (NDT) debate today is only decipherable to other NDT debaters and debate coaches. Likewise, National Forensic Association (NFA) individual event speeches are crafted for NFA judges, but rarely delivered to other listeners. Students would benefit from speaking before community audiences, and audiences, in turn, might benefit as well.

The main way that we might extend civic engagement outside the classroom, however, is through the pedagogy of service learning, a subset of experiential education. According to Bringle and Hatcher, service learn-ing is a planned pedagogical activity in which students draw on course concepts to fulfill a community need and to extend their own learning; they further learn from the experience through a classroom assignment that requires them to reflect on the relationship of the experience to course content and their own development.[75] For ten years at Purdue University, for example, I taught and/or directed a service-learning course called "Problems in Public Relations" in which students wrote, presented, and enacted proposals for local nonprofit organizations like the Tippeca-noe Arts Federation, the Women in Crisis Shelter, and the Community and Family Resource Center.[76] Students learned a great deal about craft-ing their written and oral messages for particular audiences, but they also discovered the virtues of civic engagement by working with worthy organizations to complete projects that otherwise might not be done.

Several years later, I turned to this model again for a political-rhetoric course. Students typically had come to my courses on political rhetoric and public issues with a high degree of cynicism, but without the skills necessary to analyze critically; in teaching them to be more analytical, however, I often found that—try as I might not to—I fed their cynicism as well. So it was in the fall of 2000 that I created a Politics-in-Action Project at Wooster modeled on the Problems in Public Relations course at Purdue. In this project, students had to choose a political problem, write and enact a proposal for some form of communication action that might help alleviate the problem, and reflect on their project through a formal presentation. The projects themselves varied a great deal, including a voter-registration program, an information campaign and petition drive on behalf of Afghan women (a full year prior to 9/11), and an issue campaign for the Wayne County Office of Rural Land Preservation. Through the Politics-in-Action Project, students gained a better understanding of concepts related to political rhetoric, learned skills needed to be meaningfully involved in politics, and developed a greater appreciation for both the difficulties and rewards associated with political action. As one student observed midway through his group's project, "This is harder than it looks."[77]

Many other service learning possibilities also exist. Through the National Communication Association's Communicating Common Ground (CCG) Initiative with the Southern Poverty Law Center, Campus Compact, and the American Association for Higher Education, students in Fundamentals of Public Speaking at Coe College teach elementary students how to give speeches on topics related to their elementary curriculum on tolerance.[78] At Loyola University, Chicago, Pollock's argumentation students created three 30-minute radio programs about the school's controversial proposed strategic plan; the programs included interviews with students and administrators, as well as the class's analysis of the arguments involved.[79] Students in communication departments across the country have also organized Debate Watch programs during presidential elections.

My own perceptions of the benefits of service learning are borne out in research that shows that service learning helps students learn the course material better than they otherwise would, and also enhances critical thinking.[80] In addition, service learning is more successful at promoting a sense of civic responsibility than service that is done independently by the student or through other organized activities.[81] Service learning combines two forms of learning that have been closely associated with civic education: problem-based learning, where students focus on real-world problems, and collaborative learning, where students have to work with others. Depending upon the project, service learning has the potential to enhance the civic engagement of community members who participate, too.[82]

Service learning also provides the advantage that Brigance's multiple public-speaking courses gave him for the speakers bureau: service learning builds on classroom instruction. This fact ensures that students begin their service-learning projects with relatively the same base of knowledge, and that instructors can use classroom instruction to improve the quality of off-campus student work. Like Brigance's speakers bureau, service learning provides a wide range of students with an opportunity that enhances classroom learning and teaches civic engagement, while benefiting the community as well. Instructors who adopt this pedagogical approach find it does take extra effort, but the ability to make use of classroom instruction and course assignments to prepare students helps lighten the load, while experience enables instructors to implement service learning with greater ease over time. Furthermore, instructors may well find the additional time and energy worthwhile in exchange for service learning's pedagogical payoff for students and potential to deepen instructors' own understanding of rhetorical principles as actualized in specific situations.

A second way in which we can extend civic engagement beyond the classroom is by modeling it for our students. While academics of Brigance's generation were involved in their communities and, indeed, thought it their civic duty to contribute as both citizens and academics to the public realm, faculty members today are far less involved. The pressures of modern life and—in the case of many colleges and universities—the demand that professors do more with fewer resources have taken their toll. Nonetheless, Smith found that professionals outside of academe, who certainly are no less busy, tended to be far more active in their communities.[83] Many American professors simply do not identify with their fellow citizens and so have withdrawn to the ivory tower, thereby exacerbating what Boyte and Kari call "democracy's crisis."[84] Only a few years ago, I recall a colleague from another department telling me that faculty members should remain unsullied from involvement in the public realm, and that our students learned good citizenship from us simply by observing that we showed up on time and taught our classes well. While I would not dispute that students learn from our example, I fear the lesson they may be learning is that one's professional life is important, while one's civic life is not. Moreover, in our case, rhetorical scholars may despair at the quality of public deliberation, but if we retreat from the civic realm then we are doing nothing to improve it.

In this regard, we might take a lesson from Professor Brigance by involving ourselves in our communities so that students can, on occasion, witness and/or work with us on issues. Additionally, we can draw upon relevant examples from our experiences in our classroom teaching. Engagement in this way is at odds with the image of the detached scholar that disciplines tend to revere, but it is important. First, our communities need informed, engaged citizens. Second, we can learn a great deal ourselves about rhetoric through such involvement. Third, mentoring relationships with students in this context encourages their own civic participation.[85] Finally, discussion of one's work—accompanied by a willingness to analyze all positions critically, including one's own—demonstrates to students that people can disagree, but still deliberate without being enemies.

This last point is key. For many years, while teaching my rhetoric courses, I tried to remain inscrutable in regard to my own opinions on issues, candidates, and government officials, but I decided a few years ago that this facade of objectivity had to end. When students outside of class were working with me on particular issues, it seemed silly, even disingenuous, to pretend in class that I had no political opinions. This more open approach is not without its risks, however. Discussing one's public-speaking program for a local 4-H club is not controversial, but talking about one's work for the local Kerry headquarters during a highly contentious presidential election, or for a rally against the war in Iraq, very well could be. Nevertheless, I have persisted in drawing upon these experiences in the classroom as a way to illustrate points, demonstrate the relationship between rhetoric and the public realm, and model civic engagement for my students. The response to this new approach has been positive, and although one student wrote in a teaching evaluation that "some" of my information was "biased," students—including that particular individual—have consistently evaluated my classroom as one "open to ideas," and one that treats individuals in a manner "free of bias or discrimination." We live in a period of highly polarized politics, and many of our students have learned to duck this topic—even when they are interested—as a way to avoid the unpleasant interactions that political issues can provoke. We need to show students that one can deliberate and be involved in politics without being mean-spirited, and that our expertise in rhetoric permits us to point out the strengths and weaknesses in any argument, regardless of our stated views. In other words, scholar-teachers of rhetoric can and should discuss their political experiences and, when relevant, their opinions in class, but they must do so in a way that reflects the same openness to deliberation and critical thinking that we desire for the public realm as a whole. Again, we might look no further than to Brigance himself, who felt no compunction about warning his listeners and readers—including his students—about the dangerous rhetoric of McCarthyism, yet still managed to maintain good relations with these groups because of his obvious commitment to ethical standards that he applied to every speaker, regardless of his/her political views.[86]

BRIGANCE AND CIVIC ENGAGEMENT THROUGH RESEARCH

One characteristic that Brigance held in common with scholar-teachers of rhetoric today is that his research was extremely important to him. During the school year, however, Brigance found it impossible to write. He told a colleague, "I know of no way to teach except to give full time to students, and when a student wants my time, he can stop in my office. You can't have students in your hair—and that's where they belong—and write."[87] It is a sentiment that those of us who teach at small liberal-arts colleges can appreciate quite well. Given the constraints on his time during the school year, Brigance worked on his research in the summers for about four or five hours each morning—and then devoted himself to golf.[88]

As Medhurst's analysis in this volume demonstrates, Brigance was amazingly prolific for the time, even in comparison to his colleagues at schools with graduate programs. However, not all of Brigance's work was aimed at college students and professional colleagues; he also saw his writing as a way to reach out to the larger public on pragmatic issues relevant to the discipline. Indeed, Brigance regularly published articles in popular magazines. For example, he wrote pieces such as "How Good Is Your Speech?" and "Has Your Child Defective Speech?" for *Women's*

Home Companion and *Ladies' Home Journal*, respectively. These essays were republished, along with new ones, in a 1937 book aimed at the lay public, *Your Everyday Speech*.[89] In 1939, Brigance coauthored a book with Florence M. Henderson of the University of Hawaii entitled *A Drill Manual for Improving Speech*. The book grew out of his experience as a visiting professor at the University of Hawaii, where many of the students were not native speakers of English; the book contained a set of drills intended to help students learn to speak English more understandably.[90] In 1942, Brigance took his expertise on public speaking to high school students. He coauthored a secondary-school textbook, *American Speech*, with Wilhelmina G. Hedde, a teacher at W. H. Adamson High School in Dallas, Texas. In it, they emphasized that the goal of speech training in high school was to prepare students for citizenship. Hedde and Brigance noted that speaking in public put great responsibility on the shoulders of the speaker. In addition, they wrote, "In a slave state, speakers are trained in *what* to think. In this book, you will be given training in *how* to think."[91] While Hedde and Brigance's observation here clearly reflected the World War II context in which they wrote, it also emphasized the linkage between a rhetorical education and critical thinking skills. Finally, as noted earlier, Brigance also spoke to civic groups quite regularly, and many of those presentations apparently dealt with issues directly related to his disciplinary expertise.

Brigance clearly believed that the insights of his scholarly work should not be limited to college students and other professors of rhetoric. Yet, I fear that many in our discipline have tended to limit themselves in exactly this way, although there are, happily, notable exceptions. To uphold Brigance's legacy, then, one obvious step for rhetorical scholars is to talk more often to people other than ourselves—a goal that can be reached through multiple avenues. Marty Medhurst, for example, has encouraged scholars from a variety of disciplines to share their ideas on political discourse through his founding of *Rhetoric & Public Affairs* and the presidential rhetoric conferences that were held at Texas A&M for a decade. He and Paul Stob have also attempted to bridge the academic and public realms through their website, *PresidentialRhetoric.com*. Many rhetorical critics have shared either our research or our rhetorical insights with journalists and lay publics through interviews, op-ed pieces, articles, public presentations, and television programs. If we hope to contribute to society at large, then our discipline needs to communicate with individuals and groups outside our discipline more often. And if any discipline were capable of translating its research into clear language that is well adapted to lay audiences, then surely it has to be ours.

A second way in which we can enhance civic engagement is by promoting undergraduate research. I am adamant on this point—in part because I am blessed to work at an institution that puts undergraduate research at the core of its mission, and I have seen its benefits firsthand. At The College of Wooster, all graduating seniors must complete a two-semester research project called Independent Study, or "IS" for short, in which they work with a faculty mentor on a project of their choosing. Most departments also require a one-semester Junior IS prior to the senior year. In addition, seniors in many departments—including ours—do formal presentations of their ongoing research to faculty and their peers, and every senior must defend his/her thesis in an oral examination with the advisor and a second reader.

The kinds of projects that students undertake vary a great deal. During the 2004–2005 academic year, for example, one of my students conducted in-depth interviews with nurses about how they communicate with the families of terminally ill children, while another conducted a rhetorical analysis of the two presidential candidates' discourse about the issues of terrorism and national security on their websites. A third student examined how campus newspapers across Ohio construct the relationship between college students and permanent residents through their coverage.

During my years at Wooster, my experiences have mirrored the conclusions of studies on undergraduate research that find it not only prepares students for graduate school, but also benefits students who choose not to continue their formal education.[92] According to Chapman, "The ability to develop a nuanced thesis, to seek out supporting materials, and to organize these into a coherent research paper are not simply the tools of graduate research; they are the essential abilities developed through a good liberal education."[93] They are also, one might add, attributes that can help make one a good citizen.

A second effect of undergraduate research is the way in which it empowers students. On IS Monday at the end of March, the day that all Senior IS theses are due at the registrar's office, students gather at Kauke Arch for a parade, wearing their IS button ("I was #210"), carrying their Tootsie Roll (the piece of candy that the registrar has traditionally given to each Senior handing in his/her thesis), and accompanied by bagpipe players (we are the Fighting Scots, after all). The air is charged with student euphoria over having completed such a challenging project. Beyond this transitory group celebration, however, one can witness a more lasting sense of empowerment on an individual level. Students frequently make comments like, "I can't believe I did this" upon completing their IS and their oral defense, and that confidence seems to carry over to their other endeavors as well, with students considering lines of work or post-baccalaureate education that they never would have considered previously. My observations are consistent with Lopatto's study that found that undergraduates who have been involved in research projects with faculty mentors "reported gains in personal development, including self confidence, sense of accomplishment, patience and tolerance."[94] Students who feel empowered through a project that stretches their research, writing, analytic, and speaking skills are more apt to feel confident in using those skills in the public realm—if they are motivated to do so.

A third impact of undergraduate research is that it helps students to see the connections between their disciplinary knowledge and the public realm—connections that may continue to enrich their perspective long after they have graduated. The student who interviewed nurses who care for terminally ill children, for instance, has started nursing school, while another student—who worked on a farmland preservation campaign with me and then coauthored a publication about it[95]—is now doing grassroots organizing on behalf of immigration reform for the U.S. Catholic Conference of Bishops. Yet a third student, who completed his IS on President Bush's political discourse, went to Vermont in the fall of 2003 and lived in his car until the Howard Dean campaign hired him for an internship and found him a place to live. Today, he is Midwest finance director for Senator Barack Obama's presidential campaign. While not all undergraduates' eventual career paths will directly align with the research projects that they undertake, the communication education that they glean from such research will continue to shape the way that they perceive and analyze issues within their professional realm—be it law, medicine, education, business, religion, politics, journalism, or even science—and, if we are lucky, their action in regard to the civic realm as well.

Because of the benefits that undergraduate research may bring to all students, we need to broaden our conception of the type of student who can and should be involved in such endeavors. Kinkead found, for instance, that undergraduate research particularly benefits "the student defined as at risk or underrepresented in a field of study."[96] During my years at Purdue, I participated in a highly successful summer research program, Access Internally for Minorities (AIM), in which undergraduate students worked with faculty mentors and also developed their own research projects. I describe it as highly successful because even the students who did not go to graduate school—and there were many—became stronger students as a result. They were better able to make sense of published research and news coverage about research, better able to organize their thoughts, and better able to articulate their arguments and to support them. Again, I see a correlation between such skills and the skills needed to be effective citizens. At Wooster, first-generation college students from the inner city and a variety of other locales—who often arrive not fully prepared for college and/or confident in their ability to succeed—likewise appear to benefit from research experience with a faculty mentor. Another important target audience for undergraduate research programs are prospective teachers who can pass along discovery learning to their own charges.[97] Finally, undergraduate research need not be limited to junior and senior majors. For young students, research experiences can serve as "a way of focusing and guiding the undergraduate experience."[98] I frequently have had sophomores and even second-semester first-year students serve ably as research assistants—I have acknowledged the help of one such student for this very chapter, in fact.

To support undergraduate research, we must, at base, provide students with the knowledge and skills that they need to carry out research—knowledge and skills that they presumably should get in their coursework. We also must mentor students and encourage their research efforts by involving them in our research, helping them with their own, and letting them know about conference opportunities. Finally, we must celebrate their research and encourage them to share it with others. When students have papers accepted at conferences, for example, we need to celebrate these successes with public notices on campus, press releases to hometown newspapers, articles in the departmental alumni/student newsletter, and—when we are also in attendance at the conference—by going to the student's presentation and sharing a meal afterwards. At Wooster, we honor the research of every student who completes IS with an informal poster session at our Senior Open House on graduation weekend. It is often the highlight of the year.

Placing the Focus on Undergraduates and Civic Engagement in Our Institutions and in Our Discipline

Thus far in this essay, I have argued that we can best respond to the troubling trends in civic engagement by providing our undergraduates with a rhetorical education that will prepare them for citizenship. I have further argued that this goal can be fulfilled through several means: (1) using the classroom as a forum for civic engagement, (2) extending pedagogy beyond the classroom by employing service learning and by modeling civic engagement ourselves, and (3) sharing our research with the public and supporting undergraduate research.

In order to carry out this program for civic engagement, we also must place the focus on undergraduates and civic engagement in our institutions and in our discipline.[99] First, departments in research institutions must alter their rewards systems to give greater recognition for undergraduate teaching and work in the area of civic engagement. I am not arguing that research should no longer be considered important, but what I am saying is that the attention given to undergraduate teaching and public pedagogy, on the one hand, and to graduate teaching and research, on the other, has become greatly unbalanced at research institutions, particularly if we take seriously our commitment to civic engagement.[100] While no department would be wise to reward a career trajectory that the institution as a whole will not approve, it is also true that senior faculty members in research institutions can make small changes within their own departments and, through their positions of leadership within the larger university, begin to exert influence there as well. Successfully working toward institutional change is never easy, of course, but it can only happen if faculty members exert the influence that they do possess. In an era when both government officials and parents often express concern over what they see as higher education's lackadaisical approach to educating undergraduates, faculty and administrators may be able to use such concerns to advocate internally for greater attention to undergraduate pedagogy and civic engagement.

And what of us in small liberal-arts colleges? We, too, have our tasks, for while we concern ourselves with undergraduates and teach smaller classes, thereby permitting us to employ teaching methods beyond straight lecture, it is still important that we provide guidance and support for faculty who wish to cultivate civic engagement through their pedagogy. Moreover, we, too, need to work on subtle changes in our rewards systems on both the departmental and institutional levels. We are evaluated primarily on our ability to teach and, secondarily, on our research, but many faculty members in small liberal-arts settings have not yet accepted the need to promote the civic engagement of our students, or the call to share our expertise with the public. We also must continue to educate our colleagues—many of whom have little or no experience with communication departments—on the enduring importance of rhetoric to a liberal-arts education.

Beyond the steps we need to take at our own institutions—and I have outlined only a few here—scholar-teachers of rhetoric also must exert our influence at the disciplinary level. The NCA has, in many ways, already taken significant steps to place the focus back on undergraduates: it has promoted our undergraduate honor society and communication club, recognized undergraduate research, and begun initiatives in service learning. However, we will not make additional headway in our efforts to promote attention to undergraduate teaching and civic engagement without action that rewards such efforts on the part of members of the discipline.

First, we should recognize outstanding undergraduate teaching. The NCA has an award for K–12 teaching and for community-college teaching; it also rewards individuals who have mentored other scholars in our discipline. In addition, the NCA has the Donald H. Ecroyd Award for Outstanding Teaching in Higher Education, but the winners of this award have often been honored as much—perhaps more—for their graduate teaching as for their undergraduate work. The student testimonies shared through NCA messages about the award winners frequently come exclusively from current and former graduate students. This is not to disparage the winners of this award—one of them was a very fine instructor in my own graduate training! Rather, if we wish scholar-teachers of rhetoric to operate on the premise that undergraduate teaching is important, then our discipline needs to treat it that way by recognizing undergraduate teaching as worthy in its own right.

Second, the NCA needs to recognize exemplary efforts at civic engagement. Again, we have an abundance of research awards that, in turn, communicate very clearly what is most valued by our discipline. In this regard, we are no different than any other scholarly discipline. What if we had a national award, however, that regularly honored endeavors like Diana Carlin's role as director of Debate Watch, Kathleen Hall Jamieson's educational work on public broadcasting, Robert Cox's contributions to environmental advocacy, or Rod Hart's direction of the Annette Strauss Institute for Civic Participation? Only by changing our disciplinary reward system can we begin to encourage more widespread efforts at civic engagement.

In *Scholarship Reconsidered: Priorities of the Professoriate*, Ernest Boyer argued, "What we urgently need today is a more inclusive view of what it means to be a scholar—a recognition that knowledge is acquired through research, through synthesis, through practice, and through teaching."[101] In looking back at the career of W. Norwood Brigance, we catch a glimmer of what such an inclusive view might look like for scholars of rhetoric. He was an outstanding undergraduate teacher and researcher who fostered his students' civic engagement both inside and outside the classroom, all the while modeling civic engagement himself and sharing his expertise with the public. By following Brigance's lead, within the context of our own time, we can offer our undergraduates the best rhetorical education possible and, in so doing, attempt to improve the quality of democratic practices. The challenge posed by the current state of civic engagement is great, but our obligations as both scholar-teachers of rhetoric and as citizens implore our action.

NOTES

The author is Professor of Communication and Associate Dean for the Class of 2012 at The College of Wooster in Wooster, Ohio. She wishes to thank Kathryn Gabriele (Class of '07) for her research assistance on this paper, and the Office of the Vice President for Academic Affairs' Sophomore Research Program that made her participation possible. The author also thanks David Timmerman, Todd McDorman, and, especially, Joseph O'Rourke for their generous provision of archival materials and David Burns's dissertation chapter on Brigance's teaching, all of which proved invaluable.

1. William Norwood Brigance, *Speech: Its Techniques and Disciplines in a Free Society* (New York: Appleton-Century-Crofts, Inc., 1952), viii, his emphasis.

2. Ibid., ix, his emphasis.

3. David G. Burns, "William Norwood Brigance and Wabash College," *Communication Quarterly* 34 (1986): 351–55.

4. Isocrates, "Antidosis," *Isocrates*, ed. and trans. George Norlin, vol. 3 (London: William Heinemann Ltd., 1929), 267–77, 285, 292, 295; Susan C. Jarratt, *Rereading the Sophists: Classical Rhetoric Refigured* (Carbondale and Edwardsville: Southern Illinois University Press, 1991), 98; Edward Schiappa with David M. Timmerman, "Aristotle's Disciplining of Epideictic," in *The Beginnings of Rhetorical Theory in Classical Greece*, ed. Edward Schiappa (New Haven and London: Yale University Press, 1999), 191–92; Wilhelmina G. Hedde and William Norwood Brigance, *American Speech*, 3rd ed. (1942; Chicago: J. B. Lippincott, 1951), 3; Brigance, *Speech*, xvi.

5. Robert D. Putnam, *Bowling Alone: The Collapse and Revival of American Community* (New York: Simon and Schuster, 2000), 31–147.

6. Robert B. Reich, *The Future of Success* (New York: Alfred A. Knopf, 2001), 158–75, 194–213, 101–4, 125–31; Joseph Turow, *Breaking Up America: Advertisers and the New Media World* (Chicago: University of Chicago Press, 1997), 37–156, 184–200.

7. John F. Freie, *Counterfeit Community: The Exploitation of Our Longings for Connectedness* (Lanham, Md.: Rowman & Littlefield, 1998), 39–154.

8. See, for example, Joseph N. Cappella and Kathleen Hall Jamieson, *Spiral of Cynicism: The Press and the Public Good* (New York: Oxford University Press, 1997); Robert M. Entman, *Democracy without Citizens: Media and the Decay of American Politics* (New York: Oxford University Press, 1989); James Fallows, *Breaking the News: How the Media Undermine American Democracy* (New York: Pantheon Books, 1996); Kathleen Hall Jamieson and Paul Waldman, *The Press Effect: Politicians, Journalists, and the Stories That Shape the Political World* (New York: Oxford University Press, 2003).

9. David Zarefsky, "Spectator Politics and the Revival of Public Argument," *Communication Monographs* 59 (1992): 413, his emphasis.

10. Carol E. Hays, "Alienation, Engagement, and the College Student: A Focus Group Study," in *Engaging the Public: How Government and the Media Can Reinvigorate American Democracy*, ed. Thomas J. Johnson, Carol E. Hays, and Scott P. Hays (Lanham, Md.: Rowman & Littlefield, 1998), 45; Joseph Cammarano and Linda L. Fowler, "Enhancing Citizenship through Active Learning: Simulations on the Policy Process," in *Education for Citizenship: Ideas and Innovations in Political Learning*, ed. Grant Reeher and Joseph Cammarano (Lanham, Md.: Rowman & Littlefield, 1997), 103.

11. W. Lance Bennett, "The Uncivic Culture: Communication, Identity, and the Rise of Lifestyle Politics," *PS: Political Science and Politics* 31 (1998): 741–61.

12. Putnam, *Bowling Alone*, 265.

13. James Youniss, Susan Bales, Verona Christmas-Best, Marcelo Diversi, Milbrey McLaughlin, and Rainer Silbereisen, "Youth Civic Engagement in the Twenty-First Century," *Journal of Research on Adolescence* 12 (2002): 126, 128. Also see Daniel M. Shea and John C. Green, "The Turned-Off Generation: Fact and Fiction?" in *Fountain of Youth: Strategies and Tactics for Mobilizing America's Young Voters*, ed. Daniel M. Shea and John C. Green (Lanham, Md.: Rowman & Littlefield, 2007), 9, 4.

14. Elizabeth F. Farrell, "More Students Plan to Work to Help Pay for College," *Chronicle of Higher Education*, February 4, 2005, A34.

15. Kavita Kumar, "Young People Rocked the Vote: Despite Belief Voters Age 18 to 29 Opted Out, Turnout Was Biggest U.S. Has Seen since 1972," *St. Louis Post-Dispatch*, November 9, 2004, A22, http://web.lexis-nexis.com/ (viewed January 25, 2005).

16. Farrell, "More Students Plan to Work to Help Pay for College," A34.

17. Joel Spoonheim, Founding Member of Active Citizens School in Minnesota, quoted in Elizabeth Van Benschoten, "Youth-Led Civic Organizing: Countering Perceptions of Apathy and Redefining Civic Engagement (a Conversation with Joel Spoonheim of the Active Citizens School)," *National Civic Review* 89 (2000): 305.

18. William A. Galston, "Civic Knowledge, Civic Education, and Civic Engagement," in *Fountain of Youth: Strategies and Tactics for Mobilizing America's Young Voters*, ed. Daniel M. Shea and John C. Green (Lanham, Md.: Rowman & Littlefield, 2007), 101; also see Michael X. Delli Carpini and Scott Keeter, *What Americans Know about Politics and Why It Matters* (New Haven, Conn.: Yale University Press, 1996).

19. David T. Z. Mindich, *Tuned Out: Why Americans under 40 Don't Follow the News* (New York: Oxford University Press, 2005), 20–21, 28–33.

20. Kumar, "Young People Rocked the Vote," A22.

21. Carol Geary Schneider, "Educational Missions and Civic Responsibility: Toward the Engaged Academy," in *Civic Responsibility and Higher Education*, ed. Thomas Ehrlich (Westport, Conn.: American Council on Education and Onyx Press, 2000), 102.

22. Edward Zlotkowski, "Civic Engagement and the Academic Disciplines," in *Civic Responsibility and Higher Education*, ed. Thomas Ehrlich (Westport, Conn.: American Council on Education and Onyx Press, 2000), 313–14.

23. Ernest L. Boyer for the Carnegie Foundation for the Advancement of Teaching, *College: The Undergraduate Experience in America* (New York: Harper and Row, 1987), 120–21, 125; Laurence R. Veysey, *The Emergence of the American University* (Chicago: University of Chicago Press, 1965), 57–179.

24. David Mathews, "How Concepts of Politics Control Concepts of Civic Responsibility," in *Civic Responsibility and Higher Education*, ed. Thomas Ehrlich (Westport, Conn.: American Council on Education and Onyx Press, 2000), 157–58.

25. Ibid., 158.

26. Zlotkowski, "Civic," 314–15.

27. Schneider, "Educational Missions and Civic Responsibility," 120.

28. Harry C. Boyte and Nancy N. Kari, "Renewing the Democratic Spirit in American Colleges and Universities," in *Civic Responsibility and Higher Education*, ed. Thomas Ehrlich (Westport, Conn.: American Council on Education and Onyx Press, 2000), 49–50.

29. Frank Newman, *Higher Education and the American Resurgence* (Princeton, N.J.: Carnegie Foundation for the Advancement of Teaching, 1985), 31, also 58–60.

30. See, for example, Anne Colby, Thomas Ehrlich, Elizabeth Beaumont, and Jason Stephens, *Educating Citizens: Preparing America's Undergraduates for Lives of Moral and Civic Responsibility* (San Francisco: Jossey-Bass in partnership with the Carnegie Foundation for the Advancement of Teaching, 2003); Thomas Ehrlich, ed., *Civic Responsibility and Higher Education* (Westport, Conn.: American Council on Education and Onyx Press, 2000); Grant Reeher and Joseph Cammarano, eds., *Education for Citizenship: Ideas and Innovations in Political Learning* (Lanham, Md.: Rowman & Littlefield, 1997); Edward Zlotkowski, ed., *Service-Learning in the Disciplines* (Washington, D.C.: American Association for Higher Education, 1998).

31. Benjamin R. Barber, *Jihad vs. McWorld: Terrorism's Challenge to Democracy* (1994; reprint, New York: Ballantine Books, 2001), 282.

32. Mathews, "How Concepts of Politics Control," 150; also see Boyte and Kari, "Renewing the Democratic Spirit," 40.

33. Isocrates, "Antidosis," 267–77, 285, 292, 295; Sherwyn P. Morreale and David Droge, "Service Learning Grows in Popularity and Enhances Communication Study in Higher Education," *Spectra* 34 (November 1998): 6. Also see James L. Applegate and Sherwyn P. Morreale, "Service-Learning in Communication: A Natural Partnership," in *Voices of Strong Democracy: Concepts and Models for Service-Learning in Communication Studies*, ed. David Droge and Bren Ortega Murphy (Washington, D.C.: American Association for Higher Education in Cooperation with the National Communication Association, 1999), xi.

34. Zlotkowski, "Civic," 315.

35. Brigance, *Speech*, 8.

36. Brigance, *Speech*, xvi. Also see John Dewey, *Democracy and Education: An Introduction to the Philosophy of Education* (New York: Macmillan, 1916), 100–102.

37. Brigance, quoted in David Burns, "The Contributions of William Norwood Brigance to the Field of Speech," Ph.D. diss., Indiana University, 1970, 82.

38. Brigance, *Speech*, 186–298, 185. Also see Burns, "The Contributions," 82.

39. Plate 3 in Burns, "The Contributions," 72.

40. Brigance, *Speech*, 185. Also see Burns, "The Contributions," 82.

41. Brigance, *Speech*, 11, his emphasis.

42. Robert A. Stephens, quoted in Burns, "The Contributions," 68, also see 94, 107; Brigance, *Speech*, 543–74.

43. William Norwood Brigance, *Classified Speech Models of Eighteen Forms of Public Address* (New York: F.S. Crofts & Company, 1928), xi–xii.

44. Brigance, quoted in Burns, "The Contributions," 120; Burns, "William Norwood Brigance," 351.

45. Campus newspaper quoted in Burns, "The Contributions," 121.

46. See, for example, Jill J. McMillan and Katy J. Harriger, "College Students and Deliberation: A Benchmark Study," *Communication Education* 51 (2002): 242.

47. Roderick P. Hart, "Why Communication? Why Education? Toward a Politics of Teaching," *Communication Education* 42 (1993): 101, 102. Also see Gerard A. Hauser, "Rhetorical Democracy and Civic Engagement," in *Rhetorical Democracy: Discursive Practices of Civic Engagement*, ed. Gerard A. Hauser and Amy Grim (Mahwah, N.J.: Lawrence Erlbaum Associates, 2004), 13.

48. Rosa A. Eberly, "Rhetoric and the Anti-Logos Doughball: Teaching Deliberating Bodies the Practices of Participatory Democracy," *Rhetoric & Public Affairs* 5 (2002): 296; John Angus Campbell, "Oratory, Democracy, and the Classroom," in *Democracy, Education, and the Schools*, ed. Roger Soder (San Francisco: Jossey-Bass, 1996), 211, 221.

49. Robert L. Ivie, "Rhetorical Deliberation and Democratic Politics in the Here and Now," *Rhetoric & Public Affairs* 5 (2002): 280.

50. Gerard A. Hauser and Chantal Benoit-Barné, "Reflections on Rhetoric, Deliberative Democracy, Civil Society, and Trust," *Rhetoric & Public Affairs* 5 (2002): 266, their emphasis.

51. This approach is what Griffin calls invitational speaking. Cindy L. Griffin, *Invitation to Public Speaking* (Belmont, Calif.: Thomson/Wadsworth, 2004), 372–99.

52. McMillan and Harriger, "College Students and Deliberation," 244–49.

53. Campbell, "Oratory, Democracy, and the Classroom," 232.

54. Darrin Hicks, "The Promise(s) of Deliberative Democracy," *Rhetoric & Public Affairs* 5 (2002): 253–54.

55. Eberly, "Rhetoric and the Anti-Logos Doughball," 293–94.

56. Scott Welsh, "Deliberative Democracy and the Rhetorical Production of Political Culture," *Rhetoric & Public Affairs* 5 (2002): 689.

57. See Garry Wills, *Lincoln at Gettysburg: The Words That Remade America* (New York: Simon & Schuster, 1992), 121–47; Denise M. Bostdorff and Steven R. Goldzwig, "History, Collective Memory, and the Appropriation of Martin Luther King, Jr.: The Reagan Rhetorical Legacy," *Presidential Studies Quarterly* 35 (2005): 661–90.

58. Colby, Ehlrich, Beaumont, and Stephens, *Educating Citizens*, 135.

59. Eberly, "Rhetoric and the Anti-Logos Doughball," 294.

60. Roderick P. Hart, *Modern Rhetorical Criticism*, 2nd ed. (Boston: Allyn and Bacon, 1997), 2, his emphasis.

61. Pew Research Center for the People and the Press, "How Young People View Their Lives, Futures, and Politics: A Portrait of 'Generation Next,'" January 9, 2007, http://209.85.165.104/u/peoplepress (viewed February 20, 2007).

62. See William Keith, "Democratic Revival and the Promise of Cyberspace: Lessons from the Forum Movement," *Rhetoric & Public Affairs* 5 (2002): 317. Also see Hart, "Why," 102.

63. William Norwood Brigance, "Training Intercollegiate Orators at Wabash College," *The Speaker* 12 (January 1927): 1.

64. Burns, "The Contributions," 99, 94, 89–90, 59.

65. Burns, "William Norwood Brigance," 354–55.

66. Burns, "The Contributions," 104–5.

67. Wabash College, *Wabash College Announces the Establishment of the Speakers' Bureau*, January 1, 1928, n.p.

68. Burns, "The Contributions," 114.

69. Wabash College, *The Speakers Bureau of Wabash College*, 1928–1929, February 1929, February 1931–1937, Spring 1940, n.p.

70. Wabash College, *The Speakers Bureau*, February 1932; Lee Nance, "Student Defends Cuba before JC's," undated newspaper article from Department of Speech files at Wabash College, 1–2.

71. J. Jeffery Auer, *The Forensic Union and the Department of Public Speaking of Oberlin College Announce the 1937–1938 Program of Extension Debates* (Oberlin, Ohio: Oberlin College, 1937), n.p.

72. Burns, "William Norwood Brigance," 354.

73. Ibid.; Burns, "The Contributions," 107.

74. Burns, "The Contributions," 94; Brigance, "Training," 1.

75. Robert G. Bringle and Julie A. Hatcher, "A Service-Learning Curriculum for Faculty," *Michigan Journal of Community Service Learning* 2 (Fall 1995): 112.

76. I wish to acknowledge Steven L. Vibbert, who provided me with the opportunity to begin teaching this course as a second-year doctoral student, and who also provided the initial structure for the course.

77. See Denise M. Bostdorff, "Learning How to Make a Difference: Politics-in-Action Projects in the College-Level Political Communication Course," *Communication Teacher* 17 (2003): 11–13, special issue on service learning.

78. "Communicating Common Ground at Coe College," http://www.coe.edu/academics/CCG/program.htm (viewed March 21, 2005).

79. Mark A. Pollock, "Advocacy in Service of Others: Service-Learning in Argumentation Courses," in *Voices of Strong Democracy: Concepts and Models for Service-Learning in Communication Studies*, ed. David Droge and Bren Ortega Murphy (Washington, D.C.: American Association for Higher Education with the National Communication Association, 1999), 114.

80. Anne Colby and Thomas Ehlrich with Elizabeth Beaumont, Jennifer Rosner, and Jason Stephens, "Introduction: Higher Education and the Development of Civic Responsibility," in *Civic Responsibility and Higher Education*, ed. Thomas Ehrlich (Westport, Conn.: American Council on Education and Onyx Press, 2000), xxxv; Robert G. Bringle and Julie A. Hatcher, "Implementing Service Learning in Higher Education," *Journal of Higher Education* 67 (March–April 1996): 223. Also see J. Eyler and D. Giles, *Where's the Learning in Service-Learning?* (San Francisco: Jossey-Bass, 1999).

81. Linda Sax, "Citizenship Development and the American College Student," in *Civic Responsibility and Higher Education*, ed. Thomas Ehrlich (Westport, Conn.: American Council on Education and Onyx Press, 2000), 5. Also see A. W. Astin and Linda J. Sax, "How Undergraduates Are Affected by Service Participation," *Journal of College Student Development* 39 (May/June 1998): 251–63; Richard M. Battistoni, "Service Learning as Civic Learning: Lessons We Can Learn from Our Students," in *Education for Citizenship: Ideas and Innovations in Political Learning*, ed. Grant Reeher and Joseph Cammarano (Lanham, Md.: Rowman & Littlefield, 1997), 32; Bringle and Hatcher, "Implementing," 223; Laura Shue O'Hara, "Service Learning: Students' Transformative Journey from Communication Student to Civic-Minded Professional," *Southern Communication Journal* 66 (2001): 251–66.

82. Colby, Ehrlich, Beaumont, and Stephens, *Educating Citizens*, 135. For an example of how service learning may enhance civic engagement, see John Gastil and James P. Dillard, "The Aims, Methods, and Effects of Deliberative Civic

Education through the National Issues Forums," *Communication Education* 48 (1999): 186–89.

83. David C. Smith, "Academic Life and Civic Engagement: Tensions and Strains," *Soundings* 82 (Spring–Summer 1999): 69.

84. Boyte and Kari, "Renewing the Democratic Spirit," 38. Also see Boyer, *College*, 6.

85. Colby and Ehrlich, "Introduction: Higher Education and the Development of Civic Responsibility," xxxiii.

86. William Norwood Brigance, "Demagogues, 'Good' People, and Teachers of Speech," *The Speech Teacher* 1 (September 1952): 161. Also see W. Norwood Brigance, "The Backwash of War," *Vital Speeches* 12 (1946): 105–8. Brigance's former students and colleagues, along with his grandson, attested to his ability to take unpopular political stands and yet maintain positive relationships with others at the colloquy held in Brigance's honor at Wabash College on April 14–16, 2005. In addition, Medhurst's chapter deals with this issue in fuller detail.

87. Brigance, quoted in Burns, "William Norwood Brigance," 351. Also see W. Norwood Brigance, interview by Professor Vic Powell, December 3, 1959, produced for the 2005 Brigance Colloquy by Wabash College, 2005, CD.

88. Burns, "William Norwood Brigance," 351.

89. William Norwood Brigance, *Your Everyday Speech* (New York: McGraw-Hill, 1937), vii.

90. William Norwood Brigance and Florence M. Henderson, *A Drill for Improving Speech* (Chicago: J. B. Lippincott, 1939), v.

91. Hedde and Brigance, *American Speech*, v, 5, 8, their emphasis.

92. David J. Hartmann, "Undergraduate Research Experience as Preparation for Graduate School," *American Sociologist* 21 (June 1990): 179–89, EBSCO, (viewed January 21, 2005); Joyce Kinkead, "Learning through Inquiry: An Overview of Undergraduate Research," in *Valuing and Supporting Undergraduate Research*, ed. Joyce Kinkead, special issue, *New Directions for Teaching and Learning* 93 (2003): 10.

93. David W. Chapman, "Undergraduate Research and the Mandate for Writing Assessment," *PeerReview* (Fall 2003): 8–11.

94. David Lopatto, "The Benefits of Undergraduate Research," *Academic Leader* 21 (February 2005): 3.

95. Denise M. Bostdorff and Julie L. Woods, "Lessons from a Failed PDR (Purchase of Development Rights) Campaign in Wayne County, Ohio," *Journal of Applied Environmental Education and Communication* 2 (2003): 169–75.

96. Kinkead, "Learning through Inquiry," 11.

97. Ibid., 11–12.

98. Chapman, "Undergraduate Research and the Mandate for Writing Assessment," 10.

99. There are, of course, other types of institutions too, such as community colleges and medium-sized state universities, but I have not dealt with them here for two reasons. First, space constraints do not permit additional elaboration, and second, I have chosen to speak about those two institutions that I know best: the R1 institution that now dominates the leadership of our national disciplinary association, and the small liberal-arts college where Brigance chose to spend his professorial career.

100. See Boyer, *College*, 12; Nancy L. Thomas, "The College and University as Citizen," in *Civic Responsibility and Higher Education*, ed. Thomas Ehrlich (Westport, Conn.: American Council on Education and Onyx Press, 2000), 84; Stanley N. Katz, "Liberal Education on the Ropes," *Chronicle of Higher Education*, April 1, 2005, B8.

101. Ernest L. Boyer, *Scholarship Reconsidered: Priorities of the Professoriate* (Princeton, N.J.: Carnegie Foundation for the Advancement of Teaching, 1990), 24.

3

Rhetorical Pedagogy and Democratic Citizenship: Reviving the Traditions of Civic Engagement and Public Deliberation

J. Michael Hogan

In the second edition of his brief textbook on public speaking, W. Norwood Brigance took a radical approach. Instead of celebrating our right to speak, Brigance declared that public address in a free society existed "to serve listeners, not speakers," and he proclaimed it our "inalienable right" to hear speech "worth listening to." We are "beset by choices and temptations," Brigance wrote, and we listen to speakers "because we hope they will throw light on our problems, temptations, and fears. We listen because we hope they will give us new information, new ideas, or will simply water and cultivate old ideas. We listen because we want to be given encouragement, to renew our faith, to strengthen our determination." For Brigance, the measure of a speaker's worth was not personal success but service to democracy, and he proclaimed all who failed to meet that test "parasites" who ought to be "put out of business."[1]

Today, of course, our public discourse is thoroughly infested with "parasites"—extremist and polarizing voices on the political scene, irresponsible journalists and political commentators on cable television and talk radio, and actors and pop stars who exploit their celebrity for political purposes. Meanwhile, our mainstream politicians duck the really tough issues, delivering "quantifiably safe" speeches and devising ever more clever ways to confuse, deceive, and manipulate public opinion—or, at least, to move the poll numbers that now substitute for public opinion.[2] Even our college campuses have become a "wasteland of public dialogue," as Barry Checkoway has observed, with very little real debate of the crucial issues of the day.[3] Not only is there less speech "worth listening to" these days, but the very institutions that ought to be promoting free speech—the schools, the mass media, and the government—are instead stifling it. No wonder so many young people have "tuned out," refusing even to vote and concluding in increasing numbers that the "political process is both morally bankrupt and completely insulated from public pressure."[4] For young people today, the decision not to participate in politics is entirely rational.

The problem is not limited to young people, of course. Robert Putnam's best-selling book *Bowling Alone* has spawned a cottage industry of scholars, civic leaders, and foundations concerned with the decline of civic engagement in America.[5] Many new initiatives are now underway in an effort to replenish the nation's "social capital" and rebuild our deliberative communities.[6] Surprisingly, however, few of these efforts emphasize the most fundamental requirement of a sustainable deliberative democracy: citizens with the communicative competencies needed to participate in civic life. If citizens are to get involved, they need to know how to articulate their own views and to listen to others. They need to understand the rules and procedures of democratic deliberation, and they need at least some sense of America's history and rhetorical traditions. They need forums where they can come together to deliberate, and they need assurances that their deliberations matter. Above all, they need an ethical commitment to deliberating together in pursuit of the common good. In the final analysis, a good citizen is one who subordinates selfish interests to some larger vision of the "public interest."

In this essay, I elaborate on some of the ways that rhetorical scholarship and pedagogy might contribute to efforts to revive civic engagement and democratic deliberation in America. My approach is, on the one hand, historical and traditional; it is grounded in the same neoclassical conception of rhetoric and "civic virtue" that inspired a revival of democratic deliberation at the start of the last century—during the so-called

Progressive Era. On the other hand, we must acknowledge the changing political and cultural realities of our age and recognize the need for radical, even revolutionary critique of the forces that have stifled public debate and silenced ordinary Americans. Like many of the Progressive reformers, my emphasis is not on the rights but the responsibilities of citizenship, insisting—with Brigance—upon speech "worth listening to." At the same time, a rhetoric for the modern age must take into account dramatic changes in the contemporary political and social landscape, including the growing diversity of American culture and new media technologies.

I begin by discussing some of the political and social problems that have inspired the revival of scholarly interest in civic engagement and democratic deliberation. I then move on to explain just a few of the ways that scholarship and teaching grounded in the rhetorical tradition might contribute to the effort to build sustainable deliberative communities. My argument is that the best answers to problems of political alienation and civic disengagement are to be found not in new information technologies, but in a revival of some of the oldest traditions in rhetorical theory and criticism. Along the way, I will discuss how some of my own research and teaching might contribute to this effort to revitalize democratic deliberation.

The Eclipse of the Democratic Public

The American democracy of the twenty-first century is threatened by a generational phenomenon of growing disinterest in, and disengagement from, the civic life of both local communities and the nation. Documented most famously in Putnam's *Bowling Alone*, this threat is manifested both in familiar ways, such as the abysmally low voter turnout among young people in America, and in less obvious ways, including sharp declines in both newspaper readership and participation in voluntary and charitable associations. Some of the discouraging facts are well-known: voter turnout in presidential elections declined from 62.8 percent in 1960 to 48.9 percent in 1996, despite greatly relaxed voter-registration requirements, "motor voter" laws, and massive "get-out-the-vote" campaigns.[7] This decline in voter turnout has been especially pronounced among young people. Since eighteen-year-olds got the right to vote in 1971, turnout among voters aged eighteen to twenty-four has declined from about 50

percent in 1972 to only about 32 percent in the 1996 election. Among
all age groups, turnout was up slightly in 2000 and still more in 2004.[8]
Nevertheless, the United States continues to trail all but a handful of the
world's democracies in voter turnout.[9]

Other signs of civic decay in America are more subtle, yet even more
discouraging. The number of people under thirty-five who read a newspaper daily, for example, has dropped from two-thirds in 1965 to one-third
in 1990, and this is not, as some have suggested, just a reflection of young
people turning to "new media." Young people are turning away from
news altogether, even on television and the Internet.[10] Indeed, many
young people no longer seem to distinguish between news and entertainment at all, as evidenced by a 2004 Pew Center poll which showed more
than a fifth of young people claiming to get their news about politics
from *Saturday Night Live* or *The Daily Show*.[11] When told about the findings,
even Jon Stewart seemed concerned. "A lot of them are probably high,"
Stewart cracked. "I'm not sure, coming off of robots fighting and into our
show, what we're dealing with out there."[12]

Given these trends, it hardly comes as a surprise that the number
of people who attend political meetings or work for a political party has
declined by more than half since the 1970s. Between 1973 and 1994, the
number of Americans who attended even one public meeting in the previous year declined by about 40 percent. In raw numbers, this means that
we now have about 16 million fewer Americans participating in public
meetings than we did twenty years ago. As Putnam summarized the bad
news, "Year after year, fewer and fewer of us took part in the everyday
deliberations that constitute grassroots democracy. In effect, more than
a third of America's civic infrastructure simply evaporated between the
mid-1970s and the mid-1990s."[13]

In a nation that prides itself on free speech, the most discouraging
trends relate to how Americans publicly express themselves. According
to the Roper Center, there has been a steady decline over the past several
decades in the number of people signing petitions, writing letters to their
elected representatives or to their local newspapers, giving speeches at
meetings and political rallies, or writing articles for a magazine or newspaper. The proportion of the American public who engaged in none of these
civic activities rose by nearly one-third through the 1970s and 1980s.
By the mid-1990s, thirty-two million fewer Americans were involved
in these sorts of activities than was the case just two decades earlier. In

1973, most Americans participated in at least one of these forms of civic expression. By 1994, most Americans did not engage in any of them. Significantly, the forms of civic engagement that declined the most were those involving collaborating or talking with other people, such as giving and listening to speeches at public meetings.[14]

Some data suggest that the situation may not be as bad as it seems. Americans actually donate more money to political and civic causes today than ever before, and the number of nonprofit organizations in America actually has doubled over the last thirty years—from 10,299 in 1968 to 22,901 in 1997.[15] Self-help and issue-advocacy groups also are prospering, and volunteering—especially among young people—has been on the rise.[16] According to Everett Carll Ladd, among others, these data suggest that civic engagement is not on the decline, but rather is being "renewed and extended," as Americans find new outlets for their political expression and form new associations to replace traditional civic groups like the PTA, the Lions Club, or the League of Women Voters.[17] Some of Putnam's critics also point to the proliferation of Internet chat rooms and weblogs as evidence that civic engagement is not on the decline, but simply assuming new forms.[18]

Yet one might argue that these developments actually confirm that America is becoming a nation of spectators rather than participants in civic life. For many Americans today, civic engagement means writing a check, and most of those checks are sent not to State College, Pennsylvania, or Crawfordsville, Indiana, but to New York or Washington, D.C. What this means is that these are not membership organizations—that is, groups that have meetings where ordinary people gather to deliberate. Rather, they are groups of paid professionals—"hired guns," if you will—whose business is to raise and spend money promoting particular causes. In other words, they are "professionalized" or "astroturf" movements,[19] organized by powerful special interests and consisting of a relatively small number of fund-raising and public-relations experts masquerading as "grassroots" movements. Ordinary citizens might support such groups by sending money or logging on to their websites. But they have no say in how their money is spent, and online "chats" are a poor substitute for town-hall debates. Not only do blogs and chatrooms lack the personal accountability of face-to-face interactions, but they tend to attract only like-minded participants and reinforce rather than challenge existing beliefs.

All this has troubling implications for the character and quality of public discourse in America. With the proliferation of special-interest groups, the rhetoric of public relations has displaced the collective voice of ordinary people deliberating over matters of public importance. Principled leadership has given way to appeals shaped by polling and focus groups, and we see more and more of the techniques of the propagandist and the demagogue in our mainstream political talk. In political campaigns, what Bill Clinton called the "politics of personal destruction" prevails, while in legislative debates, the rhetoric of negotiation and compromise has given way to political posturing and gridlock. Scholars and politicians alike have lamented this loss of substance and civility in our nation's political talk. But the real losers are ordinary citizens, whose voices have been squeezed out of the public dialogue by paid rhetorical "hit men." No longer are we a nation of citizens deliberating among ourselves, committed to discovering the common good through the process of collective deliberation. When special interests dominate public discussion, the rhetoric of polarization and vilification prevails. And when that sort of rhetoric prevails, as James Davison Hunter has argued, the "quiet" and "reflective" voices of the majority of Americans are, "for all practical purposes," rendered *silent* in the broader public discussion."[20]

So, what has been the response of higher education to these troubling trends? Unfortunately, colleges and universities have been part of the problem rather than the solution, not only stifling free expression on campus but also abandoning the civic mission that inspired the land-grant movement of the nineteenth century. As historian Thomas Bender has argued, the American research university at one time successfully combined specialized research with education for citizenship, and the first Ph.D. programs in America produced not "scholars alone" but also "educated civic leaders and journalists"—including such towering figures as Theodore Roosevelt and Woodrow Wilson.[21] Over time, however, American universities have lost that sense of mission, as the drive toward academic professionalization transformed American universities from "civic institutions into some of the world's most powerful research engines."[22] Today, even the humanities have been corrupted by an "academic meritocracy" that undermines both the "populist mystique inherent in the land grant mission" and the altruistic and moral enterprise of teaching undergraduates. With the "clamber for display, recognition, self-promotion, and fame" undermining their ethical foundations, even the land-grant colleges have lost touch with their civic mission.[23] As the late Ernest Boyer of the Carnegie Foundation summarized the situation in the mid-1990s: "Higher education is suffering from a loss of overall direction, a nagging feeling that it is no longer at the vital center of the nation's work."[24]

In just the past few years, there have been a number of efforts to rediscover the civic mission of America's colleges and universities. Conferences have been convened to discuss how higher education might promote civic engagement,[25] and a number of educational associations and foundations have called for reform.[26] Meanwhile, service-learning programs have proliferated around the country, and colleges and universities have launched a variety of new programs promoting civic engagement and education for citizenship.[27] My own university president, Graham B. Spanier, has played at least a small part in these efforts. He has led the campaign nationally to reduce binge drinking on campuses, and he inaugurated a newspaper readership program that now has Penn State students reading some 1.8 million free newspapers a year—the largest such program in the nation. He has even given his blessing to "public scholarship" and is channeling new resources into undergraduate education. In his 2001 "State of the University" address, however, Spanier did not talk about how sober or better-informed students grow up to be good citizens, nor did he champion education for citizenship as central to Penn State's land-grant mission. Instead, he devoted his entire address to the "promise of information technology," sounding almost giddy as he imagined all the various ways that "emerging technologies" might create "unprecedented opportunities for us to develop a true learning society."[28] Unfortunately, Spanier could not promise us that this new "learning society" would also be more civil, cohesive, or politically engaged. The cynic might even suggest that for Spanier, the real "promise of technology" lies in the $4.5 million in external funding that Penn State's online World Campus has generated for the university—or in Penn State's participation in a five-year, $453 million program to provide distance learning for the U.S. Army.[29]

It is important to recognize that technological dreamers and entrepreneurs have always promised that new technologies could save democracy. Television, for example, was once touted as a magical new tool of civic engagement—a technology that would inform and inspire the citizenry with "public interest" programming and even provide ways for citizens to "talk back" to their leaders. Instead, of course, television became what former FCC chairman Newton N. Minow famously called a "vast waste-land," dominated by mindless entertainment programming and increas-ingly devoid of serious public-interest programming, documentaries, and news. In the 1990s, we heard similarly optimistic predictions that the Internet would revive grass-roots democracy by providing ordinary citi-zens with unprecedented information resources and a powerful new tool for interacting with their fellow citizens.[30] Instead, the Internet has too often become a refuge for purveyors of political disinformation, bizarre conspiracy theories, and the rhetoric of hate. Even mainstream political websites reek of ideological parochialism and rhetorical excess.[31] Clearly, technology—in and of itself—is not the answer. It seems more than just coincidence that the generation that came of age with these two great advances in information technology—television and the Internet—is arguably the least politically literate and engaged in U.S. history. If any-thing, these technologies have only exacerbated the problems that have undermined our public deliberations.

So if technology is not the answer, how do we address the problem of civic decay in America? And what might colleges and universities con-tribute to the effort? My answer, as I already suggested, lies in a revival of three of the oldest traditions in rhetorical scholarship and pedagogy: (1) the classical or neoclassical tradition of rhetorical theory—a tradition that is still reflected, although incompletely, in the textbooks we use to teach public speaking and persuasion; (2) the tradition of rhetorical criticism, which today emphasizes the critique of public discourse in all of its vari-ous manifestations, including mass-mediated discourse and the rhetoric of popular culture; and (3) the tradition of historical studies in public ad-dress, which emphasizes the lessons that we might learn from the speak-ers, speeches, political campaigns, and social movements of the past. Each of these traditions has something important to contribute to a revival of civic engagement. All can help promote the rhetorical and civic literacy needed for a healthy deliberative democracy. Yet if rhetorical scholarship and pedagogy are to contribute to a revival of public deliberation, they must eschew narrow ideological agendas and reemphasize the practical tools of democratic citizenship. In the remainder of this essay, I sketch a broad overview of how the rhetorical tradition might supply some of the knowledge and competencies essential to an engaged democratic public. In the process, I'll suggest how some of my own research and teaching hopefully contribute to that effort.

Reviving the Rhetorical Tradition

Historically, the rhetorical tradition has been all about civic engagement. Inspired by the need to train citizens for the legal and deliberative assemblies of the Greek city-state, the earliest rhetorical treatises, such as Aristotle's *Rhetoric*,[32] taught rhetoric as the handmaiden of politics and as education for citizenship. Passed down across centuries, the classical tradition evolved in response to changing political and social conditions, most notably the inexorable expansion of the democratic "public." By the early twentieth century, that tradition had evolved into a neoclassicism that acknowledged forms and forums of public discourse never imagined by the ancients. The neoclassicism of the Progressive Era reflected both the growing diversity of the mass public and the development of new communication technologies, like the mass-circulation magazine and the "magnivox," or electronic public-address system. Yet despite these changes, two elements of the classical tradition remained unchanged: its emphasis on the practical skills of democratic citizenship, and its ethical foundations in notions of "character" and "civic virtue." In ethical terms, it suggested a particular conception of citizenship: "civic republicanism," or the idea that citizens had a moral obligation to put the "common good" ahead of their own "private interests."[33]

CLASSICAL AND NEOCLASSICAL RHETORICAL THEORY

When the Roman rhetorician Quintilian described the ideal orator as a "good man skilled in speaking," he envisioned much more than an effective platform speaker. Quintilian's orator-statesman was, first and foremost, a person of high moral character and a servant of the people. Before he could be "skilled in speaking," he had to be a virtuous citizen, a lover of wisdom and truth, and a champion of the "common good" rather than his own private or personal ambitions. So too did the neoclassicism of the early twentieth century uphold a model of the ideal orator grounded in character and civic virtue. During the "oratorical renaissance" of the Progressive Era, as Robert Kraig has noted, both educators and the popular media celebrated an "orator-statesman" who was both a nostalgic throwback to the Golden Age of American Oratory and a forward-looking reformer. As Kraig concludes, the neoclassicism of the Progressive Era was more than a theory of effective public speaking, or even a "cultural style." It was, "at base," an "ethical tradition" that "required its adherents to live up to an exalted code of conduct."[34]

Today, most of our basic public-speaking textbooks are still grounded in the classical or neoclassical tradition. Yet they tend to be "classical" only in the sense that they treat the mechanics of public speaking much as the ancients did, dividing the subject into the five classical "canons" and distinguishing among Aristotle's three "modes of proof." The typical public-speaking text touches upon the ethics of speech, but most only treat such mundane matters as plagiarism or the ethics of emotional appeal. No existing public-speaking text treats the responsibilities of citizenship as a core concern. None endorses civic republicanism or has anything even remotely resembling Quintilian's portrait of the ideal orator. Indeed, the trend in recent years has been in precisely the opposite direction: toward rejection of the ethical foundations of the classical tradition. In place of that tradition, two very different paradigms have been competing to define the public-speaking text of the future. One we might call the corporate or Dale Carnegie model; the second is driven by ideological concerns.

The Dale Carnegie approach to public speaking holds that it is more important to teach students about personal advancement than citizenship. Typically employed in courses with titles like "Presentational Speaking" or "Corporate Communication," the Dale Carnegie approach is all about showmanship and "winning," not disinterested leadership, civic engagement, or the "common good." Worse yet, these texts often celebrate the most manipulative, even demagogic communicators among us as models of the ideal orator: the flamboyant ideologues on the political scene, the icons of big business and consumer culture, and the celebrity-heroes of the sports-entertainment and pop-culture industries. Upholding the molding of consumer preferences or the manipulation of public opinion as the measures of "success," the Dale Carnegie approach teaches public speaking not as a liberal art, but as a tool of professional advancement—a skill that one needs to "beat the competition."[35] Needless to say, this view of public speaking encourages rather than checks some of the worst tendencies in our already degraded public discourse. It barely acknowledges the importance of personal character, much less some larger conception of "civic virtue" or the "common good."

Others have abandoned the classical or neoclassical tradition for a very different reason: they think it inconsistent with their multicultural, feminist, or postmodern ideological agenda. And while it remains difficult to imagine a postmodern public-speaking textbook, a few multicultural and feminist texts have appeared, capturing a small but significant portion of that huge undergraduate market. At first glance, of course, these texts do not seem all that different from traditional texts; most treat the mechanics of public speaking much like those grounded in the classical tradition.[36] Yet they do paint a very different portrait of the ideal orator, and the personal and political values they celebrate are antithetical to the classical tradition. Emphasizing personal identity rather than our common heritage, diversity and separatism rather than some larger "public good," the ideological approach to public speaking rejects what the famed historian Arthur M. Schlesinger Jr. once described as "the historic theory of America as one people—the theory that has thus far managed to keep American society whole." Like most politicized educational curricula, the ideological approach to public speaking promotes not unity and common purpose, but "the fragmentation, resegregation, and tribalization of American life."[37]

Nobody disputes that our public-speaking textbooks must change with the times. Even Schlesinger conceded that multicultural education has helped Americans to develop a "more complex and invigorating sense of the world—and of themselves."[38] And that broader cultural awareness will only become more important in the years to come. We must acknowledge the greater challenges of public deliberation in a diverse, multicultural society, and we need to take account of globalization, new information technologies, and the realities of the Consumer Age. But that does not mean that we cannot uphold a model of the ideal orator—an orator with the civic virtues of Quintilian's "good man skilled in speaking." Nor does it mean that we cannot aspire to some larger vision of our common purposes and values as a nation. Our success as a deliberative democracy depends upon our ability to teach all of our citizens how to participate in civic life. To do anything less is to surrender to the forces of polarization and division that have been tearing our democracy apart.

A sustainable revival of civic engagement in America must begin with the basics: teaching young people about responsible public advocacy and democratic deliberation, with a renewed emphasis on character, civic virtue, and the larger "public good." In our public-speaking courses, we need to revive the neoclassical tradition's emphasis on the ethics of speech, and we need to stress the responsibilities of citizenship, not personal advancement. Yet rhetoric's contributions to a renewal of civic engagement should extend well beyond the public-speaking classroom. The neoclassical model of the ideal orator should be promoted throughout the undergraduate curriculum and in our culture at large. We need to encourage citizens not only to become responsible speakers themselves, but also to insist upon responsible speech from those in positions of leadership and social influence. And that is where the second tradition in rhetorical pedagogy comes in—the tradition of rhetorical criticism. No less than virtuous public speakers, we need both professional rhetorical critics and engaged "citizen critics" to hold all who speak in public to higher standards.

RHETORICAL CRITICISM AND THE CITIZEN CRITIC

Like consumer watchdogs who protect the public against unscrupulous merchants and unsafe products, the professional rhetorical critic can help guard against deception and fraud in the "marketplace of ideas." Trained both in rhetoric and more broadly in the liberal arts, the rhetorical critic can play an important role in a revival of democratic culture by helping others to make the right choices as citizens. Born out of a separatist movement within literary criticism in the early twentieth century, the academic practice of rhetorical criticism originally reflected the Progressive Era's obsession with improving the character and quality of public discourse. Today, we have a pressing need not only for professional rhetorical critics with that same reform spirit, but also for a citizenry educated to be more critical themselves—"citizen critics," as my colleague Rosa Eberly might put it.[39] More than ever, we need rhetorical critics not only to expose the deceptions of demagogues, but also to teach the rest of the citizenry to be more critical consumers of public discourse.

My own work as a rhetorical critic has ranged over a broad terrain, from critiques of presidential rhetoric and electoral campaigns, to studies of congressional foreign-policy debates, direct-mail campaigns, television news, political films, and documentaries. I have even written about junior-high-school curricula that, to my mind, promote ignorance and ideological conformity rather than engaged democratic citizenship.[40] Not everything I study as a rhetorical critic represents deceptive or manipulative propaganda; some of what I study is not even intentionally designed to persuade. Still, if it impacts the character and quality of public deliberations, I consider it fair game for the rhetorical critic. Indeed, one of my hobbyhorses over the past decade has been something that most people do not even consider a communicative form: the public-opinion poll. So while much more might be said about how rhetorical critics might hold our political orators to higher standards or do more to expose the biases and distortions of today's celebrity journalists, I will focus for just a moment on what I have called "the rhetoric of polling."

When I first submitted an essay on polling to *Communication Monographs*, one reviewer quoted the mission statement of the journal and declared that polling had nothing to do with communication. Even a brief moment's reflection should reveal the folly of that statement. Presidents routinely use polls to decide what to say in their speeches. The news media spend millions on polls, both to help predict the outcome of elections, and to create news about issues and trends. In Congress, legislators sometimes talk more about the polls than the merits of the policy being debated, and during election campaigns, polls not only dictate candidates' strategies but also drive the "horse race" media coverage. In a number of my books and essays, I have elaborated on these and other deleterious effects of the rhetoric of polling, and even some of the pollsters have now come to agree with me that their industry has evolved into a grotesque distortion of George Gallup's original vision. Polling is no longer the "pulse of democracy," as Gallup envisioned, but rather serves to trivialize and oversimplify complex issues, discourage public discussion, and distort the "will of the people." Whatever its potential to serve democracy, polling now does more to silence than to give voice to public opinion.[41]

Since September 11, 2001, we have witnessed fresh examples of how polling's mission has been corrupted by the media "takeover" of the industry that began in the early 1980s. Instead of polls assessing just how far the public was willing to go in combating terrorism—what freedoms people were willing to sacrifice, for example, or just how much of our blood and treasure they were willing to expend in the fight—we saw polls on how many people "cried" after the terrorist attacks, how many still felt "scared," and how many thought Osama Bin Laden was dead or alive. The same sort of thing occurred during the first Persian Gulf War in 1990. Despite asking some 5,000 questions, the pollsters never really answered "the crucial question of whether the public supported or opposed a war with Iraq," as David Moore has noted.[42] Instead they asked the public to speculate about the unknowable: "How long do you think the war will last?" Or "How many Americans do you think will be killed before the war is over?" The Gallup poll even asked Americans whether they thought that "prayers" might be "effective" in bringing the Persian Gulf War to an end.[43]

Perhaps the best example of how media polling trivializes and subverts public deliberation came during the Monica Lewinsky scandal in 1998–99. In a study published in 2003, I showed how the news media's obsession with so-called "presidential approval" polls protected Clinton from impeachment and diverted attention from evidence of a widespread loss of faith in his honesty and moral integrity.[44] I also showed how Clinton's high approval ratings may have reflected not support for Clinton, but a backlash against a media "feeding frenzy" that treated the Lewinsky scandal as the most important "issue" facing America for more than a year. I will not rehash my entire argument here, but suffice it to say that despite asking literally thousands of questions, the pollsters did little to shed light on the real issue at stake: should the President of the United States be impeached and removed from office? Instead, they fueled what I dubbed a sort of "journalistic voyeurism," asking question after question about Clinton's sexual proclivities but almost nothing about impeachment. One poll, for example, asked whether Americans thought Clinton suffered from a "sex addiction." Another asked who we thought made the "first move," Clinton or Lewinsky. Still another asked us to reflect on whether the sex acts described in the Starr report were "normal or kinky." And yet another asked whether we would trust Bill Clinton to "babysit" our teenage daughter. One poll even asked us to imagine how we would respond if President Clinton tried to kiss us: Would we let him? Would we slap him in the face?

Now, perhaps there is nothing wrong with a few silly polls—polls designed merely to entertain or amuse. During the Lewinsky scandal, however, these sorts of polls were the rule rather than the exception, obscuring the vital issue at stake: should the President of the United States be impeached and removed from office? In the final analysis, the pollsters may have even misrepresented the "will of the people" altogether by emphasizing a measure that revealed absolutely nothing about public reactions to the scandal: the so-called presidential-approval rating. To my mind, that represents a subversion of public deliberation and a serious breach of the pollsters' public trust. It is precisely the sort of thing that can and should be exposed—in scholarship, in the classroom, and in the popular media—by the professional rhetorical critic. And it is precisely the sort of thing that rhetorical critics might teach the rest of the citizenry to guard against themselves.

THE "LESSONS" OF HISTORY

Finally, what might we learn from that last tradition in rhetorical scholarship and pedagogy—the tradition of historical studies in public address? How can studying dead orators, or dead issues like slavery or woman's suffrage, contribute to a revival of civic engagement and democratic deliberation? For some, like Kenneth Burke, the answer comes couched largely in negative terms. By studying the rhetoric of Adolph Hitler, Burke insisted, we could "discover what kind of 'medicine' this medicine-man has concocted," so that we would know "what to guard against, if we are to forestall the concocting of similar medicine in America."[45] Yet there are other, more positive lessons to be learned from the history of public address, including lessons about how to revive civic engagement and how to revitalize public deliberation. My own work on the Progressive Era, both in the edited volume *Rhetoric and Reform in the Progressive Era*,[46] and in a new book on Woodrow Wilson,[47] illuminates some of those lessons.

The Progressive Era—the period between the turn of the twentieth century and World War I—was hardly a "golden age" of enlightened, forward-looking policies. Especially in race relations and foreign affairs, it was arguably among the most reactionary periods in U.S. history, as blacks suffered through an epidemic of lynchings and the United States warred ruthlessly against "barbarian" peoples overseas. At the same time, however, the Progressive Era brought a "remarkable renaissance of public discussion and deliberation," as ordinary Americans of all political stripes "gathered in schools, in churches, and even in tents to listen to speakers, to debate among themselves, and to render their judgments on the issues of the day." As I concluded in *Rhetoric and Reform in the Progressive Era*, the so-called Progressive Era may not have been all that "progressive," but it was a time of revived civic engagement and democratic deliberation. It was, in short, a most "rhetorical" of times.[48]

Americans in the Progressive Era confronted challenges that were strikingly similar to those that we confront today: rapid technological change, economic inequality, environmental degradation, racial tensions, the loss of community, and political disaffection. And contrary to conventional wisdom, the Progressive reformers did not address such problems solely through new laws and governmental programs. Progressives actually disagreed over specific measures, but they all shared an abiding faith in democratic deliberation. For Progressives, the essential problem of the era was what John Dewey would later call "the problem of the public": the need for improvements in "the methods and conditions of debate, discussion, and persuasion."[49] Progressives feared that, in an increasingly complex world, powerful special interests had supplanted the "voice of the people," and whatever their other differences, they agreed on the need to reinvent and revitalize the public sphere.

This concern with public deliberation was at the core of the reform program of that great Progressive crusader, Wisconsin's Robert La Follette. As Peter Levine has noted, La Follette believed that the "surest way for voters to form wise judgments . . . was for them to *deliberate* together about public affairs," and so he proposed a number of "practical measures to increase the quantity, quality, and inclusiveness of public deliberation."[50] Other Progressives joined with La Follette in this effort to create regular forums of public debate and decision making—forums where an active, enlightened, and freely deliberating democratic public might emerge. The result was a long list of initiatives designed to revitalize public discussion. Among these was a "social centers" movement that opened school buildings to town meetings and public debates. The Progressives also founded many of the civic and voluntary associations that still exist today. In their efforts to cultivate public discussion, Progressives turned settlement houses into community forums, and they revived the Chautauqua movement—a national program of educational meetings and discussions "organized for—and by—farmers."[51] In small Midwestern cities, they appointed "civic secretaries" to organize public meetings and debates, and they invented school newspapers and student governments to teach young people about politics. Meanwhile, debate and forensics clubs flourished in colleges and universities, and the University of Wisconsin even established a Department of Debating and Public Discussion, which encouraged off-campus public debates by distributing background papers on such issues as the income tax and woman suffrage.[52] The Progressive Era also gave birth to public radio and the "university extension," which brought academic knowledge to the common folk in hopes of promoting more informed public discussion.[53] Even the movement to build municipal parks and playgrounds grew out of this concern with democratic community, as Progressives viewed such spaces as investments in "neighborliness" and good citizenship.[54]

Again, the citizens of the Progressive Era did not always arrive at decisions that we would today call "progressive." But by participating in community debates and deliberations, they "learned the necessary skills of a democratic public: how to listen, how to argue, and how to deliberate."[55] They also learned a larger lesson essential to a healthy deliberative democracy: that citizens in a diverse, democratic society must be willing to search for common ground, to compromise, and to show respect for those who disagree with their own points of view. Finally, they learned what Woodrow Wilson himself taught throughout his scholarly career: that true eloquence consists not merely of "a good voice and a few ringing sentences," but rather must be grounded in the "character, spirit, and thought of the nation."[56] If citizens are to participate meaningfully in public deliberations, as Wilson concluded, they needed at least some understanding of "the history and leading conceptions" of the nation's political institutions and traditions.[57]

We need to reinvent the twenty-first-century equivalents of the Chautauqua and the "civic secretaries" of the Progressive Era. We need to create new spaces for public deliberation, and we need to rebuild the institutional infrastructure of our deliberative democracy. Above all, we need to nurture the values and skills necessary for a genuine and sustainable democratic public: the ability to articulate one's own views, a willingness to listen to others, an understanding of the differences between eloquence and demagoguery, an appreciation for the wide range of views and interests in our diverse democratic society, and a commitment to working with others to promote the common good. In our schools, we need to teach rhetoric as the practical art of democratic citizenship, and we need to emphasize not just the skills of public advocacy and debate, but also history, ethics, and the responsibilities of citizenship. Finally, we need to speak out more vigorously against the "parasites" who have degraded and debased our public discourse: the demagogues on the political scene, the cynical celebrity journalists, the strident and uncompromising advocates of single-issue politics, and the "true believers" whose "grammar of hostility" fuels the "culture wars."[58] And we need to speak out against such "parasites" even when we happen to agree with their politics.

A healthy democratic republic requires more than access to new technologies or new institutional spaces for public deliberation. It also requires a common store of political knowledge and a shared sense of history. It requires an appreciation for the well-crafted argument and the eloquent speech, as well as the ability to recognize and resist the diversions and deceptions of the propagandist and the demagogue. For self-government to succeed, there must not only be some common understanding of the methods and conventions of public discussion, but also a shared rhetorical ethic and a commitment to what E. J. Dionne Jr. has called "serious speech"—speech "in search of truth"; speech designed not just to defeat political adversaries, but to aid citizens in their "common search for understanding"; speech that engages citizens in "a continuous and ongoing effort to balance worthy but competing values, to mediate conflicts, to resolve disputes, to solve problems."[59] That, in the final analysis, is what the rhetorical tradition has to offer: a renewed commitment to "serious speech" in America.

NOTES

1. William Norwood Brigance, *Speech Communication*, 2nd ed. (New York: Appleton-Century-Crofts, Inc., 1955), 2–3.

2. See Wynton C. Hall, "The Invention of 'Quantifiably Safe Rhetoric': Richard Wirthlin and Ronald Reagan's Instrumental Use of Public Opinion Research in Presidential Discourse," *Western Journal of Communication* 66 (2002): 319–46.

3. Barry Checkoway, "Renewing the Civic Mission of the American Research University," *Journal of Higher Education* 72 (March/April 2001): 129.

4. David T. Z. Mindich, *Tuned Out: Why Americans under 40 Don't Follow the News* (New York: Oxford University Press, 2005), 6.

5. Robert D. Putnam, *Bowling Alone: The Collapse and Revival of American Community* (New York: Simon and Schuster, 2000).

6. For some examples, see Robert D. Putnam and Lewis M. Feldstein, *Better Together: Restoring the American Community* (New York: Simon and Schuster, 2003).

7. Putnam, *Bowling Alone*, 31–32.

8. About 51 percent of eligible voters turned out in 2000, and initial estimates in 2004 point to the highest turnout since 1968. Nearly 60 percent of eligible voters turned out in the most recent presidential election. Turnout among young voters also was up, to about 42 percent. Yet young people still voted at less than half the rate of older Americans. See "National Voter Turnout in Federal Elections, 1960–2000," http://www.infoplease.com/ipa/A0781453.html (accessed

February 18, 2005); Committee for the Study of the American Electorate, "President Bush, Mobilization Drives Propel Turnout to Post-1968 High," news release, November 4, 2004, http://www.fairvote.org/reports/CSAE2004election report.pdf (accessed May 17, 2005); Center for Information and Research on Civic Learning and Engagement, "Youth Voting in the 2004 Election," *Fact Sheet*, November 8, 2004 (updated January 25, 2005), http://www.civicyouth. org/PopUps/FactSheets/FS-PresElection04.pdf (accessed May 17, 2005).

9. Center for Voting and Democracy, "International Voter Turnout, 1991–2000," http://www.fairvote.org/turnout/intturnout.htm (accessed May 18, 2005).

10. See Mindich, *Tuned Out*, 18–33.

11. In the 2004 poll, 21 percent of respondents between the ages of 18 and 29 cited the comedy shows as regular sources of political news, up from just 9 percent who cited such shows in 2000. Meanwhile, the percentage of young people getting their news from the network evening news dropped from 39 percent in 2000 to just 23 percent in 2004. The findings point to a remarkable change in how young people get their news and, one might argue, in the very meaning of "news" itself. See Pew Research Center for the People and the Press, "Cable and the Internet Loom Large in Fragmented Political News Universe," news release, January 11, 2004, http://people-press.org/reports/pdf/200.pdf (accessed February 18, 2005).

12. "Young America's News Source: Jon Stewart," CNN.com, March 2, 2004, http://www.cnn.com/2004/SHOWBIZ/TV/03/02/apontv.stewarts.stature.ap/ (accessed June 14, 2005).

13. Putnam, *Bowling Alone*, 31–43.

14. Ibid., 43–45.

15. Ibid., 49.

16. See Peter D. Hart and Mario A. Brossard, "A Generation to Be Proud Of," *Brookings Review* 20 (Fall 2002): 36–37.

17. Everett Carll Ladd, "The American Way—Civic Engagement—Contrary to Cynical Conventional Wisdom, US Citizens Are Not Increasingly Bowling Alone," *Christian Science Monitor*, March 1, 1999, 9.

18. Richard Stengel, for example, has argued that Americans may not be going to political meetings anymore, but they are "discussing politics in the Internet equivalent of smokefilled rooms." Richard Stengel, "Bowling Together," *Time*, July 22, 1996, 35–36.

19. On "professional" and "astroturf" movements, see John D. McCarthy and Mayer N. Zald, "The Trend in Social Movements in America: Professionalized Movements and Resource Mobilization," in *Social Movements in an Organizational*

Society, ed. Mayer N. Zald and John D. McCarthy (New Brunswick: Transaction Press, 1987); and Samantha Sanchez, "How the West Is Won: Astroturf Lobbying and the 'Wise Use' Movement," *American Prospect*, no. 25 (March–April 1996): 37–42.

20. James Davison Hunter, *Culture Wars: The Struggle to Define America* (New York: Basic Books, 1991), 159.

21. Thomas Bender, "Then and Now: The Disciplines and Civic Engagement," *Liberal Education* 87 (Winter 2001): 6.

22. Checkoway, "Renewing the Civic Mission of the American Research University," 128.

23. David D. Cooper, "Academic Professionalism and the Betrayal of the Land-Grant Tradition," *American Behavioral Scientist* 42 (February 1999): 776–77.

24. Ernest L. Boyer, "Creating the New American College," *Chronicle of Higher Education*, March 9, 1994, A48.

25. In 1998, for example, a group of college administrators and faculty, foundation officers, and representatives from educational associations began a series of meetings at the Wingspread Conference Center in Racine, Wisconsin, to discuss ways to better prepare college students for citizenship. The recommendations of the Wingspread Conference continue to frame much of the discussion of the role of higher education in promoting civic engagement. See Johnnella E. Butler, "Democracy, Diversity, and Civic Engagement," *Academe* 86 (July/August 2000): 52–56; and Barry Checkoway, "Public Service: Our New Mission," *Academe* 86 (July/August 2000): 24–29.

26. Among these calls for reform are the Association of American Colleges and Universities' report "Greater Expectations: A New Vision for Learning as a Nation Goes to College," and the Carnegie Foundation's publication "The Civic Mission of Schools." See Carol G. Schneider, "President's Message: Greater Expectations and Civic Engagement," *Liberal Education* 88 (Fall 2002): 2; and Joseph O'Brien and Jada Kohlmeier, "Leadership: Part of the Civic Mission of School?" *Social Studies* 94 (July/August 2003): 161.

27. For some examples, see Pierre M. Omidyar, "Public Service's Profile Is Rising in Many College Curriculums," *New York Times*, April 24, 2000, A21; Susan A. Ostrander, "Democracy, Civic Participation, and the University: A Comparative Study of Civic Engagement on Five Campuses," *Nonprofit and Voluntary Sector Quarterly* 33 (March 2004): 74–94; and Jeffrey R. Young, "Persuading Students to Care: Eugene Lang's Program Aims to Prod Colleges into Encouraging Civic Involvement," *Chronicle of Higher Education*, April 11, 2003, A47.

28. Graham B. Spanier, *State-of-the-University Address, September 21, 2001* (University Park: Penn State Department of University Publications, 2001), 5.

29. Ibid., 7.

30. See, for example, Brock N. Meeks, "Better Democracy through Technology," *Communications of the ACM* 40 (February 1997): 75–78; and Jerry Berman and Daniel J. Weitzner, "Technology and Democracy," *Social Research* 64 (Fall 1997): 1313–19.

31. On the Republican National Committee's website, for example, RNC chairman Ken Mehlman warns that Democrats—presumably all of them—favor "weakening our national security," while the DNC website demonizes the GOP for a "culture of corruption." See Katie MacGuidwin, "Dems Seek to Further Weaken National Security," *GOP.com*, online at http://www.rnc.org/ (accessed March 22, 2006); Ken Mehlman, "Their Real Agenda," *GOP.com*, online at: http://www.rnc.org/ (accessed March 22, 2006); and "Unsweet Sixteen: Breaking Down Republican Culture of Corruption," *The Democratic Party*, online at http://www.democrats.org/ (accessed March 25, 2006).

32. Aristotle, *Rhetoric*, trans. W. Rhys Roberts (Chicago: University of Chicago Press, 1952).

33. For a discussion of the relationship between classical rhetoric and civic republicanism, see Robert Hariman, *Political Style: The Artistry of Power* (Chicago: University of Chicago Press, 1995), 95–149.

34. Robert Alexander Kraig, "The Second Oratorical Renaissance," in *Rhetoric and Reform in the Progressive Era*, ed. J. Michael Hogan (East Lansing: Michigan State University Press, 2003), 32.

35. Among many examples of texts that take such an approach, one of the most recent is Gary Hankins, *The Power of the Pitch: Transform Yourself into a Persuasive Presenter and Win More Business* (Chicago: Dearborn Trade Publishing, 2005).

36. In *Invitation to Public Speaking*, for example, Cindy L. Griffin incorporates the theory of "invitational rhetoric" into the basic public-speaking text, yet she still structures the book around the Aristotelian "canons" of rhetoric. The table of contents of the book differs little from traditional texts, with chapters on developing one's topic, audience analysis, research, supporting materials, reasoning, organization, style, and delivery. See Cindy L. Griffin, *Invitation to Public Speaking* (New York: Wadsworth, 2004).

37. Arthur M. Schlesinger Jr., *The Disuniting of America: Reflections on a Multicultural Society* (New York: W.W. Norton, 1992), 16, 18.

38. Ibid., 156.

39. Rosa A. Eberly, *Citizen Critics: Literary Public Spheres* (Urbana: University of Illinois Press, 2000).

40. See J. Michael Hogan and David Olsen, "The Rhetoric of Nuclear Education," in *Propaganda: A Pluralistic Perspective*, ed. Ted J. Smith III (New York: Praeger, 1989), 165–79.

41. See J. Michael Hogan, "George Gallup and the Rhetoric of Scientific Democracy," *Communication Monographs* 64 (June 1997): 161–79.

42. David W. Moore, *The Superpollsters: How They Measure and Manipulate Public Opinion* (New York: Four Walls, Eight Windows, 1992), 353.

43. *Gallup Poll Monthly*, no. 304 (January 1991), 7, 25.

44. J. Michael Hogan, "The Rhetoric of Presidential Approval: Media Polling and the White House Intern Scandal," in *Images, Scandal, and Communication Strategies of the Clinton Presidency*, ed. Robert E. Denton Jr. and Rachel L. Holloway (New York: Praeger, 2003), 271–98.

45. Kenneth Burke, *The Philosophy of Literary Form* (Baton Rouge: Louisiana State University Press, 1941), 191.

46. J. Michael Hogan, ed. *Rhetoric and Reform in the Progressive Era* (East Lansing: Michigan State University Press, 2003).

47. J. Michael Hogan, *Woodrow Wilson's Western Tour: Rhetoric, Public Opinion, and the League of Nations* (College Station: Texas A&M University Press, 2006).

48. J. Michael Hogan, "Introduction: Rhetoric and Reform in the Progressive Era," in *Rhetoric and Reform in the Progressive Era*, xiii–xv.

49. John Dewey, *The Public and Its Problems* (1927; Athens, Ohio: Swallow Press, 1991), 208.

50. Peter Levine, *The New Progressive Era: Toward a Fair and Deliberative Democracy* (Lanham, Md.: Rowman and Littlefield, 2000), xiii.

51. Ibid., 16.

52. Ibid.

53. Kevin Mattson, *Creating a Democratic Public: The Struggle for Urban Participatory Democracy during the Progressive Era* (University Park: Pennsylvania State University Press, 1998), 25–29.

54. Michael J. Sandel, *Democracy's Discontent: America in Search of a Public Philosophy* (Cambridge, Mass.: Harvard University Press, 1996), 209–10.

55. Mattson, *Creating a Democratic Public*, 45.

56. Woodrow Wilson, "The Making of a Nation," in *The Papers of Woodrow Wilson*, ed. Arthur S. Link et al. (Princeton, N.J.: Princeton University Press, 1966–94), 10:233.

57. Woodrow Wilson, "University Training and Citizenship," in *The Papers of Woodrow Wilson*, 8:589.

58. See Hunter, *Culture Wars*, 143–56.

59. E. J. Dionne Jr., *They Only Look Dead: Why Progressives Will Dominate the Next Political Era* (New York: Touchstone Books, 1997), 261.

4

Democracy and Rhetorical Education in Lithuania

James A. Herrick

There is no simple set of instructions on how to proceed. A moral and intellectual state cannot be established through a constitution, or through laws, or through directives, but only through a complex, long-term, and never ending work involving education and self-education.

—Vaclav Havel, *Summer Meditations*

Dramatic events in Eastern and Central European countries such as Ukraine and Kyrgyzstan reminded Westerners at the beginning of the millennium that the hope of democracy still drives people to risk everything in its pursuit. For the Baltic States of Lithuania, Latvia, and Estonia, the leap from state control of life into a democratic experiment occurred in 1991. Admission to the EU and NATO in 2005 signaled that the Baltic States' association with Western democracies likely constitutes a long-term arrangement. The development of flourishing and self-sustaining democracies, however, requires more than national autonomy and association with other democracies.

Still, there are today many hopeful signs of thriving democracies in these former Soviet republics, including free elections and open public debate. Moreover, the modern Baltic democracies have already demonstrated their resilience in the face of considerable testing. For instance, the Lithuanian Parliament peacefully removed a corrupt president in April 2004, an arduous process that involved lengthy and sometimes tumultuous debate.

At this juncture, it seems clear that the development of stable democracies in countries that had for five decades known Soviet repression requires that, in addition to basic political freedom, certain social conditions be present. Citizens must have access to information about candidates and issues, must be allowed and encouraged to vote, and must be allowed opportunities for free expression. But, it is equally evident that if these new democracies are to do well over the long term, various educational conditions must also be met. As Kurtis S. Meredith notes, "The evolving societies of CEE [Central and Eastern Europe] and CA [Central Asia] are contending simultaneously with assembling civil, democratic societies and restructuring schools in ways that will sustain and nurture a new social order."[1] During a four-month sabbatical spent teaching university students in Lithuania, I became convinced that the most critical of the educational conditions necessary to "sustain a new social order" are rhetorical in nature. Specifically, instruction in argumentation and public speaking, the core elements of the rhetorical tradition, will be essential to the flourishing of these new democracies.

Important work toward meeting such educational goals in the former Soviet republics has already been done, with these nations receiving vital assistance from Western agencies such as the United States Agency for International Development, and international foundations such as the Soros Foundation's Open Societies Institute. Smaller organizations are also working toward crucial educational reform centered on the teaching of subjects closely related to rhetoric. For instance, a network of teachers engaged in the Reading and Writing for Critical Thinking (RWCT) project is represented in more than twenty countries in Eastern and Central Europe.[2]

My recent experiences in Lithuania served as an important reminder of just how intimately linked are education in rhetoric and the success of democratic institutions. It is my view that teaching rhetorical skills such as argumentation in culturally sensitive ways, as well as propagating the interconnected set of values closely associated with the rhetorical tradition, are educational goals crucial to achieving stable democracies in Eastern Europe. While in Lithuania, I was also convinced of the crucial role played by public enactment of rhetorical processes—and thus public propagation of rhetorical values—in an emerging democracy. Though rhetorical education is critical to young democracies, not all educating in rhetoric is accomplished by educators.

This essay, then, offers a reflection on the close relationship between the rhetorical tradition and successful democracies. As part of this reflection, I will suggest several cultural factors that Western educators must recognize and accommodate when engaged in the crucial task of teaching rhetoric in Eastern Europe. This consideration of culture will prepare the way for discussing the foundational elements of what I will term a "rhetorical worldview"—interrelated public values associated with the rhetorical tradition and crucial to democratic practices. Finally, I will provide a brief case study in how rhetorical values may be cultivated by public enactment in political discourse. My central contention is that propagating rhetorical skills *and* values by means of both education and enactment is essential to the long-term success of emerging democracies.

Cultural Assumptions and Rhetorical Education

I will begin by exploring some cultural elements in Eastern Europe that are germane both to teaching rhetoric and to growing healthy democracies. As regards the future of democracy, there is much good news about the rising generation in Eastern Europe. Intellectual energy is in great supply among students; they are curious, ambitious, witty, bold, and determined. On standard academic measures, "The young people of the region have demonstrated over the years . . . that they can compete with their peers on a global level and come out on top."[3] Moreover, students possess an intense interest in the social issues facing their recently liberated nations. For instance, several of my students were "children of Chernobyl," either infants or in utero at the time of the reactor meltdown in 1986. Each had suffered personal setbacks as a result, and each knew that bad government had contributed to her or his injuries. Such students know from personal experience the significance of Richard Weaver's famous phrase "Ideas have consequences."[4] They are thus aware that thinking and speaking skills are critical to the success of their countries. To this awareness they add moral courage learned from their parents and grandparents, who, at extreme personal cost, suffered under and threw off political tyranny. In short, the human resources are in place here for vital democracies to develop.

Indeed, we in the West have much to learn from Eastern Europeans about what it takes to maintain basic freedoms. Any successful educational assistance, whether rhetorical or otherwise, must recognize and honor the fact that international cooperation is a two-way street. As Vaclav Havel told the United States Congress in 1989, "We must all learn many things from you [Americans], from how to educate our offspring and how to elect our representatives, to how to organize our economic life so that it will lead to prosperity and not poverty. But this doesn't have to be merely assistance from the well-educated, the powerful, and the wealthy to those who have nothing to offer in return. We, too, can offer something to you: our experience and the knowledge that has come from it."[5] Havel's point is well taken, and education about the relationship between rhetoric and democracy—like other East-West educational efforts—must be cooperative. With this caveat in place, what do we in the West have to offer Eastern Europe in this regard?

Though we usually take it for granted (or are unaware of the fact at all), our long experience with the rhetorical tradition has taught us a great deal about the conduct and the benefits of open public discourse. Indeed, foundational rhetorical norms and expectations are accepted and endorsed by the broad majority of citizens of Western democracies, though most are no longer directly familiar with the rhetorical tradition itself. This often is not the case in Eastern Europe. My conversations with students from Lithuania, Latvia, Estonia, Albania, Ukraine, Belarus, Kyrgyzstan and Russia, as well as with several Lithuanian educators, revealed that knowledge of rhetoric—Greco-Roman or otherwise—is almost wholly lacking in the region. This is perhaps not surprising, given several important historical and cultural factors.

First, Soviet educational policy—in place for fifty years—prohibited teaching the skills of independent thinking and public speaking. As Meredith writes, "The hallmark of the Soviet system was centralized control" that limited the potential for personal expression on the part of both teachers and students.[6] Learning in Soviet schools was largely by rote, and independent thought was discouraged. Self-expression of the type that is at the very center of the rhetorical tradition was associated with Western individualism, a notion that dovetailed with Baltic communitarian culture.

Second, though Western popular culture is widely admired and emulated in the East, the Western cultural heritage is often unknown or treated with suspicion as a potential usurper of regional traditions. This underlying apprehension about Western cultural dominance extends to rhetoric and the rhetorical tradition. Moreover, explaining that rhetoric is not of modern American but of ancient Greek and Roman origin does not help allay suspicions or provide credibility for the tradition. Athens and Rome are not the sources of cultural legitimation that they typically are in the West. For instance, I learned this when I introduced Greek or Latin terms to describe rhetorical concepts; students reacted with amused curiosity as if I had for no apparent reason shown them the Chinese character for ocean or house. Nor did it validate rhetorical concepts as inherently worthy of study to say that Aristotle or Cicero had endorsed them.

Third, because individualism is not a widely accepted value in communitarian Lithuania (and much of the rest of Eastern Europe), speechmaking is not a widely venerated skill. "Egoism" of any type is frowned upon, and nothing is considered more egoistic than making a speech, especially a speech about one's own opinions. Speechmaking, to the extent that it is esteemed at all, is seen as a public exhibition of cleverness—a skill valued only for keeping things moving at a wedding reception or anniversary celebration. During one class session, I set out ten reasons why being an able speaker was a valuable skill—such as presenting one's ideas effectively in a business setting. Following the class, a student earnestly informed me, "You left out the most important one—telling jokes and making toasts at wedding receptions." The kind of speechmaking characteristic of public officials elicited near-contempt, a reaction that reflects the nation's and the region's near-Platonic suspicion of professional persuaders. To stand up in front of a group and present your personal views on a topic as if you should be listened to and believed, as if your opinions were any more important that anyone else's, was considered an embarrassing display of ego worthy of a politician—or an American.

Finally, the understanding of what makes a claim appealing or persuasive seems to be quite different in Eastern Europe than it is in the West. It is not widely assumed that the claim supported by the best evidence is the most convincing. I soon learned from my students that

Western conceptions of evidence are either unknown or not endorsed. "Good evidence" is that which is cleverly or passionately asserted; claims are found convincing because they are intriguing. Subjective response to an idea or a "fact" is more important than its objective evaluation. What is fascinating, shocking, or mysterious is convincing because it is captivating. Riveting an audience's attention is more compelling than engaging its rational faculties. Canons of evidence such as accuracy, recency, consistency, or source credibility, unless also emotionally moving, are viewed as mere pedantry—boring, unconvincing, worthy of a stuffy academic or a devious bureaucrat. Above all, a speech must be interesting, and issues of evidence take a back seat to eliciting a strong audience reaction.

Cultivating a Rhetorical Worldview

Cultural differences between East and West regarding that most fundamental rhetorical form—the public speech—pointed to an even deeper divide regarding all things rhetorical. My experience in Lithuania suggested that a number of fundamental values undergirding the practice of public discourse in the West were not widely embraced there. For instance, open debate of issues of public significance was not typically seen as a good in itself. Moreover, access to information was an almost unknown concept, as was the notion that an ordinary citizen might make an important public statement on a substantial matter of public controversy.

These observations illustrate that what I term the rhetorical worldview is not widely embraced in Eastern Europe. This is perhaps not surprising, as training in both critical thinking and expository writing—potential sources of such a worldview—were unknown under Soviet dominance. By rhetorical worldview, I mean the presuppositions and values embedded in the rhetorical tradition that nurture, and provide the preconditions for, vibrant public discourse. These presuppositions and values are crucial to the flourishing of democracy, and as such must be central to the ongoing educational reform taking place in Eastern Europe. But, education alone is not sufficient to the propagation of such a worldview. Rhetorical values and practices must also be modeled by cultural leaders in the marketplace of ideas.

Western rhetorical theorists reveal their acceptance of a range of rhetorical values crucial to effective public discourse, each deeply rooted in the

Western cultural experience. I would like to highlight three such values particularly crucial to democratic processes. The first of these we might call the value for rhetorical agents and process. This value is affirmed by the late American rhetorical theorist Thomas Farrell when he writes that the norms of rhetorical culture assume that "interested advocates and agents may deal with radical contingencies in the human condition better through the shared disputation of practical reason than through other available means."[7] Such a commitment to "advocates and agents" engaging in "shared disputation" as a means of addressing "radical contingencies" is largely unquestioned in, for example, Western political contexts. Farrell's statement rests upon a taken-for-granted, axiomatic building block of any effective practice of rhetoric—a component in a discursive worldview founded on the West's accumulated rhetorical wisdom.

The value for rhetorical agents and practices affirms that public discourse is the preferred means of resolving disputes, discovering solutions to pressing problems, and bringing harmony out of discord. Public discourse, though not always the actual means, is considered the proper means of addressing the "radical contingencies of the human condition" to which Farrell refers. This value insists that the public practice of rhetoric is the only democratic, and the most reliable, means of achieving rational decisions about matters of civic significance, and a guard against deferring to absolutes or to the rule of the expert.

The value for rhetorical agents and processes, so crucial to healthy democracies, implies an equally crucial educational goal, for such a value involves developing skilled rhetorical agents familiar with tested rhetorical processes. Regard for rhetorical skill is itself a component in the values that make up the rhetorical worldview. But, for reasons already noted, in Eastern Europe this skill is not likely to be regarded for its capacity to elevate the individual capable of making an impressive display in public. Rather, in these communitarian states, cultivating a culturally adapted value for rhetorical skill would mean educating students in the reliable performance of public reasoning and speaking for the good of the community.

Education in rhetorical skill could be promoted in new democracies as a means of democratically distributing power. But, of course, with wider access to power comes a concern for the ethical practice of rhetoric, suggesting yet another goal of rhetorical education. Fundamental ethical commitments implied in sound rhetorical practice and characteristic of the most reliable rhetorical agents—virtues such as such as honesty, cooperation in discursive process, and the courage to defend unpopular ideas—would need to be taught and modeled as part of the effort to cultivate a practice of rhetoric that sustains and nourishes democracy.

The second foundational value I will term the value for rhetorical agreements. German social theorist Jürgen Habermas, for instance, draws our attention to the "healing power of unification and reconciliation" that comes about through the "unforced intersubjectivity of rational agreement." Such trust in "intersubjectivity" provides a foundational component of his celebrated view of rationality in the public sphere.[8] But, as with Farrell, such a view is not assumed to be true in many parts of the world desperately in need of the very "healing power" of which Habermas speaks. It is not everywhere intuitively obvious that "unification and reconciliation" might be achieved through agreements arising from the practice of rational public rhetoric. Again, a crucial commitment of a rhetorical worldview—the value for rhetorical agreements—is evident in Habermas's confidence in the power of rhetorical agreements. Moreover, other dimensions of that worldview are also at work in his affirmation.

Habermas's value for rhetorically achieved agreements rests on the deep presupposition that humans are by nature givers and hearers of reasons, and thus the corporate reasoning process issues in a reliable product. Such basic regard for human rhetorical capacity and its products was unknown in Eastern Europe during the Soviet decades, when students "spent their school life in a relatively voiceless, autocratic setting where dialogue, problem solving, collaborative work, and sharing ideas and the formation of ideals and beliefs [was] discouraged."[9] The value for human beings as independent reasoners—a sine qua non of the rhetorical worldview—will have to be retrieved and propagated in efforts to educate for citizenship in the East's emerging democracies.

Belgian legal theorist Chaim Perelman and L. Olbrechts-Tyteca draw our attention to a third value foundational to rhetoric and democracy—a value for rhetorical communities. Perelman and Olbrechts-Tyteca noted that in order for constructive public discourse to occur, "an effective community of minds must be realized at a given moment." But, they added, "this does not come about automatically."[10] Indeed, an effective rhetorical community develops over time, and only in the presence of certain carefully cultivated and intentionally enacted values and practices.

Perelman and Olbrechts-Tyteca studied the master texts of Western rhetoric in their search for the components of the rational-discourse community, finally distilling the rhetorical tradition's essence into two critical components: argumentation and the audience. Embedded, then, in the value for rational rhetorical communities is a commitment to sound arguments as essential to rational discourse, and a high regard for the rhetorical audience (their "particular audience") as one develops such arguments. Again, they would remind us that rhetorical communities only develop over time, and only as components of the rhetorical worldview establish themselves in a culture's soul.

Perelman and Olbrechts-Tyteca's notion of maturing rhetorical communities rests on a respect for tested methods of public rationality. Implicit in the idea of a "community of minds" is the complementary value for the community's traditional methods or argument—the kind of catalog of arguments that Aristotle referred to in his *Rhetoric* as *topoi*—being valued, preserved, and refined.[11] The effort to identify and refine distinctly Eastern European methods of public reasoning might, therefore, constitute an element of effective rhetorical education in the region.

The rhetorical worldview affirms that democracies flourish when rhetoric is practiced well. And, in order for this value to serve as a foundational commitment for the development of lasting democracies, it must be joined to a firm belief that the audience of the general public ought to be treated as trustworthy to manage public affairs. It is vacuous to hope that new democracies can flourish and develop without a commitment to rhetorical practices, and a concomitant commitment to the public as audience. Rhetoric, democracy, and the public audience are inextricably linked concepts. Thus, a bedrock commitment to rhetorically educating the public audience must be a feature of any plan for the development of lasting democratic institutions.

In sum, when the rhetorical tradition is introduced in culturally appropriate ways, the values I have identified as constituting a rhetorical worldview will slowly take hold. When such values are in place, and as they become integral to the practice of public discourse, then democratic practices and institutions will be enhanced in such a way as to be more likely to succeed over the long haul. Farrell, Habermas, and Perelman point us toward foundational value commitments essential to a vibrant practice of rhetoric—the kind of practice that encourages confidence in public rhetorical agents and processes, that strives for intersubjective agreements, and that is constitutive of rhetorical communities. Such community-endorsed values are essential to the successful maintenance of democracy.

Publicly Enacting a Rhetorical Worldview

The long Soviet experience destroyed any conception of public rationality in the former Soviet republics. I have been arguing that a vital sense of such a possibility must be retrieved if democracy is to flourish in these emerging democracies. The destruction of a public sphere drove citizens into radically private lives—the only safe place to speak was within the confines of one's own home. Consequently, belief in the safety of public expression, even of dissenting opinions, must be reestablished as a condition of democratic success. But more than this, a belief in the efficacy of rhetorical practices within a safe public sphere must be cultivated and propagated. Educational reform centered on the teaching of critical thinking, public speaking, and other rhetorical skills is part of this process. However, the public enactment of rhetorical skills and values can also play an important role in the process of cultivating a rhetorical worldview in the nations once dominated by the USSR.

During my stay in Lithuania, President Rolandas Paksas was impeached and expelled from office as the result of a lengthy investigative and deliberative process that tested the mettle of this young democracy. Paksas had been accused of various constitutional violations, including leaking state secrets and granting Lithuanian citizenship to a wealthy supporter—Russian businessman Yuri Borasov. Simonas Girdzijauskas writes that "the impeachment capped more than five months of investigative processes."[12]

Though the process was a painful one, out of the publicly televised parliamentary debate that eventually led to Paksas's ouster, elements of a rhetorical worldview began to emerge in dramatic relief. Moreover, the contrast with all-too-familiar Soviet practices that had radically suppressed critical thought and public discourse, and that had forcefully transformed all public discourse into innocuous commentary or outright praise for the state, could not have been more striking. The stage was set for a decisive encounter between two discursive worldviews.

The weeks-long processes of bringing evidence against Paksas before a national audience through the auspices of Lithuanian State Television (TVLT) helped Lithuanians begin to develop confidence in the kind of public rationality that makes democracy possible. Paksas resisted the public debate, refusing to answer the constitutional charges against him, and resorting to "emotional speeches and personal appeals."[13] His dismissive response itself provided the public with a vivid contrast between a rhetorical worldview that venerated public rationality, and the evasive practices of an older system of power politics that refused to engage the citizenry rhetorically on issues of public import. What was learned through the process of trying a president before a public audience?

First, public presentation of the evidence and charges against Paksas modeled for Lithuanians that issues engaging public values ought properly to be resolved rhetorically in public settings, not behind closed doors by experts and insiders in government agencies. Thus, the value for rhetorical agents and processes was publicly enacted during the Paksas trial, placing in bold relief a commitment so often taken for granted in the West—that the resolution of "radically contingent" issues rightly belongs in the public domain of non-experts engaged in an open process of argumentation. Through the process of impeaching and expelling Paksas, Lithuanians began to appreciate that public rationality on such weighty issues is possible.

Second, Lithuanians began to understand themselves as an adjudicating audience—a rhetorical community—seeking reliable agreements. The decision to bring the parliamentary debate before a national audience was a demonstration that the public was to be treated with regard as rational decision makers. The courageous leadership of a few younger parliamentary representatives ensured that constitutional procedures were followed, but also that regard was paid to the important role played by agreement within the public audience. Various reemerging community values, such as those for honesty and the rule of law, were thus shown to hold a central place in public rationality. Moreover, foundational rhetorical practices such as public debate, the testing of evidence, and public speaking were demonstrated to be means of distributing power within the community. Power no longer belonged only to the well-connected and the wealthy; it was also a function of the rhetorical community.

Third, throughout the impeachment debate, various public officials demonstrated publicly the crucial role played by skill in reasoning and argument. Members of Parliament skillfully countered the deceptive rhetorical tactics employed by Paksas, his attorneys, and his supporters in Parliament. The discursive performance of Paksas's accusers underlined the importance of cultivating rhetorical skills as a means of improving both public discourse and democratic government. Paksas and his attorneys unwittingly provided a contrasting model by repeatedly refusing to engage the evidence, answer accusations, and respond to arguments. Girdzijauskas notes, "During the proceedings, the privately hired presidential defense team did not argue or challenge the dozens of phone recordings" brought in evidence against Paksas.[14] Nor did they bother to answer specific charges against Paksas. An important point was being made through the public enactment of contrasting rhetorical models—skillful rhetoricians in possession of sound evidence can effectively counteract the evasive tactics of political power.

Finally, the openness with which the presidential impeachment process played itself out in the spring of 2004 illuminated the fact that high ethical standards are crucial to regulating the conduct of public argument. Radio Free Europe followed the proceedings closely and provided favorable press coverage for the Lithuanian Constitutional Court's, as well as the Lithuanian Parliament's, determination to discover the facts in the case.[15] Standards such as honesty before the public, determination to search out the facts and make them part of the public record, and the rhetorical courage to face down entrenched power were repeatedly demonstrated. Such standards would constitute important components in the educational agenda of all such emerging democracies, for skill in rhetoric alone without a commitment to rhetorical ethics will not support democracy over long periods of time.

Conclusion

I left Lithuania cautiously hopeful about the possibilities for its future as a democracy. My hope was founded on witnessing firsthand how courage, intellect, and political tenacity brought the nation successfully through a major constitutional crisis. My caution was rooted in the fact that a number of foundational values and assumptions crucial to public rationality, and thus to democracy, are not widely embraced or taught. My experiences in Lithuania convinced me that democracies do not grow in a rhetorical vacuum, but that the interconnected commitments that I have termed the rhetorical worldview have to be nurtured alongside democracy. This means, I believe, that these commitments must constitute an intentional educational goal, and must also be publicly enacted to reinforce their close connection to properly functioning democratic processes.

Lithuanians learned valuable lessons through the public rhetorical performance that transpired during the televised proceedings against Rolandas Paksas. These lessons included the necessity of publicly debating "radically contingent" issues, recognizing the rationality of "intersubjective agreements," and accepting the public's role as "rhetorical community" in a democracy. Moreover, the centrality of skillful rhetorical practice to sound public rationality, as well as the important role played by rhetorical ethics in public discourse were also clearly evidenced.

But public enactment of rhetorical values is not sufficient to sustain a democracy; its citizens must be purposefully prepared for democracy's demands. This means that a rhetorically oriented education in Eastern Europe ought to actively propagate the presuppositions, values, and skills crucial to the future of democracy. But, as noted, such educational goals will need to be pursued in culturally appropriate ways. If fledgling democracies such as those recently established in several former Soviet Republics are to last, the basic values and skills that have attended rhetoric throughout its long history need to be propagated and practiced. This will occur most effectively through the combined efforts of educational, business, and government institutions.

NOTES

1. Kurtis S. Meredith, "The Political and Historical Context for Educational Reform in Central and Eastern Europe and Central Asia," in *Ideas without Boundaries: International Education Reform through Reading and Writing for Critical Thinking*, ed. David Klooster, Jeanine Steele, Patricia Bloem (Newark, Del.: International Reading Association, 2001), 23.

2. *Ideas without Boundaries: International Education Reform through Reading and Writing for Critical Thinking*, ed. David Klooster, Jeanine Steele, Patricia Bloem (Newark, Del.: International Reading Association, 2001).

3. Meredith, "Political and Historical Context," 36.

4. Richard M. Weaver, *Ideas Have Consequences*, reprint (Chicago: University of Chicago Press, 1984).

5. Vaclav Havel, "Address to Joint Session of US Congress (1989)," in *The Art of the Impossible* (New York: Alfred A. Knopf, Inc., 1997), 17–18.

6. Meredith, "Political and Historical Context," 25.

7. Thomas B. Farrell, *Norms of Rhetorical Culture* (New Haven: Yale University Press, 1993), 229.

8. Thomas McCarthy, Introduction to Jürgen Habermas, *The Philosophical Discourse of Modernity: Twelve Lectures*, trans. Frederick Lawrence (Cambridge, Mass.: MIT Press, 1987), x, xii.

9. Meredith, "Political and Historical Context," 30.

10. Chaim Perelman and L. Olbrechts-Tyteca, *The New Rhetoric: A Treatise on Argumentation*, trans. John Wilkinson and Purcell Weaver (Notre Dame, Ind.: University of Notre Dame Press, 1969), 14.

11. Aristotle, *Rhetoric*, trans. George A. Kennedy (Oxford: Oxford University Press, 1991), 190–204.

12. Simonas Girdzijauskas, "Issues Backgrounder #5" (Rockville, Md.: The Joint Baltic American National Committee, 2004), 1.

13. Ibid., 2.

14. Ibid., 1.

15. Radio Free Europe, "Lithuania: President Looks Likely to Lose Job Next Week," April 1, 2004.

PART 2

Rhetoric, Democracy, and the Critique of Political Practices

5

Two Faces of Democratic Rhetoric

David Zarefsky

braham Lincoln began his memorable 1860 speech at Cooper Union by saying, "The facts with which I shall deal this evening are mainly old and familiar; nor is there anything new in the general use I shall make of them. If there shall be any novelty, it will be in the mode of presenting the facts, and the inferences and observations following that presentation."[1]

If there was little new in Lincoln's remarks about the founders' view of Congress's power to restrict the spread of slavery, even less is there likely to be news in my thoughts about rhetoric and democracy. I doubt that any of us would challenge the claim that democracy is the best form of government—or at least, as Churchill said, the worst except for all the others. And I suspect we would all resonate with the claim that rhetoric is a powerful, perhaps essential instrument in the service of democracy—since that is a claim we have heard from our earliest public-speaking courses and probably have repeated from time to time when we thought it necessary to justify what we do. And while this next assertion is more speculative, I believe that most of us harbor some anxiety about the state of contemporary rhetoric, or of contemporary democracy, or perhaps both. Even as the years since 1990 have seen nations unfamiliar with democratic traditions move fitfully to claim them, many in the United States have worried not only that our brand of democracy may be unsuitable for export but also that it may not be healthy here at home. These beliefs—the materials with which I will work—are old and familiar. If there is anything new here, it will be in the mode of describing them and in the inferences following from them. Because I know it best, I will talk mainly about rhetoric and democracy in the United States. Specifically, I want to argue that democratic rhetoric has two faces—one benign, one threatening—that exist in tension, that the balance between them is jeopardized, and that our active efforts are needed to restore it.

Understanding Democracy

I want to begin with a working definition of democracy, and again, Lincoln's formulation is as good as any. After the assault on Fort Sumter, he summoned Congress into special session to consider measures to suppress the rebellion. In his message opening the session, he presented the issue as whether or not "a constitutional republic, or a democracy . . . can, or cannot, maintain its territorial integrity, against its own domestic foes." Midway through that sentence, he defined democracy as "a government of the people, by the same people"[2]—a formulation that prefigured the Gettysburg Address and that offers a good touchstone for us. In a democracy, sovereignty resides with the people. They grant power to their leaders, expect their leaders to act as their agents on their behalf, and know that they can hold their leaders accountable. For the secular, sovereignty resides in the people by virtue of natural law; for the religious, as the gift of God. In any case, this is an inversion of the hierarchy in nondemocratic regimes, in which sovereignty resides in leaders by virtue of heredity, or wealth, or power. Leaders grant liberties to, or withhold them from, the people as they choose, taking care only to prevent or defeat any possible revolutionary upheaval so that they might retain sovereignty. Conversely, only the success of revolution can change the locus of sovereignty.

From this very general formulation of democracy, we can derive at least three corollaries. One is political equality. Sovereignty resides not in any particular person, but in the people generically—so one person's claims to rule are just as strong as another's. Obviously I do not claim that in fact, people are equal in their access to power and influence, but that in principle, decision-making authority is allocated per capita and not on the basis of wealth, race, gender, religion, heredity, occupation, or even intelligence.

A second corollary is majority rule. Democracy does not assume that all people will think alike; it anticipates that conflicts will arise. If sovereignty resides in the people equally, then the only way to make decisions in the face of conflict is by the weight of greater numbers. Advocates may claim that their ideas are buttressed by economic power, military might, or the word of the Almighty, but only the judgment of a majority of their fellows will settle a conflict in their favor. If we want to discourage hasty action, we may insist on a larger majority, or we may require more than one vote. But these are simply refinements that do not alter the basic principle.

And the third corollary is minority rights. While the position of the minority does not prevail, the members of the minority lose none of their legitimacy or sovereignty. The Talmud embodies this principle by preserving and honoring both the majority and the minority views; courts and committees do so through the device of the minority report. Members of the minority share the same human and civil rights as do their majority counterparts, and that means that the minority could become the majority another day. In democracies, there are no final victories.

I suspect that this principle and its corollaries will not be found controversial by readers of this volume. They are consistent with the values with which we have been socialized, and most of us—however we feel about this or that contemporary event—will find them generally to be borne out by history and experience. And we will endorse the principle.

But why? Other than habit, why is it that we so readily regard democracy as a superior system? If called upon to justify it, how would we do so?

When I studied American political thought as an undergraduate, in addition to the usual texts (*The Federalist Papers*, Tocqueville, Calhoun's Disquisition on Government, and so on), I read a small book by Thomas Landon Thorson called *The Logic of Democracy*.[3] Thorson's goal is to answer the question "Why are democratic political values to be preferred over authoritarian ones?"[4] and his answer is that democracy is the political system most consistent with human fallibility. It is the system of government that most clearly acknowledges that we can be wrong, and permits the correction of error.

Implicit in Thorson's argument is that human fallibility is both a necessary and a sufficient condition for preferring democracy. To see why it is necessary, try a simple thought experiment. Suppose that we knew for sure when life begins, or what is our responsibility to the elderly, or whether multilateral or unilateral action is more likely to deter terrorism. If we really knew any of these things, we ought to do whatever is necessary to act upon that knowledge. And if ignorant people disagreed with our advice, we should spare no effort to be sure that we prevailed—not so much for our own satisfaction as to save the world from the consequences of error. Perhaps this thought experiment helps us to understand, even as we condemn, the actions of people who think they do know for sure. As Thorson rhetorically asks, "If there is an absolute good, why let an obviously ignorant majority make political decisions?"[5] It is the very fact that we do not know for sure (even if we think we do) that deters us from such no-holds-barred action and leads us to seek the assent of others. "Only by denying absolute values," Thorson concludes, "does democracy make sense."

Equally so, the very fact that we cannot be sure of our knowledge is the sufficient condition for preferring democracy. Drawing an analogy to the scientific method, Thorson suggests that "we are never justified in behaving as if we knew [the truth]. That is to say, we are never justified in refusing to consider the possibility that we might be wrong."[6] Precisely because there are no final victories, because the principle of political equality protects minorities while permitting majorities to rule, and because "decisions on public policy always involve matters of preference, the ultimate 'rightness' of which cannot be demonstrated,"[7] it makes sense to favor a system that does not in principle exclude anyone's views and preferences and that vests sovereignty in the same people who must live with the consequences of decisions.

Noting that the advocates of democracy nevertheless seem to defend absolute values, such as "equality, life, liberty, the pursuit of happiness, limited government, and revolution," Thorson explains that these cannot be strictly deduced from any general theory about the nature of humanity or the universe, so they are not self-evident.[8] Rather, they function instead as recommendations for how we should conduct political deliberation in recognition of human fallibility. They are what the command "Be rational!" means when applied to the sphere of politics. To complete the circle, Thorson maintains that were it not for fallibility, there would be no need for politics at all: "If perfect knowledge were to be obtained," then, like philosophy or science, politics "would be as useless as a telescope is to God."[9] So if politics exists in the first place because of human fallibility, then it is only rational to favor the political system that comports best with the condition of fallibility, and democracy is that system.

The First Face of Democratic Rhetoric: An Invitation to Deliberate

Among the reasons that I have been so influenced by Thorson's argument is that it is congruent with my understanding of rhetoric. I believe that the fundamental defining condition of the rhetorical situation is the need to make collective decisions under conditions of uncertainty. The uncertainty of the situation may stem from the fact that there is not enough time to contemplate our choices thoroughly. Or it may stem from the fact that our choice cannot be deduced from a set of facts. This is what argumentation theorists refer to as the "is-ought problem."[10] Facts may be relevant to a decision about what should be done, but they do not compel a decision about what should be done. Therefore, choices are grounded in the beliefs and values of an audience and a culture—the classical understanding of the enthymeme.

Or, even more commonly, the situation is uncertain because the audience holds beliefs and values in dialectical tension. We favor both civil liberties and national security, both individualism and equality, both order and justice, both independence and interdependence. These are essentially contested concepts; that is, they derive their meaning by comparison with their opposite, and the underlying contests are impossible to resolve in the abstract. People settle them in the context of particular situations.[11] And so, imagining Protagoras speaking in gender-neutral language, we would say that humanity is the measure of all things.

This understanding of rhetoric is either classically sophistic or decidedly postmodern, or perhaps both. It distinguishes rhetoric from philosophy on the basis that rhetoric is anti-foundational and grounded in contingency. It deals with human action, not detached contemplation. As a middle ground between the seeming certainty of deduction and the anarchy of vicious relativism, rhetoric emphasizes justification, but grounds it in the beliefs and values of an audience in a given context or situation. Notice the close parallels between these understandings of rhetoric and of democracy. First, people respond to choices that are grounded in their beliefs and values. The same people make the decisions and are guided by them. That sounds very much like government of the people, by the same people. Second, appeal is made to audience beliefs and values in a given case. That sounds very much like saying that there are no final victories, that both majority and minority positions are honored, and that although one position will prevail today, the argument can circle back around and the other position might prevail tomorrow.

This sketch represents one face of democratic rhetoric. It is invitational. In this view, we recognize that all discourses are partial, put forward as ways to formulate and test claims. Speakers and listeners together are engaged in the search for *phronesis*—for practical wisdom—which is the guide to conduct in the given case. They assume that such guidance will emerge as the outcome of their deliberations, rather than already existing prior to them. We might say that the participants in these exchanges are together constructing the social reality in which they live—government of the people, by the same people.

Although I am describing an ideal, one can identify occasions when rhetoric has served the cause of democratic leadership in about this way. Problem-solving discussions in small groups often fit this model. So do court decisions that weigh and balance the competing stories and worldviews of the different advocates. Even some congressional debates and national policy decisions approximate this model. I would regard the debate over authorizing force in the 1991 Persian Gulf war, the mid1990's "national conversation" on affirmative action, the 1980's debates about the future of Social Security (as opposed to those of 2005), and the public debate of 1951–52 about whether Europe or Asia should take precedence in our foreign policy as fairly clear examples. Others will have their own lists.

I do not mean to suggest that rhetoric functions only in this invitational way. To be sure, Plato regarded it as a *techne* for use by the philosopher-kings in order effectively to convey truth that had been determined by other means. Throughout history, it has been a tool for demagogues and an instrument for charismatic totalitarian leaders to use in order to thwart, rather than encourage, reflective deliberation. But I do mean to suggest that a strong rhetorical culture—in the sense in which that term is used by my late colleague Thomas Farrell—can be sustained only in a democracy. Farrell regards rhetoric as "the collaborative art of addressing and guiding decision and judgment—usually public judgment about matters that cannot be decided by force or expertise"—and regards a rhetorical culture as "an institutional formation in which motives of competing parties are intelligible, audiences available, expressions reciprocal, norms translatable, and silences noticeable."[12] Democracy is not a sufficient condition for nurturing such a culture, but I believe that it is necessary for that project, because only people who believe themselves sovereign will seriously engage public issues. And I think it is something like this conception of rhetoric that we have in mind when we proclaim, in our public-speaking textbooks and elsewhere, that rhetoric is an essential tool of democratic leadership.

Can the First Face of Democratic Rhetoric Be Maintained?

It may give us pause, however, to realize that this is not the view of democracy or of rhetoric that guided the United States at its founding. Most of those whom we memorialize as the founding fathers did not believe either that democracy was the most desirable form of government or that people responded to the public-spirited appeal of an invitational rhetoric to come and reason together in pursuit of the common good.

Most of the founders, at least those who prevailed in the discussions about the shape of the U.S. government, took a less optimistic view of human nature. Even as they engaged in rhetoric directed to a variety of audiences—perhaps because they could not avoid it—their more reflective writings cast doubt on the capacity of the people to judge. Democracy was one of three pure forms of government, the others being monarchy and aristocracy. Monarchy was rule by the one; aristocracy, by the few; and democracy, by the many. Each had its accompanying vice. The dark side of monarchy was tyranny; that of aristocracy, oligarchy with its resulting concentration of power; and that of democracy, mob rule. The danger of mob rule was real because, the founders believed, the mass of the population was easily swayed by demagogues. In a pure democracy, rhetors who harnessed an ancient art for their own selfish and ignoble purposes would warp public judgment, leading the mass of the people actually to surrender their hard-won freedoms and liberties and to follow a siren song. The solution adopted by the founders was to incorporate elements of all three forms in the new government, but to check them one against another so that none could be taken to its logical conclusion. This was the reason for separation of powers, checks and balances. *The Federalist* argues, in essence, that the Constitution provides for the government the right mix of energy and restraint so that it will achieve equilibrium among the three pure forms. The anti-Federalists were not so much convinced of the capacity of the people as they were distrustful that the Constitution would be enough of a check on the power of the rulers.

The founders were influenced by an eighteenth-century concept of virtue, which was understood as a preference for the public good over personal self-interest. They assumed that the public good was self-evident, so there was no need for rhetorical deliberation to discern what it was. If some people could not see it, that was because they were not sufficiently virtuous. They should not be trusted with the decisions about policy, or even about who should hold office. But what even they *could* do was to identify the most virtuous among their neighbors, who in turn could identify the most virtuous in a wider circle, and eventually a group could deliberate among themselves and, on the basis of character, select a virtuous person to administer the government as president. That is why the Electoral College was created. That is why, as the Supreme Court reminded us in *Bush v. Gore*,[13] the Constitution did not grant citizens the right to vote in presidential elections, but instead left the method of selecting electors up to the state legislatures—several of whom, at least initially, did not defer to direct popular vote.

If the founders did not embrace democracy, then how can we describe their view of the government they created? Essentially, it combined the democratic assumption that sovereignty ultimately rested with the people, with the assumption of civic republicanism that the task of government was to make the choices that were in the public interest, and with the belief that it was self-evident to any virtuous person what these were. We might say that it was an attempt to protect democracy from what the founders regarded as the inherent tendency of democratic rhetoric. Of course, this view had the consequence of eliminating space for legitimate political disagreement and controversy. The existence of controversy must mean that one's opponent is lacking in virtue. Rather than offering a legitimate alternative position, one's opponent was threatening the very stability of the political system by failing to heed the call of virtue. Seeing things this way, of course, quickly escalated the stakes of any conflict. This may help to explain the heated temperature of the rhetoric of the 1790s and the fact that the election campaign of 1800 was one of the meanest and most bitterly fought that we have had.[14]

For the founders, then, only a relatively small coterie of the most virtuous were capable of participating in the sort of rhetorical culture I have described above. This conviction, as much as outright racist or sexist prejudice, explains why political participation was so circumscribed. Of course, the nation evolved in a very different way from what the founders had anticipated. The consistent tendencies were to expand the body politic by weakening barriers to participation, to legitimize but sublimate political conflict, and yet to maintain the assumption that political processes would produce results that would be for the common good.

The Second Face of Democratic Rhetoric: The Engineering of Consent

The democratizing trends are easy to discern. State constitutional conventions beginning in the 1820s rewrote the organic acts to remove property restrictions on the franchise. By the 1840s, every state except South Carolina had adopted direct popular vote as the means of selecting presidential electors. Racial restrictions, at least in theory, were eliminated by the ratification of the 15th Amendment in 1870—and gender restrictions with the 19th Amendment, ratified in 1920. The 26th Amendment, adopted in 1971, weakened age restrictions by lowering the voting age to eighteen, and in recent years such initiatives as provisional ballots and motor-voter registration are attempts to limit barriers posed by the growing mobility of the population. Voting is not the only dimension of political involvement, to be sure. But the expansion of the franchise is indicative of larger democratizing tendencies as they applied to political participation.

For a long time, these expansions of the political audience were not accompanied by widespread concern that the electorate might be victimized by the perverse use of rhetoric or that the demagogue might hold sway, the fears of the founders notwithstanding. This was true even though in practice, as Michael Schudson has demonstrated, votes were influenced by deference to one's social "betters," or by the discipline of the early party organizations, or by the hoopla of songs and parades.[15] There was fairly widespread confidence in the judgment of the people. Thomas Paine had claimed in 1795, "Certain I am that when opinions are free, either in matters of government or religion, truth will finally and powerfully prevail."[16] In the 1840s the democratic historian George Bancroft was even more optimistic, proclaiming that "The common judgment in matters of taste, politics, and religion is the highest authority on earth."[17] As late as 1909, Herbert Croly wrote in *The Promise of American Life*, "The American people are absolutely right in insisting that an aspirant for popular eminence shall be compelled to make himself interesting to them, and shall not be welcomed as a fountain of excellence and enlightenment until he has found some means of forcing his meat and his wine down their reluctant throats."[18] This nineteenth-century romanticism about the power of rational judgment survived long after underlying social and cultural changes had rendered the Enlightenment project largely obsolete. This was true even as the late nineteenth century witnessed the advent of the social sciences, which shifted attention from the normative question of how people should behave to the empirical question of how they actually did; the advent of Freudian psychoanalysis, which emphasized the role of unconscious and hence nonrational motivation; and the study of crowds and mobs, which encouraged the belief that crowds were likely to make manifest our otherwise latent animal instincts.

In my judgment, the defining event that led to a much more pessimistic portrayal of the human potential and the rhetorical prospect was a massive sense of disillusionment that set in after World War I. This is when propaganda was "discovered."[19] Both the Allies and the Central Powers were shown to have mobilized support for the war with atrocity stories, blatant appeals to fear, ethnocentric—even jingoistic—messages, and other techniques of persuasion that did not conform to the expectations of the Enlightenment. The realization that people were, in fact, influenced by such messages gave pause to those who had been confident that even a large democratic public could reason rhetorically in search of practical wisdom. This was a second face of democratic rhetoric, one that was manipulative rather than deliberative. It was the rhetoric of the closed fist, not the open hand.

A convenient marker of this change in American thinking about the potential of rhetoric can be found in the early writings of Walter Lippmann.

In 1922 he published *Public Opinion*,[20] notable especially for its theory of the stereotype as a force guiding people's opinions. Lippmann's thesis was that public opinion had been disastrously wrong at the critical junctures in history. Why? Because of the false ideal of the competent citizen who is capable of making judgments in the realm of public affairs. The sad truth is that the average citizen responds instead to mental images of the world that are the product of stereotypes and that do not match reality. Guided by stereotypes and intellectually lazy, the citizen enacts a kind of Gresham's Law of ideas: Cheap arguments drive out the good. Weaker arguments, intuitively appealing and easy to grasp, will entice people away from the serious thought and mental energy that good arguments usually require. And the willingness of the public to settle for cheap arguments is what leads public opinion astray. Lippmann's critique of over eighty years ago has contemporary resonance; it reads like many more current analyses of American public discourse.

Three years later, Lippmann published *The Phantom Public*,[21] a work in which he was even more pessimistic. He extended his earlier argument by claiming that the ordinary citizen cannot possibly be made competent, because education always lags behind reality in the world of public affairs. It cannot encompass change quickly enough. Hence, he reasoned, we must abandon even the ideal of the competent public and defer instead to expert decision makers. This completed a line of thought that had its roots in the Progressive movement and that had the effect of discouraging active public participation in the making of policy decisions.[22] Again, this critique has a contemporary ring, although it has been more common for critics to decry than to excuse the displacement of the public sphere by the technical.[23]

At various times over the past century, theorists and pundits have lamented the atrophy of the public sphere. Some have pointed to indicators of apathy about public affairs; others, to embarrassingly low levels of public knowledge of such basic matters as the names of incumbent officeholders; others, to the growing influence of money in politics. If we have a democracy, but with a weak public sphere, the likelihood is that we will see the second face of democratic rhetoric to which I have alluded. Since sovereignty still resides in the people, they must be appealed to. But since they lack the time, experience, and motivation to participate actively, the appeal takes on a grotesque form. It represents the appearance of deliberation, but not the substance—a simulacrum, in the postmodern vocabulary. Citizens are not offered arguments that they are invited to test, compare, and join, but instead are appealed to with slogans, half-truths, and condensation symbols in a bid for their unreasoned support.[24] Rather than co-creating social reality and thereby discovering *phronesis* in the given case, they are led to acquiesce in a vision of the good that has been determined in advance. Consent is not cultivated; it is engineered. The second face of democratic rhetoric is to be feared, not encouraged. It is what the American founders rightly warned against. And if this second face is the very essence of what rhetoric *is* (as in the public understanding it often seems to be), then rhetoric eminently deserves the scorn bestowed upon it for the past century or more.

So runs the critique. In fairness, I should make clear that I have overstated the case and perhaps indulged in a stereotype of my own. For one thing, the second face of democratic rhetoric is not new; we have not just recently fallen from grace. As Michael Schudson's study of the changing understandings of citizenship makes clear, romantic nostalgia for an imagined golden age misleads us about both our history and our current prospects.[25] Moreover, there is substantial evidence to suggest that the public does behave rationally—that people use reasonable and efficient heuristics to simplify complex problems, that they understand the basics of the issues they are cailed upon to decide, that they do not blindly follow opinion leaders, and that they vote in a way that is consistent with their own interests and values.[26]

In his provocatively titled book *What's the Matter with Kansas?* Thomas Frank maintains that significant numbers of Americans are voting for Republicans against their own self-interest, and he explains this phenomenon by noting that rhetors' invocation of cultural values such as abortion and gay rights has blinded people to their own interests.[27] As an explanation for why so much of the South and Midwest, which once harbored radical populists, has become solid red states, I find Frank's book insightful. But if it is offered as evidence for the irrationality of the American people, I am less convinced. After all, many prosperous Democrats who opposed tax cuts also voted against their own self-interest, and probably liked to think they did so in the belief that other considerations affecting the public interest were more important. Is this not what the eighteenth-century thinkers called virtue?

The Imbalance between the Two Faces of Democratic Rhetoric

The invitation to deliberate undergirds the assumptions of democracy; the engineering of consent seems to subvert them. Yet we cannot have one without the other. A commitment to political equality, majority rule, and minority rights requires collective decision making under uncertainty. But the space we open for deliberation about these decisions is also, necessarily, open for the manipulative engineering of consent. We cannot separate the two faces, but we must try for a healthy balance between them.

If the critique of the contemporary public sphere is overblown, still there is reason for concern about the balance between the two faces of democratic rhetoric. It seems to have tilted in the direction of engineered consent. For some writers, the focus of concern is the corporatization of the media. The suggestion is that mergers and acquisitions have made media organizations parts of larger conglomerates whose corporate values, ideology, and self-interest restrict the content of what is broadcast. As a result, citizens do not receive enough different points of view to enable them to participate meaningfully in the public dialogue. For other writers, on the opposite side of the political spectrum, the same constriction of access to diverse viewpoints is thought to be caused by the persistently liberal ideology of the news media.

There is a long-standing controversy about whether the media are biased and, if so, in what way. I suppose we all have our favorite examples of inappropriate media influence. Mine is the premature call of Florida for George W. Bush in 2000 by a Bush relative on the news desk at FOX. For others, the example might be Dan Rather's broadcast in September 2004 of inadequately substantiated reports about President Bush's attendance record while on duty at the National Guard. But I must say that despite these examples, I am not too worried about the charge of excessive media influence. I do not think the evidence of political communication research supports the allegation of consistent liberal bias. And while media corporatization is undeniable,[28] the danger of constricted viewpoints is offset by the fact that fewer and fewer people get their news from television networks in any event. The average viewer of network news is now sixty years old.[29] A vast array of other information sources, including especially the Internet, are revitalizing the notion of freedom of the press and making a seemingly unlimited range of information and perspectives available to those who wish to seek them out.

My conviction of the empowering potential of the Internet was reinforced in a taxi ride en route to Chicago's O'Hare Airport. After ascertaining that I was a college professor, the cab driver explained that although he had no academic degrees, he was a teacher too. "I teach bad politicians to do what is right," he said. "How do you do that?" I asked. The reply: "With a stick." So I said, "Tell me about it." It turns out that he has a weblog on which he posts, in pungent language, his views on world problems and what should be done. Then, when he identifies politicians in need of his instruction, he e-mails them a link to his blog and tells them to heed his warnings. I asked how he knows that his teaching is effective. "Well," he replied, "I sent a message to Condoleezza Rice that she should be less warlike in the Middle East, and, look, she is following my advice."

Say what you will about this man's naive assurance of his political efficacy, about the logical fallacy of affirming the consequent—there is no denying that he is an engaged participant in important public deliberation. I am convinced that new technologies will create even more opportunities for this sort of engagement and personal empowerment that serve to connect the individual to the political process. What I worry about is not whether we will have the opportunities for such engagement, but whether we will have the motivation. If the Internet recapitulates shallow discussions, unreflective judgments, and stereotypes, it will be the fault not of the technology but of the lack of demand for anything else. My concern stems both from what I see as problematic elements in political discourse and from the danger of unreflective responses by audiences.

Let me begin with the discourse of our leaders, and I will highlight only three from a potentially longer list of problems. One is the tendency to substitute valence issues for position issues. Scholars of contemporary politics such as Donald Stokes and John DiIulio explain the difference.[30] A position issue is one on which people take different positions: I am in favor of the North American Free Trade Agreement; you are opposed to it. By contrast, a valence issue is one on which everyone supports the same value—such as "protecting the homeland," "keeping our promise to seniors," or similar phrases that appear on the backdrops when the president speaks—and competing advocates try to identify their proposals with that value. The unstated but implicit message is that the phrase on the backdrop is what the speech is about, and that the policy the president proposes is identical to the value displayed on the backdrop. Any other policy deviates from that value. So "keeping our promise to seniors" is taken to mean carving private (or, if you prefer, personal) accounts out of Social Security. The danger with this sort of rhetorical identification is that it eliminates the possibility of agreeing about goals while disagreeing about means. If private accounts is what keeping our promise *means*, then to oppose private accounts is to oppose keeping our promise. This logic invites a discourse in which opponents of a specific proposal can be portrayed as beyond the pale, challenging a value that enjoys near-universal support. Supporters of an early withdrawal from Iraq are presented as encouraging terrorism, not as proposing a different way to fight it. Those who oppose tax cuts are presented as wanting to weaken the economy, not as preferring a different way to strengthen it.

Paradoxically, this recreates the conditions of political dispute in the 1790s, when disagreement was seen not as legitimate questioning of a proposal, but as a challenge to the political system itself. The use of valence issues is neither a new thing nor unique to Republicans. Champions of President Johnson's War on Poverty, for example, portrayed the program's opponents as being opposed to trying to do anything about poverty.[31] But it is my sense that the reliance on valence issues and the resulting polarization of discourse have intensified in recent years.

A second disturbing tendency is the growing use of what I have elsewhere called "argument by definition."[32] This is a discourse pattern in which a "loaded" definition, containing an incipient argument, is simply applied to a controversial topic, as if there were no controversy. Rather than being presented and defended, the incipient argument is simply stipulated and, unless specifically challenged, is not advanced and defended. Recent examples that come to mind are the definition of the estate tax as the "death tax," references to slowdowns in the rate of increased spending as a "spending cut," regarding the medical procedure of intact dilation and extraction as "partial birth abortion," characterizing the withdrawal of Terri Schiavo's feeding tube as "starvation," and the aforementioned choice of either "personal" or "private" to describe individual accounts that the George W. Bush administration proposed to carve out of Social Security. Defining election results as "mandates"—implying that the outcome of an election is to be taken as the end of a discussion—is another long-standing example of argument by definition.[33] The effect of such strategies is to beg the question—to assume rather than to defend a controversial proposition. Instead of arguing that the estate tax penalizes death rather than takes a share of unearned, inherited wealth, this is stipulated in the very act of calling it a "death tax." Instead of arguing that responsible personal behavior is enhanced by limiting access to welfare, this assertion is simply proclaimed by calling welfare reform the Personal Responsibility and Work Opportunity Act. This relocates presumption and shifts the argumentative ground. For our purposes what is especially important is that it does so by stealth, by removing from discussion important subjects about which deliberation would help to identify and test assumptions and thereby promote the search for practical wisdom.

My final example of problematic rhetorical moves is the one that has been most obvious in the time since September 11, 2001—the proclamation of crisis. When matters are in crisis, reaching a decision is particularly urgent. There is not time to deliberate about what to do. When the crisis is seen as threatening the nation or society itself, people naturally rally around their leaders, so long as the leaders convey the impression that they are in charge. In this environment, questioning of fundamental premises is not only inconvenient, but unpatriotic. Crisis, then, creates pressures for consensus in support of whatever measures leaders advance as an appropriate response.[34] Like argument by definition, it shifts the rhetorical landscape, but it has a more powerful effect. It not only discourages assessment of a particular claim, it discourages deliberation itself. For this reason, the ability to proclaim a situation as a crisis is a valuable rhetorical tool for leaders. In my judgment, this is why the metaphor of war has been used so frequently, whether to refer to poverty, drugs, street crime, or energy independence. It harnesses the tendency of people to unite in support of their leaders' efforts, and it discourages questioning of assumptions.

Since September 11, of course, the frame of war has been applied to the U.S. response to terrorism. It is an open question whether "war on terror" is literal or metaphorical, since the terrorist attacks had some, but not all, of the characteristics of war.[35] But a war on terrorism is inherently open-ended. Terrorism by its nature is planned and organized in secret. As a result, there is no way to know whether we have "won" this war—hence no basis on which to judge the war to be over, and hence no justification for returning to the "normal" conditions of discourse. By construing any proposal as part of the war on terror, critical scrutiny and deliberation about that proposal are delegitimized—even without the occasional clumsy statements by administration officials that dissent and disagreement give aid and comfort to the terrorists. Without such scrutiny, power is ceded and restraints on official action are weakened. The cause of deliberation is hurt; consent can more easily be engineered. Unless and until the frame cracks of its own weight, as may happen with regard to some provisions of the Patriot Act, the invocation of crisis trumps the encouragement of deliberative discourse.

Indeed, each of these three problematic moves—recourse to valence issues, argument by definition, and the proclamation of crisis—trumps the encouragement of deliberative discourse. Since that is a key element of the first face of democratic rhetoric, without deliberation the first face is subordinated to the second. Rhetoric is less a means of ascertaining practical wisdom than a *techne* to serve a cause chosen in advance.

Since I have identified problems in the production of political discourse, I do not want altogether to exonerate the audiences to whom such discourse is directed. There, too, I see cause for concern. The increased sophistication of polling and information technologies makes it possible to know instantly what the public "thinks" about an event or appeal. People who express their preferences immediately, by clicking a box on the computer screen or calling a toll-free number, are offering their first-impression, knee-jerk response, not one that has been tempered by deliberation. This is also true of those who respond viscerally to appeals to mobilize the "base" and therefore send telegrams, sign petitions, boycott products, or contribute money without stopping to examine the reasons they have been urged to do so. And the interpretation of these instant responses as "public opinion" gives them added weight.

Rebalancing the Two Faces of Democratic Rhetoric

It should be apparent that I regard a culture that values deliberation as necessary in order to keep the two faces of democratic rhetoric in balance. Without it, the first aspect will wither and the second will predominate, with the tragic result that a democratic instrument could undermine democracy. It stands to reason, therefore, that promoting deliberation may be the way to secure democracy. This is very close to the position that the more mature Walter Lippmann reached in the 1950s, when he wrote that the conscious cultivation of a "public philosophy" could offset the workings of Gresham's Law of ideas.[36]

Recently, a number of scholars of politics have begun to theorize about what they call "deliberative democracy." The term was coined by Joseph M. Bessette in 1980 and refers to a system in which conflict is resolved and disagreement addressed through "open and uncoerced discussion."[37] The assumption is that "political agreement should be reached on the basis of principles that can be justified to others."[38] This occurs through discussion characterized by reason-giving and reason-seeking. What will emerge from the "solicitous search for right solutions in circumstances of conflict"[39] is collective rationality—what the decision-making group as a whole considers to be reasonable. This is not necessarily the same as a simple aggregation of individuals' preferences, because individuals will transform their own preferences to take others' views into account. Rather, it is similar to what Lincoln meant by the "public mind": the judgment that members of a political community would make together if they were being reflective and exercising their best judgment. It is a normative concept of public opinion, and the goal of deliberative democracy is to structure decision-making processes to bring the empirical more into line with the normative. Of course, rhetoric is a central instrument of deliberative democracy, because the justifications people provide are rhetorically grounded—not deduced like syllogisms, but premised on the beliefs and values of members of the deliberating community. And deliberation builds community; that and openness to change over time are the principal byproducts of the search for right decisions in cases of conflict and uncertainty.

The deliberative democracy literature is almost completely theoretical. There are but a few empirical applications: cases of deliberative polling, in which people are asked their opinions after they have had a chance to discuss a question with others; the deliberative convention organized by James Fishkin; proposals for a national Deliberation Day; and, in our own field, the "Debate Watch" initiative for discussions following the presidential debates. The limited available evidence suggests that deliberation does make a difference, that participants do develop a sense of "public philosophy" and make decisions to promote collective rationality rather than narrow self-interest.[40] But deliberative democracy is a set of attitudes and values, not a particular set of procedures and actions. It does not tell us what to do. So it is not saying enough to simply recommend deliberative democracy as the way to restore balance between the two faces of democratic rhetoric.

Instead, let me offer two suggestions that would go a long way to implement the norms of deliberative democracy. First, leaders must become more sensitive to their role as rhetorical leaders. This is about agenda-setting, setting forth templates for understanding issues, modeling reason-giving, and inviting participation. All of these tasks are approached with sensitivity to public opinion, but are not performed simply in reaction to it. Thinking of rhetorical leadership brings us back to Abraham Lincoln. I have described elsewhere how Lincoln carefully prepared public opinion to accept the reality of emancipation—by modulating his own support for colonization; acknowledging its practical difficulties as well as its intuitive appeal; making his own assumptions, definitions, and premises clear; and inviting others to participate in working through to the solution.[41] Offering visions that acknowledge the empirical state of public opinion while inspiring people to move toward a stronger sense of collective rationality is the essence of rhetorical leadership. And if Lincoln is the exemplar, surely he is not alone. In my opinion, President Kennedy attempted the same task at American University in 1963 as he tried to inspire the American people to think beyond the boundaries of the Cold War and to recognize peace as the overarching goal shared by all. And while I personally am less sanguine about either his motives or his methods, surely this is what President George W. Bush was trying to do in asking his countrymen to rethink the assumptions of Social Security.

Beyond calling on our leaders to be rhetorical leaders, the other way we can further the goals of deliberative democracy is through our pedagogy. It is in our classrooms that we can best cultivate what Walter Lippmann called "the public philosophy." That involves addressing significant public issues. It involves exploring why they are uncertain and controversial. It involves recognizing and appreciating the competing values and beliefs that underlie different choices. It involves deciding upon a position and trying to justify it in the face of critical scrutiny. It involves revising our understanding based on what others might have to say. It involves effective advocacy that is sensitive to audience beliefs without pandering to them. And it involves prompting students not to sit on the sidelines, but to be actively involved as members of a deliberating and decision-making public. These values were embodied in the pedagogy of W. Norwood Brigance.

Sometimes we teach those who will become political leaders; it is not hubris to imagine that they will benefit from what we offer. In his 1956 Harvard commencement address, then Senator John F. Kennedy told the story of an English mother who told the provost at Harrow, "Don't teach my boy poetry; he's going to stand for Parliament." Kennedy added, "Well, perhaps she was right. But if more politicians knew poetry, and more poets knew politics, I am convinced that the world would be a better place to live on this Commencement Day of 1956."[42] What Kennedy said about poetry, I would say about rhetoric. And I think more than fifty years later that his sentiment is still true.

But while leaders can benefit from education that stresses the link between rhetoric and democracy, even more so can the citizenry at large. The habits and attitudes that constitute the "public philosophy" make for an exalted conception of rhetorical education, making it far more than skills-training in composition or public speaking. Reconciling the two faces of democratic rhetoric, making rhetoric democracy's instrument rather than its threat, demands no less of us.

NOTES

1. *Collected Works of Abraham Lincoln*, ed. Roy P. Basler (New Brunswick, N.J.: Rutgers University Press, 1953), 3:522.

2. *Collected Works of Abraham Lincoln*, 4:426.

3. Thomas Landon Thorson, *The Logic of Democracy* (New York: Holt, Rinehart, and Winston, 1962).

4. Ibid., viii.

5. Ibid., 22.

6. Ibid., 122.

7. Ibid., 141.

8. Ibid., 23.

9. Ibid., 139.

10. For a representative selection of readings on the is-ought problem, see W. D. Hudson, ed., *The Is-Ought Problem* (London: Macmillan, 1969).

11. See John Kekes, "Essentially Contested Concepts: A Reconsideration," *Philosophy and Rhetoric* 10 (1977): 71–89.

12. Thomas B. Farrell, *Norms of Rhetorical Culture* (New Haven: Yale University Press, 1993), 1.

13. *Bush v. Gore*, 531 US 98 (2000), 104.

14. On the 1800 election campaign, see especially John Ferling, *Adams vs. Jefferson: The Tumultuous Election of 1800* (New York: Oxford University Press, 2004); Joanne B. Freeman, *Affairs of Honor: National Politics in the New Republic* (New Haven: Yale University Press, 2001), 199–261.

15. Michael Schudson, *The Good Citizen: A History of American Civic Life* (New York: Free Press, 1998), esp. 11–132.

16. Thomas Paine, *The Age of Reason*, in *Basic Writings of Thomas Paine* (New York: Willey, 1942), 256. The pamphlet is also reprinted in the 1995 Library of America edition of Paine's works, where the quotation is on page 830.

17. George Bancroft, "The Office of the People in Art, Government, and Religion," rpt. in *American Forum*, ed. Ernest J. Wrage and Barnet Baskerville (New York: Harper and Row, 1960), 68.

18. Herbert Croly, *The Promise of American Life* (New York: Macmillan, 1911), 443.

19. See Lee W. Huebner, "The Discovery of Propaganda: Changing Attitudes toward Public Communication in America, 1900–1930," Ph.D. diss., Harvard University, 1968.

20. Walter Lippmann, *Public Opinion* (1922; rpt. New York: Free Press, 1965).

21. Walter Lippmann, *The Phantom Public* (New York: Harcourt, Brace, 1925), 27, 39, 143, 147.

22. Lippmann represented one side of an intellectual controversy during the 1920s. The other side was represented by John Dewey, who believed that, though weak, the public sphere could be rehabilitated. His major work on this topic is *The Public and Its Problems* (New York: Henry Holt, 1927). For analyses of Dewey's thought about the public sphere, see Robert Asen, "The Multiple Mr. Dewey: Multiple Publics and Permeable Borders in John Dewey's Theory of the Public Sphere," *Argumentation and Advocacy* 39 (2003): 174–88.

23. See, for example, G. Thomas Goodnight, "The Personal, Technical, and Public Spheres of Argument: A Speculative Inquiry into the Art of Public Deliberation," *Argumentation and Advocacy* 18 (1982): 214–27.

24. On condensation symbols, see Edward Sapir, "Symbolism," in *Encyclopedia of the Social Sciences*, ed. E. R. A. Seligman (New York: Macmillan, 1934), 492–95; Murray Edelman, *The Symbolic Uses of Politics* (Urbana: University of Illinois Press, 1964), 6.

25. Schudson, 9–10.

26. See, for example, Benjamin I. Page and Robert Y. Shapiro, *The Rational Public* (Chicago: University of Chicago Press, 1992); Lawrence R. Jacobs and Robert

Y. Shapiro, *Politicians Don't Pander: Political Manipulation and the Loss of Democratic Responsiveness* (Chicago: University of Chicago Press, 2000), esp. 3–71.

27. Thomas Frank, *What's the Matter with Kansas? How Conservatives Won the Heart of America* (New York: Henry Holt, 2004).

28. The evidence for this claim is clearly presented in Karlyn Kohrs Campbell, "Marketing Public Discourse," *Hedgehog Review* 6 (Fall 2004): 39–54.

29. Jacques Steinberg, "CBS News Makeover, by Four Kibitzers," *New York Times*, April 10, 2005, sec. 4, p. 1, cites Nielsen Media Research as the source for this claim.

30. John J. DiIulio Jr., "A View from Within," in *The George W. Bush Presidency: An Early Assessment*, ed. Fred I. Greenstein (Baltimore: Johns Hopkins University Press, 2003), 258; Donald E. Stokes and John J. DiIulio Jr., "Valence Politics in Modern Elections," in *The 1992 Elections*, ed. Michael J. Nelson (Washington, D.C.: Congressional Quarterly Press, 1993), chap. 1.

31. For example, President Johnson himself disparaged objections raised to his program by Representative Peter H. B. Frelinghuysen, Republican of New Jersey, by saying, "Why anyone should hate an antipoverty program, I don't know." *Public Papers of the Presidents: Lyndon B. Johnson, 1963–64* (Washington, D.C.: U.S. Government Printing Office, 1965), 1:597.

32. David Zarefsky, "Definitions," in *Argument in a Time of Change*, ed. James F. Klumpp (Annandale, Va.: National Communication Association, 1998), 1–11.

33. On the definition of election results as mandates, see especially Patricia Heidotting Conley, *Presidential Mandates: How Elections Shape the National Agenda* (Chicago: University of Chicago Press, 2001).

34. There is a growing literature on crisis rhetoric and the American presidency. See especially Denise M. Bostdorff, *The Presidency and the Rhetoric of Foreign Crisis* (Columbia: University of South Carolina Press, 1994); Amos Kiewe, ed., *The Modern Presidency and Crisis Rhetoric* (Westport, Conn.: Praeger, 1994).

35. On the implications of defining the response to terrorism as war, see David Zarefsky, "George W. Bush Discovers Rhetoric: September 20, 2001 and the U.S. Response to Terrorism," in *The Ethos of Rhetoric*, ed. Michael J. Hyde (Columbia: University of South Carolina Press, 2004), 136–55.

36. See Walter Lippmann, *Essays in the Public Philosophy* (Boston: Atlantic, Little, Brown, 1955). Gresham's Law was advanced during the late nineteenth-century debates about whether gold or silver should be the basis of the money supply. Advocates of bimetallism (using both) were countered by opponents who cited Gresham's Law: the cheaper metal would be used exclusively because holders

of the more expensive metal would keep it out of circulation. The "Law" was summarized as "Cheap money drives out good."

37. Joseph M. Bessette, "Deliberative Democracy: The Majority Principle in Republican Government," in *How Democratic is the Constitution?*, ed. Robert A. Goldwin and William A. Schambra (Washington, D.C.: American Enterprise Institute, 1980); David Miller, "Deliberative Democracy and Social Choice," *Debating Deliberative Democracy*, ed. James S. Fishkin and Peter Laslett (Malden, Mass.: Blackwell, 2003), 183. Basic sources on deliberative democracy are James S. Fishkin, *Democracy and Deliberation* (New Haven: Yale University Press, 1991); and Amy Gutmann and Dennis Thompson, *Democracy and Disagreement* (Cambridge, Mass.: Harvard University Press, 1996). For more recent treatments of deliberative democracy, see Bruce Ackerman and James S. Fishkin, *Deliberation Day* (New Haven: Yale University Press, 2004); Ethan Leib, *Deliberative Democracy in America: A Proposal for a Popular Branch of Government* (University Park: Penn State University Press, 2004). I am indebted to Timothy Quinn for reviewing the deliberative-democracy literature.

38. Amy Gutmann and Dennis Thompson, "Deliberative Democracy beyond Process," in *Debating Deliberative Democracy*, ed. James S. Fishkin and Peter Laslett, 33.

39. Ian Shapiro, "Optimal Deliberation?" in *Debating Deliberative Democracy*, ed. James S. Fishkin and Peter Laslett, 122.

40. For a recent study of the effects of deliberation, see Jason Barabas, "How Deliberation Affects Policy Opinions," *American Political Science Review* 98 (2004): 687–701.

41. David Zarefsky, "Lincoln's 1862 Annual Message: A Paradigm of Rhetorical Leadership," *Rhetoric & Public Affairs* 3 (2000), 5–14.

42. John F. Kennedy, "Address to the Annual Meeting of the Harvard Alumni Association," Cambridge, Mass., June 14, 1956, rpt. *U. S. Congressional Record*, 84th Cong., 2d sess., 102, pt. 8 (Washington, D.C.: U.S. Government Printing Office, 1956), 10800–10801. The speech is sometimes titled "The Intellectual and the Politician."

6

Constituting Presidentiality and U.S. Citizenship in Campaign 2004: NASCAR Dads, Security Moms, and Single Women Voters

Shawn J. Parry-Giles

The main thing is Kerry has to prove that he is tough enough to protect America and better than George Bush, so he has to prove he's a manly man.

—Maureen Dowd

Such press quotations offer a mere glimpse into the status of politics, gender, and citizenship in 2004, particularly as presidential candidates competed to become the nation's next commander in chief. A heightened masculinization of the presidential imaginary is not that surprising given the state of war that framed the 2004 presidential election.[1] As J. Ann Tickner contends, the "states' national-security policies are often legitimated by appealing to masculine characteristics." In the process, "not only does war mobilize the national consciousness, it also provides the myths and memories that create a sense of national identity."[2]

Within this ritualized process that recurs every four years, presidential campaign rhetoric works to (re)constitute citizenry roles for the democratic nation. Roderick P. Hart argues: "During elections, a democracy is re-performed. Through its rituals, its pacing, its daily unfoldings, a campaign makes a population a citizenry."[3] Extending the constitutive role of language, James Jasinski suggests that political narratives enact the "ongoing project of communal (re)constitution: a continual process of shaping and reshaping our possibilities for collective action."[4]

Utilizing a perspective that intersects theories of gendered, racialized, and militarized nationalism and assumes a constitutive role for rhetoric, this chapter examines how presidentiality and citizen identity is construed in the rhetoric of the 2004 presidential election. Of critical interest is the discourse of the presidential candidates, the news media coverage, as well as the political advertisements featured in the campaign.[5] From such a perspective, the presidential campaign rhetoric reified a hypermasculinized and all-empowered presidency, often in familial and militarized terms, with the white presidential candidates functioning as the would-be "citizen-protectors" of the democratic nation, preserving patriarchal structures in the nation and in the home.

In the process, such discourse constituted a white, gendered citizenry with limited political power in a wartime context through a familial framework that depoliticized their citizen identity. More specifically, political agency for white males was reduced to their sports-centered activities, rendering them "citizen-spectators" rather than engaged civic actors. Political agency for women, conversely, was reduced to their familial status as either "citizen-mothers" or as single women constituted as sexualized and politically naive "citizen-ingénues," reflecting the historical legacies where women were either excluded from or marginalized in the contested political terrain. Throughout, a discourse of whiteness framed the "citizen imaginary,"[6] as voters of color were either discursively absent or limitedly visible in the presidential rhetoric of campaign 2004.

In the end, the act of voting represented the quintessential democratic activity for upper- to lower-middle-class white men and women, hailed as the nation's swing voters and thus nonpartisan citizens from battleground states. Most others, particularly those aligned with identity politics or with clear political convictions, were considerably less visible in the campaign discourse—due, in part, to their assumed partisan identities. Before moving to the rhetorical constructions of NASCAR dads, security moms, and "sex and the city" single women, I first historicize the familial, racialized, and militarized implications of U.S. nationalism and citizenship.

The Familial, Racialized, and Militarized Nation

The link between images of nationhood and "familial motifs"[7] is centuries old. George L. Mosse maintains that the "triumph of the nuclear family. . . coincided with the rise of nationalism" in eighteenth-century Europe.[8] Such national and familial conflations are rooted in the rhetoric of the French Revolution; these familial images represented "a timeless and global unity of loyalty," which "served as a guarantee for the continuation of traditional bonds" between the individual and the nation.[9] The British, of course, conceived of themselves as the mother country to the children of the American colonies. Those presidents who helped forge the political design of the new nation—George Washington, John Adams, Thomas Jefferson, and James Madison—have historically been described as the nation's "founding fathers." Phrases like "sexual union" were also commonplace in public discourse of the early 1800s, which Rogan Kersh maintains "drew parallels to the union of wife and husband," representing the symbolic foundation that underlay many of these nationalist constructs.[10]

Such familial images privileged European whites as the natural forebears of the new nation. Legally, such a white (male) citizenry was established early on with the Nationalization Law of 1790, which stipulated that "Any alien, being a free white person, who shall have resided within the limits and under the jurisdiction of the United States for two terms, may be admitted to become a citizen thereof."[11] The history of U.S. nationalism thus perpetuated not only gender prescriptions but also ones pertaining to race. Anthony W. Marx argues that "states reinforce[d] race to unify the nation," as European heritage, especially from northern and western Europe, was equated with "natural white superiority," a "color line" seemingly "drawn by God or biology."[12] Even northerners who abhorred slavery did not conceive of blacks in citizenship terms. Paul Goodman writes that "So unprepared were whites for black citizenship that the suffrage laws enacted during the Revolutionary era failed to specify whites only until a wave of black voting triggered a wave of exclusions from many northern states."[13]

Conceiving of the nation as a white family arguably influenced the power dynamics within the nation and the family.[14] Those family metaphors that constituted a white male citizenry offered, Anne McClintock asserted, "a 'natural' figure for sanctioning national hierarchy." Depicting the nation in familial terms helped "guarantee social difference as a category of nature," since "the subordination of woman to man and child to adult was deemed a natural fact."[15] For women, their relationship to the nation was "submerged as a *social* relation to a man through marriage."[16] A key focus then and now was the patriarchal power that extended from the family to the nation and back to the family. As Tamar Mayer argues, "Nation remains . . . emphatically, historically, and globally—the property of men," that "enable[s] [white] men and nation to achieve superiority over women and a different Other by controlling them."[17]

Athletics became an important means of socializing white male children of elites for participation in the public world; "a direct link [was] made between all-male games and sport . . . and patriotism and Empire-building,"[18] which helped inspirit feelings of "national superiority."[19] The growth of athletics in the United States paralleled the rise of U.S. nationalism in the nineteenth century, intensifying the separate spheres between men and women and strengthening the psychological divisions among whites and persons of color, inside and outside the nation's borders. Varda Burstyn argues that the growth of sports represented "a dynamic cultural response to the changes and challenges of industrialization, urbanization, nation-building, imperialism, and gender order flux." As more white fathers began working outside of the home within a U.S. industrial context, sports represented a key socializing force for young white boys in their fathers' absence, providing "training in manly pursuits—war, commerce, and government—and a stepping stone out of the family of women and into the world of men."[20] Accordingly, appropriate male citizenship was associated early on with exhibiting athletic prowess and success.

Sports participation, of course, represented a prelude for the ultimate act of citizenship—military and wartime service. Although women were seemingly devoid of the necessary "physical strength and martial skills [needed] to defend their nation's . . . honour,"[21] masculinity and militarism intersected and were naturalized as the domain of male citizenry. Women's citizenry, conversely, was associated with the home. Theodore Roosevelt's turn-of-the-century discourse reveals such gendered, familial, and militarized conceptions of U.S. nationalism. Then Governor Roosevelt argued in "The Strenuous Life" speech of April 10, 1899, that "A man's first duty is to his own home, but he is not thereby excused from doing his duty to the State. . . . In the same way, while a nation's first duty is within its own borders, it is not thereby absolved from facing its duties in the world as a whole."[22] As president, Roosevelt reinforced traditional gender roles that held out national consequences: "When men fear work or fear righteous war, when women fear motherhood, they tremble on the brink of doom; and well it is they should vanish from the earth."[23] For Roosevelt, who equated the skills of soldiering and governing, the readiness for battle was the key component of U.S. nationalism: "A peaceful and commercial civilization is always in danger of suffering the loss of the virile fighting qualities without which no nation . . . can ever amount to anything."[24] As Roosevelt's discourse reveals, clear conceptions of U.S. nationalism, steeped in familial and martial terms, were well formed by the turn of the twentieth century, offering insight into the ideological conflations of U.S. politics, citizenry, and war.

As "fatherland" served as the "force behind government,"[25] the nation's "mothers" were expected to fulfill their own unique citizenry roles as well.[26] Even though "Classical republicanism had . . . banished women from the political arena," Carroll Smith-Rosenberg contends,[27] women's national roles were important in their own right as exemplified by the ideology of republican motherhood. Mothers of the revolutionary era and beyond were expected to commit themselves to the promulgation of "civic virtue,"[28] "by their refusal to countenance lovers who were not devoted to the service of the state" and to "raise sons who were educated for . . . responsible citizenship."[29] The republican mother thus was imbued with the power to prepare her children, particularly the male members of her family, for citizenship by instilling moral and religious commitments in the private spaces of the home.

U.S. women also held important homeland duties as their husbands trekked off to war, propelling more white women into public roles during wartime, evidencing what James Dawes describes as the "dissolution of the public-private border."[30] In the wars of the eighteenth and nineteenth centuries, more middle- and upper-class white women attended to wounded soldiers in campsites and hospital settings, making bandages for the wounded. By the twentieth century, such women were volunteering with the Red Cross and knitting items of clothing for U.S. soldiers.[31] Women's contributions to the labor force expanded during both world wars, with some women becoming casualties of war. An April 14, 1917, article in *The Suffragist* of the National Woman's Party reports on an explosion at Eddystone Ammunition Corporation in Chester, Pennsylvania, which killed 118 "munition workers, mostly women," injuring over 150 others.[32] During World War II, women also entered the work force, and were called on to build wartime weaponry and machinery throughout the war. Elaine Tyler May notes, however, that World War II also accentuated "women's tasks as homemakers, consumers, and mothers" even as they moved into the work force.[33] In more contemporary wartime battles, women continue to serve as medical professionals and hold military posts within all branches of the U.S. armed forces. In 2005, approximately 10.4 percent of the total U.S. forces in Iraq and Afghanistan were women, totaling nearly 60,000 serving in the region.[34]

In many ways, men's and women's historical responsibilities to the nation represent divergent constructions with differing implications. Whereas men serve as the "protectors" of the nation, women are conceived of as "protectors of the integrity of the family and its individual members."[35] Whereas men "defend the national image," women are depicted as the nation's "biological and symbolic reproducers"[36] and the "bearers of national traditions."[37] Whereas the male physique "is connotative of power and strength," women's bodies represent sites of control as "variations of struggles . . . played out over the feminine body."[38] Conflicts over race and citizenship also persist in U.S. political culture. Marx reminds us that "Gradual expansion of citizenship is . . . gained through protracted contestation,"[39] often enacted by those outside of the government. While gains are apparent, the legacies of exclusion are mindfully visible. The campaign discourse of 2004 reflects many of these gendered, racialized, and militarized ideologies and hegemonies, which suggests much about the president and U.S. citizens at the start of the new millennium.

The Presidential Imaginary

In previous scholarship, Trevor Parry-Giles and I discuss a concept we call "presidentiality," which represents a discourse that demarcates the cultural and ideological meaning of the presidency for the larger community. A given presidentiality thus is responsive to context and collective memory, and it defines, in part, the national community by offering a vision of this vital office. Given its constitutive character, "presidentiality" invites the continued scrutiny of the ideologies and boundaries that circumscribe the presidency in U.S. political discourse.[40] Certainly, presidential campaign rhetoric, particularly disseminated during wartime, contributes ritually to our understanding of presidentiality. Such discursive presidential constructions in turn reinforce a power dynamic between the citizenry and the president. Especially relevant for campaign 2004 is the presidential role of commander in chief—the one who promises to protect the nation and its citizens from external harm. In the end, the presidential candidates associated themselves with the ultimate citizenship enactment, through their service as commander in chief (Bush) and as a decorated war hero (Kerry). Either way, both promised to fulfill the role of citizen-protector.

During the wartime election of 2004, both the Bush and Kerry campaigns promulgated images of a strong commander in chief who represented a heroic contender for the most visible and powerful embodiment of U.S. nationalism. Susan Jeffords identifies the rhetoric of war as the primary site for the "remasculization of U.S. society"[41]—an effort emboldened by the September 11, 2001, attack on American soil. Within the process of creating images of a citizen-protector who vowed to keep U.S. citizens safe, hypermasculine images dominated the campaign, reifying the president's patriarchal authority within the U.S. political process and the democratic nation.[42]

From the beginning of the campaign, the candidates portrayed themselves as strong, and their opponents as weak, through images of a presidential protectorate in the war on terrorism.[43] When reviewing President Bush's agenda for "Building a Safer, Stronger and Better America," the Republican National Committee (RNC) declared that the "President's most important job is to protect and defend the American homeland." Throughout the online position piece, the RNC urged that the president was "Protecting the American People" by "Protecting Our Skies. . . . Protecting Our Borders. . . . Protecting Our Ports. . . . Protecting Our Critical Infrastructure. . . . [and] Protecting Your Health." The RNC concluded that President Bush was thus "Protecting America."[44] Bush emphasized such protective themes in his September 2, 2004, acceptance speech before the Republican National Convention: "Three days after September 11th, I stood where Americans died, in the ruins of the Twin Towers. Workers in hard hats were shouting to me, 'Whatever it takes.' A fellow grabbed me by the arm and he said, 'Do not let me down.' Since that day, I wake up every morning thinking about how to better protect our country. I will never relent in defending America whatever it takes."[45]

The theme of "whatever it takes" dominated Bush's rhetoric and became the title of a campaign ad where the president delivered the phrase "I will never relent in defending America, whatever it takes."[46] Such a protective discourse, reflective of the patriarchal role of fathers, imbues a president with the power, control, and authority to protect the country's citizenry from evil acts, through virtually any means necessary. George Lakoff details a "Strict Father model" reflective in certain conservative logic, which insists that "life is difficult and the world is fundamentally dangerous,"[47] granting the father-figure president full authority. Elaborating on the consequences of such assumptions, Alexander DeConde asserts: "Regardless of the flaws in their presidents, in times of real or imagined international crises Americans rallied around them as though they were father figures."[48]

Some of Bush's masculine imaging as commander in chief, though, became the centerpiece of controversy during the 2004 campaign. Of particular note was his May 2003 landing on the USS *Abraham Lincoln* by way of a Navy S-3B, the president dressed in a flight suit and subsequently delivering a speech before the backdrop of a "Mission Accomplished" banner. Bush was also derided for phrases like "Bring it on"[49] when responding to counterinsurgency efforts in Iraq. Challenging the commander in chief's displays of masculinity in such wartime spectacles, General Wesley Clark spoke of George Bush "*prancing* around on the deck of an aircraft carrier" in a flight suit, while Kerry accused the president of "playing dress up" on the same aircraft carrier.[50] Such a battle over the national protectorate reflects a common machismo of presidentiality.

Kerry's military experience proved to be a central feature of his own campaign image, predicated on a "Lifetime of Service and Strength,"[51] which furthered his qualifications as the nation's citizen-protector. During his July 29, 2004, acceptance speech before the Democratic National Convention, Kerry used his military service as a premonition of his ethos as commander in chief and as the ultimate act of citizenship: "I defended this country as a young man and I will defend it as President."[52] In his online "Biography," Kerry's campaign touted his voluntary decision "to serve on a Swift Boat in the deltas, one of the most dangerous assignments of the war. His leadership, courage, and sacrifice earned him a Silver Star, Bronze Star with Combat V, and three Purple Hearts."[53] Historically, such military force and experience reveals, DeConde contends, a presidential "virility" that is beneficial to the men who would occupy the nation's highest office.[54] Kerry's campaign also reinforced a protectorate role for the presidency while questioning the country's security under President Bush during a campaign ad entitled "Obligation": "The obligation of a commander-in-chief is to keep our country safe. In Iraq, George Bush has overextended our troops and now failed to secure 380 tons of deadly explosives. . . . His Iraq misjudgments put our soldiers at risk and make our country less secure" (male voiceover),[55] challenging Bush's citizen-protector role.

A key component of Kerry's image was linked to his decorated military service depicted in familial terms. Despite his military record, though, Kerry's own military gestures attracted attention and scrutiny. On July 29, 2004, as candidate Kerry prepared to receive his party's nomination, he greeted the Democratic delegates with a salute and an utterance: "I'm John Kerry and I'm reporting for duty." He often traveled with other Vietnam veterans, whom he fondly introduced as the "extraordinary band of brothers" in the same convention speech: "Our band of brothers doesn't march together because of who we are as veterans, but because of what we learned as soldiers. . . . We may be a little older now, we may be a little grayer, but we still know how to fight for our country."[56]

Shortly after the convention, several advertisements by the 527 group Swift Boat Veterans for Truth worked to challenge Kerry's wartime heroism, as well as his "band of brothers" mantra. Vietnam veterans associated with the group claimed that Kerry was "no war hero," because he "lied" to receive certain medals, "betrayed his shipmates," and "dishonor[ed] his country" by alleging U.S. war crimes before the Senate Committee on Foreign Relations on April 22, 1971.[57] Regardless of the veracity of the allegations, to be accused of such unpatriotic and perhaps treasonous acts undermined Kerry's claims of valorized heroism and citizenship that were central to his campaign image, raising doubts about his ability to protect U.S. citizens.

Attacks also persisted against Kerry's contemporary statements about war, suggesting that he and the Democratic Party would implement a weakened and thus unsafe war plan. In a Bush ad entitled "Peace and Security," the narrator asserted: "History's lesson. . . . Strength builds peace. . . . Weakness invites those who would do us harm. Unfortunately, after the first World Trade Center attack, John Kerry and congressional liberals tried to slash six billion dollars from intelligence budgets. . . . And refused to support our troops in combat with the latest weapons and body armor."[58] Other campaign messages furthered the suggestion that a Kerry presidency threatened the security of the United States while justifying the Bush administration's preemptive strike against Iraq: "Some are now attacking the President for attacking the terrorists. . . . Some have called for us to retreat, putting our national security in the hands of others. . . . Tell them to support the President's policy of preemptive self-defense."[59] Bush explained his preemptive acts in unabashed terms during his 2004 State of the Union address: "America will never seek a permission slip to defend the security of our country."[60]

Within the United States, the president and the first lady are often referred to as the "first family." Such familial symbolism combines with the president's commander-in-chief role to depoliticize his citizen-protector image as a key component of presidentiality. Kerry's band-of-brothers reference reified the role of men in conducting the nation's military business, linking images of male bonding, family ties, and protectionist obligations with presidentiality and visions of U.S. citizenship. As Dawes notes, "War is [often] an extension of the home,"[61] which reenforces familial power dynamics in the enactment of U.S. nationalism. Within such discursive logic, presidential authority over the nation's citizenry is strengthened, granting presidents immeasurable decision-making power once in office. In the process, such campaign rhetoric offered clear, yet disempowering roles for the U.S. electorate, hailing their familial and nonpolitical commitments as badges of ideal citizenship.

The Citizen Imaginary

The 2004 campaign rhetoric revealed the valorization of nonpartisan swing voters in battleground states who have been a feature of U.S. elections since at least the 1960s. Such so-called Independent voters are of key interest to pollsters, candidates, and the news media, acting on the assumption that these voters "share some characteristics that differentiate them in important ways from Republicans and Democrats." Even though a thirty-year study by Bruce E. Keith et al. suggests that Independent voters "are more diverse than either Republicans or Democrats," are generally "not uncommitted," and "are not a [voting] bloc,"[62] political operatives persist in naming and thus constituting such independent voting groups during U.S. elections. For 2004, such constituted groups, formed through "discursive action,"[63] included NASCAR dads, security moms, and single women. These groups shared a common symbolism reliant on familial characteristics often personified by white voters, further reifying their status as nonpartisan swing voters removed from the vagaries of identity politics. Indecisive voters from battleground states were especially encouraged and empowered to carry out their ultimate act of citizenship by voting for that white male president who would keep the nation safer. Images of a white citizenry constituted through a familial rhetoric seemingly depoliticized voter participation, as well as the presidential candidates and the U.S. news media that identified and targeted these depoliticized citizens.

NASCAR DADS

The creation of such swing-voter labels is often attributed to polling professionals. The *Denver Post*, for example, credited Democratic pollster Celinda Lake with developing the NASCAR dad descriptor in 2002.[64] Others, like Mark Mellman, challenge such labeling on the grounds that they serve the "political agenda[s]" of those who create them, are too "vaguely defined" to know who fits the category, and lack predictive value in determining the election outcome.[65] Despite such challenges, the labels still hold significant rhetorical sway because of their massive popularization among journalists and political campaigns that target these constituted voting blocs.

To evidence the importance of the NASCAR voter to the Bush campaign, the president opened the Daytona 500 on February 14, when Air Force One flew over the track, the presidential motorcade took a lap around the track, and the president waved the checkered flag to start the race. The president also yelled, "Start Your Engines" at the New Hampshire International Speedway in September.[66] By October, some seven NASCAR drivers appeared at fourteen Bush campaign events. The campaign issued a statement justifying the importance of such voters: "NASCAR fans present a pivotal voting block in this election, and these NASCAR celebrities' enthusiastic support for President Bush will have a real impact in driving voters to the polls."[67]

Throughout the campaign, journalists expended considerable news space defining the NASCAR dad. While some articles noted that women

also attend NASCAR events and that their fans are racially and economically diverse,[68] most articles defined such sports-minded dads as southern,
blue-collar, white males who drink beer, chew tobacco, listen to country
music, love guns, tout Confederate flags, and especially love their country.[69] In discussing the expansion of NASCAR beyond the South, the *Seattle Weekly* featured an article on the "Dixiefication of America," where a
sociologist claimed that the "cultural ethos of guns, cars . . . and masculinity" was spreading across the nation.[70] In a September 27 report, National
Public Radio (NPR) referred to NASCAR dads as the "forgotten man" of
the 1930s and the contemporary "bubbas"—"the kind of white Southern-
ers, working- to middle-class men who wanted to see NASCAR drivers in
the Rose Garden."[71] The *Denver Post* suggested that these dads were "men
moved by guns, God and gays,"[72] with such companies as Viagra sponsor-
ing drivers.[73] Writing about the ideological connection between sport and
nation, Burstyn notes that athletics represent a "coded symbolic system
that embodies a template of . . . 'manly' values—as social values."[74]

In conflating masculinity, sports, and citizenship, though, NASCAR
dads were constituted as "citizen-spectators," synecdochically sidelined
in the political process, rather than empowered as engaged citizens. Although judged as socially conservative Republicans who were Democrats
prior to the Reagan revolution, such white male voters were moved into
the undecided voter column of 2004 because of economic conditions.[75]
Dubbed the "angry white males" of the 2004 campaign, some journalists
accentuated NASCAR dads' "feelings of disenfranchisement," reflecting
the outsider status of the rural "rebel" who rejected team sports in favor of
"heroic individuals defying the laws of man and physics."[76] For the *Seattle
Weekly*, the popularization of NASCAR represented the "decline of the
idea that we're all in this together. In a NASCAR world, we're all in this
alone."[77] NASCAR's promotion of masculine individualism and defiance
of course is reflective of its heritage, when Appalachian bootleggers used
rebuilt cars to enhance their speed in order to evade law-enforcement
officers.[78] Such language constitutes NASCAR dads as a rebellious voting
bloc—one that is void of real political power to affect change over their
own lives, or else one that rebels against the political process altogether
by not voting.

Democrats saw potential in this typically Republican voting bloc because of such perceived alienation.[79] Democratic presidential candidate
Howard Dean, for example, attempted to target "white guys" who drive

"pick-up trucks" with "confederate flags" in their windows.[80] Kerry instead focused less controversially on the loss of jobs and other economic
hardships; his campaign website noted, for instance, that "as fathers, both
John Kerry and John Edwards learned how important it is for a family
to have health care and for children to have a good education."[81] Yet
by the end of the campaign, many political pundits moved the NASCAR
dads to the column of decided Bush voters, lessening their importance to
the political landscape. Public-opinion polls showed minimal shifting of
southern white males away from their Republican Party allegiances.[82] Tim
Appelo of *Seattle Weekly* wondered if Kerry seemed too "mushy, wimpy,
mealymouthed—that kind of wuss who thinks that there's more than
one kinda Arab, disrespects guns and medals, and doubts Saddam was
Osama's 9/11 copilot."[83]

Regardless of the reasons, the news media shifted their interests
away from NASCAR dads, sensing a return to partisanship that lessened
their political capital as swing voters. Once dubbed a decided voter,
their importance as citizen-voters dissipated, lessening their importance
to the election and in turn to the national imaginary. Most central to
their persona as NASCAR dads were such factors as masculinity, sports,
southern whiteness, and lifestyle issues. Historically, white men prepared
for citizenship through participating in sports. By 2004, sports, and thus
politics, symbolically represented a spectator activity rather than one of
active civic engagement. By the election, even the act of voting for white
southern males lacked civic salience, further marginalizing their role in
the democracy. Such discourse ultimately suggested that changing their
own economic conditions involved not working with others to affect
change, but rather voting for the right white male who reflected their
values, seemingly reducing economic obstacles to personal rather than
political or systemic exigencies.

Noticeably absent in such depictions is the role that dads play in the
U.S. family. Although labeled "dads," the descriptions seldom mentioned
their parenting involvement or their concern with issues affecting the
family beyond jobs. Ironically, while the news media noted the alienation
of NASCAR dads, press coverage furthered a sense of their irrelevance to
their families and ultimately to the nation as citizens, downplaying their
problems and potential contributions to the national dialogue. The media
instead placed greater focus on the newly dubbed "security mom," who
promised to be the most influential voter of the 2004 campaign.

SECURITY MOMS

Not surprisingly, family matters were central to the swing-voter demographics aligned with women. Titling this phenomenon the "new momism," Susan J. Douglas and Meredith Michaels argue that the media insist that "no woman is truly complete or fulfilled unless she has kids . . . and that to be a remotely decent mother, a woman has to devote her entire physical, psychological, emotional, and intellectual being . . . to her children."[84] Security moms throughout 2004 were depicted almost exclusively as concerned with the protection of their children in the wake of 9/11. Fathers were virtually invisible in such depictions, even though safety issues would seemingly concern all parents. Because moms worried over the safety of their children, the discursive logic suggested, they became "citizen-mothers" who sought a president who would not only protect the entire nation, but their own family in particular.

The absenteeism of fathers in this cultural discourse (and in the lives of some children) is not a new phenomenon. And the concept of the new momism may well explain the media's focus on the obsession that women may have, or are supposed to have, with their children's well-being. Miriam Cooke and Angela Woollacott also note that new gender realities exist in wartime as "war transforms motherhood from a social to a political factor."[85] Regardless of the causes of such constructions, the implication is that women's political focus is reduced to voting for a white, male, protector president to keep her family safe. In the process, women's political agency is limited, and also depoliticized, by associating women's primary civic contribution to motherhood and swing voting. Like NASCAR dads, security moms were often portrayed as white and undecided in their presidential preference; yet unlike NASCAR dads, they were economically more secure, transforming the soccer moms of 1996 from consumers to family protectors. Reflecting the historical tenets of Republican motherhood, such citizen participation is depoliticized and turned inward to the family, rather than outward to the myriad of institutional problems that affect women's lives (e.g., pay equity, sexual harassment, affordable child and health care, abortion rights).

Many news articles suggested that women were the primary target voters in campaign 2004, particularly throughout the summer and fall.[86] White women in particular were categorized into groups according to their motherhood or marital status as married mothers, single women, or single mothers (the ones more likely to be identified as women of color). Security moms attracted the most attention and became what the soccer moms were to the 1996 election. Defining the soccer moms' role in the 1996 campaign, Mary Douglas Vavrus asserts that their "power was constructed discursively from a nexus of factors, including their domestic relations, their household income levels, and their somewhat uncertain political leanings, a feature that could work for or against candidates until the very last minute of the election."[87] A key change in this voting bloc, pollsters and the press suggested, was an intense concern about their children's safety in the aftermath of September 11. Even though their swing-voter status and the uniqueness of their heightened security concerns were challenged by many pollsters, both campaigns targeted security moms.[88] The Bush campaign, for example, initiated a "W Stands for Women" drive; Laura Bush addressed security issues before women-only audiences; and even Vice President Dick Cheney's (heterosexual) daughter identified herself as a security mom.[89] In the latter weeks of the campaign, widows of 9/11 traveled with Kerry as he targeted security issues toward women in particular.[90] Throughout, white women's citizenry is conflated with their familial roles, focusing their attention on one issue—that of selecting a white father figure to protect their family.

Security moms represented the same women as those who constituted the soccer moms of 1996—"white, suburban, middle- and upper-middle class, college educated," swing voters, married with kids, and living in battleground states.[91] The *Philadelphia Inquirer* suggested that "A lot of Soccer Moms have dropped the water bottles and picked up the worry beads."[92] Rather than driving minivans, though, the *Pitt News* declared that security moms were driving more security-conscious "SUVS instead."[93] The key for security moms, the UPI reported, is that they "look at the world through the prism of their children" and are living "child-centered lives in the suburbs."[94] When reviewing a play about a security mom, the *Arkansas Democrat-Gazette* depicted this woman as a "housewife who obsesses about terrorism."[95] Such images reflect the new momism that Douglas and Michaels call "intensive mothering," which reveals a media fixation where mothers are the "main caregivers" and "their kids are the center of the universe."[96] Their actions as citizens apart from the home are absent from such characterizations.

Rather than focus on issues like education, equal pay, health care, and prescription drugs, security moms were depicted as single-issue voters, concerned almost exclusively with national security and, most particularly, the protection of their children. Many journalists and political observers attributed their increased focus on security to the "terrorist takeover of the Russian elementary school" in September of 2004, reflecting "the worst nightmare a mother could have"[97] (which curiously is not a nightmare for fathers). The *Philadelphia Inquirer* elaborated the concern: "It's not that class size, mammograms and flex time no longer matter. But those preoccupations of a sunnier time now pale next to Job One: Don't ever let what happened in Breslan [Russia] happen to my children."[98] For security moms, then, their vote was driven by "fear" as well as a keen sense of "vulnerability." As conservative columnist and self-identified security mom Michelle Malkin suggested, "I have not settled back casually into a Sept. 10 way of life. I have studied the faces on the FBI's most wanted-terrorist list. When I ride the train, I watch for suspicious packages in empty seats." Because of her fears, Malkin concluded, "I own a gun. And I vote."[99] Such concerns, pollsters suggested, made security moms more concerned about the war on terrorism than the war in Iraq, constituting them as single-issue citizens.[100]

According to such media logic, the solution to such security fears involved the identification of a white president who would protect the nation, particularly the children. Malkin explained, "I want a president who is of one mind, not two, about what must be done to protect our freedom and our borders."[101] Journalist Ellen Goodman noted that undecided women voters are "looking for a guy [president] who is strong."[102] Similarly, the *Christian Science Monitor* reported that security moms "want a little more macho in the White House (or a lot)," and often "roll their eyes" at "guys' softer sides."[103] The *NBC Nightly News* concluded that "security moms [are] voting not only for a president but for peace of mind."[104] Their political agency, as a result, is limited to their vote.

Absent, of course, in any of this discourse is the role of Congress, the FBI, the CIA, the Department of Homeland Security, the military, the national guard, or other law-enforcement agencies at the national, state, or local levels in combating terrorism—the actual women and men who work daily to protect the country, or pass laws that help secure its safety. Such security measures, rather, are instantiated in the machismo of the individual white man who would become president, disconnected from the state and local communities, neighborhood watches, and other family members in such protective actions. Mothers assumed the burden of worry over such matters, but had minimal recourse other than their one person, one vote.

To that end, such discourse, which paralleled the campaign rhetoric articulated by the candidates themselves, constituted the president as the protector-in-chief, assuming a more fatherly role over the entire nation as well as individual families. In an article entitled "Two Projections of the Father Image," the *Los Angeles Times* explicitly used such paternal images in its coverage of the first presidential debate, with Paul Brownfield asking, "Who's your daddy?"[105] White mothers' primary mission, then, was to answer this question, selecting the appropriate white father figure for their families—the "essence" of their citizenship role in the 2004 election.

In press coverage, President Bush emerged as the one who would most likely secure national and familial safety. Even though a government professor writing for *Newsday* reported that security moms "normally vote Democratic," they "shifted to President George W. Bush because they think he will do a better job of protecting the nation from terrorism."[106] When deciphering polling data, the *Charleston Gazette* noted that "so many [women] are in the unenviable pickle of hating the war and thinking the commander-in-chief is a strong leader."[107] *USA Today* interviewed one security mom who was a registered Democrat but planned to vote for Bush because "'He had the gumption and the nerve to not just sit there and keep getting hit in the face' after 9/11."[108] Another Bush supporter and security mom concluded that she had to know that "my president is watching my back."[109] Throughout the campaign, numerous organizations led by mothers formed to support a particular candidate or to promote a specific position on the U.S./Iraq war. The leader of one such Republican group, SecurityMoms4Bush, declared, "I am just a mom . . . a mom that dreams of a day when all mothers will again feel safe."[110] Such constructions reified white women's role in the democracy as citizen-mothers, reflective of the historical depictions where women are excluded from the contested political terrain in favor of the depoliticized domestic spaces.

Contrastingly, concerns surfaced in the press over whether Kerry was "strong enough to protect them [security moms and their children] from terrorists."[111] The *New York Times* noted that "Kerry's failure to fight back" against the Swift Boat Veterans for Truth "fed a perception, particularly among married women, that he would not fight for them and their children."[112] A reporter for the *New York Sun* editorialized that "Mr. Kerry's behavior after the war and his record in the Senate demonstrate that he has no real love for the military or any war," which was not "reassuring to a security or soccer mom in 2004."[113] Part of this issue, of course, is linked to the feminization of Democrats as weak on foreign policy—a political construction that became increasingly visible in the earliest years of the Cold War. Men of the New Left and antiwar movements worried about the "loss and recovery of manhood"[114]—anxieties that continue to haunt liberals and any antiwar positions that they might assume. In the wake of Governor Arnold Schwarzenegger's (R-CA) pronouncement that Democrats were "girly men" for not passing his proposed budget in California, an editorial writer for the *Minnesota Star Tribune* concluded: "Democrats haven't been acting like girly-men. We've acted like girly-girls, specifically the dreaded nice ones."[115] And the *New York Times* also featured an article, entitled "How Kerry Became a Girlie-Man."[116] Such hypermasculine rhetoric reified notions of patriarchy, creating limited options for performing masculinity while also preserving women's submission to men in the home and in the nation.

Kerry, though, did attract a following from security moms. Several pro-Kerry or antiwar groups with familial-titled organizations emerged during the campaign, including Mothers Opposing Bush (MOB), Mainline Moms for Kerry, Military Moms with a Mission, and the Band of Sisters. MOB, whose slogan read, "Because Mother Knows Best," defined its mission as "harnessing the power of mothers (and others) across the country to get the facts out, get the voters out and to get this president out of office."[117] The Band of Sisters organization was a branch of the liberal 527 group Win Back Respect, which was partially funded by Moveon.org. Members of this group traveled with General Wesley Clark as he campaigned for Kerry, and were comprised of sisters, wives, and mothers of U.S. soldiers stationed in Iraq—some of whom were killed or wounded in combat. In one campaign ad sponsored by Win Back Respect ("He Doesn't Get It"), a sister of a U.S. soldier killed in Iraq condemned President Bush for laughing about not finding the weapons of mass destruction in Iraq.[118] The "band of sisters" metaphor represents the female counterpart to the "band of brothers" that Kerry referenced throughout his campaign. Rather than serving in the enemy war zone, though, this "band of sisters" combated the political war at home, voicing opposition to a commander in chief who, in their minds, betrayed the nation and the men who fought the war. Such characteristics suggest that the men of the country fight the wars while the women stay home to battle the wartime exigencies domestically, even though women are placed in combat positions in Iraq. Referring to such constructions as the "myth" of war, Miriam Cooke details the "mystique of the unquestionable masculinity of soldiering, of the essential femininity of peace advocacy."[119]

The activities of such political groups centering on the actions of mothers across the country reflected the historical practices of (republican) mothers "to stop the violence against their children, their families, and their communities," or to promote other forms of social change.[120] Using a familial term like "mothers" rather than "women" worked to depoliticize their actions. Women within many of these groups were defined by their familial relationships rather than their status as women. Such symbolic choices helped blunt the partisan actions of mother and sister organizations that targeted other women characterized as wavering in their selection of a presidential protectorate (even though many were leaning toward Bush). In the process, security moms were portrayed as active and engaged voters—voters whose democratic participation was limited to casting a ballot for the white father-like president who would keep their families safe, normalizing subservient prescriptions for women in the nation and the family. Other issues affecting women were missing from the political landscape that could help erode such systemic oppressions. Single women, conversely, were portrayed as disengaged women, too busy with work, kids, and/or fun to be bothered with the civic act of casting a ballot.

SINGLE WOMEN—UNMARRIED MOMS
AND SINGLES IN THE CITY

In campaign 2004, single women were dubbed the "hottest" swing-voting bloc, making up some 20 million potential voters in twelve battleground states.[121] Single women were also characterized as the largest nonvoting group,[122] which inspired various initiatives, among Democrats in particular, to target them. The constructions of such voters varied depending on their motherhood status; women without children were portrayed as more urban and "sex and the city" style voters, while single mothers were represented as more diverse economically and racially. Yet, these women were similarly defined in large measure by their sexuality and their marital status. Susan Page of *USA Today* queried: "Want to know which candidate a woman is likely to support for president?" The answer:

"Look at her ring finger."[123] Sexualizing women's political participation is also historically rooted, evidencing the double bind of women's citizenry that is continually anchored to the men in their lives. Women are thus either depoliticized as mothers (wives of men) or as sexual objects (of men), with limited political power or voice in either case.

Although pollsters predicted that single women would vote for Kerry, they were still pegged as swing voters with unpredictable voting habits caused by the distractions of work, dating, and other narcissistic matters that kept many willfully disengaged from U.S. politics. In characterizing such women, a rhetoric of dating dominated, which treated the presidential candidates not as father figures, but as surrogate husbands for these available women. The campaign, thus, was constructed as a dating scene where the white presidential contenders courted single women for their vote, constituting them as "citizen-ingénues"—politically naive and decidedly sexualized.

The demographics offered for the single-women voter bloc were broader than for NASCAR dads or security moms. *USA Today* posited that "Some are divorced, some never married, some have kids, and their ages range from 18 to 64."[124] The *San Antonio Express-News* also accentuated the group's economic diversity, concluding that they "represent a wide swath of socioeconomic America. They are young women fresh out of college. They are single moms with kids. They are working professional women. They are widows living on a fixed income."[125] Finally, the *Hartford Courant* furthered the focus on this group's racial, economic, and geographical diversity: "The demographics of these women cut across, age, race, geography and income level. But, when they vote, they tend to vote Democratic by a ratio of nearly 2-to-1."[126] Unlike married women, who were portrayed as more focused on the war on terrorism, pollsters and journalists suggested that single women were more concerned about domestic violence, health care, daycare, education, crime, and the war in Iraq, if they were described as issue-conscious at all.[127] Single women, though, were predominantly portrayed as disengaged and uninspired citizens.

Even though expected to support Kerry, their swing status was justified on the uncertainty surrounding their voter turnout, with some calling them "disengaged" and others suggesting that such women embodied "poor citizenship."[128] Some pollsters and journalists linked their nonvoting decisions to a lack of information. The Associated Press, for example, quoted a member of the League of Women Voters who concluded that such single women "are so uninformed and don't seem to fully understand the process."[129] Others asserted that single women were "cynical about politics" because they tend to be ignored by politicians represented mostly by "powerful men."[130] Single women were also portrayed as "too busy" to think about politics as they tried to "juggle complicated work and family schedules."[131] Still other journalists justified single women as swing voters on the stereotypical grounds that they were "gutsy, wonderfully unpredictable wom[e]n" who "hate [nothing] worse than being taken for granted."[132]

Democratic pollsters like Anna Greenberg concluded that had some 6 million more single women voted in 2000, Al Gore would be president. As a result, the Democratic Party, and to a lesser extent the Republican Party, targeted this constituted group of citizens. Unmistakably, a discourse of dating dominated the media coverage, especially for those single women dubbed as "Sex and the City Voters"[133] after the popular HBO series, evidencing the sexualization of women's political participation. The headlines of newspapers and magazines reveal such dating symbolism, with some resembling a singles ad. One *Business Week* headline read, "Desperately Seeking Single Women Voters," while the *Memphis Commercial Appeal* featured a headline that queried, "Come Here Often? Apparently Not." The *San Francisco Chronicle* also issued the following headline: "Courting the Single Female Voter."[134] Other dating metaphors were also commonplace. Bush and Kerry were portrayed as "courting," "luring," "wooing," and "pursu[ing]" while also "turning on the charm" for these "unattached femmes" and "swinging singles" with "commitment issues."[135] In the process, single-women citizens were depicted as "tantalizing to Democratic partisans."[136]

In other news features, dating discourse framed entire news stories. The *Arkansas Democrat-Gazette*, for example, began its article entitled "What's in a Dame: Something Old, New, Borrowed and . . . Red?" with the sentence "Do you promise to love, honor and vote Republican?" In answering the question, the journalist replied, "Politics is not a part of the wedding vows, but it might as well be."[137] The *San Francisco Chronicle* also noted that the "political arena has never been considered good hunting ground for hunks," which advantages "handsome politicians . . . because there are so few sexy senators and politicians." The journalist also detailed a poll taken by the dating website "It's Just Lunch," which surveyed whether single women would rather be set up on a blind date with Kerry,

Bush, or other political officials like Colin Powell and John McCain. Some 53 percent indicated "they'd skip" the lunch "altogether." The journalist reassured readers, though, that "surveys have shown that single women won't vote for someone whose policies they don't support just because he's a hunk" (like John Edwards).[138]

Attempting to increase voter registration of single women in campaign 2004 clearly represented an important mission for both political parties, but especially for more progressive-leaning organizations. Groups registering single women included one pro-Kerry group entitled Belles against Bush, and a subsequent Republican organization called Belles at the Ballot.[139] Other organizations like Women at the Table and Women's Voices Women's Vote (WVWV) likewise sought to increase voter registration for their demographic group.[140] Laudably, the goal of WVWV, which is officially nonpartisan yet partially financed by Moveon.org and the Heinz foundation, was to show women the power that they could have over the outcome of elections. The group targeted women through public-service announcements with celebrities like Jennifer Aniston, Sarah Jessica Parker, Christina Applegate, and Helen Hunt on the E! Entertainment Television network. Such women gained their political celebrity not from their collective involvement or interrogation of public/social matters, but from their own personal angst regarding such issues as sex, marriage, and children. Citizenship was reduced once again to individual and private, rather than collective and systemic, matters.

Despite such important voter-registration efforts, the strategies reflected the sexualized expressions of women's citizenship, which trivialized and depoliticized women's civic contributions. The nonpartisan group 1000 Flowers sent beauty salons voter-registration kits that contained nail files with the slogan "Nailing the election one vote at a time."[141] A group entitled Code Pink sold pink lingerie as part of its "Give Bush the Pink Slip" campaign. And the Democratic National Committee explicitly sexualized single women voters by offering "panties with . . . slogans like 'Kiss Bush Goodbye,'" which were disseminated at "PantyWare" parties and nightclubs. As a writer for the *New York Times* queried, "Want to attract single voters? Drop the underpants." Such efforts were depicted by the *San Francisco Chronicle* as "unusual, sexy, irrelevant and often highly creative efforts aimed at a tech-savvy, media-savvy younger generation."[142] Such sexualization of women's civic engagement is not surprisingly associated with presidentiality, constituted as the white masculine embodiment of nationalism and the receptacle of female heterosexual love and admiration.[143] As Yuval-Davis asserts, "Gendered bodies and sexuality play pivotal roles as territorialities, markers and reproducers of narratives of nations."[144]

Several journalists and group organizers maintained that the work to register single women represented the group's "collectivity" and "empowerment." Targeting college students, one writer urged: "Voting empowers you as a citizen and as a woman. Your voice is your vote."[145] While voting is clearly a necessary act of citizenship, it also is an individual act of political participation reflective of postfeminism that represents both the means and the ends of civic participation. As Vavrus explains, postfeminism epitomizes "a shift from a vision of collective politics for social change to an individualistic focus; successes *and* failures are attributed to individual women [not voting] rather than to a complex formula of individual work, group efforts, and structural influences."[146] While such voting drives require group efforts, the ultimate goal is the one person, one vote to elect a white male figure using dating criteria to address issues affecting single women. Such voter mobilization ignored women's collective work to change policies affecting their lives. Such campaigns also lacked noteworthy educational efforts to help single women overcome their political naiveté. As long as they voted, they could return to their politically disengaged and narcissistic lives, the discourse implied. Bonnie Dow suggests that the "most radical aspects of feminism . . . a profound awareness of power differences between the sexes at all levels and in all areas, ha[s] been discarded as irrelevant and threatening."[147] As one leader of Mainstreet Moms Oppose Bush assured when selling necklaces to single women, "It's not an angry movement—it's joyful,"[148] portraying single women as happily oblivious in their oppressive citizenry roles.

Rhetoric, Democratic Citizenship, and Identity Politics in U.S. Political Culture

John Collins and Ross Glover remind us that "Processes of meaning-making don't happen overnight; rather, they happen historically, through repeated . . . and generally selective usage."[149] Grounding this study of contemporary citizenship constructs in the history of U.S. nationalism demonstrates that many of the earliest ideological formations of the gendered, racialized, and militarized nation are still visible at the turn of the twenty-first century. Throughout this contested and ongoing process of defining the national imaginary, rhetoric assumes the means of (re)constituting democratic citizenship. As Murray Edelman contends, "political language" creates "political reality."[150] In the process of linguistically constituting such citizen realities, Jasinski suggests, "Discursive action. . . enable[s] and constrain[s] subsequent thought and action."[151] Discourse by and about the white male president serves as a key site for "articulating the collective culture" and "managing the collective action."[152]

Multiple implications emerge out of this examination of the 2004 presidential-campaign discourse. First, as military power and masculinity have come to represent central features of U.S. national identity, so too have they evolved to define the key criteria of a successful president—the lone white male political figure in whom the nation invests its hope for security. DeConde believes that "presidential machismo could not thrive without the awe most Americans have for the presidency."[153] As the presidency gained political force over the past two centuries, the role of Congress in matters of war dissipated, allowing a commander in chief considerable power to constitute the nation's identity around matters that invested his office with increased authority. Not surprisingly, the U.S. people often condone such militaristic responses as the epitome of patriotism.[154] In times of greatest threat, presidential power expands as he alone becomes the predominant promise of national and familial security.[155]

The discourse further reified the president's position of white, patriarchal power through a familial discourse. The reliance on a family framework helps naturalize such power dynamics because of its historical and ideological legacy in the U.S. national imaginary. French philosopher Etienne Balibar suggests that expressions of suppressive nationalisms are generally invisible and "present themselves, rather, as political and cultural universalisms."[156] The end result of such "telling of history," Otto Bauer contends, is that "The nation is linked with the idea of its destiny, with the memory of heroic struggles. . . . The whole rapport that someone today may feel with the struggling people in the past is then transformed into love for the bearers of this motley fate, the nation."[157] White male presidents often fulfill the role of romantic protagonist in such national romance narratives, becoming the benefactors of such love during turbulent times in particular. Presidential-campaign rhetoric thus helps reconstitute the nation's identity and strengthen the love that citizens hold toward (some) of their presidents—the embodiment of the nation's patriotism, the white male protector-father, and the surrogate husband. Given that presidentiality reifies national whiteness, the familial conflations normalize a homogenized and idealized white citizenry.

As the presidency is empowered by the campaign rhetoric of 2004, the same discourse delimits citizenship engagement and responsibilities, depoliticizing citizen participation through the use of a white familial framework. For the groups discussed, voting represented the ultimate act and end of civic engagement. NASCAR dads were constituted as alienated and disenfranchised sports spectators, voting for a candidate who protected their southern, white male values, rather than as citizen-actors poised to collectively change their own economic conditions. In the process, NASCAR dads were sidelined from the political spaces of democracy and their own homes. In the end, southern white males disappeared from the campaign landscape when their status as nonpartisan voters dissipated, reducing their capital as citizen-voters.

Conversely, security moms were selecting an appropriate family protector in a post-9/11 world, while single women were expected to judge the presidential candidates like a dating partner, rather than becoming citizens engaged in and informed about the issues affecting their lives. Such pollster-derived swing voters thus were not encouraged to engage politically beyond their vote, especially given the political naiveté of many single women. Gerard A. Hauser reflects on the "defining characteristic of a modern democracy" and its central "problem," which is "the creation of a discursive practice in which citizens may pursue the possibilities of civic engagement."[158] Certainly, voting is a place to begin such engagement, but its presence as the essence of democratic participation is limiting and only promises enhanced alienation; voters likely do not feel any more secure after the election, and no more engaged once the excitement of voting dissipates. And for those who vote for the losing candidate, feelings of despair can foster further civic estrangement. A rhetoric of citizenship, thus, must transcend campaign discourse and offer citizens additional means of civic participation and meaning.

Yet, even though the political power of security moms, NASCAR dads, and sex-in-the-city citizens was depoliticized and limited to voting, such groups were legitimated as ideal citizen participants in the presidential contest. Many "others" were virtually ignored in the presidential campaign advertisements, news-media coverage, and public-opinion polls, suggesting that their vote, and thus their voice were somehow less valued. The targeted focus of candidates, journalists, and pollsters also may have unintended consequences. Focusing on the swing voter in battleground states suggests that the most important citizens are those who are undecided, judged as more nonpartisan, and in some instances, lacking in political knowledge and conviction.[159] Such rhetorical choices further what Amy Gutmann calls the "myth that superior citizens are independent voters."[160] Voters who are decisive, aligned with party or identity politics, and/or reside in non-battleground states like Indiana, Kansas, Maryland, and Montana often lack a discursive presence in the national campaign rhetoric rather than reaping the benefits of "general uplift [that] elections inspire."[161] Decisive voters, thus, are often devalued in the electoral process, which can further alienation and exacerbate divisions in U.S. political culture.[162]

There are other consequences, though, of legitimizing swing voters identified during campaign 2004. The familial metaphors linked to swing voters in battleground states worked to privilege white middle-class men and women in the electoral process. Although single women were depicted as more diverse, NASCAR dads and security moms were uniformly labeled white. Latino/a voters also attracted more attention than other racial or ethnic groups as potential swing voters, yet the national discourse did not raise such voters to the same level as white NASCAR dads, security moms, or single women. Consequently, the campaign rhetoric of 2004 reconstituted whiteness as a central characteristic of U.S. nationalism and citizenship. Such continued rhetorical patterns reflect what Ian F. Haney López explains is the historical assumption that "Whites qualified for citizenship because they were fit by nature for republican government."[163]

Finally, the campaign rhetoric of 2004 says much about identity politics at the turn of the twenty-first century. The conflict surrounding identity politics aligned with groups of color, labor unions, and feminist or gay organizations is too explosive for candidates or the media elites to include routinely in their national messages. Such exclusions reflect a fear of appearing beholden to political correctness and misguided leftists rather than at home with white, mainstream centrism. In the process, Victor Burgin asserts, "Institutional racism may ensure that racial minorities live in a condition of internal exile within the nation of which they are citizens—an exile that, if it is not legal, cannot be named."[164] Yet despite all of the objections to identity politics, Todd Gitlin contends that "The identity obsession is not just practiced by history's most beleaguered people. American culture in the late twentieth century is a very stewpot of separate identities."[165] Arguably, the valorization of such white swing-voter groups also represents a legacy of identity politics fashioned in the 1960s and 1970s as the national civil rights discourse moved away from equality toward matters of identity and diversity.[166]

White identity groups that candidates target and the press uplifts, though, do not attract the scorn that appealing to African Americans or labor-union voters incites. The circulation of groups like NASCAR dads and security moms as an extension of identity politics is masked by their whiteness, their so-called swing-voter status, and by the use of familial discourse that naturalizes their role in the nation state. As Gutmann concludes, "Nationalism is part of identity politics," and the nation state "cannot be culturally neutral" as governmental discourse (and news-media coverage) "protects the dominant culture, whether intentionally or not, through the language it uses, the education it accredits, the history it honors."[167] Toward that end, undecided voters are not neutral and should not be exclusively valorized as citizens who exist above politics.[168] Instead, the rhetoric that imagines such citizenry participation should offer spaces for inclusive civic-engagement opportunities that avoid privileging some groups and states while exiling others to the political margins. If this country is to transcend the political divides, it must work to overcome such divisiveness with a national rhetoric of diversity and inclusivity to help ensure that presidential campaigns achieve Hart's ideal political campaign goal of "re-democratizing and "invigorat[ing] the nation."[169]

NOTES

1. Susan Jeffords, *The Remasculinization of America: Gender and the Vietnam War* (Bloomington: Indiana University Press, 1989).

2. J. Ann Tickner, *Gendering World Politics: Issues and Approaches in the Post–Cold War Era* (New York: Columbia University Press, 2001), 52, 56.

3. Roderick P. Hart, *Campaign Talk: Why Elections Are Good for Us* (Princeton, N.J.: Princeton University Press, 2000), 9.

4. James Jasinski, "(Re)constituting Community through Narrative Argument: *Eros* and *Philia* in *The Big Chill*," *Quarterly Journal of Speech* 79 (1993): 480.

5. The use of this critical perspective, these sources, the discourse of campaigns, as well as the media coverage, is of course one of several approaches to the study of these matters. This approach is focused upon public and mediated political communication and is both enriched and restricted by that perspective. Other examinations might utilize alternative sources such as vernacular discourses, satire and comedic parodies, direct polling, independent focus groups and survey data, the examination of live campaign events, or the analysis of debates.

6. Benedict Anderson defines "nation" as "an imagined political community." See *Imagined Communities* (London: Verso, 1983), 6. When referring to the "citizen imaginary," I mean to suggest that constructions of citizenship are likewise discursively constituted through discourse in the same way that conceptions of "nation" are constituted through the language that circulates over time to create understandings of political culture and its participants. Political elites (e.g., political officials, pundits, the press) are key participants in such constitutive activities. Nevertheless, members of the nation-state can likewise influence the constitutive processes of creating the national and citizen imaginary.

7. Gopal Balakrishnan, ed., "The National Imagination," in *Mapping the Nation* (London: Verso, 1996), 206.

8. George L. Mosse, *Nationalism and Sexuality: Respectability and Abnormal Sexuality in Modern Europe* (New York: Howard Fertig, 1985), 18.

9. Ida Blom, "Gender and Nation in International Comparison," in *Gendered Nations: Nationalisms and Gender Order in the Long Nineteenth Century*, ed. Ida Blom, Karen Hagemann, and Catherine Hall (New York: Oxford University Press, 2000), 8.

10. Rogan Kersh, *Dreams of a More Perfect Union* (Ithaca, N.Y.: Cornell University Press, 2001), 26, 44, 94, 118.

11. *Act of March 26, 1790* (Naturalization Law of 1790), 1 Stat 103–104.

12. Anthony W. Marx, *Making Race and Nation: A Comparison of South Africa, the United States, and Brazil* (Cambridge: Cambridge University Press, 1998), 268, 3.

13. States that sought to block African Americans from entry included Maryland (1783), Connecticut (1814), New York (1821), and Pennsylvania (1838). Many of the northern states, such as Massachusetts, discouraged free blacks from settling in their region; other newer states, such as Ohio, also attempted to ban blacks. See Paul Goodman, *Of One Blood: Abolitionism and the Origins of Racial Equality* (Berkeley: University of California Press, 1998), 6–7.

14. Nira Yuval-Davis, *Gender and Nation* (London: Sage, 1997), 92.

15. Anne McClintock, "'No Longer in a Future Heaven': Gender, Race and Nationalism," in *Dangerous Liaisons: Gender, Nation, and Postcolonial Perspectives*, ed.

Anne McClintock, Aamir Mufti, and Ella Shohat (Minneapolis: University of Minnesota Press, 1997), 91.

16. McClintock, "'No Longer in a Future Heaven,'" 91.

17. Tamar Mayer, *Gender Ironies of Nationalism: Sexing the Nation* (London: Routledge, 2000), 1–2, 6.

18. John Beynon, *Masculinities and Culture* (Buckingham, UK: Open University Press, 2002), 27, 28, 33.

19. Blom, "Gender and Nation in International Comparison," 17.

20. Varda Burstyn, *The Rights of Men: Manhood, Politics, and the Culture of Sport* (Toronto, Canada: University of Toronto Press, 2000), 45. See also R. W. Connell, *Masculinities* (Berkeley: University of California Press, 1995), 68.

21. Carroll Smith-Rosenberg, "Political Camp or the Ambiguous Engendering of the American Republic," in *Gendered Nations: Nationalisms and Gender Order in the Long Nineteenth Century*, ed. Ida Blom, Karen Hagemann, and Catherine Hall (Oxford, UK: Berg, 2000), 275.

22. See Theodore Roosevelt, ed., "The Strenuous Life," in *The Strenuous Life: Essays and Addresses* (New York: The Century Company, 1901), 16.

23. Roosevelt, "The Strenuous Life," 4.

24. Theodore Roosevelt, *American Ideals and Other Essays, Social and Political* (Philadelphia: Gebbie and Company, 1903), 46–47.

25. Julie Mostov, "Sexing the Nation/Desexing the Body: Politics of National Identity in the Former Yugoslavia," in *Gender Ironies of Nationalism: Sexing the Nation*, ed. Tamar Mayer (London: Routledge, 2000), 91.

26. Hannah Arendt reminds us that such discernments between the public political sphere versus private domestic space has roots in antiquity: "The *polis* was distinguished from the household in that it knew only 'equals,' whereas the household was the center of the strictest inequality." See *The Human Condition* (Chicago: University of Chicago Press, 1958), 32.

27. Smith-Rosenberg, "Political Camp or the Ambiguous Engendering of the American Republic," 275.

28. Linda K. Kerber, *Women of the Republic: Intellect and Ideology in Revolutionary America* (Chapel Hill: University of North Carolina Press, 1980).

29. Linda K. Kerber, *No Constitutional Rights to Be Ladies: Women and the Obligations of Citizenship* (New York: Hill and Wang, 1998), 146.

30. James Dawes, *The Language of War: Literature and Culture in the U.S. from the Civil War through World War II* (Cambridge, Mass.: Harvard University Press, 2002), 133. It is important to note that women of color, poorer white women, and

women from rural farming communities had been in the U.S. workforce for decades.

31. See Kerber, *Women of the Republic*; Glenna Matthews, *The Rise of Public Woman: Woman's Power and Woman's Place in the United States, 1630–1970* (New York: Oxford University Press, 1992); and Judith Ann Giesberg, *Civil War Sisterhood: The U.S. Sanitary Commission and Women's Politics in Transition* (Boston: Northeastern University Press, 2000).

32. "The First War Losses," *The Suffragist*, April 14, 1917, 4.

33. Elaine Tyler May, *Homeward Bound: American Families in the Cold War Era* (New York: Basic Books, 1996), 65.

34. Miles Moffeit and Amy Herdy, "Female GIs Report Rapes in Iraq War," *Denver Post*, January 25, 2005, 1, http://www.denverpost.com/cda/article/print/0,1674,36%257E643 (accessed February 2, 2005).

35. See Mayer, "Gender Ironies of Nationalism," 6; and Pnina Werbner, "Political Motherhood and the Feminisation of Citizenship: Women's Activisms and the Transformation of the Public Sphere," in *Women, Citizenship, and Difference*, ed. Nira Yuval-Davis and Pnina Werbner (London: Zed Books, 1999), 221–22.

36. Mayer, "Gender Ironies of Nationalism," 6.

37. Cynthia Enloe, *The Morning After: Sexual Politics at the End of the Cold War* (Berkeley: University of California Press, 1993), 238.

38. See Beynon, *Masculinities and Culture*, 65; and Mostov, "Sexing the Nation/De-sexing the Body," 91.

39. Marx, *Making Race and Nation*, 5, 270.

40. Shawn J. Parry-Giles and Trevor Parry-Giles, *Constructing Clinton: Hyperreality and Presidential Image-Making in Postmodern Politics* (New York: Peter Lang, 2002), 3. "Presidentiality" is the discursive manifestation of Bruce Buchanan's discussion of "presidential culture" that involves citizens and the psychological impressions of the presidency that are "embedded in the public mind." See Bruce Buchanan, *The Citizen's Presidency: Standards of Choice and Judgment* (Washington, D.C.: CQ Press, 1987), 26. My concern, of course, is with how these impressions are expressed rhetorically with ideological resonance for the U.S. political culture. See also Trevor Parry-Giles and Shawn J. Parry-Giles, *The Prime-Time Presidency: The West Wing and U.S. Nationalism* (Urbana: University of Illinois Press, 2006).

41. Jeffords, *The Remasculinization of America*, 186.

42. Of course, the presidency has been the site of masculine enactments since the country's inception. See Alexander DeConde, *Presidential Machismo: Executive Authority, Military Intervention, and Foreign Relations* (Boston: Northeastern University Press, 2000).

43. George W. Bush, "Policy in Focus: Compassionate Conservatism," online at http://www.whitehouse.gov/news/releases/2002/07/20020701–1.html (accessed December 1, 2004).

44. "Homeland Security: Protecting the American People," Republican National Committee, online at http://www.gop.com/GOPAgenda/AgendaPage.aspx?id=6 (accessed December 1, 2004).

45. George W. Bush, "Acceptance Speech"—Republican National Convention, September 2, 2004, Republican National Committee, online at http://www.gop.com/News/Read.aspx?ID=5054 (accessed September 5, 2004).

46. "Whatever It Takes," Bush/Cheney 04, Inc., Political Advertising Resource Center, online at http://www.umdparc.org/AdAnalysisWhateverItTakes.htm (accessed January 12, 2005).

47. George Lakoff, *Moral Politics: How Liberals and Conservatives Think*, 2nd ed. (Chicago: University of Chicago Press, 2002), 65, 67. Mothers, of course, can also be protectionist; as Lakoff acknowledges, there are also strict mothers who assume the same behavioral characteristics as strict fathers.

48. DeConde, *Presidential Machismo*, 292–93.

49. See "Commander in Chief Lands on USS Lincoln," CNN.com/Inside Politics, May 2, 2003, online at http://www.cnn.com/2003/ALLPOLITICS/05/01/bush.carrier.landing (accessed January 20, 2004); and James W. Pindell, "In NH, Democrats Criticize Bush's Language over Iraq," PoliticsNH.com, July 4, 2003, New Hampshire's Online Political Network, online at http://www.politicsnh.com/archives/pindell/2003/July/7_4.shtml (accessed January 20, 2004).

50. The author attended a pancake breakfast in Keene, New Hampshire, where General Clark uttered the phrase on Sunday, January 18, 2004. He also repeated the phrase in a "Conversation with Clark" in Newport, New Hampshire, later that same evening. See also Edward Wyatt, "The 2004 Campaign: The Stump Speech/General Wesley Clark; Rising Above Politics, as High as Commander in Chief," *New York Times* (January 15, 2004), online at http://query.nytimes.com/search/restricted/article?res=F30C10F73 (accessed January 20, 2004); and John Kerry, "Iowa Jefferson Jackson Day Dinner," online at http://www.johnkerry.com/pressroom/speeches/spc_2003_1115.html (accessed January 20, 2004) (emphasis added).

51. John Kerry.com, "A Lifetime of Service and Strength," online at http://www.johnkerry.com/about/john_kerry/ (accessed January 12, 2005).

52. John Kerry, "Acceptance Speech"—Democratic National Convention, July 29, 2004, online at http://www.washingtonpost.com/wp-dyn/articles/A25678–2004Jul29.html (accessed January 4, 2006).

53. John Kerry.com, "Biography," online at http://www.johnkerry.com/about/john_kerry/bio.html (accessed January 12, 2005).

54. DeConde, *Presidential Machismo*, 286.

55. John Kerry.com, "Obligation," online at http://www.johnkerry.com/tv/ (accessed January 12, 2005).

56. Kerry, "Acceptance Speech."

57. Swift Boat Veterans for Truth, "Any Questions," online at the Political Advertising Resource Center, http://www.umdparc.org/AdAnalysisAnyQuestions.htm (accessed January 12, 2005).

58. Bush/Cheney '04, Inc., "Peace and Security," online at the Political Advertising Resource Center, http://www.umdparc.org/AdAnalysisPeaceAndSecurity.htm (accessed January 12, 2005).

59. See Mike Allen, "Bush Ad Criticizes Democrats on Defense: Doctrine of Preemption is Touted as Effective," *Washington Post*, November 22, 2003, A03.

60. George W. Bush, "State of the Union" address, January 20, 2004, online at http://www.whitehouse.gov/news/releases/2004/01/print/20040120-7.html (accessed December 1, 2004).

61. Dawes, *The Language of War*, 87.

62. Bruce E. Keith, David B. Magleby, Candice J. Nelson, Elizabeth Orr, Mark C. Westlye, and Raymond E. Wolfinger, *The Myth of the Independent Voter* (Berkeley: University of California Press, 1992), 1–4.

63. James Jasinski, "A Constitutive Framework for Rhetorical Historiography: Toward an Understanding of the Discursive (Re)constitution of 'Constitution' in *The Federalist Papers*," in *Doing Rhetorical History: Concepts and Cases*, ed. Kathleen J. Turner (Tuscaloosa: University of Alabama Press, 1998), 80.

64. Dana Coffield, "NASCAR Dads Who Voted for Bush Less Pack-Minded in '04," *Denver Post*, June 20, 2004, 1, online at http://academic.lexisnexis.com/ (accessed December 1, 2004).

65. Mark S. Mellman, "Name That Voter," *The Hill*, September 29, 2004, 1, online at http://academic.lexisnexis.com/ (accessed December 1, 2004).

66. See Dana Coffield, "Searching for the Real NASCAR Dad: Just Who Are These Guys, Whose Votes Politicians Crave?" *Denver Post*, June 20, 2004, 1, online at http://academic.lexisnexis.com/ (accessed December 1, 2004); and Noelle Straub, "Prez Revs Up for NASCAR Appearance," *Boston Herald*, September 11, 2004, 1, online at http://academic.lexisnexis.com/ (accessed December 1, 2004).

67. "Bush-Cheney '04 Launches NASCAR Campaign," UPI, October 19, 2004, 1, online at http://academic.lexisnexis.com/ (accessed December 1, 2004). Journalists

identify NASCAR as the second most popular sport in the United States behind professional football, further evidencing the political importance of these events that attract large media audiences. See John Hanc, "Confessions of a NASCAR Dad," *Newsday*, August 31, 2004, 1–4, online at http://academic.lexisnexis.com/ (accessed December 1, 2004).

68. See Genaro C. Armas, "From NASCAR Dad to Soccer Mom: Campaigns Drawn to Political Labels," *Associated Press*, June 11, 2004, 2, online at http://academic. lexisnexis.com/ (accessed December 1, 2004); and Tim Appelo, "The NASCAR-ing of the Northwest," *Seattle Weekly*, June 30, 2004, 1–6, online at http://academic.lexisnexis.com/ (accessed December 1, 2004).

69. See Appelo, "The NASCARING of the Northwest," 1–6; and Hanc, "Confessions of a NASCAR Dad," 1–4.

70. Appelo, "The NASCARing of the Northwest," 2.

71. Juan Williams, "Security Moms, NASCAR Dads, Soccer Moms, and Waitress Moms," *National Public Radio*, September 27, 2004, 1–2, online at http://academic.lexisnexis.com/ (accessed November 18, 2004).

72. Coffield, "Searching for the Real NASCAR Dad," 1.

73. Appelo, "The NASCARing of the Northwest," 1–6.

74. Varda, *The Rites of Men*, 22.

75. Armas, "From NASCAR Dad to Soccer Mom," 2.

76. See Mary Diebel, "Almost Everyone's in a Voter Bloc This Year," *Scripps Howard News Service*, October 28, 2004, 1, online at http://academic.lexisnexis.com/ (accessed December 1, 2004); Dana Coffield, "These Guys Are a Far Cry from the Soccer-Mom Bloc," *Denver Post*, October 19, 2004, 1, online at http://academic. lexisnexis.com/ (accessed December 1, 2004); and Appelo, "The NASCARing of the Northwest," 1–6.

77. Appelo, "The NASCARing of the Northwest," 1–6.

78. For more on NASCAR's history, see Mark D. Howell, *From Moonshine to Madison Avenue: A Cultural History of the NASCAR Winston Cup Series* (Bowling Green, Ohio: Bowling Green State University Popular Press, 1997).

79. Straub, "Prez Revs Up for NASCAR Appearance," 1.

80. CNN.com, "Analysis of 'Rock the Vote' Debate: Interviews with Democratic Presidential Candidates," *Paula Zahn Now*, November 4, 2003, online at http://www-cgi.cnn.com/TRANSCRIPTS/0311/04/pzn.00.html (accessed January 12, 2005).

81. John Kerry.com, "Building a Stronger America," online at http://www.johnkerry.com/about/john_kerry/vision.html (accessed January 12, 2005).

82. Jonathan E. Kaplan, "The NASCAR Voter That Never Was," *The Hill*, October 13, 2004, 1, online at http://academic.lexisnexis.com/ (accessed December 1, 2004).

83. Appelo, "The NASCARing of the Northwest," 2.

84. Susan J. Douglas and Meredith W. Michaels, *The Mommy Myth: The Idealization of Motherhood and How It Has Undermined Women* (New York: Free Press, 2004), 4.

85. Miriam Cooke and Angela Woollacott, eds., *Gendering War Talk* (Princeton, N.J.: Princeton University Press, 1993), xii.

86. See Jo Mannies, "Laura Bush Rally Spotlights Appeals to Women Voters: Democrats Get Ready to Mobilize This Week," *St. Louis Post-Dispatch*, August 18, 2004, 2, online at http://academic.lexisnexis.com/ (accessed November 18, 2004); Carla Marinucci, "Terror Concerns Move More Women into Bush Camp," *San Francisco Chronicle*, September 22, 2004, 1, online at http://academic.lexisnexis.com/ (accessed November 18, 2004); and CNN.com., "Can Kerry Turn Iraq on Bush? Campaigns Target Security Moms . . . ," *Paula Zahn Now*, September 23, 2004, 1, online at http://academic.lexisnexis.com/ (accessed November 18, 2004).

87. Mary Douglas Vavrus, *Postfeminist News: Political Women in Media Culture* (New York: State University of New York Press, 2002), 113.

88. "'Security Moms' Not the 'Soccer Moms' of 2004," *U.S. Newswire*, September 28, 2004, 1, online at http://academic.lexisnexis.com/ (accessed November 18, 2004); and Richard Louv, "Myth of the 'Security Mom,'" *San Diego Union-Tribune*, October 3, 2004, 2, online at http://academic.lexisnexis.com/ (accessed November 18, 2004).

89. See Marinucci, "Terror Concerns Move More Women," 1; John Seewer, "Laura Bush Touts President's Tax Relief Plans in Toledo," *Associated Press*, August 9, 2004, 1, online at http://academic.lexisnexis.com/ (accessed November 18, 2004); Ken Fireman, "'Security Moms' in Suburbs," *Newsday*, September 26, 2004, 3, online at http://academic.lexisnexis.com/ (accessed November 18, 2004); and Lynn Sweet, "Courting the Ladies," *Chicago-Sun Times*, October 13, 2004, 1, online at http://academic.lexisnexis.com/ (accessed November 18, 2004).

90. Charles Hurt, "Kerry Losing Ground with Women, *Washington Times*, September 29, 2004, 2, online at http://academic.lexisnexis.com/ (accessed November 18, 2004).

91. See Alicia Colon, "Security Moms Tilting toward President Bush," *New York Sun*, October 15, 2004, 1, online at http://academic.lexisnexis.com/ (accessed November 18, 2004). See also Kathleen Megan, "'Security' Parents," *Hartford Courant*,

October 30, 2004, 1, online at http://academic.lexisnexis.com/ (accessed November 18, 2004); and Al Swanson, "Analysis: 'Security' Moms Decided Election," UPI, November 12, 2004, 1, online at http://academic.lexisnexis.com/ (accessed November 18, 2004).

92. "Security Moms: Doomsday Is Haunting Election Day," *Philadelphia Inquirer*, September 27, 2004, 1, online at http://academic.lexisnexis.com/ (accessed November 18, 2004).

93. Jen Stephan, "Single Women Have Political Life beyond Shoes," *Pitt News*, October 21, 2004, 2, online at http://academic.lexisnexis.com/ (accessed November 18, 2004).

94. Peter Roff, "Analysis: Security Moms May Swing Election," UPI, September 23, 2004, online at http://academic.lexisnexis.com/ (accessed November 18, 2004).

95. Werner Trieschmann, "Rep's Prize-Winning Sleeper Tells Story of 'Security Mom,'" *Arkansas Democrat-Gazette*, October 24, 2004, 1, online at http://academic.lexisnexis.com/ (accessed November 18, 2004).

96. Douglas and Michaels, *The Mommy Myth*, 6–7. Such intensive mothering trends, of course, are not new and are visible as well in the earliest years of the Cold War, where issues of domesticity, motherhood, and safety were conflated in political and popular culture. See May, *Homeward Bound*.

97. Marinucci, "Terror Concerns Move More Women into Bush Camp," 2.

98. "Security Moms: Doomsday is Haunting Election Day," 1.

99. Michelle Malkin, "Candidates Ignore 'Security Moms,' at Their Peril," *USA Today*, July 21, 2004, 1, online at http://academic.lexisnexis.com/ (accessed November 18, 2004).

100. Roff, "Analysis: Security Moms May Swing Election," 1.

101. Malkin, "Candidates Ignore 'Security Moms,'" 1.

102. Ellen Goodman, "Hard-Pressed Moms May Decide It: They Have Strong, but Conflicted, Political Opinions," *Charleston Gazette*, July 31, 2004, 2, online at http://academic.lexisnexis.com/ (accessed November 18, 2004).

103. Linda Feldmann, "Why Women Are Edging toward Bush," *Christian Science Monitor*, September 23, 2004, 2, online at http://academic.lexisnexis.com/ (accessed November 18, 2004).

104. "Security Moms Big Swing Voter Group in This Election," *NBC Nightly News*, September 28, 2004, 2, online at http://academic.lexisnexis.com/ (accessed November 18, 2004).

105. Paul Brownfield, "In a Rigid Setting: Two Projections of the Father Image," *Los Angeles Times*, October 1, 2004, 1, online at http://academic.lexisnexis.com/ (accessed November 18, 2004).

106. Philip A. Klinkner, "Deflating the 'Security Mom' Angle," *Newsday*, October 5, 2005, 1, online at http://academic.lexisnexis.com/ (accessed November 18, 2004).

107. Goodman, "Hard-Pressed Moms May Decide It," 2.

108. Susan Page, "Married? Single? Status Affects How Women Vote," *USA Today*, August 26, 2004, 3, online at http://academic.lexisnexis.com/ (accessed November 18, 2004).

109. Marinucci, "Terror Concerns Move More Women into Bush Camp," 1.

110. Stephan, "Single Women Have Political Life beyond Shoes," 2.

111. Goodman, "Hard-Pressed Moms May Decide It," 2.

112. Katherine Q. Seelye, "Kerry Tries to Win Back Natural Allies—Women," *New York Times*, September 23, 2004, 2, online at http://academic.lexisnexis.com/ (accessed November 18, 2004).

113. Alicia Colon, "Security Moms Tilting toward President Bush," *New York Sun*, October 15, 2004, 1–2, online at http://academic.lexisnexis.com/ (accessed November 18, 2004).

114. Doug Rossinow, *The Politics of Authenticity: Liberalism, Christianity, and the New Left in America* (New York: Columbia University Press, 1998), 298.

115. Lynnell Mickelsen, "Democrats Need to Stop Playing the Nice Girl Rules," *Star Tribune*, September 5, 2004, online at http://academic.lexisnexis.com/ (accessed November 18, 2004).

116. Frank Rich, "How Kerry Became a Girlie-Man," *New York Times*, September 5, 2004, 1, online at http://academic.lexisnexis.com/ (accessed September 24, 2004).

117. Mothers Opposing Bush, "Mothers Opposing Bush: About Us," online at http://www.mob.org/_new/_pages/about/_ab_about_us?intro.htm/ (accessed December 1, 2004).

118. "Sister of U.S. Soldier Killed in Search for WMD Slams Bush for Crude Joke," *U.S. Newswire*, October 22, 2004, 1, online at http://academic.lexisnexis.com/ (accessed October 25, 2004).

119. Miriam Cooke, "Wo-man, Retelling the War Myth," in *Gendering War Talk*, ed. *Miriam Cooke and Angela Woollacott* (Princeton, N.J.: Princeton University Press, 1993), 178.

120. See Guida West and Rhoda Lois Blumberg, eds., *Women and Social Protest* (New York: Oxford, 1990), 205.

121. See Page, "Married? Single? Status Affects How Women Vote," 4; Trish Regan, "Efforts to Register and Urge Single Women to Vote," CBS's *The Early Show*, September 6, 2004, 1, online at http://academic.lexisnexis.com/ (accessed

November 18, 2004); and Grace Helms, "Single Women Count, Too," *Badger Herald*, September 15, 2004, 1, online at http://academic.lexisnexis.com/ (accessed November 18, 2004).

122. See Margaret Bernstein, "Courting Unmarried, Nonvoting Women; Experts: Untapped Bloc Could Decide Election," *Cleveland Plain Dealer*, June 20, 2004, 1, online at http://academic.lexisnexis.com/ (accessed November 18, 2004); and "Single Women Should Use Their Power at the Polls," *Allentown (Pa.) Morning Call* , July 7, 2004, 1, online at http://academic.lexisnexis.com/ (accessed November 18, 2004).

123. Page, "Married? Single? Status Affects How Women Vote," 1.

124. Page, "Married? Single? Status Affects How Women Vote," 1.

125. Melissa Fletcher Stoeltje, "Single Women Aren't Married to Voting Booth: 22 Million Who Skipped 2000 Election Are Untapped Market," *San Antonio Express-News*, July 25, 2004, 1, online at http://academic.lexisnexis.com/ (accessed November 18, 2004).

126. Michele Jacklin, "Single Women: The Overlooked Constituency," *Hartford Courant*, July 28, 2004, online at http://academic.lexisnexis.com/ (accessed November 18, 2004).

127. Helms, "Single Women Count, Too," 2; Jacklin, "Single Women: The Overlooked Constituency," 1; "New Poll Shows Women's Vote Critical in Final Days," *PR Newswire*, October 25, 2004, 1–3, online at http://academic.lexisnexis.com/ (accessed November 18, 2004); and Stoeltje, "Single Women Aren't Married to Voting Booths," 1.

129. Melissa Trujillo, "Women Using Visits, Phone Calls to Encourage Single Women to Vote," *Associated Press*, October 3, 2004, 1, online at http://academic.lexisnexis.com/ (accessed November 18, 2004).

130. Renee Busby, "Voter Registration Drives Target Single Women," *Associated Press*, September 4, 2004, 2, online at http://academic.lexisnexis.com/ (accessed November 18, 2004).

131. See Stoeltje, "Single Women Aren't Married to Voting Booths," 2; and Stephanie R. Jones, "Come Here Often?—Apparently Not: Single Women Vote in Lower Numbers Than Other Demographic Group, But That May be Changing," *The Commercial Appeal* (Memphis), September 26, 2004, 1, online at http://academic.lexisnexis.com/ (accessed November 18, 2004).

132. See Jones, "Come Here Often?" 2; and Alexander Starr, "Desperately Seeking Single Women," *Business Week*, June 21, 2004, 1, online at http://academic.lexisnexis.com/ (accessed November 18, 2004).

133. Jane Ganahl, "Query for Candidates: Is Hope on the Way for Single Women?" *San Francisco Chronicle*, August 8, 2004, online at http://academic.lexisnexis.com/ (accessed November 18, 2004).

134. See DePaulo, "Sex and the Single Voter," 1; and Ganahl, "Query for Candidates: Is Hope on the Way for Single Women?" 1.

135. See Starr, "Desperately Seeking Single Women Voters," 1; and Carla Marinucci, "Courting the Single Female Voter," *San Francisco Chronicle*, May 23, 2004, 1, online at http://academic.lexisnexis.com/ (accessed November 18, 2004).

136. See Bernstein, "Courting Unmarried, Nonvoting Women," 1–3; April Bethea, "Single Women Want to Hear about Health Care, Jobs," *Dayton Daily News*, September 29, 2004, 1, online at http://academic.lexisnexis.com/ (accessed November 18, 2004); Dan Rather, "Presidential Candidates Seek the Votes of Single Women," *CBS Evening News*, October 5, 2004, 1, online at http://academic.lexisnexis.com/ (accessed November 18, 2004); Charles Osgood, "Single Women Often Don't Vote," *The Osgood File*, October 6, 2004, 1, online at http://academic.lexisnexis.com/ (accessed November 18, 2004); Dana Calvo, "Stars Shine Light on Potent Voting Block: Single Women," *Los Angeles Times*, October 8, 2004, 1, online at http://academic.lexisnexis.com/ (accessed November 18, 2004); and "MapInfo Profiles Undecided Women Voters in Battleground States," *Business Wire*, October 12, 2004, 1, online at http://academic.lexisnexis.com/ (accessed November 18, 2004).

137. Stoeltje, "Single Women Aren't Married to Voting Booth," 1.

138. Jennifer Christman, "What's in a Dame: Something Old, New, Borrowed and . . . Red?" *Arkansas Democrat-Gazette*, August 31, 2004, 1, online at http://academic.lexisnexis.com/ (accessed November 18, 2004).

139. Ganahl, "Will Candidates' Sex Appeal Sway Single Women Voters?" 1–2.

140. Renee Busby, "Voter Registration Drives Target Single Women," *Associated Press*, September 4, 2004, online at http://academic.lexisnexis.com/ (accessed November 18, 2004).

141. Jones, "Come Here Often?" 1–2.

142. "Jennifer Aniston Urges Single Women to Vote," *U.S. Newswire*, October 4, 2004, 1, online at http://academic.lexisnexis.com/ (accessed November 18, 2004); Calvo, "Stars Shine Light on a Potential Voting Bloc," 1–2; and Starr, "Desperately Seeking Single Women Voters," 1.

143. DePaulo, "Sex and the Single Voter," 1; and Marinucci, "Courting the Single Voter," 1–3.

144. It is important to note that some journalists, while positive about the attempts to target single women, were likewise critical of the tendency to overlook the

number of single women who were poorer. See Michele Norris, "Single Women as a Force in the Presidential Election," NPR, July 5, 2004, 1, online at http://academic.lexisnexis.com/ (accessed November 18, 2004); and Swanee Hunt, "Moms on the Margins: Your Country Needs You," *Scripps Howard News Service,* 1, online at http://academic.lexisnexis.com/ (accessed November 18, 2004).

145. Yuval-Davis, *Gender and Nation,* 39.

146. Helms, "Single Women Count, Too," 2. See also Busby, "Voter Registration Drives Target Single Women," 1–3; and Jones, "Come Here Often?" 1–3.

147. Vavrus, *Postfeminist News,* 23.

148. Bonnie J. Dow, *Prime-Time Feminism: Television, Media Culture, and the Women's Movement since 1970* (Philadelphia: University of Pennsylvania Press, 1996), 88.

149. Marinucci, "Courting the Single Female Voter," 2.

150. John Collins and Ross Glover, eds., *Collateral Language: A User's Guide to America's New War* (New York: New York University Press, 2002), 9.

151. Murray Edelman, *Constructing the Political Spectacle* (Chicago: University of Chicago Press, 1988), 104.

152. Jasinski, "A Constitutive Framework for Rhetorical Historiography," 80.

153. Mary E. Stuckey, *Defining Americans: The Presidency and National Identity* (Lawrence: University Press of Kansas, 2004), 7.

154. DeConde, *Presidential Machismo,* 5.

155. Walter Russell Mead, *Special Providence: American Foreign Policy and How It Changed the World* (New York: Routledge, 2002), 220–21. See also James K. Oliver, "The Foreign Policy Presidency after the Cold War: New Uncertainty and Old Problems," in *The Post-Cold War Presidency,* ed. Anthony J. Eksterowicz and Glenn P. Hastedt (Lanham, Md.: Rowman & Littlefield Publishers, 1999), 35–36.

156. There are risks, of course, for such a masculine and militarized presidentiality. Should a president fail in such protective tasks, he may well lose the mythic allure of omnipotence that has become central to presidential ethos in wartime. Also, congressional or state campaigns lack the media spectacle of presidential contests that entice people to become engaged in the voting process, making the representative role of government less inspirational for citizens.

157. Etienne Balibar, *Politics and the Other Scene,* translated by Christine Jones, James Swenson, and Chris Turner (London: Verso, 2002), 61.

158. Otto Bauer, "The Nation," in *Mapping the Nation,* ed. Gopal Balakrishnan (London: Verso, 1996), 63.

159. Gerard A. Hauser and Amy Grim, eds., "Rhetorical Democracy and Civic Engagement," in *Rhetorical Democracy: Discursive Practices of Civic Engagement* (Mahwah, N.J.: Lawrence Erlbaum, 2004), 12.

160. Amy Gutmann discusses research that suggests the independent voter may be less informed about political issues and less interested in U.S. political practice. See *Identity in Democracy* (Princeton, N.J.: Princeton University Press, 2003), 4.

161. Gutmann, *Identity in Democracy*, 4.

162. Hart, *Campaign Talk*, 80.

163. Certainly, the campaigns did not forget about the need to turn out their base. However, to the extent that the decided voters are no longer newsworthy for journalists, the swing voter in the battleground state becomes the site of potential news and political uncertainty. As the candidates work to influence the undecided voters, their energies too become preoccupied in the general election with those yet to make up their minds, even as their campaigns work diligently to get their base to the polls. Evan Thomas of *Newsweek* argues that Karl Rove, the primary architect of the Bush campaign, believed the key to the 2004 election was to get out the swing voters. In the aftermath of the 2004 presidential campaign, the Christian Right voter grew in importance when many exit pollsters concluded that such conservative voters influenced the final outcome of the vote. See Evan Thomas, *Election 2004: How Bush Won and What You Can Expect in the Future* (New York: Public Affairs, 2004), 168–69.

164. Ian F. Haney López, *White By Law: The Construction of Race* (New York: New York University Press, 1996), 162.

165. Victor Burgin, *In/Different Spaces: Place and Memory in Visual Culture* (Berkeley: University of California Press, 1996), 130.

166. Todd Gitlin, *The Twilight of Common Dreams: Why America Is Wracked by Culture Wars* (New York: Henry Holt, 1995), 227. It is important to note that Gitlin is very critical of the move away from a politics of equality to a politics of identity.

167. For a discussion of the transition from a politics of equality to a politics of diversity and identity in U.S. political culture during the 1960s, 1970s, and beyond, see Rossinow, *The Politics of Authenticity*; and Bruce Shulman, *The Seventies: The Great Shift in American Culture, Society, and Politics* (New York: The Free Press, 2001).

168. Gutmann, *Identity in Democracy*, 4, 43.

169. Based on survey data, Penny S. Visser et al. conclude that many voters who identify themselves as undecided have a particular preference for a candidate when asked to make a decision, further challenging the indecisiveness of the undecided voter. See Penny S. Visser, Jon A. Krosnick, Jesse F. Marquette, and Michael F. Curtin, "Improving Election Forecasting: Allocation of Undecided Respondents, Identification of Likely Voters, and Response Order Effects," in

Election Polls, the News Media, and Democracy, ed. Paul J. Lavrakas and Michael W. Traugott (New York: Chatham House Publishers, 2000), 224–60.

170. Hart, *Campaign Talk*, 229, 230.

7

Debating "The Means of Apocalypse": The Defense Science Board, the Military-Industrial Complex, and the Production of Imperial Propaganda

Stephen John Hartnett and Greg Goodale

The Defense Science Board (DSB) is the most powerful institution you have never heard of. As of January 2007, its "32 members and seven ex-officio members," overseeing working groups known as Task Forces, were in the process of producing fifteen blue-ribbon reports on such topics as "Nuclear Weapons Effects National Enterprise"[*sic*], "Directed Energy," "Nuclear Deterrence Skills," "Defense Biometrics Program," "Improvised Explosive Devices," and "Critical Homeland Infrastructure Protection," thus amounting to a catalog of the nation's military concerns. Such reports are written to advise the Defense Department (DoD) regarding "the fields of science, technology and its application in military operations, research, engineering, manufacturing, and acquisition."[1] From its founding at the heart of the Cold War in 1956 up through its current role in producing reports about the U.S. occupation of Iraq, the DSB has played a complicated role, not only fulfilling an advisory capacity, but in many cases functioning as a weapons-program catalyst, a procurement advocate, and sometimes a policy critic. An elite think tank contributing to planning U.S. military operations—think of it as a part of the brain of the military-industrial complex—the DSB is one of the many government organizations, private contractors, and multinational corporations advising the DoD regarding the development of weapons systems, operational strategies, and propaganda campaigns for current and future wars.[2] Tracking the activities of the DSB therefore means studying the intellectual architects of the U.S.' global military dominance, the Washington elites whose work, even while ostensibly conducted on our behalf, takes place largely behind closed doors. Analyzing the DSB amounts, then, to a case study in the balancing (or unbalancing) of the delicate relationship between national security and democratic deliberation.[3]

More than a think tank for military planning, however, the DSB is also one of the Washington institutions that play crucial roles in shaping U.S. public discourse about foreign policy. For example, numerous scholars have noted how, from 9/11 to the close of its first term in office, the Bush administration portrayed the Global War on Terrorism (GWT) as a struggle against enemies opposed not to specific U.S. foreign policies, but to the broad contours of modern Western life. Even while explicitly denying the charge, the Bush administration relied upon rhetorical strategies pointing toward what Samuel Huntington famously characterized as a "clash of civilizations." The DSB's September 2004 *Report of the Defense Science Board Task Force on Strategic Communication* found, however, that such arguments are contrivances, and that foreign anger toward the United States is not directed at our values, but at specific military and economic policies. In response to these findings, however, the DSB's *Strategic Communication* report did not propose changes in U.S. foreign policy; rather, it called for the production of new propaganda intended to make those policies more palatable to the world. It is not clear if the DSB's report catalyzed action in the White House or simply reflected changes that were already in the air in Washington, but beginning in the autumn of 2004 and building momentum up to President Bush's State of the Union address on February 2, 2005, the Bush administration dramatically shifted rhetorical strategies, turning from "clash of civilizations" attacks against terrifying Others to trumpeting the genius of freedom and democracy; swaggering anger was replaced with benevolent cheerleading for the American way. The DSB's *Strategic Communication* report called for this rhetorical transformation and hence, whether as catalyst or bellwether, marks a significant change in the tenor of post-9/11 U.S. political discourse.[4]

Because the DSB is an institution most Americans have never heard of, and because its leaders are not found giving public speeches, its work falls outside the purview of what rhetorical and public-address scholars have traditionally considered relevant objects of analysis. However, given the DSB's historical role in shaping U.S. military policy, and given its more recent roles in both theorizing about and organizing the production of post-9/11 propaganda—and hence U.S. public address—the DSB surely demands attention from those of us concerned with the norms of democratic deliberation. Addressing the DSB as part of a rhetorical critique of U.S. foreign policy responds to one of our field's learned incapacities—for as Bryan Taylor has argued, "Speech communication scholars have been shy about studying the actual military and industrial institutions involved in producing the Cold War. While they have persistently scrutinized the elite rhetors of government and science, they have been less attentive to the mundane and rationalized interactions occurring on factory floors, in Pentagon offices, and down-below in missile-silos. And with good reason: these hidden places of power have been well-defended and mystified by coercive secrecy rules and heavily-armed security forces."[5]

While noting his colleagues' reticence in tackling these "hidden places of power," Taylor's hard-nosed digging through the "military and industrial institutions involved in producing the Cold War" and its aftermath provides compelling evidence of how to merge fine-tuned rhetorical criticism of public texts with investigative work on the institutions that make such texts possible. Thus, following Taylor's lead (and the leads of others, to whom we turn below), we propose here to study the institutional parameters of public address about the military-industrial complex, and hence to explore the intricate relationships between backroom deals and public speaking, between budgetary imperatives and philosophical questions, between institutions and individual actors, between military policies abroad and democratic practices at home.[6]

Conducting such research has led us to conclude that the DSB is not only one of the architects of a foreign policy that we believe is imperialist in nature, but also one of the lead forces in an ongoing (and long-standing) battle between those who see national security as a necessarily secrecy-cloaked operation and those (like us) who believe it should be vetted according to the public norms of democratic deliberation.[7] For example, along with its 2004 *Strategic Communication* report's call for better propaganda, the DSB's 2002 study of *Special Operations and Joint Forces in*

Countering Terrorism called for deploying assassination teams and other clandestine military and paramilitary operations planned outside the rubric of congressional oversight. As Chalmers Johnson has observed, such proposals "threaten to institutionalize the acts behind the Iran-Contra scandal of the 1980s as a way of life." Indeed, whereas the DSB's 2002 *Special Operations* report proposes to subvert congressional norms of checks and balances by pursuing secret means of military dominance, its 2004 *Strategic Communication* report calls for spinning such actions via enhanced propaganda efforts; the DSB thus stands as a threat to preserving any sense of democratic deliberation regarding U.S. foreign policy.[8]

The DSB does not act alone in this regard, of course, as observers have charged a variety of actors with degrading the norms of democratic deliberation. For example, Russell Baker has characterized Washington, D.C., as sinking, under the Bush White House's leadership, into "an age of moral and philosophical sterility." Expanding from Washington to the nation as a whole, Wendell Berry has argued that post-9/11 America has slouched toward a "new strategy" of politics that "depends on the acquiescence of a public kept fearful and ignorant, subject to manipulation by the executive power, and on the compliance of an intimidated and office-dependent legislature." Joan Didion has diagnosed the nation as suffering from an "enthusiasm for bellicose fantasy." For Baker, Berry, and Didion, respected longtime observers of our national scene, post-9/11 America has lost its habit of reveling in the messy and sometimes ennobling elegance of public debate, instead succumbing to the communication dilemmas noted above.[9] As Lisa Keranen, the Union of Concerned Scientists, and others have argued, the practical consequences of this loss of deliberation are especially damaging to science, which requires robust idea testing and countertesting—all premised on the norms of democratic deliberation—to rise to standards of verifiability that transcend political whimsy. From this perspective, losing our sense of what it means to celebrate and engage in public deliberation—especially about the life-and-death matters of foreign policy and science—leaves the nation with a government that, according to Berry, "cannot be democratic," and a citizenry that cannot be free.[10]

To track the DSB's complicated roles in these processes, this essay unfolds in four stages. First, we offer a brief history of the DSB's Cold War founding, hence situating the institution within the military, scientific, economic, and rhetorical struggles against communism. Second, to review the DSB's more contemporary incarnations, we track its role in shaping public discourse in the age of President Ronald Reagan's Star Wars program. Third, to follow the DSB into post-9/11 American life, we turn to its 2004 *Strategic Communication* report, where the DSB calls for a new age of imperial propaganda. To situate the DSB's report within the wider body of public deliberation about the GWT, we review President George W. Bush's early post-9/11 comments on the subject, hence establishing the "clash of civilizations" theme, and then analyze the dramatic rhetorical change in the president's speaking following the release of the DSB *Strategic Communication* report. Fourth, to raise the intellectual and political stakes of the essay, we appeal to rhetorical and public-address scholars to rethink what we mean by democratic deliberation and rhetorical criticism; this final section of the essay challenges our colleagues to think more creatively about the circulation of power, the institutional frameworks that enable public arguments, and the relationship between textual criticism and imperial domination.

The Defense Science Board: Its Pre-History and Cold War Founding

It should be stated at the outset that the DSB fulfills an important role: no nation of our size and importance can survive long without professional intelligence and military apparatuses. If it is not to fall into the hands of cronies and charlatans, the nation's intelligence and military capabilities must be professionalized and their modes of procurement rationalized according to democratic norms of public checks and balances. Such claims appear obvious, yet this has not always been the case. During the U.S. Revolutionary War, for example, just about everyone who could charge extortionate prices—whether for food, horses, guns, or ammunition, or beer for the troops, or via inflated interest on loans for the effort—did so. By December 1778, George Washington was trembling with rage at the ways the war effort was being hampered by profiteering; in fact, he wrote a letter to Joseph Reed calling for "bringing those murderers of our cause (the monopolizers, forestallers, and engrossers) to condign punishment." Using a metaphor usually reserved for dehumanizing Indians, Washington seethed, "It is much to be lamented that each state long ere this has not hunted them down as the pests of society." Illustrating his then-famous but since-largely-forgotten penchant for employing murderous violence as a means of coercing allegiance, Washington went so far as to offer a prayer to "God that one of the most atrocious of each State was hung in Gibbets upon a gallows. . . . No punishment in my opinion is too great for the Man who can build his greatness upon his Country's ruin." The future president thus proposed public hangings and mutilations for war profiteers. By the time of the U.S. Civil War, President Abraham Lincoln hoped to avoid such unsightly punishments, in part by organizing the research and development of the Union's army under the leadership of the National Academy of Science (NAS, founded in 1863).[11]

As the U.S. waged ever more complicated wars with ever more complicated weapons, and as the pace of scientific discovery accelerated exponentially, general advisory bodies like the NAS became obsolete. Hence, in 1944 the U.S. Air Force established its Air Force Advisory Board, in 1946 the navy launched its Naval Research Advisory Committee, and then in 1951 the army founded its Army Science Advisory Panel. During roughly this same period, Congress formed overarching organizations as well, including in 1940 the National Defense Research Committee, which was superseded in 1941 by the Office of Scientific Research and Development (OSRD), which was then subsumed in 1947 by the Research and Development Board. The formation of these bodies was driven both by a pragmatic desire to provide the U.S. military with the best available technology and by a strain of thinking perhaps best described as the "technological sublime." For example, in his now canonical 1945 "The Endless Frontier" essay, Vannevar Bush argued that "Advances in science when put to practical use mean more jobs, higher wages, shorter hours, more abundant crops, more leisure for recreation, for study, for learning how to live without the deadening drudgery which has been the burden of the common man for ages past. Advances in science will also bring higher standards of living . . . and will assure means of defense against aggression." Bush was the wartime director of the OSRD and among the most important figures advocating for founding the institutions and arguments that eventually coalesced in the military-industrial complex. Written at the request of President Franklin D. Roosevelt, Bush's "Frontier" essay envisioned science as a sublime force capable of producing stunning achievements in almost every avenue of human existence. As we shall see when we turn to President Reagan's Star Wars program, this trope of the scientific sublime pervades military-industrial complex rhetoric, often draping military planning in visionary, even utopian tones.[12]

Despite Vannevar Bush's vision, the post–World War II multiplication of military-linked research-and-development boards, panels, and committees could not prevent the opportunism that drove George Washington into a murderous rage. For example, when President John Kennedy nominated John McCone to serve as director of the CIA in 1961, McCone's opponents focused on his former war-profiteering. McCone had made a killing during World War II, when his California Shipbuilding Company turned a $100,000 investment into $44 million worth of war-related business. Testifying before Congress in 1946 about McCone's wartime dealings, Ralph E. Casey of the General Accounting Office argued that "At no time in the history of American business, whether in wartime or peacetime, have so few men made so much money with so little risk and all at the expense of the taxpayers." (In addition to his shipbuilding profiteering, McCone had longstanding ties to international oil companies, leading some observers to question his ability to manage the CIA in an impartial manner; he was nonetheless confirmed for the position in January 1962.) Thus, from Washington's murderous rage in 1778 through Casey's lament in 1946 to McCone's contested nomination in 1961—to say nothing of the boondoggles unfolding in occupied Afghanistan and Iraq—Americans have worried about the ways profiteering clouds war planning and management, and about the ways capitalist opportunism compromises the national interest. It is therefore not difficult to discern how founding the DSB in 1956 was seen as a common-sense attempt to institutionalize relationships that had previously been made on the fly. From this perspective, you can see the logic: better to rationalize the scientific, military, and corporate relationships that will henceforward protect the nation than to see them subject to profiteering of the kind lamented by Washington and Casey.[13]

The April 1955 *Subcommittee Report on Research Activities in the Department of Defense and Defense Related Agencies* therefore responded to specific Cold War exigencies, Bush's vision of the technological sublime, and long-standing concerns about the efficiency of weapons planning. In its "Recommendation No. 5," the report argued that "the Assistant Secretary of Defense (Research and Development) [should] appoint a standing committee, reporting directly to him, of outstanding basic and applied scientists. This committee should canvass periodically the needs and opportunity for studies leading to *radically new weapons systems*." As a first step toward building such "radically new weapons systems," the DoD drafted the DSB charter in June 1956; although not formally approved until that December, the Defense Science Board convened its first meeting on September 20, 1956.[14]

That autumn found President Dwight Eisenhower straddling two contradictory trends. Internationally, the Cold War was in a shambles: China had fallen to communist forces, the Russians had gone nuclear, the Middle East was—then as now—a mess, the Korean peninsula bristled with hundreds of thousands of troops held in check by an armistice that left no one satisfied, and U.S. exports were down. The U.S. was thus mired in a grueling global war for international political, military, and economic supremacy. Domestically, however, the United States was enjoying an economic boom, fueled in part by defense spending (between 1950 and 1953, arms spending jumped from $14.3 billion to $49.3 billion), the rise of credit cards (Diners Club was founded in 1950, Carte Blanche in 1958, American Express and BankAmericard in 1959), and the emerging advertising industry. Supporting this alliance between weapons, manufactured needs, and expensive credit meant neglecting key aspects of domestic life. In fact, by 1951 U.S. corporations were spending as much as $6.5 billion on annual advertising fees, while the federal government was spending only $1.5 billion per year on schools. Thus, for Eisenhower in 1956—as for President Bush in 2007—the political task was trying to convince Americans to support foreign entanglements that did not help the domestic scene, while trying to persuade foreigners to welcome a U.S. lifestyle that was fraught with such contradictions as spending more money on manufacturing capitalism's latest silky desires than educating citizens to play responsible roles in the republic. The DSB was formed, then, in an era marked by the pressing needs to produce "radically new" Cold War weaponry, to accelerate the use of defense spending to spur domestic economic production, and to create more persuasive Cold War propaganda both at home and abroad.[15]

Within a year of the DSB's founding, the Cold War appeared to be slipping out of control. The Soviet's launching of Sputnik on October 4, 1957, greeted with a media barrage that accelerated general Cold War dismay, left many Americans wondering if the communists had surpassed U.S. technical capabilities. *Newsweek* stoked the concerns of many Americans when its first post-Sputnik cover promised answers to "Why We're Lagging." As David Henry has shown, President Eisenhower's initial response to this crisis was uninspiring and slow-footed, as it took a month

for Eisenhower to prepare his November 7, 1957, "Science in National Security" speech. The president's response was complicated by the fact that
he did not want to disclose information acquired via secret U-2 flights,
and so, in his nationally televised talk from the White House, Eisenhower
sought to decouple the Soviet Union's scientific achievement from any
presumed military superiority. Eisenhower also announced the appointment of James Killian, the president of MIT, as special assistant to the
president for Science and Technology. The president did not mention the
DSB in his speech, because at the time the organization was embroiled in
bitter DoD infighting; as Kevin Cunningham argues, the DSB was "lost in
the cross-currents of technological, political, and bureaucratic events." No
sleek juggernaut, the DSB appears at this early point in its history to be a
marginal player in an emerging, yet highly contested and organizationally
confused, military-industrial complex.[16]

At the same time as it was handling the political concerns triggered by
Sputnik, and while the DSB was in organizational turmoil, the Eisenhower
administration faced a budgetary crisis, for despite the escalating costs of
the Cold War, the Defense Department had pledged in 1957 not to raise
its annual budget. This fiscal cap on defense spending left the DoD scrambling to pay its bills, hence forcing it to shift considerable funds from R&D
to simple maintenance. Critics worried that shorting Cold War–related
R&D would have dire long-term consequences. In fact, the *New York Times*
reported in October 1957 that "there is a feeling in scientific and military circles that irreparable harm already has been done to the research
programs." To underscore that point, the *Times* printed this story with a
photograph of wide-eyed New Yorkers pressing against the window of the
New York Trade Center (then at Eighth Avenue and Thirty-Fifth Street)
to watch an oscilloscope tracking the Sputnik satellite. The story's textual
message and visual cues were clear: the U.S. was losing the fight for Cold
War scientific—and therefore military—supremacy.[17]

The *New York Times* thus observed in January 1958 that President
Eisenhower confronted "a hurricane of problems beating around him."
Along with the technical, scientific, and R&D issues raised above, another
key question was how to balance national-security needs against the deliberative practices that sustain U.S. democracy. In short, can democratic
deliberation survive war? The Cold War presented a complicated version
of this question, for while the U.S. desperately needed to forge ahead in
scientific discoveries in order to keep pace with Soviet developments, it

also felt compelled to keep scientific work under tight scrutiny—hence preventing leaks of useful information to Cold War enemies. Intellectual progress, however, requires open deliberation, meaning the trajectory of scientific discovery and Cold War concerns over secrecy were in constant tension. It comes as no surprise, then, to find the Eisenhower administration bristling at critics who charged that Cold War secrecy was hampering scientific discoveries and jeopardizing the health of democratic deliberation. For example, when Assistant Secretary of Defense Murray Snyder addressed the 1958 convention of the American Society of Newspaper Editors, he chastised the gathered newspaper men (for they were overwhelmingly men) for "the unfortunate tendency to characterize the valid exercise of considered judgment by responsible Government officials as an illegal or otherwise wrongful act." Translated, Snyder was arguing that censorship of matters relating to national security was justified, and that critics should grant the Eisenhower administration more slack when addressing its handling of the Cold War. J. Russell Wiggins, then editor of the *Washington Post*, responded by charging that a "secret voluntary war-time censorship agreement" had been made between some newspapers and the Eisenhower administration, hence trampling on the First Amendment and the free exchange of information that enables scientific advancement and healthy democratic deliberation.[18]

While showing up only rarely in the day's public arguments, the DSB, once it got its house in order, slowly became central to both of the crises addressed above. First, it created an institutional framework for funneling advanced technical work and cutting-edge economic developments into Cold War applications. Linking private sector to public sector, independent R&D to state-driven Cold War functions, the DSB harnessed the U.S.' best scientific minds to the needs of the state, hence institutionalizing the networks of knowledge and power that would come to be known as the military-industrial complex. Second, by publishing some—but not all—DSB reports, the government was able to create a sense of transparency, hence aping the norms of democratic deliberation even while the bulk of the DSB's work was conducted under the cover of national-security-driven secrecy.[19] President Eisenhower famously lamented the rise of the military-industrial complex in his 1961 Farewell Address (to which we turn below), yet the DSB, formed under his watch, was a key component in that process. Publicly fearing the same dilemma that he was privately creating was typical of Eisenhower's Cold War strategy, as he claimed to be pursuing peace while in fact, as Robert Ivie has put it, "institutional-izing an age of peril." Indeed, the gap here between public rhetoric and military-industrial-complex action is glaring, suggesting that even the president, that actor invested with such awesome rhetorical power, was compelled to respond to institutional forces beyond his control and out-side the purview of his public address.[20]

Locating Eisenhower in this delicate position, where he bemoans the rise of the military-industrial complex while institutionalizing the DSB's pursuit of "radically new weapons systems," should come as no surprise, for he is widely recognized as a hard-nosed politician who understood the difference between exercising power behind closed doors and justify-ing power in public forums. In fact, Eisenhower's use of psychological warfare was well known, especially after he appointed C. D. Jackson as his special assistant to the president for Psychological Warfare. Ivie has discovered a 1953 letter from Eisenhower to William Benton where the president admits that "The job of presenting the American story to the world. . . . must be done in many ways. And in most of it the hand of the government must be carefully concealed, and, in some cases I should say, wholly eliminated." Heard with this 1953 letter in mind, Eisenhower's 1961 warning about the rise of the military-industrial complex, intoned after founding the DSB, can be appreciated for its representative clarity: American interests would be advanced on the ground via "radically new weapons systems" developed by the DSB in particular, and the military-industrial complex in general, while "the American story" would be pro-mulgated in public address that bore little relation to the facts.[21]

We hope these opening historical comments further stoke the inter-est of communication scholars in the DSB, for studying this institution offers paths of insight into the inner—and contested—workings of the military-industrial complex, hence enabling us to garner a more com-plete picture of the ways U.S. foreign policy has been shaped since the Cold War. Unfortunately, however, and perhaps as a testament to the ways the military-industrial complex has shrouded much of its activity in secrecy, no communication scholar has written about the DSB, and only one monograph-length study (Cunningham's unpublished Ph.D. dissertation) has tackled the organization. Surely our understanding of the Cold War, Eisenhower's presidency, and the formation of the military-industrial complex would be enhanced by rectifying this glaring gap in our scholarship. Space does not permit us to provide a complete history here, yet by reviewing the early days of the DSB we have suggested that the institution has been linked, ever since its founding, with the needs of producing weapons, jump-starting domestic economic growth and scientific research via defense spending, and influencing the ways U.S. foreign policy is discussed in public. While our brief overview of the DSB's founding situates it within a Cold War narrative of superpowers dueling for technical (and hence military) supremacy, we also learn here that the DSB's function has always been rhetorical. Indeed, because the DSB helped to fulfill foreign-policy imperatives in ways that appeared to honor the norms of democratic deliberation even while burying them under a barrage of (some would say necessary) Cold War secrecy, the DSB stands among our nation's largely unseen but perpetually important forces shaping public arguments about U.S. foreign policy. Whereas Robert Hariman and John Lucaites, Cara Finnegan, Lester Olson, and others have begun mapping the forms of "visual citizenship," arguing about the public norms of looking and being seen that underwrite U.S. democracy, studying the DSB enables us to begin the process of mapping one of the structural *forces of invisibility*—one of those government organizations that shape public discourse while functioning largely behind closed doors.[22]

The DSB and the Military-Industrial Complex in the Age of Star Wars

By the early 1980s, the DSB had become an essential part of the very thing Eisenhower had warned against in his Farewell Address. Delivered January 17, 1961, the president observed that

> This conjunction of an immense military establishment and a large arms industry is new in the American experience. The total influence— economic, political, even spiritual—is felt in every city, every Statehouse, every office of the Federal government. . . . In the councils of government, we must guard against the acquisition of unwarranted influence, whether sought or unsought, by the military-industrial complex. . . . We must never let the weight of this combination endanger our liberties or democratic processes. . . . Only an alert and knowledgeable citizenry can compel the proper meshing of the huge industrial and military machine of defense with our peaceful methods and goals.[23]

The fact that Eisenhower saw the "total influence" of the military-industrial complex reaching even "spiritual" dimensions should alert us to just how powerful it had become by 1961. Despite Eisenhower's warning, ongoing Cold War tensions and then the Vietnam War drove the military-industrial complex's growth into a behemoth capable of undermining democracy itself.

In fact, by February of 1983, with President Ronald Reagan escalating tensions with the USSR—leading some scholars to call the period a *new* Cold War—the *New York Times* reported that "The Reagan administration is cutting social programs for the poor and whittling away entitlement programs for the middle class, but it seems determined to pour ever larger amounts of money into scientific research." Given the barrage of encomiums to President Reagan following his death on June 5, 2004, we should note that what the *Times* called "cutting social programs for the poor" was in fact part of one of the largest transfers of wealth in the modern world. In fact, based on his analysis of information provided by the Congressional Budget Office, Mike Davis reports that between 1980 and 1984, cuts in programs for the poor cost them $23 billion in lost income and benefits, while tax cuts for the rich enabled them to pocket $35 billion.[24] While orchestrating this redistribution of wealth away from the poor and into the hands of the rich, President Reagan pushed through Congress a federal budget in 1983 that allocated $47 billion for research and development, with 70 percent of this money going to military-industrial-complex projects (and as much as 25 percent of that money going to his home state of California alone). Garry Wills has referred to this ballooning weapons-research budget as part of President Reagan's first term "spending spree." In fact, between 1980 and 1985, President Reagan's defense budget jumped from $196.9 billion to $296.1 billion.[25]

The Strategic Defense Initiative (SDI) was among President Reagan's favored spending-spree items; mockingly referred to by critics as Star Wars, hence linking the president's plan to the popular science-fiction films, SDI was a space-based anti-missile system that would supposedly use nuclear-powered x-ray lasers to shoot down incoming Soviet rockets, hence ending the age of nuclear terror and ushering in an age of guaranteed safety. Few scientists believed SDI would do what was proposed; an anonymous Reagan science advisor confessed to Robert Scheer that White House speechwriters had spent the final days before the president's March 23, 1983, speech announcing the program scrambling to find some rationale for Star Wars. "The whole thing was just nutty," the unnamed source revealed, "because it was content free—it was a challenge to the technical community to go invent something."[26] While SDI was "nutty" as an actual weapons proposal, it nonetheless offered an attractive rhetorical strategy: imagine, an impenetrable defensive shield that would make nuclear-tipped rockets useless, hence amounting to a weapon for peace, an end to fear! In fact, during a preliminary White House meeting regarding Star Wars on September 14, 1981, Edward Teller counseled President Reagan to argue for Star Wars as a way of ending the capricious reign of Mutually Assured Destruction (MAD) with a program of "assured survival." While this pie-in-the-sky (or lasers-in-the-sky) fantasy of "assured survival" was not believed by most scientists or defense experts, Wills has noted that the fantasy was useful for a number of political reasons, as it enabled the U.S. government to "take the next step in weapons technology, to establish supremacy in space, to frighten the Russians, to force them into overspending, to weaken their economic system, to please American contractors and entice those in other countries, [and] to keep America number one in science." Thus, much like President Eisenhower's capitalizing upon his largely manufactured "age of peril" to found the DSB and institutionalize the military-industrial complex, so President Reagan's SDI provided cover for a range of activities, few of which had much to do with making nuclear weapons obsolete. As Wills notes wryly, "All these motives were jostling along together under the cover of the Reagan fairy tale, each gaining advantages so long as the fairy tale was neither questioned *nor taken seriously.*"[27]

David Meyer has argued that by claiming the rhetorical high ground of hoping to make nuclear weapons irrelevant, SDI enabled Reagan to outflank anti-nuclear-weapons and peace activists. In fact, Gordon Mitchell has obtained a copy of "High Frontier: A New Option in Space," a classified Heritage Foundation report that circulated in the White House in the early days of Star Wars, where the authors argue that SDI would enable the president to "unambiguously seek to recapture the term 'arms control' and all of the idealistic images and language attached to this term." Acknowledging that the science needed to propel SDI was lagging behind the president's dreamy vision, "High Frontier" argues that Star Wars "will be driven by ethical urgency rather than by technological availability." "High Frontier" thus proposes SDI not as a functional weapons systems, but as a rhetorical device for countering the arguments made by anti-nuclear activists.[28] The president desperately needed to engage this rhetorical struggle, for by the early 1980s the peace and anti-nuclear movements were peaking. Elise Boulding has studied these movements, concluding that by 1983 the United States was home to 140 chapters of the Women's International League for Peace and Freedom, 83 of the Fellowship of Reconciliation, 47 of the American Friends Service Committee, 32 of the War Resisters League, 26 of SANE, 132 of Mobilization for Survival, 52 of Clergy and Laity Concerned, 109 of Freeze Campaign, 80 of Jobs with Peace, and 40 of Women's Action for Nuclear Disarmament—and this list just scratches the surface of groups mobilizing against the foreign policies and nuclear ambitions of the Reagan administration.[29]

The rising power of these peace and anti-nuke groups helps to explain President Reagan's March 23, 1983, nationally televised address, where, despite the fact that the science involved was nothing less than "nutty," he unveiled Star Wars as "a new hope for our children in the 21st century." Co-opting the language of activists, President Reagan argued that Star Wars would "give us the means of rendering these nuclear weapons impotent and obsolete." Thus repeating the same strategy employed by President Eisenhower in his 1961 Farewell Address and by President Bush in his 2005 Fort Hood speech (to which we turn below), President Reagan opened a new frontier of military-industrial-complex spending and propaganda by claiming that he was seeking peace: "Our only purpose—one all people share—is to search for ways to reduce the danger of nuclear war."[30]

While Star Wars sought to enable President Reagan to counteract the surging popularity of peace and anti-nuclear groups, it played an economic role as well. For the domestic economy was in a shambles: January 1982 found the United States suffering an unemployment rate of 8.9 percent, a figure reported by William Broad as "the second highest monthly level since the start of World War II." Facing a successful anti-nuclear-weapons movement fueled by citizens tired of living under the shadow of nuclear war and millions of Americans worn down from living within a crumbling economy, SDI provided both a rhetorical blast of hope and a national-security-driven excuse for redoubling the use of military Keynesianism to jump-start the economy. For while few key players—other than the president and perhaps Edward Teller—actually believed SDI would ever do what it was supposed to do, and while its chief functions were therefore rhetorical rather than military, Star Wars opened the floodgates for an unprecedented rush of weapons research and contracts, hopefully serving as a gravitational force for pulling the U.S. economy out of its doldrums. Broad accordingly characterizes these early days of Star Wars as "a scientific free-for-all, a license to spend tens of billions of dollars as creatively as possible." Although he campaigned on promises of getting Big Government off the backs of everyday Americans, President Reagan's Star Wars initiative thus amounted, as Thomas McCormick has put it, to "Keynesian pump-priming with a vengeance."[31]

The Star Wars "free-for-all" funded a remarkable number of boon-doggles (which Broad chronicles with gleeful venom) and led to a number of scandals, including the revelation in the pages of the *New York Times* in April 1983 that "the principal owner of a small laser company that could benefit from President Reagan's program to develop a futuristic missile defense system has given or offered company stock now valued at mil-lions of dollars to leading scientific and military experts and others with connections to the Reagan Administration." The *Times* reported that Dr. Edward Teller—known as the father of the hydrogen bomb; the founder of the Lawrence Livermore National Laboratory in Berkeley, California; a member of President Reagan's White House Science Council; and the figure widely credited with persuading the president to pursue Star Wars in the first place—held "a financial stake currently valued at more than $800,000" in the company. While offering company stocks as induce-ments to influence policymakers is illegal, the story also focused on the dealings of Helionetics, a company that saw its stock rise 30 percent, from $13.50 a share to $17.50 a share, in the week before the president's March 23 speech where he first unveiled his Star Wars scheme. That is, before Star Wars was revealed as a public plan, Washington's military-industrial-complex insiders were likely acting on secret information on Wall Street. Helionetics denied any wrongdoing, arguing that its astronomically rising stock reflected "a combination of general market conditions, the compa-ny's history of increasing sales and earnings and increased acceptance of its non-laser product lines." Teller defended his actions in a legalistic letter to the editor of the *New York Times* on July 1, 1983; anyone who has studied Teller's influential role in pushing Star Wars in general, and laser technol-ogy in particular will find the letter nothing short of embarrassing.[32]

Critics raising questions regarding the relationships among Teller, Helionetics, SDI, and the DSB received further fuel for suspicion when, in July 1983, the inspector general of the Department of Defense (IGDoD) released a scathing report charging the DSB with a number of serious infractions. Responding to the IGDoD report and cascading news stories of military-industrial-complex improprieties, Congress hauled various military-industrial-complex elites, including the leadership of the DSB, before the Subcommittee of the House of Representatives' Committee on Government Operations. Entitled "Favoritism and Bias within the Defense Science Board and Other Military Advisory Panels," the hearings offer a damning glance inside the workings of the DSB and the military-industrial complex in the age of President Reagan. Congressman Jack Brooks (D-TX) opened the hearings on September 22 by acknowledging that the IGDoD's report "found that the DSB and its 33 advisory task forces suffer from apparent conflict of interest problems, favoritism, and non-enforcement of financial disclosure requirements and other ethical standards." Brooks announced that "this subcommittee uncovered the complete disregard for all legal and ethical standards"; even after the DSB responded to those initial findings via a series of negotiated changes in policy, Brooks worried that "there are still potential criminal violations in their procedures."[33]

Nations must have competent militaries to defend themselves from possible attack by enemies. But if the apparatus for planning, building, and maintaining those weapons is rife with "potential criminal violations," then President Eisenhower's warning about the military-industrial complex infringing on democracy is well on the way to being realized. For a telling glimpse into the inner workings of the military-industrial complex, and to begin to fathom how it has hijacked U.S. resources, influences U.S. policy, and treads close to "criminal violations," consider this testy exchange between Congressman Brooks, Deputy Secretary of Defense Paul Thayer, and Undersecretary of Defense for Research and Engineering Richard DeLauer, a former member of the DSB and then the DoD official to whom the DSB reported. Brooks was a longtime Texas Democrat (he was first elected to Congress in 1953), a former Marine, and an ornery rhetorical pugilist both respected and feared on the Hill—he was a thorn in the side of Regan-era appointees and programs. Brooks was pushing Thayer and DeLauer about excesses in military-industrial-complex spending, wondering if they were anything other than handouts for friends, when he noted with a tone of amazement that the DoD had recently commissioned "1,000 [studies] on laser weapons, 2,600 on cruise missiles, 11,000 plus on electronic warfare, and 12,000 on countermeasures":

BROOKS: I wondered what it cost for all those studies?

THAYER: I don't know where those numbers come from.

BROOKS: From the Defense—

THAYER: I can't believe there have been 12,000 studies on—

BROOKS: We got them from the Defense Department. Mr. DeLauer?

DELAUER: Yes sir, Mr. Chairman, that included all contractual studies over a period of five years.

BROOKS: Yes sir.

DELAUER: It included all studies on particular issues. . . . When you have studies on generic topics such as electronic warfare, I can talk about jamming, I can talk about anti-jamming, I can talk about self-protection, I can talk about non-self-protection . . .

BROOKS: Countermeasures. 12,000. Fascinating subject.

DELAUER: Oh. And is it against aircraft? Is it against submarines? Is it against satellites?[34]

This exchange is revelatory for three reasons. First, when confronted with the absurdity of commissioning the 26,600 studies cited by Congressman Brooks, Thayer's initial reaction is to deny the number by questioning its accuracy. For even Thayer, ensconced among the military-industrial-complex elite, is apparently stunned by the profligacy of the operation: "I don't know. . . . I can't believe there have been 12,000 studies." The deputy secretary of defense, when face-to-face with the immensity of the military-industrial-complex's waste—26,600 studies!—is dumbfounded. The routes of communication within the military-industrial complex are so garbled, so complicated, so immense, that apparently even the deputy secretary of defense has little idea what is happening under his watch. Thayer's evasions may also have served the legalistic rhetorical purpose of shielding him from responsibility for the enormous waste attacked by Brooks; nonetheless, despite such responsibility-denying testimony, Thayer was thereafter "convicted and imprisoned for stock fraud and perjury." This first exchange, when coupled with Thayer's and many of his colleagues' subsequent criminal convictions, portrays the military-industrial complex in the age of Star Wars less as a monolithic behemoth than as an organizational nightmare, less as a sleek war-fighting machine than as a bloated raft of mismanaged and illegal cronyism. If the health of the nation depends in no small part on balancing our norms of democratic deliberation with the needs of national security, then Brooks's sharp questioning indicates one small moment of the former trying to correct the excesses of the latter.[35]

The exchange quoted above is telling for a second reason: for in recognizing the rhetorical damage of Brooks's questioning of Thayer, Undersecretary of Defense for Research and Engineering DeLauer jumps in, hoping to right the listing ship. Struggling to retrieve the studies under question from the oblivion of waste and excess, DeLauer explains their necessity, suggesting that "I can talk about jamming . . . anti-jamming . . . self-protection . . . [and] non-self protection." Recognizing the absurdity of providing these four examples to explain the commissioning of 26,600 studies, DeLauer lamely adds: "And is it against aircraft? . . . submarines? . . . satellites?" DeLauer thus appears incapable of explaining the sophisticated weapons research taking place under his leadership, let alone justifying why it would require the immense expenditures floating 26,600 studies. Whereas Thayer denies responsibility for or knowledge of the information conveyed by Brooks—*I don't know. . . . I can't believe*—DeLauer responds like a well-practiced prevaricator, offering dissembling non-answers to Brooks's challenging questions. This second exchange illustrates how the military-industrial complex in the age of Star Wars is literally beyond description: its excesses are so vast that even its highest-ranking elites cannot begin to justify the system. Thayer's and DeLauer's answers, then, vary from stunned denials to shallow justifications, and then off toward comic absurdity. To his credit, Congressman Brooks responds to the tag-team performance of Thayer and DeLauer with deadpan venom: "Countermeasures. 12,000. Fascinating."[36]

Brooks's sarcasm points to the third important aspect of this exchange: that despite Brooks's searing contempt, Thayer's repeated denials, and DeLauer's bumbling excuses, very little changed at the DSB in general, or in the DSB's relationship to Star Wars in particular following these hearings. In fact, when the SDI Advisory Committee (SDIAC) was established in 1985, Frederick Seitz, Robert Everett, and William Nierenberg— all DSB members—were placed on the committee. Edward Reiss reports that by 1987, perhaps because of these DSB/SDIAC connections, "31 of the 48 members of the DSB belonged to organizations profiting from SDI programs." We do not have the space here to track the intricacies of these thirty-one cases, but Reiss's study suggests the presence of cronyism, if not illegalities. Indeed, based on his evaluation of this too-cozy relationship between DSB members, the SDIAC, and the corporations reaping vast profits from Star Wars, Reiss argues that the military-industrial complex was run during the Reagan years as "a system of mutual informal favors, conflicts of interest, and cavalier contempt for federal regulations." That is, the DSB functioned in 1987 pretty much as it did in 1983, when Brooks characterized the outfit as being laced with "apparent conflict of interest problems, favoritism," and lapses in "other ethical standards," thus verging on "potential criminal violations in their procedures." This takes us back to the anonymous Reagan science advisor's confession that in the days before the president's March 23, 1983 speech, White House writers struggled to justify the "content free" SDI program; that is, explaining Star Wars would require a new round of propaganda.[37]

The DSB's relationship to Star Wars is rendered doubly confusing by noting that its April 1988 *Strategic Air Defense* report was deeply critical of President Regan's SDI. In fact, Tom Wicker observed in the *New York Times* that the DSB's report dealt a "serious blow to SDI." Reconciling this critical report with the institutional connections uncovered by Reiss demonstrates how the institution's public address and its behind-closed-doors business practices were in conflict. Indeed, while the DSB was issuing a "serious blow to SDI" in public, Reiss shows that thirty-one of its members were at the heart of the Star Wars "free for all," hence profiting privately from the same program their outfit was criticizing publicly. Studying the DSB in the age of Star Wars thus suggests how our nation's elite military-industrial-complex institutions muddy our democratic deliberation, in this case empowering citizens by offering a critique of a "nutty" weapons system while, at the same time, enabling military-industrial-complex elites to enrich themselves at the cost of taxpayers. In this case, public address was little more than a cover for private excess. As Congressman Brooks argued in a second hearing about the DSB and other advisory committees, this one held on November 28, 1983: "If DoD does not move quickly to remedy deficiencies in the administration of these scientific advisory boards, they will, for all practical purposes, become an arena for the advancement of private interests under the guise of scientific advice. If this should happen, the Pentagon will be relying solely on the military-industrial complex for advice on how to spend hundreds of billions of dollars." Brooks was arguing that even the slimmest notions of democratic deliberation and checks and balances were being compromised by the military-industrial complex running an essentially private operation funded with tax dollars, all the while creating some of the most deadly weapons in the history of the planet. What the congressman could not have foreseen in 1983 was the DSB becoming both a military-industrial-complex feeding trough and an outfit proposing new strategies for producing propaganda.[38]

The DSB and Post-9/11 Propaganda

Having established the contours of its Cold War–era founding and its implication in the Reagan-era's slew of weapons-related illegalities, waste, and subterfuge, we turn now to the DSB's call for a new age of propaganda and its relationship to President George Bush's rhetoric since September 11, 2001. Before tackling this topic, however, it is important to note that the DSB's 2004 *Strategic Communication* report offers a sharp critique of how the post-9/11 United States is losing "a generational and global struggle about ideas" (p. 2). Considering the source, this is a remarkable claim, for it demonstrates that some of Washington's most powerful military-industrial-complex elites know that President Bush's clash-of-civilizations rhetoric is ineffective, and that his prosecution of the GWT has been counterproductive. For example, the DSB *Strategic Communication* report shows that U.S. international credibility is plummeting, and that following the U.S. invasion of Iraq, "Arab/Muslim anger has intensified. . . . The U.S. is viewed unfavorably by overwhelming majorities in Egypt (98 percent), Saudi Arabia (94 percent), Morocco (88 percent), and Jordan (78 percent). The war has increased mistrust of America in Europe, weakened support for the war on terrorism, and undermined U.S. credibility worldwide" (p. 15). Hence, offering a stunning moment of elite truth-telling—one worthy of Brooks's crisp cross-questioning of Thayer and DeLauer—the DSB *Strategic Communication* report depicts post-9/11 U.S. foreign policy as an unmitigated disaster.[39]

Indeed, based on a Zogby International poll conducted in July 2004, the *Strategic Communication* report measures public opinion about the United States in Morocco, Saudi Arabia, Jordan, Lebanon, and the United Arab Emirates. The poll is broken down into ten categories: four aspects of U.S. foreign policy and six aspects of U.S. culture. To take Morocco as an example, its favorable ratings for the cultural categories are 90 percent for science/technology, 53 percent for freedom/democracy, 59 percent for people, 60 percent for movies/TV, 73 percent for products, and 61 percent for education. However, its unfavorable ratings for foreign policy aspects

are 90 percent for policy toward Arabs, 93 percent for policy toward Pal-
estinians, 82 percent for policy on terrorism, and 98 percent for policy
on Iraq (p. 45). Moroccans therefore have strongly favorable views of
U.S. values and cultural practices, and intensely unfavorable views of U.S.
foreign policy. In sum, respondents to the poll do not hate Americans because of who we are and how we live—the essentialist argument fueling
the Bush administration's early post-9/11 claims—but because of what
we do as an international colossus. Moreover, the *Strategic Communication*
report notes that the unfavorable numbers have been rising since the U.S.
invasion of Iraq, and that throughout the Islamic world "Americans have
become the enemy" (p. 46). The report concludes that "opinion is hard-
est against America in precisely those places ruled by what Muslims call
'apostates' and tyrants" including "the tyrannies of Egypt, Saudi Arabia,
Pakistan, Jordan, and the Gulf states"—all U.S. allies. "This," the report
suggests, "should give us pause" (p. 46). Moreover, the DSB's *Strategic
Communication* report makes it painfully clear that one of the fundamental
causes of rising global terrorism is opposition to a U.S. foreign policy committed to supporting oil-rich authoritarian regimes. Michael Klare has
characterized this mutual dance of dependence—with the United States
desperate for oil and Middle Eastern monarchies desperate for U.S. military protection—as amounting to a "lethal embrace" likely to continue
producing waves of political violence.[40]

Considering the glaring gap between the DSB *Strategic Communication*
report's assessment of why U.S. foreign policy is failing and of the Bush
administration's escalatory clash-of-civilizations rhetoric, readers might
expect the DSB to call for reconsidering both White House policies and
the president's modes of public address. But in fact, the authors of the
DSB report call for a revamped propaganda machine to help change the
minds of the disaffected foreigners described above. Rather than addressing the deep historical, economic, and political reasons why the U.S. is
losing the global war of ideas, the *Strategic Communication* report offers
bureaucratically thick, labyrinthine recipes for making current U.S. policies more attractive. For example, offered under the heading of "The Case
for a New Vision," the report argues that "strategic communication can
help to shape context and build relationships that enhance the achievement of political, economic, and military objectives. It can be used to
mobilize publics in support of major policy initiatives" (p. 11). The report
proposes that such mobilization will take place under the leadership of

an "Office of Strategic Influence," which will manage "tactical influence efforts (PSYOP) and broader influence efforts like Public Diplomacy (PD)" (p. 78). So rather than addressing the root causes of the U.S.' precipitous nosedive in international legitimacy, the DSB's *Strategic Communication* report repeated a pattern we saw established with Eisenhower: the report calls for improved "strategic communication" and enhanced "tactical influence efforts"—what it later calls "managed information dissemination" (p. 99)—that is, for "mobiliz[ing] publics" via better propaganda.[41]

The *Strategic Communication* report's findings should "give us pause" indeed, for they suggest, counter to everything the president and his allies postulate, that international anger is not directed at broad U.S. values, but at specific U.S. policies. The report therefore suggests that the Bush administration's missionary rhetoric regarding the GWT and the clash of civilizations has inflamed already rising anger toward the United States. As we shall see below, these frightening conclusions may explain why the Bush administration has so drastically changed its rhetorical justifications for recent U.S. military actions from prosecuting a "clash of civilizations" war against inhuman Others, to extending the benign hand of Freedom and Democracy to all those wise enough to grab hold. To pursue this thesis, let us watch the transformation in Bush-administration rhetoric. Initially, the Bush administration turned 9/11 into the opening shot of a cultural war between the forces of Modern Goodness and Pre-Historic Evil. For example, in the first days following 9/11, the president described the U.S response to al Qaeda's strikes as part of a "crusade." Speaking from the South Lawn of the White House on Sunday afternoon, September 16, 2001—"on the Lord's Day," as he said in his opening remarks— President Bush fielded questions from the media. After being pressed for a timeline of possible U.S. responses to 9/11, the president blurted out: "The American people are beginning to understand. This crusade, this war on terrorism is going to take a while." To make sure the president's crusade quip was not interpreted as calling for a clash of civilizations, the White House acted quickly to defuse the scandal; the very next day, the president gave a widely celebrated speech entitled "Islam is Peace" at the Islamic Center of Washington, D.C.[42]

Regardless of the White House's quick-footed reaching out to the Islamic community, the president's "crusade" comment elicited a firestorm of domestic and international criticism. Given this eruption of concern over President Bush's rhetoric, one might imagine that the White House

would have tried to moderate the president's clash-of-civilizations arguments. But in fact, the president continued to hammer on this theme. On
October 11, 2001, roughly one month following his first use of "crusade"
to characterize U.S. foreign policy, the president claimed in a press conference that al Qaeda's strikes were "an attack on the heart and soul of
the civilized world." This was the same speech in which he referred to
terrorists as "the parasites." One month later the president again relied
on these clash-of-civilization terms in a speech on homeland security in
Atlanta, where he said that "We wage a war to save civilization itself."
Two months later, in his January 2002 State of the Union Address, the
president pledged to "eliminate the terrorist parasites." Four months later,
speaking in the German Bundestag on May 23, 2002, President Bush
again claimed that "We are defending civilization itself." Six months later,
when he signed the Homeland Security Act into legislation on November
25, 2002, the president noted that the war to save civilization was being
fought against foes who "hate us because of what we love." The war to
save civilization is therefore waged between the moral and God-loving
United States and foes who are devoid of basic human values: they are
parasites, inhuman foes of "what we love."[43]

These themes were encapsulated in September 2004, when David
Brooks argued in the *New York Times* that the world was under assault by
a "cult of death" that thrives on "the sheer pleasure of killing and dying.
It's about massacring people. . . . It's about experiencing the total freedom
of barbarism. . . . It's about the joy of sadism and suicide." Rather than
seeing global terrorism in political terms, Brooks, like Bush before him,
diagnosed this "cult of death" as "pathological," thus turning its members
into monstrous, disease-riddled deviants. For the president, Brooks, and
their supporters, the GWT is therefore nothing less than a war of civilizations being fought to defend Modernity against the barbarism of those
who hate everything that makes life worth living.[44]

Much of President Bush's domestic success since 9/11 has rested on
his ability to turn that terrible day into a call for a crusade, a rally to arms
with religious overtones. And while we could spend pages detailing the
seductive nature of such calls (they are, after all, very persuasive for many
Americans) or addressing the international dangers inherent in them
(they are, after all, very alienating for most everyone outside the United
States), we are interested in the following pages in tracking how such
claims have changed following the publication of the DSB's *Task Force on*

Strategic Communication. One of the president's early attempts at this shift in tone was bungled, for while speaking at the Ellipse in Washington, D.C., during a nighttime concert in January 2005, President Bush opined that "We have a calling from beyond the stars to stand for freedom, and America will always be faithful to that cause." Invoking Heavenly guidance to wage his wars for freedom, and referring to such an endeavor as a call of faith, could only further stoke the concerns of those afraid of a religiously driven clash of civilizations. Two weeks later, on February 2, 2005, while delivering his State of the Union Address, the president scrupulously avoided such crusader implications, instead arguing that "The only force powerful enough to stop the rise of tyranny and terror, and replace hatred with hope, is the force of human freedom." Cementing these secular and humanist claims, the president pledged that "America will stand with the allies of freedom to support democratic movements in the Middle East and beyond, with the ultimate goal of ending tyranny in our world." That last sentence echoes the DSB's findings, which explained how U.S. support for Middle Eastern monarchies is among the chief reasons for international anger toward the United States. Little has changed in terms of U.S. foreign policy since this speech, but at a rhetorical level, one has to grant the felicity of switching from the president's earlier clash-of-civilizations terms to this "allies of freedom" position. Indeed, President Bush and his handlers have apparently decided that successful GWT propaganda depends not on righteous denunciations of loathsome Others, but on celebratory tributes to democracy as the higher cause for waging global wars for peace.[45]

Thus, by March 2005 the president was triumphantly proclaiming from the Rose Garden that "Freedom is on the march"; by April he was speaking before troops in Texas of "the global democratic revolution." In both cases, President Bush tried to situate the U.S. occupations of Iraq and Afghanistan, and its prosecution of the GWT more generally, as central components of a universalizing U.S.-led push for freedom. The rhetorical tenor of these speeches suggests, however, that freedom and democracy will henceforward be less political goals than propagandistic tools. For example, in the third sentence of the April speech, the president greeted the troops with what he called the "proper Army greeting: Hoo-ah!" Grateful for the president's praise of their service to the nation and the cause of globalizing freedom, and responding to the president's invitation to regale him with the "Army greeting," the assembled troops proceeded to interrupt the president's speech with the "Hoo-ah" chant sixteen times, hence turning the occasion into a raucous call-and-response. Completing this masterpiece of propaganda, the president praised the troops assembled at Fort Hood, Texas—the single largest collection of conventional military weaponry in the world, accounting in one estimate for as much as 40 percent of U.S. combat power—for "making the world more peaceful." Eschewing clash-of-civilizations rhetoric, keeping religious references to a minimum, and issuing buoyant proclamations to repeated "Hoo-ah!"s from the troops, the president offered the world a vision of the U.S. pursuing what I (SJH) and Laura Stengrim have characterized elsewhere as "globalization-through-benevolent-empire." This is an oxymoronic formula where the U.S. acts as a globalizing agent for enforced freedom, as a military superpower waging wars for peace, as an imperial republic spreading the American way accompanied by roaring rounds of democracy-loving Hoo-ahs.[46]

A key question, then, is whether this new rhetorical pattern was spurred by the DSB report, or whether the report reflected already-changing norms in discourse; that is, was the DSB report *causal of* or *consistent with* the rhetorical transformation from a swaggering clash-of-civilizations genre to what we have called globalization-through-benevolent-empire? This question cannot be answered definitively, at least not until classified White House papers are made available to scholars. But we can gather a sense of the working processes that fueled the DSB report by noting that some of its nongovernmental members work with the nation's elite strategic-communication firms, each of which profits handsomely from U.S. military entanglements abroad. Moreover, the task force that produced the DSB report consulted not only with a wide array of government figures (from DoD, State, the White House Office of Global Communications, the NSC, the CPA, and others) but also with representatives of the American Enterprise Institute and the Rendon Group. That is, while the DSB task force did not consult with a single independent critic of either the Bush administration in particular or the military-industrial complex in general, it did consult with a bevy of elites whose careers are linked directly to the extension of U.S. military power. As we have argued here, the result of that skewed consultation process was a document that did not propose fundamental changes in U.S. foreign policy, but rather—as apparently pushed by a number of government officials, corporate contractors, and strategic-communication experts—a renewed propaganda effort to make those policies look better to an outraged world. Rather than thinking of the DSB report as playing a role that was either causal of, or consistent with the rhetorical transformations discussed here, then, we would propose that it should be situated as one player within a larger network of military-industrial-complex forces.[47]

We turn to the interpretive dilemmas raised by this conclusion in the following section of this essay, but want first to observe that the transformation in rhetorical strategy addressed here carries serious implications for the health of democratic deliberation. For while the clash-of-civilizations rhetoric issued in the early days following 9/11 brought to mind some of the worst stereotypes of the ugly American—xenophobic, provincial, self-righteous, racist, culturally obtuse—hence igniting a wave of outraged international repercussions, this turn to the trope of globalization-through-benevolent-empire puts international and domestic critics in a difficult, almost impossible position. Like peace activists facing President Reagan's visionary Star Wars rhetoric, so critics of President Bush's handling of U.S. foreign policy in general and the DSB report in particular have been placed in the difficult situation of having to explain why they oppose ideas as unopposable as freedom and democracy. Along with being factually deceptive, this new rhetorical strategy therefore makes it even more difficult for dissent to sound legitimate, hence curtailing the health of our public deliberation about the nation's policies. We may be stuck, then, in a situation imagined almost fifty years ago by Aldous Huxley, who warned in *Brave New World Revisited*, his prophetic 1958 cry against Cold War–era propaganda and the rising culture of mass-produced consumerism, that "The democracies will change their nature; the quaint old forms—elections, parliaments, Supreme Courts and all the rest—will remain. [But] the underlying substance will be a new kind of . . . totalitarianism. All the traditional names, all the hallowed slogans will remain exactly what they were in the good old days: democracy and freedom will be the theme of every broadcast and editorial. . . . Meanwhile the ruling oligarchy and its highly trained elite of soldiers, policemen, thought-manufacturers and mind-manipulators will quietly run the show as they see fit."[48]

Some readers may find Huxley's vision overwrought, but our analysis of the military-industrial complex, the DSB report, and Bush White House rhetoric suggests that it is largely accurate. In fact, Ivie demonstrates in *Democracy and America's War on Terror* that the United States has been committed—since the Cold War, if not before—"to rationaliz[ing] war as the work of peace." The rationalization depends on the claim that "war and domination (represented as national defense and global leadership) are deemed the only realistic options for protecting freedom and preserving civilization against ubiquitous forces of death, destruction, and chaos." Post-9/11 U.S. rhetoric, both driven by and reflected in the DSB's 2004 *Strategic Communication* report, appears more than ever committed to this rhetorical construction, wherein war equals peace and imperialism is extended in the name of democracy—Hoo-ah indeed.[49]

Implications for Rhetorical Scholarship and Democratic Deliberation

Like other mature academic disciplines, rhetorical criticism and public address are practiced in divergent schools of thought, are supported by contrasting ideals, and are institutionalized in competing departments, organizations, and journals. Finding common ground regarding the definition of what is or is not rhetorical criticism or public address is therefore difficult; agreement on what counts as democratic deliberation is equally hard to come by. Asking about the relationship between rhetorical criticism, public address, and democracy—the question driving the 2005 Brigance Colloquy that led to this volume—is therefore bound to elicit widely divergent responses. Nonetheless, we may discern some broad patterns within the vast body of work affiliated with these fields. First, our objects of analysis are remarkably complex, as we range from considering single orators (speakers in the most traditional sense) to addressing the most diffuse subcultural artifacts (the detritus of discourse in the postmodern sense). Second, notions of democratic deliberation cross from the great-men-persuading-specific-audiences model to layered analyses of networked communities and mass media to the farthest edges of embodied performance studies. Third, because of this spread of ideas about what counts as relevant objects of rhetorical criticism and what counts as moments of public address and democratic deliberation, the political, cultural, and personal implications of our work is heavily (and healthily) contested. Fourth, because of these first three observations, it follows that the field is marked by strong differences regarding what counts as persuasion, how it happens, and to what effect. Fifth—and here is where we circle back to the DSB—we see an almost complete lack of attention to what might be called the institutional contexts of rhetorical production. That is, while each of the many forms of thought described here understand the complexities of thinking about a given rhetorical situation, few of them ask questions about the ways their objects of analysis reflect deep institutional imperatives. With some notable exceptions (to which we turn below), even the best rhetorical criticism and public-address scholarship still reproduce what Dilip Gaonkar sees as one of the central, and often blindly followed, assumptions of the field: its "view of speakers as seats of origin rather than points of articulation."[50]

Gaonkar's critique of traditional rhetorical criticism is particularly apt regarding the work we have done on the Cold War and the military-industrial complex. As we argued above, rhetorical critics would do well to rethink our commitment to "speakers as seats of origin," instead locating individual acts of persuasion within larger institutional frameworks. One example of this work is Bryan Taylor's analysis of nuclear-weapons scientists as nodes in the circulation of professional discourse developed to manage the national-security state.[51] Another example is Gordon Mitchell's "Placebo Defense," an essay debunking propaganda about Patriot missile accuracy in the first Gulf War. Mitchell uses the traditional close-reading tactics of rhetorical critics to peel back the deceptions offered in the first Bush administration's "hyper-real rhetorical frame," yet he also layers this interpretive work against a review of the evidence from the battlefield, a journey into the weapons-manufacturing industry, analysis of the mass media's role in disseminating propaganda, and political observations on the possible "ways of resisting the massive institutional inertia" that has been created by the convergence of presidential and DoD deception, military-industrial-complex opportunism, and corporate mass-media irresponsibility. Mitchell's essay thus relies upon a heroic notion of agency-as-resistance, even while demonstrating the multiple ways institutionalized powers constrain both individual agency and collective forms of democratic deliberation. In a related essay from 2001, this one examining the deceptions used to push the selling of U.S. Theatre Missile Defense systems to Japan, Mitchell summarizes how the military-industrial complex constrains democratic deliberation: "Excessive secrecy locks in Cold War patterns of public discourse, where defense officials and industry representatives monopolize arguments, sealing their positions with the unassailable proof of classified evidence.

Threat assessments drift toward worst-case scenarios generated from simulation and speculation, rather than more sober appraisals. . . . Military officials who see the idea of public debate as superfluous luxury skirt critical arguments, removing issues of grave national importance from arenas of democratic deliberation."[52]

For Mitchell and Taylor, then, two of our best critics of the military-industrial complex as a manufacturing network of both weaponry and rhetorical artifacts, the most pressing issues of the day—questions affecting nothing less than life and death, war and peace, and the long-term health of the republic—are shrouded in democratic-deliberation-destroying secrecy. This means not only that citizens are excluded from the decision-making processes that make democratic governance legitimate, but that military-industrial-complex elites, by proceeding without facing critical questioning and public idea testing, may veer into weapons programs and war plans that jeopardize rather than protect the nation's best interests. The invasion and occupation of Iraq is a recent case in point; as noted above, Star Wars also illustrates this point—both examples demonstrate how by circumventing robust democratic deliberation, the decision-making processes of the military-industrial complex devolve into what Scheer calls "political whim and ideological obsession."[53]

It may simply be too much to ask the many practitioners of rhetorical criticism and public address to take institutional formations more seriously, for after all, that is what organizational scholars already do—yet organizational scholars have tended to frame their analyses within tightly delineated institutional parameters (how does communication work within this company or hospital or school?) rather than working from institutional powers outward to public, persuasive actions.[54] In contrast to this communication-within-the-discreet-institution model, Mitchell's work on Patriot missiles, Taylor's work on nuclear weapons, and our reading of the DSB suggest aspects of the ways Washington's military-industrial-complex institutions influence the public persuasive acts that we rhetorical critics have traditionally considered the purview of our expertise. Analyzing an institution like the DSB therefore enables us to tackle the institutional frameworks underpinning the production of presidential speeches, congressional debates, and other public documents. This in turn means giving up any lingering romanticism regarding the "view of speakers as seats of origin," instead suggesting that speakers—even presidents—are both independent agents and also nodal points, negotiated catchments, conflicted filters, and, in worst-case scenarios, even compromised mouth-pieces of much larger institutional forces. This claim neither devalues the importance of individual speech acts nor denies the modulated agency of individual agents engaged in acts of persuasion, but rather supplements our traditional understanding of rhetorical production, reception, and interpretation with a realpolitik perspective—what Martin Medhurst calls a "strategic approach"—that strives to make better sense of the ways power circulates throughout military-industrial-complex institutions, and from them into the public realm.[55]

Conclusion: Facing Apocalypse

As archival scholars, we are trained to find obscure and even hidden documents; as rhetorical critics and public-address scholars, we are uniquely practiced in analyzing public texts; as teachers of public speaking we should, at least in theory, be well-versed in the means of persuasion; and as historians of the republic, we are intimately familiar with the nation's deep fears and loves, its ambivalences and its ambitions. Combining these four skill sets makes for citizens who should be especially powerful champions of, and participants in, our democracy. We have argued here that fulfilling that promise also requires focusing more attention on the DSB and the other military-industrial-complex institutions charged with managing the empire. From this perspective, tracking the relationships among DSB task forces, the military-industrial complex in general, and particular examples of public address will lead not only to stronger intellectual work, but to more important political work. Rather than bemoaning the demise of democratic deliberation, such a project would enable its practitioners to begin the much-needed task of building a community of engaged scholars, albeit one washed clean of the naive assumptions regarding heroic individual agency that mark so much prior work in the field.[56]

To escalate the political stakes involved in proposing such work, we will close this essay by turning to Don DeLillo's *Underworld*, his magisterial novel of American life from 1951 through the present. Musing on the military-industrial complex, nuclear weapons, and a century's worth of state-produced violence, DeLillo wanders off on one of his brilliant, and in this case, prophetic tangents:

Through the battered century of world wars and massive violence by other means, there had always been an undervoice that spoke through the cannon fire and ack-ack and that sometimes grew strong enough to merge with the battle sounds. It was the struggle between the state and secret groups of insurgents, state-born, wild-eyed—the anarchists, terrorists, assassins and revolutionaries who tried to bring about apocalyptic change. . . . The passionate task of the state was to hold on, stiffening its grip and preserving its claim to the most destructive power available. With nuclear weapons this power became identifiable totally with the state. . . . The state controlled the means of apocalypse.[57]

This is the DSB's function: to control "the means of apocalypse"—what we saw its charter call "radically new weapons systems"—while holding at bay those who would rather see historical change, even if brought about by anarchic violence, than spend another day under stifling imperial oppression. We are not advocates of "wild-eyed" violence, but it is nonetheless chilling to realize, along with DeLillo, that because apocalypse has been threatened for so long to keep so many in check, it has slowly lost its persuasive power; post-9/11 America has entered a terrifying historical space where its universally acknowledged mastery over the means of apocalypse no longer scares anyone, leaving the United States all-powerful yet all-vulnerable all the time.

The DSB's task, given this daunting situation, is to devise new weapons to kill those undeterred by the threat of nuclear apocalypse, to produce new modes of propaganda to convince us that forthcoming wars will be fought in our best interest, and to funnel the profits from these endeavors to fellow military-industrial-complex elites. To allow the DSB to succeed in these tasks without having to confront the critical intelligence and political energies of contemporary rhetorical critics and public-address scholars would suggest that many of us have become little more than dumbfounded observers of military grandeur, bureaucratized intellectuals complicit with the empire, "suicidal sleepwalkers," in Jacques Derrida's phrase, "blind and deaf alongside the unheard-of" catastrophe that awaits further U.S. belligerence. Addressing institutions like the DSB may enable those of us who fear this rotten fate to play some small role in renewing our norms of democratic deliberation by resisting the violence of empire.[58]

NOTES

The authors express their thanks for the editing assistance and intellectual cama-raderie of Lisa Keranen, Donovan Conley, David Zarefsky, Ned O'Gorman, Bryan Taylor, Hamilton Bean, the editors of this volume, and two anonymous reviewers for the Press.

1. For a list of DSB task forces, the DSB charter from which the personnel and purpose quotations are taken, and accessible versions of the *DSB Newsletter*, go to the DSB website: www.acq.osd.mil/dsb (last accessed January 17, 2007).

2. We recognize that using the phrase "military-industrial complex" is problematic, for it is not a monolithic entity; rather, it is a loose network of institutions laced with contradictions. For example, while Boeing, Lockheed, TRW, and other weapons manufacturers all profit from DoD largesse, they are also engaged in intense competition for contracts and elite influence; while the CIA, DIA, INR, and other intelligence agencies are meant to work together for roughly the same purposes, we know that they frequently disagree with each other's analyses and fight with each other over funds and access to the Oval Office, hence fueling what I (SJH) and Laura Stengrim have called elsewhere "intelligence turf wars"; while the DoD, Department of State, and various branches of the White House staff are meant to work together, we have ample evidence of the infighting both within each institution and between them. We could go on enumerating the many institutional fractures within the military-industrial complex, but the point should be clear: the military-industrial complex is a sprawling network of allegiances and feuds, alliances and tensions. Nonetheless, even as we recognize the military-industrial complex as a diffuse site of contestation and contradiction, we will hereafter use the term to suggest the overarching system of scientific R&D firms, weapons manufacturers, military elites, and policy experts who work, albeit in a competitive manner, to formulate, carry out, and profit from U.S. foreign policy. For a reminder that the military-industrial complex is not a "monolithic apparatus," see Bryan C. Taylor and Brian Freer, "Containing the Nuclear Past: The Politics of History and Heritage at the Hanford Plutonium Works," *Journal of Organizational Management* 15, no. 6 (2002): 563–88 in full, quotation from 570; for a dissection of the "intelligence turf wars" surrounding the U.S. invasion of Iraq, see Stephen John Hartnett and Laura Ann Stengrim, *Globalization and*

Empire: The U.S. Invasion of Iraq, Free Markets, and the Twilight of Democracy (Tuscaloosa: University of Alabama Press, 2006), 40–83; more broadly, see William Odom, *Fixing Intelligence: For a More Secure America* (New Haven: Yale University Press, 2003) and James Bamford, *Body of Secrets: Anatomy of the Ultra-Secret National Security Agency, from the Cold War through the Dawn of a New Century* (New York: Doubleday, 2002); for analyses of the intelligence community as suffering from communicative inertia, see Robert Newman, "Communication Pathologies of Intelligence Systems," *Speech Monographs* 42 (1975): 271–90, and Thomas Kean, chair, *The 9/11 Commission Report: Final Report of the National Commission on Terrorist Attacks upon the United States* (New York: Norton, 2003), esp. 399–428.

3. Edwin Black theorized this balancing act as part of a philosophical quandary involving tropes of secrecy and disclosure. See his "Secrecy and Disclosure as Rhetorical Forms," *Quarterly Journal of Speech* 74 (1988): 133–50; for historical studies of this question, see Amy B. Zegart, *Flawed by Design: The Evolution of the CIA, JCS, and NSC* (Palo Alto, Calif.: Stanford University Press, 1999), and Stephen John Hartnett and Jennifer Rose Mercieca, "'Has Your Courage Rusted?': National Security and the Contested Rhetorical Norms of Republicanism in Post-Revolutionary America, 1798–1801," *Rhetoric & Public Affairs* 9 (2006): 79–112; for a memoir along these lines, see Harold Lloyd Goodall Jr., *A Need to Know: The Clandestine History of a CIA Family* (Walnut Creek, Calif.: Left Coast, 2006).

4. Office of the Under Secretary of Defense (William Schneider Jr., DSB chairman), *Report of the Defense Science Board Task Force on Strategic Communication* (Washington, D.C., 2004), hereafter cited in the text as *Strategic Communication*. Samuel Huntington, "The Clash of Civilizations," *Foreign Affairs* 72, no. 3 (Summer 1993): 22–50; the book version appeared as *The Clash of Civilizations and the Remaking of the World* (New York: Simon and Schuster, 1996); for a critique see Tariq Ali, *The Clash of Fundamentalisms: Crusades, Jihads, and Modernity* (London: Verso, 2002), 297–310; for a conservative response see Roger Sandall, "The Politics of Oxymoron," *The New Criterion: A Web Special* (Summer 2003), available at www.newcriterion.com; for more moderate treatment, see Michael Elliott, "When Worlds Collide," *Washington Post*, December 1, 1996: Book World, p. 4.

5. Bryan Taylor and Stephen Hartnett, "'National Security, and All That It Implies . . .'": Communication and (Post-) Cold War Culture," *Quarterly Journal of Speech* 86 (2000): 465–91 in full, quotation from 472; although jointly

authored, Taylor deserves the credit for this line of argument and is thus cited in the text as the passage's author.

6. For Taylor's commentaries on these questions, see Taylor, "Nuclear Weapons and Communication Studies: A Review Essay," *Western Journal of Communication* 62 (1998): 300–315; for examples of his case studies of different aspects of the military-industrial complex, see "Register of the Repressed: Women's Voice and Body in the Nuclear Weapons Organization," *Quarterly Journal of Speech* 79 (1993): 267–85, and "Revis(it)ing Nuclear History: Narrative Conflict at the Bradbury Science Museum," *Studies in Cultures, Organizations and Societies* 3 (1997): 119–45.

7. Regarding the now ubiquitous claim that U.S. foreign policy is "imperial," see David Harvey, *The New Imperialism* (Oxford: Oxford University Press, 2003); Michael Mann, *Incoherent Empire* (London: Verso, 2003); Rashid Khalidi, *Resurrecting Empire: Western Footprints and America's Perilous Path in the Middle East* (Boston: Beacon Press, 2004); Ellen Meiksins Wood, *Empire of Capital* (London: Verso, 2003); and Hartnett and Stengrim, *Globalization and Empire*.

8. Chalmers Johnson, *The Sorrows of Empire: Militarism, Secrecy, and the End of the Republic* (New York: Metropolitan Books, 2004), 130; like much of the DSB's work, the report Johnson refers to is classified and hence not accessible on the DSB website.

9. Russell Baker, "In Bush's Washington," *New York Review of Books*, May 13, 2004, 25; Wendell Berry, "A Citizen's Response to *The National Security Strategy of the United States*," in *Citizens Dissent: Security, Morality, and Leadership in an Age of Terror*, ed. Wendell Berry (Barrington, Mass.: Orion Society, 2003), 2–3; Joan Didion, "Politics in the 'New Normal' America," *New York Review of Books*, October 21, 2004, 64–73, quotation from 63.

10. For reports of how the processes discussed here have politicized and degraded science, turning it into little more than administration propaganda, see Lisa Keranen, Lisa Irvin, Jason Lesko, and Alison Vogelaar, "'Myth, Mask, Sword and Shield': Dr. John H. Marburger III's Rhetoric of Neutral Science for the Nation," *Cultural Studies <=> Critical Methodologies* (May 2008): 159–186; the Union of Concerned Scientists, *Scientific Integrity in Policymaking: An Investigation into the Bush Administration's Misuse of Science* (Boston: Union of Concerned Scientists, 2004); and Chris Mooney, *The Republican War on Science* (New York: Basic Books, 2005).

11. George Washington to Joseph Reed, December 12, 1778, as reprinted in *The Spirit of 'Seventy-Six: The Story of the American Revolution as Told by Participants,*

ed. Henry Steele Commager and Richard B. Morris (1958; New York: Da Capo, 1995), 804, 796–814 on profiteering; on the founding of the NAS and similar institutions, see Don K. Price, "The Republican Revolution," in *The Politics of Science: Readings in Science, Technology, and Government*, ed. William Nelson (Oxford: Oxford University Press, 1968), 5–25; the NAS has an extensive website available at www.nasonline.org; on the relationship between early military and science institutions and U.S. state formation, see Stephen Skowronek, *Building a New American State: The Expansion of National Administrative Capacities, 1877–1920* (Cambridge: Cambridge University Press, 1982).

12. Vannevar Bush, "The Endless Frontier," 1945 essay reprinted in Nelson, *The Politics of Science*, 26–54 in full, quotation from 26, and see 33–34 for Bush's thoughts on science and national security; on Bush, see "National Science Foundation Report 62–37," in ibid., 56ff. On the World War II–era advisory panels noted here, see Kevin R. Cunningham, *Scientific Advisers and American Defense Policy: The Case of the Defense Science Board*, Stanford University, Ph.D. diss., 1991, 75–86; and the Commission on Organization of the Executive Branch, *Subcommittee Report on Research Activities in the Department of Defense and Defense Related Agencies* (Washington, D.C., April 1955), 5–7.

13. On McCone, see David Wise and Thomas Ross, *The Invisible Government* (1964; New York: Vintage Books, 1974), 193–99, Casey quotation from 194. On military-industrial complex-driven cronyism in the occupation of Iraq, see Hartnett and Stengrim, *Globalization and Empire*, 212–66; Pratap Chatterjee, *Iraq Incorporated: A Profitable Occupation* (New York: Seven Stories, 2004); Center for Strategic and International Studies, *Progress or Peril? Measuring Iraq's Reconstruction* (Washington, D.C.: CSIS, 2004); Christian Parenti, *The Freedom: Shadows and Hallucinations in Occupied Iraq* (New York: New Press, 2004); and the materials posted by CorpWatch at www.corpwatch.org.

14. *Report on Research Activities*, 82, emphasis added; on the DSB's founding, see Bruce L. R. Smith, *The Advisors: Scientists in the Policy Process* (Washington: Brookings Institution, 1992), 48–67.

15. Figures from Marty Jezer, *The Dark Ages: Life in the United States, 1945–1960* (Boston: South End Press, 1982), 117–33; for an unenthusiastic notice of the founding of the DSB, see J. T. (full name not used), "Defense Science Board," *Science* (31 May 1957): 1065.

16. *Newsweek* cover of October 14, 1957; David Henry, "Eisenhower and Sputnik: The Irony of Failed Leadership," in *Eisenhower's War of Words: Rhetoric and Leadership*, ed. Martin Medhurst (East Lansing: Michigan State

University Press, 1994), 223–49, 238–39 on Killian; Cunningham, *Scientific Advisers and American Defense Policy*, 114–38 on this period, quotation from 138; for public notice of the turmoil within the DSB in particular and the DoD more generally, see John Finney, "Arms Aide Quits in Research Rift," *New York Times*, April 20, 1957, A6.

17. John W. Finney, "Economy Campaign Halts Plans for New Military Research Projects," *New York Times*, October 9, 1957, A13.

18. Sidney Hyman, "Inner Circles of the White House," *New York Times*, January 5, 1958, SM10; W. H. Lawrence, "Secrecy Charges Stir New Clash: Snyder Upholds Defense Policies," *New York Times*, April 19, 1958, A6.

19. In fact, even as late as 1983, Congressman Jack Brooks observed in congressional hearings that between January 1977 and September 1982, "of 198 [DSB] meetings held . . . minutes were available for just 32, and only 158 had been announced in advance." In short, the DSB was functioning then, as in 1957, largely as a private, behind-closed-doors entity. Committee on Government Operations, Jack Brooks, chairman, *Defense Science Boards: A Question of Integrity* (Washington, D.C.: G.P.O., 1983), 5.

20. Robert Ivie, "Eisenhower as Cold Warrior," in *Eisenhower's War of Words*, 7–25 in full, quotation from p. 8; for an overview of why institutionalizing an "age of peril" served U.S. interests, see Harvey, *The New Imperialism*, 38–42; Ivie has recently characterized Eisenhower's role in even more critical terms, arguing in *Democracy and America's War on Terror* (Tuscaloosa: University of Alabama Press, 2005) that Eisenhower "dedicated his presidency to a campaign of psychological warfare aimed at totalizing a communist threat that could be met only by risking nuclear suicide" (p. 14).

21. Passage from President Dwight Eisenhower's letter to William Benton, 1 May 1953, quoted in Ivie, "Eisenhower as Cold Warrior," 23 n. 32; on Jackson and the role of psychological warfare, see J. Michael Hogan, "Eisenhower and Open Skies: A Case Study in Psychological Warfare," in *Eisenhower's War of Words*, 137–55; more broadly, see Shawn Parry-Giles, "The Eisenhower Administration's Conceptualization of the USIA: The Development of Overt and Covert Propaganda Strategies," *Presidential Studies Quarterly* 24 (2004): 263–73.

22. For case studies of the norms of "visible citizenship," see Robert Hariman and John Lucaites, *No Caption Needed: Iconic Photographs, Public Culture, and Liberal Democracy* (Chicago: University of Chicago Press, 2007); Cara Finnegan, *Picturing Poverty: Print Culture and FSA Photography* (Washington, D.C.: Smithsonian, 2003); and Lester C. Olson, *Benjamin Franklin's Vision of*

American Community: A Study in Rhetorical Iconology (Columbia, S.C.: University of South Carolina Press, 2004).

23. President Dwight Eisenhower's January 17, 1961 Farewell Address, p. 2 of the version downloaded from http://mcadams.posc.mu.edu/ike.htm.

24. Philip Boffey, "R&D Gets a Boost from Washington," *New York Times*, February 13, 1983, 4:18; Mike Davis, *Prisoners of the American Dream* (London: Verso, 1986), 234; for a welcome rejoinder to the hagiography prompted by President Reagan's death, see William Rivers Pitt, "Planet Reagan," *TruthOut* (7 June 2004), available at www.truthout.org.

25. Garry Wills, *Reagan's America* (New York: Penguin, 1987), 25% from 376, quotation from 334; defense figures from Richard Stubbing and Richard Mendel, *The Defense Game: An Insider Explores the Astonishing Realities of America's Defense Establishment* (New York: Harper & Row, 1986), 44.

26. Reagan science advisor quoted in Robert Scheer, "Teller's Obsession Became Reality in 'Star Wars' Plan," *Los Angeles Times*, July 10, 1985, 6:6–8 in full, quotation from 6; for a science-fiction rendering of the proposal, see the cover of *Newsweek* for April 4, 1983, where a satellite channels nuclear-powered x-ray lasers firing on no less than two dozen Soviet rockets at the same time.

27. The White House meeting is described in, and the "assured survival" quotation is from, William J. Broad, *Teller's War: The Top-Secret Story behind the Star Wars Deception* (New York: Simon and Schuster, 1992), 107; Wills, *Reagan's America*, 466, and see 419 on the similarities between Reagan and Eisenhower; for further insight into Star Wars as a rhetorical program rather than a weapons program, see Jack Kidd, *The Strategic Cooperation Initiative: or, The Star Lights Strategy* (Charlottesville, Va.: Three Presidents, 1988), 61–77.

28. David Meyers, "Peace Movement Demobilization: The Fading of Nuclear Freeze," in *Peace Action in the Eighties: Social Science Perspectives*, ed. Sam Marullo and John Lofland (New Brunswick, N.J.: Rutgers University Press, 1990), 53–71; "High Frontier" quotations from Gordon Mitchell, "Japan-U.S. Missile Defense Collaboration: Rhetorically Delicious, Deceptively Dangerous," *Fletcher Forum of World Affairs* 25 (2001): 85–108 in full, quotations from 88.

29. Elise Boulding, "The Early Eighties Peak of the Peace Movement," in *Peace Action in the Eighties*, 19–36, groups listed on 23; and see Rebecca Bjork, *The Strategic Defense Initiative: Symbolic Containment of the Nuclear Threat* (Albany: State University of New York Press, 1992).

30. President Ronald Reagan, "Address to the Nation on Defense and National Security" (Washington, D.C., 23 March 1983), available at http://www. reagan.utexas.edu/archives/speeches/1983/32383d.htm. For rhetorical analyses of the speech, see G. Thomas Goodnight, "Ronald Reagan's Re-Formulation of the Rhetoric of War: Analysis of the 'Zero Option,' 'Evil Empire,' and 'Star Wars' Addresses"; and Janice Hocker Rushing, "Ronald Reagan's 'Star Wars' Address: Mythic Containment of Technical Reasoning"—both in *Quarterly Journal of Speech* 72 (1986): 390–414 and 415–33.

31. Broad, *Teller's War*, 113; Thomas McCormick, *America's Half-Century: United States Foreign Policy in the Cold War* (Baltimore: Johns Hopkins University Press, 1989), 230; Broad, *Teller's War*, 138; for a concise history of the U.S.' missile-defense obsessions, see Center for Defense Information, *National Missile Defense: What Does It All Mean?* (Washington, D.C.: CDI, 2000).

32. Jeff Gerth, "Reagan Advisers Received Stocks in Laser Concern," *New York Times*, April 28, 1983, A1; Helionetics' denial from "Denial on Teller's Role," *New York Times*, April 29, 1983, D2; Edward Teller, "Of Laser Weapons and Dr. Teller's Stock," *New York Times*, July 1, 1983, A22. For the evidence proving Teller's denial was legalistically accurate (he did not advise the president on the text of his March speech) but on the whole deceptive (he was one of the chief architects and most strident boosters of Star Wars—he therefore knew what the president was about to propose), see Broad, *Teller's War*, 94–137; and Philip Boffey, William Broad, Leslie Gelb, Charles Mohr, and Holcomb Noble, *Claiming the Heavens: The New York Times Complete Guide to the Star Wars Debate* (New York: Times Books, 1988), 3–25.

33. Subcommittee of the House of Representatives' Committee on Government Operations, *Favoritism and Bias within the Defense Science Board and Other Military Advisory Panels* (Washington, D.C.: GPO, 1984), 1, 2, 66.

34. Exchange quoted from ibid., 120. For sketches of Brooks, see "Brooks Feels Right at Home in the House," *Houston Chronicle*, October 9, 1994, 1; and "Voter's Guide," *Houston Chronicle*, October 30, 1994, 6. Brooks was later implicated in his own scandal, this one involving massive stock purchases in 1991 with the First National Bank of Silsbee, Texas (see "Rep. Jack Brooks," a *Mother Jones* special report available by following the links at www.motherjones.com/news/special_report).

35. Quotation about Thayer's conviction from Cunningham, *Scientific Advisers and American Defense Policy*, 360, and see 365–471 on the DSB during the Reagan years. For stories about Thayer and Reagan-era corruption, see Philip Shenon, "Top NASA Official Indicted in Fraud on Weapons Cost,"

New York Times, December 3, 1985, A1; and Steven Roberts, "Espousing 'High Morality,' Living with Scandal," *New York Times*, May 15, 1987, B10.

36. DeLauer was USDRE from 1981–1984, when he left that post to rejoin the DSB; Cunningham, *Scientific Advisers and American Defense Policy*, 361. Brooks's 1983 report on *Defense Science Boards* notes that prior to his government service, DeLauer was an executive vice president at TRW, one of the nation's leading weapons firms (p. 6).

37. Edward Reiss, *The Strategic Defense Initiative* (New York: Cambridge University Press, 1992), 103, 104, 107.

38. Defense Science Board, *Report of the Defense Science Board Task Force Subgroup on Strategic Air Defense (SDI Milestones Panel)* (Washington, D.C., 1988); Tom Wicker, "Star Wars in Decline," *New York Times*, June 14, 1988, A27; Brooks's statement in *Defense Science Boards*, 2.

39. For a concise version of this argument, see Mark Danner, "Taking Stock of the Forever War," *New York Times Sunday Magazine*, September 11, 2005, 45–53, 68, 86–87. For longer versions, see Mann, *Incoherent Empire*; Stephen John Hartnett and Laura Ann Stengrim, "War Rhetorics: *The National Security Strategy of the United States* and President Bush's Globalization-Through-Benevolent-Empire," *South Atlantic Quarterly* 105 (2006): 175–206; and John Newhouse, *Imperial America: The Bush Assault on the World Order* (New York: Knopf, 2003).

40. Michael Klare, *Blood and Oil: The Dangers and Consequences of America's Growing Petroleum Dependency* (New York: Metropolitan Books, 2004), 26–55 on the "lethal embrace." On the relationships among U.S. imperialism, U.S. oil needs, and rising terrorism, see Aijaz Ahmad, "Imperialism of Our Time," and Michael Klare, "Blood for Oil: The Bush-Cheney Energy Strategy," both in *The New Imperial Challenge*, ed. Leo Panitch and Colin Leys (London: Palgrave, 2003), 43–62, 166–85; Michael Ruppert, *Crossing the Rubicon: The Decline of the American Empire and the End of the Age of Oil* (Gabriola Islands, B.C. [Canada]: New Society, 2004); and Peter Dale Scott, *Drugs, Oil, and War: The United States in Afghanistan, Colombia, and Indochina* (New York: Rowman & Littlefield, 2003).

41. The DSB was not acting alone in this regard; for coverage of other proposed propaganda programs, see Thom Shanker and Eric Schmitt, "Pentagon Weighs Use of Deception in a Broad Area," *New York Times*, December 13, 2004, A12.

42. President George Bush, "Remarks on Arrival at the White House and an Exchange with Reporters" (September 16, 2001); the triggering question and

the president's response are from pages 2 and 3 of the transcript downloaded from *Weekly Compilation of Presidential Documents,* available through the Government Printing Office at www.frwebgate.access.gpo.gov. For glowing responses to the president's "Islam is Peace" speech, see (no author), "Wartime Rhetoric," *New York Times,* September 19, 2001, A26, which praised the president's "high eloquence"; and Dana Milbank and Emily Wax, "Bush Visits Mosque to Forestall Hate Crimes," *Washington Post,* September 18, 2001, A1. For a more sober analysis, see Peter Waldman, "Some Muslims Fear War on Terrorism is Really a War on Them," *Wall Street Journal,* September 21, 2001, A1.

43. For critiques of the crusade comment, see Hywel Williams, "Crusade is a Dirty Word," *The Guardian,* September 18, 2001; Peter Ford, "Europe Cringes at Bush 'Crusade' against Terrorists," *Christian Science Monitor,* September 19, 2001; and Rahul Mahajan, *The New Crusade: America's War on Terrorism* (New York: Monthly Review, 2002), 16–19. Quotations of the president's speeches from President Bush, "The President's News Conference" (October 11, 2001), available from *The Weekly Compilation of Presidential Documents;* President Bush, "Address to the Nation on Homeland Security from Atlanta" (November 9, 2001), "President Delivers the State of the Union Address" (January 28, 2002), "President Bush Thanks Germany for Support against Terrorism" (May 23, 2002), and "President Bush Signs Homeland Security Act" (November 25, 2002), all available from the White House at www.whitehouse.gov.

44. David Brooks, "The Cult of Death," *New York Times,* September 7, 2004, A27; for a brilliant analysis of the usefulness of such tropes of monstrosity, see "Dialectic of Fear," chapter 3 of Franco Moretti, *Signs Taken for Wonders: Essays in the Sociology of Literary Forms,* trans. David Forgacs (London: New Left Books, 1983), 83–108.

45. President Bush, "President Thanks Military, Guests at 'Celebration of Freedom' Concert (Washington, D.C., January 19, 2005); "State of the Union Address" (Washington, D.C., February 2, 2005), page 4 of the printout available from the White House. For analyses of President Bush's rhetoric, see John M. Murphy, "'Our Mission and Our Moment': George W. Bush and September 11th," *Rhetoric & Public Affairs* 6 (2003): 607–32; Denise Bostdorff, "George W. Bush's Post–September 11 Rhetoric of Covenant Renewal: Upholding the Faith of the Greatest Generation," *Quarterly Journal of Speech* 89 (2003): 293–319; and Hartnett and Stengrim, *Globalization and Empire.*

46. President Bush, "President Discusses Freedom and Democracy (Washington, D.C., March 29, 2005), 2, and "President Discusses War on Terror" (Fort Hood, Texas, April 12, 2005), 3, both speeches available from the White House; for cheerleading coverage of the Fort Hood speech, see Richard Stevenson, "Bush Praises Troops' Role in Helping to Free Iraq," *New York Times*, April 13, 2005, A10; 40% from William Greider, *Fortress America: The American Military and the Consequences of Peace* (New York: Public Affairs, 1998), 3; quotation from Hartnett and Stengrim, "War Rhetorics," 177; for a history of this trope of warmaking-as-peace, from the Cold War through the present, see Ivie, *Democracy and America's War on Terror*, 111–16, 123–39. This reading of the president's Fort Hood speech contains material previously published in Stephen John Hartnett and Jennifer Rose Mercieca, "A Discovered Dissembler Can Achieve Nothing Great: or, Four Theses on the Death of Presidential Discourse in An Age of Empire," *Presidential Studies Quarterly* 37 (2007): 599–621.

47. *The Report on Strategic Communication* includes a list of the DSB Task Force's membership (appendix A, p. 91) and a schedule of its briefings (appendix B, p. 92); for information on the firms alluded to here, go to www.appliedminds.net, www.dmg.org, and www.mitre.org; for a sampling of the kind of advice these figures offered the DSB, see David Morey, "Winning the War of Ideas," a February 10, 2004, presentation before the U.S. Congress's Subcommittee on National Security, Emerging Threats and International Relations (accessible at www.au.af.mil/au/awc/awcgate/congress/public_diplomacy_morey_feb04.pdf); regarding the Rendon Group, see Pratap Chatterjee, "Information Warriors: Rendon Group Wins Hearts and Minds in Business, Politics, and War," *CorpWatch*, August 4, 2004, accessed at www.corpwatch.org; Norman Solomon, "War Needs Good Public Relations," *Media Beat*, October 25, 2001, accessed at www.fair.org; and James Bamford's stunning exposé "The Man Who Sold the War: Meet John Rendon, Bush's General in the Propaganda War," *Rolling Stone*, November 17, 2004, accessed at www.rollingstone.com.

48. Aldous Huxley, *Brave New World Revisited* (New York: Harper & Brothers, 1958), 137; on the notion of a new totalitarianism, see Hartnett and Stengrim, *Globalization and Empire*, 267–92; regarding the DSB's decline from an advisory panel into something closer to "a corporate board made up only of members of its own industry," see Smith, *The Advisors*, 65.

49. Ivie, *Democracy and America's War on Terror*, 5, 13. For overviews of this question about the relationship between democratization and war, see Fareed

Zakaria, *The Future of Freedom: Illiberal Democracy at Home and Abroad* (New York: W. W. Norton, 2003); and Joanne Gowa, *Ballots and Bullets: The Elusive Democratic Peace* (Princeton, N.J.: Princeton University Press, 1999).

50. Dilip Gaonkar, "The Idea of Rhetoric in the Rhetoric of Science," in *Rhetorical Hermeneutics: Invention and Interpretation in the Age of Science*, ed. Alan Gross and William Keith (Albany: State University of New York Press, 1997), 25–85 in full, quotation from 32; and see Karlyn Kohrs Campbell, "Agency: Promiscuous and Protean," *Communication and Critical Cultural Studies* 2 (2005): 1–19.

51. See Bryan C. Taylor, "The Politics of the Nuclear Text: Reading Robert Oppenheimer's Letters and Reflections," *Quarterly Journal of Speech* 78 (1992): 429–49; and "Organizing the 'Unknown Subject': Los Alamos, Espionage, and the Politics of Biography," *Quarterly Journal of Speech* 88 (2002): 33–49.

52. Gordon Mitchell, "Placebo Defense: Operation Desert Mirage? The Rhetoric of Patriot Missile Accuracy in the 1991 Persian Gulf War," *Quarterly Journal of Speech* 86, (May 2000): 121–45 in full, quotations from 123, 140; Mitchell, "Japan-U.S. Missile Defense Collaboration: Rhetorically Delicious, Deceptively Dangerous," 99; and see *Hitting First: Preventive Force in U.S. Security Strategy*, ed. William Keller and Gordon Mitchell (Pittsburgh: University of Pittsburgh Press, 2006).

53. Scheer, "Teller's Obsession," 6.

54. A new wave of organizational work is moving past this characterization. For examples, see Shiv Ganesh, Heather Zoller, and George Cheney, "Transforming Resistance, Broadening Our Boundaries: Critical Organizational Communication Meets Globalization from Below," *Communication Monographs* 72 (2005): 169–91; John C. Lammers and Joshua B. Barbour, "An Institutional Theory of Organizational Communication," *Communication Theory* 16 (2006): 356–77; and the works cited above by Bryan Taylor, Gordon Mitchell, and Lisa Keranen. These works build upon the politically oriented form of organizational communication scholarship that has been practiced by George Cheney, Stanley Deetz, and Dennis Mumby.

55. Martin Medhurst, "Rhetoric and Cold War: A Strategic Approach," in *Cold War Rhetoric: Strategy, Metaphor, and Ideology*, ed. Martin Medhurst et al. (New York: Greenwood, 1990), 19–27, where he calls for a "strategic approach" (p. 19) that recognizes how Cold War rhetorical production is constrained by "the history of superpower relations, domestic political concerns, the status of both domestic and world economies, present diplomatic negotiations, and the ever-present possibility of military engagement" (p. 21).

56. For a programmatic statement regarding engaged scholarship, see Larry Frey, Barnett Pearce, Mark Pollock, Lee Artz, and Bren Murphy, "Looking for Justice in All the Wrong Places: On a Communication Approach to Social Justice," *Communication Studies* 47 (1996): 117, 111. For case studies, see Dwight Conquergood, "Homeboys and Hoods: Gang Communication and Cultural Spaces," in *Group Communication in Context: Studies of Natural Groups*, ed. Larry Frey (Hillsdale, N.J.: Erlbaum, 1994), 23–55; Stephen John Hartnett, "Lincoln and Douglas Engage the Abolitionist David Walker in Prison Debate: Empowering Education, Applied Communication, and Social Justice," *Journal of Applied Communication Research* 26 (1998): 232–53; and the essays collected in *Communication Activism*, vol. 1, *Communication for Social Change*, ed. Larry Frey and Kevin Carragee (Cresskill, N.J.: Hampton, 2007).

57. Don DeLillo, *Underworld* (New York: Scribner, 1997), 563; for analysis of DeLillo's masterpiece, see Taylor and Hartnett, "National Security, and All That It Implies," 482–85.

58. Jacques Derrida, "No Apocalypse, Not Now (Full Speed Ahead, Seven Missiles, Seven Missives)," trans. Catherine Porter and Philip Lewis, *Diacritics* 14, no. 2 (Summer 1984): 20–31 in full, quotation from 21. For examples of work not cited elsewhere in this essay that pursues this anti-imperial agenda, see Robert Jensen, *Citizens of the Empire: The Struggle to Claim Our Humanity* (San Francisco: City Lights, 2004); Stephen John Hartnett, "'You are Fit for Something Better': Communicating Hope in Anti-War Activism," in Frey, *Communication Activism*; the essays collected in *9/11 in American Culture*, ed. Norman Denzin and Yvonna Lincoln (Walnut Creek, Calif.: AltaMira Press, 2003); and the powerful work published since 9/11 in *Cultural Studies <=> Critical Methodologies*.

8

Rethinking Deliberative Democracy:
Rhetoric, Power, and Civil Society

Gerard A. Hauser

The meaning of democracy is up for grabs. Common parlance often understands democracy as a participatory mode of decision making in which all citizens (or shareholders) have a say, after which a vote is taken and the majority rules. This naive trust of neighbors to play the game on the up-and-up opens a seeming Pandora's box of challenges to the commonplace view. For starters, only fools rush into a tyranny of the majority without the corrective of constitutional boundaries to regulate what is let into democratic procedures and practices, and to preserve minority rights.[1]

Constitutional boundaries, however, can be problematic. For example, boundaries can contain and exclude. Sometimes they contain people who are the same—autochthonous peoples, those who share the same nationality, and so forth. Foreigners, both national and cultural, are barred by those who meet criteria of "proper" identity. Although this construction of democracy excludes the cultural politics of gender and race, the politics of identity is no less conservative. By insisting on refiguring democracy to accommodate difference and identity, cultural politics switches the signs of purity and impurity; it transforms the banished into innocent victims while condemning the dominant group as tainted.[2]

It is also the case that the ideals of participatory rhetoric lead to the commodification of democracy by exporting it to "liberate" nation-states regarded as "non-democratic." Although narrated as securing a process of self-determination through a constitution that guarantees voting rights, the exported output is a state ruled by a particular form of government, usually envisioned as friendly to the exporting nation. Meanwhile, exporters, who invoke democracy as the rationale for intruding in the internal affairs of another country, sometimes use "democracy" as a rhetorical cover for a multitude of sins committed in its name. Exporting democracy as if it were a commodity ignores the political learning necessary to replace traditions of governance and political dealings in its new surroundings.[3] It took British colonials 150 years of living in the New World before they were able to envision themselves in terms other than as subjects of the British crown, and another twelve years before they adopted a democratic constitution.

Some portray democracy as a political system marked by open procedures in which all have equal access to information, media of dissemination, and participation in the political process that ultimately informs and guides action by representatives of the people's will. The romance of *vox populi, vox dei* offers a reflection of our better angels in mirrors that warp the image of advantages held by special interests, epistemic and moral elites, elites of wealth and birth, and well-positioned aides-de-camp to hoard information, access to media they often own or control, and entrée to public officials.

These formulations, among others, share in locating democracy as a political practice ultimately found in the state. However, as Sheldon Wolin observes, democracy is more than the place where the political is located; more fundamentally it is concerned with how democratic politics is experienced, including revolution. "Revolutionary transgression," he writes, "is the means by which the demos makes itself political. It is by *stasis* not *physis*, that the demos acquires a civic nature."[4] Understanding democracy as how politics is experienced entails rhetoric.

To say that democracy is inherently rhetoric-based stands either as an amendment to, or a differentiation from the current wave of scholarly work under the rubric of deliberative democracy. The deliberative-democracy discussion has theorized the quality of deliberation with respect to political choice, with most participants understanding deliberation on philosophical terms of communication as set forth in Jürgen Habermas's model of critical rationalism.[5]

This is not necessarily good news for rhetoricians. Although rhetoricians study institutional discourse and the quality of arguments that support public decisions, most do not assume that political choice is always rational, or that reason alone is the litmus test for the quality of public argument. Moreover, most contemporary rhetoricians use a broader palate of participatory discourse than that of political actors deliberating in official sites. However, the current multidisciplinary discussion has left rhetoric mostly on the sidelines, either as an assumed activity whose bearing on the meaning of deliberative democracy goes undiscussed, or as a risky form of discourse that threatens to destabilize communicative action.[6]

In response, rhetoric scholars who explore democracy's rhetorical requirements may provide excellent news for developing a more comprehensive theory of deliberative democracy, and possibly one more sensitive to the way deliberation actually occurs among the citizens of liberal democracies. One cannot imagine democratic life without it entailing conditions of public life. Nor can one imagine public life without it entailing conditions of power. There is a further entailment, often recognized but underdeveloped, that I wish to explore in this chapter: how public life and power entail rhetoric, especially as rhetorical discourse is experienced in the lives of the body politic.

My interest in this chapter is theoretical: to develop a rhetorical framework for understanding deliberative democracy, or what I have elsewhere referred to as rhetorical democracy.[7] My method will be to use a representative anecdote (the formation of the Polish trade union Solidarity) as an examplar for the theoretical claims I wish to advance about how ordinary citizens engage in public deliberation, and as a heuristic to generate these claims. I will develop my theoretical argument for situating deliberative democracy within a rhetorical framework by tacking back and forth between the theoretical and the case of Solidarity. My concern throughout is to move beyond the rhetoric of opposition found in resistance to the more general condition of opposing commitments that define the general state of public deliberation today.

I will begin, then, with a narrative of the events that led to Solidarity's founding. The aspiration for democracy that inspired Solidarity's resistance and subsequent political change in Poland is always in the background when ordinary citizens in a free society engage in public deliberation. Solidarity's dramatic unfolding is felicitous insofar as it reflects the range of free associations and ties of public life independent of the state, as well as strategies of self-organization to make civil society possible. As such, the opening section of this chapter will serve as an exemplar of the ongoing contestation for power within an active society. Next, I will use Solidarity's rhetorical manifestations of contestation with power heuristically to argue that an active society is marked by conflictive relations, and that rhetoric serves as such a society's inventional resource for establishing relations by which it continually produces itself. In the third section, I will contend that deliberation among citizens in a democracy is less formal and less tied to institutional norms than to practices of participation, that these practices occur most evidently in civil society, that they are marked by vernacular more than formal rhetoric, and that they suggest democracy requires bottom-up political relations based more on compromise than rational consensus. Finally, I will maintain that relations of mutual dependency inherent to civil society provide a basis for developing trust among partners who are marked by difference.[8]

Accommodating differences among ideas and practices circulating among interdependent partners makes it possible for us to form a civic community based on relations of collaboration and the inventive possibilities of compromise.

The Rhetorical Performance of Democracy

During August 1980, the free world was mesmerized by the drama of worker strikes spreading across Poland. If democracy is more than a governmental structure, that summer's events provided a riveting performance of political rebirth when it arrived at the denouement of an accord granting Polish workers the right to form trade unions independent of the Communist Party. Ordinary citizens were reclaiming their right to form as a public and to assert its power. A primary focus of that summer's drama was the major role of rhetoric as a public principle that breathed life into democracy's rebirth.

The story of Solidarity's[9] founding remains captivating. In the immediate aftermath of August 1980, a voluminous literature appeared

describing the movement's episodic journey into Poland's political transformation and analyzing its causes and significance.[10] These accounts
provide a fairly consistent version of how the strikes were precipitated.

Poland's First Secretary Edward Gierek came to power in 1970 amidst
widespread labor unrest. Gierek determined that Poland's economic problems stemmed from overreliance on agriculture and small industry. He
initiated policies intended to shift Poland's economy to heavy-industrial
production. Poland would compete on the world market with the economic forces of Western Europe. The support and motivation of Polish
workers were enticed by the vision of satisfying consumer wants. Ten
years later, the Polish economy was in shambles. Poland was heavily in
debt, its industrial plant was in poor repair, its international credit was
so low that it could not borrow money even to provide spare parts, its
balance of trade was in the red, and its currency was virtually worthless
beyond its own borders.[11] Moreover, Polish laborers were demoralized.
They worked long hours, including Saturday and Sunday; wages were
incommensurate with consumer needs; and food—especially meat—was
in short supply.

In the summer of 1980, exhausted and beleaguered, the regime of
party first secretary Edward Gierek decided that internal economic adjust-
ments were necessary, especially in light of the worldwide inflationary
spiral that put Polish prices out of line with its own economic realities.
Thus it initiated a steep increase in food prices. Polish workers immediately began to strike.

The strikes started in Mielec in the south and gradually worked their
way northward until they reached the Baltic coast. They were local in
nature, as plant by plant workers put down their tools. At the outset they
clearly were concerned with economic matters. The demand for higher
wages received a positive hearing from the state, and it soon became apparent that the regime was willingly giving Polish workers small economic
gains to get them back to work.

By August the strikes fanned out into the mining regions of Silesia
and the Baltic shipyards in Gdansk, Gdynia, and Szczecin, where they
almost followed the prevailing pattern of quick settlement. In fact, as late
as August 15, the day after the Gdansk strike began, the demand for a pay
increase of 2,000 zlotys per month was met, and strike leader Lech Walesa
announced that an agreement had been reached. However, the workers refused to accept it and beseeched Walesa to reconsider. It would be

wrong, they argued, to make the Lenin shipbuilders' gain everyone else's loss. The workers maintained they should not weaken their bargaining leverage by accepting the state's proposal until other Baltic workers' demands were settled. Walesa was persuaded and turned back to the rank and file to proclaim: "We must continue the strike out of solidarity, until everybody has won."[12] The Lenin shipyard remained on strike.

Now the work stoppage was a solidarity strike, and in that context, negotiations assumed a different cast. The next day, August 16, the Inter-Factory Strike Committee (MKS) was formed, with nineteen delegates representing 388 enterprises. It drafted a common set of demands that punctuated the radical nature of their joint effort, the first and most notorious of which was the insistence that Polish workers be granted the legal right to form independent trade unions.[13] Amazingly, unlike previous strikes that ended in the militia bringing them to a violent end,[14] the terms were met, and on August 31 an agreement was reached in which the regime acknowledged the workers' right to form independent unions. Immediately, the trade union known as Solidarity was formed.

Tempting though it may be to say that Solidarity was the child born from a decade of fiscal disintegration,[15] there are excellent reasons to resist economic explanations. Economic crises were endemic to the communist nations of Central and Eastern Europe. Their currencies were soft; their colonial relation to the Soviet Union deprived them of the vital goods they produced and needed, including food; their populations were impoverished—yet social movements with revolutionary portents seldom occurred. Mostly, Central and Eastern Europeans ground their way through these hardships. It seems unlikely, even in the context of Poland's then current crisis, that economic conditions were the guiding inspiration behind Solidarity's formation. If not economic gain, then what did Solidarity represent to the Polish workers?

The Gdansk Agreement speaks eloquently to this question. From a structural perspective, its points reflect a consciousness of political relations that transcend economic concerns. One must read to Point 7 of its twenty-one demands before pay is even mentioned, and then it is the right of strikers not to be docked pay as a penalty for laying down their tools. Their demands addressed the broad spectrum of grievances that prevailed in Polish social and political life, which suggests that the right to form independent trade unions was not born of dissatisfaction with wages, but with the social and political order. Theirs was the greater desire

TABLE 1. SUMMARY OF GDANSK ACCORDS

1. Accept trade unions free and independent of the party.
2. Guarantee the right to strike and safety of those who help them.
3. Respect freedom of expression and publication and grant the Church access to the media.
4. Reestablish the rights of dissenters and cease repression against people for their opinions.
5. Inform the public about the creation of the MKS and its demands, through the mass media.
6. Implement measures for resolving the economic crisis, starting with publishing relevant information and allowing all groups rights of discussion on economic reform.
7. Guarantee back-pay for all strikers to cover the duration of the strike.
8. Increase the minimum wage of all workers 2,000 zlotys per month.
9. Guarantee the sliding scale (tying wages to cost of living).
10. Ensure the domestic supply of products, exporting only the surplus.
11. Suppress commercial prices and the use of foreign currency in domestic sales.
12. Introduce ration cards for meat and meat-based products.
13. Make cadre selection on the basis of merit, not party membership, and abolish other social and economic privileges accorded only to the apparatus and the police.
14. Set retirement ages for women at fifty and men at fifty-five, or after thirty and thirty-five years of work respectively regardless of age.
15. Increase the old-style pensions to the level paid under the new system.
16. Improve work conditions and health services (to this there is an addendum of thirty specific items regarding pay and work conditions plus health and medical benefits).
17. Ensure sufficient daycare facilities for children of working women.
18. Increase the length of maternity leave to three years to allow a mother to bring up her child.
19. Reduce the waiting period for the allocation of housing.
20. Increase the traveling allowance and introduce a cost-of-living bonus.
21. Make Sunday a holiday in factories where there is continuing production, and compensate Saturday work by a commensurate increase in holidays or another free day.

for an active role in shaping the conditions of Polish life. They wanted an
active say in economic and certain social issues, which required a public
realm where they could appear and be heard (table 1).

Under each of these demands as adopted in the Gdansk accord, there
is a protocol detailing the agreements reached on specific practices to be
initiated or ceased, and the timetable for such enactments. As demands,
they contested for power at least over the conditions of their labor, and
quite possibly within Polish society. A review of these provisions and their
accompanying protocols reveals some unexpected patterns, especially in
their subordination of economics to other concerns. First, only four points
(8, 9, 15, and 20) are linked exclusively to income. Point 7 implicitly
ties back-pay to the right to strike, which was a political point especially
pertinent for this strike protesting state initiatives in pricing food. Five
points (10, 11, 12, 17, and 18) raise economic concerns but couple them
to social rights—the right to food, the right to equality, the right to equal
work opportunities for women, and the right of children to be raised by
their mothers through their toddler period. Five points (13, 14, 16, 19,
and 21) have economic implications, but are cast more as issues of social justice: a person's right to equal opportunity for advancement, to a
reasonable retirement age, to work conditions that were safe and that
provided necessities during times of illness or injury, to adequate housing,
to a day off, and to time for religious observances. In short, demands 7
through 21 were as concerned with the sociopolitical order as they were
with economic well-being, suggesting that the Polish workers at the 388
enterprises represented by the MKS had a profound dissatisfaction with
the overall conditions of their lives.

The first six demands were focused more narrowly on conditions of
communication. They provide a framework that supports the conclusion that the Agreement was more a claim to power than exclusively
driven by the desire for economic reform. The MKS demands called for
enabling structures that made it possible for Polish workers to engage in
democratic practices of assembly and free speech in order to negotiate
conditions of work and certain conditions of society. Viewed in the light of
democratic aspirations, these demands for structural change functioned
as a rhetorical performance of power. Unlike the state's use of violence
as an instrumentality to coerce compliance, the strikers' power lay in
their ability to act as a group. The legitimacy of their claims rested on
their coming together in the Gdansk shipyard as a political community

constituted through their ongoing deliberations over actions and tactics.[16] This legitimacy transferred to the negotiations, where the strike committee performed as a political community whose demands were intent on codifying workers' rights to public performances of self-defined collective identity.

Demands fall within the genre of protest rhetoric. Among the many ways to lodge dissatisfaction with objectionable conditions, demands deploy the topoi of confrontation. Their rhetorical valence unites dissenters by drawing a line in the sand. They typically are issued by those out of power with displays of non-negotiability to power. Dominant groups, by contrast, do not make demands; they issue orders. When they issue orders to their subjects, they act with unquestioned authority to discipline recalcitrance with what they consider appropriate punishment. Demands perform the counterpart act of disciplining authority. Without physical resources to enforce their will with violence or legal authority to exercise official sanctions, the powerless deploy a rhetoric of entitlement; demands are claims of autonomy. Were the powerless viewed as lacking sovereignty to defend themselves against imposed conditions that violate their own interests, which is also a claim to equality, they would lack public warrant to have their demands taken under consideration. While authority may regard demands as ridiculous or impudent, it is not necessarily the audience for which this rhetoric is intended. Demands performed on the larger stage of public awareness invoke a different set of judges to render a public verdict on the oppressors. Demands are the resource for the powerless to discipline authority through rhetorical acts designed to impose public shame.

The disciplining character of demands also performs a demythologizing function by challenging the power of authority with the counterpower of challengers. The Communist Party's merger of the political with labor had absorbed the workers' voice into state structures. By exercising the state's role in setting the conditions of work while simultaneously claiming to represent worker interests, the party created the absurdity of negotiating with itself. The workers' demands, presented through MKS, exorcised the myth of representation by a performance of collective identity that signified a counter-organization to the party's.

The demands themselves, especially the first six, focus on the conditions for a certain type of experience. Each was a claim related to discourse—to have a voice, to be heard, and to have one's arguments taken seriously.[17] The ethos of free citizens is made legible through exhibitions of self-worth. Here they were manifested in expectations to be treated in certain ways by authoritarian power: acceptance of rights, restraint from using violence, respect for free speech, access to media, cessation of repressing unwanted opinions, use of mass media to inform the public of opposition, and inclusive communication to advance discussion of economic issues. The demands protected the right and the means to live a free public life without fear of punishment for expressing one's views. Demands also dialogize the state's authoritative rhetoric through a rebellious expression of sovereign authority. The Polish state's rhetoric located political authority in the government; striker rhetoric located it in the comity of civic relations among peers. Its incivility toward authority is an ironic exhibition of its desire for a civil society.

These rhetorical features provide insight into Solidarity's revolutionary character and its subsequent history. Its original objective was to provide a voice independent of the state to present workers' needs to the state. Yet it was more than a labor union, a fact that forced Solidarity into ever more intrusive acts in the offical sphere of the state. The differences between Solidarity and a labor union were partly a function of the context and manner of its emergence—labor negotiations with the state to end a general strike. More fundamentally, however, they were a function of strikers coming together as a political community with aspirations for democratic rights and representation that exceeded conditions of labor and that legitimated its power to challenge the state's hegemony in Polish national life.

The rise of Solidarity might be construed narrowly as illustrating an alternative institutional form emerging to fill the void of popular representation within the state. But more fundamentally, Solidarity represented an alternative form of social organization to what Vaclav Havel has dubbed the post-totalitarian state, namely, the organization of civil society.[18] It is significant, for example, that the mid-1980s in Poland and elsewhere within the Warsaw bloc saw oppositional discourse shift its key term of identity from "nation" to "society."[19] In this vein, Adam Michnik's call for a bloodless revolution recognized the futility of armed resistance against a state that had the overwhelming advantage of military weapons and munitions. Poles would cede to the state its right to rule in return for a civil society. Nor was Poland alone in its call for civil society. It spread over Central and Eastern Europe, with an understanding of "civil society" as including both the range of free associations and ties of public life independent of the state, and the strategies of self-organization to make such a public life possible.[20]

The case of Solidarity mirrors the discourse and deeds found elsewhere when the aspiration for democracy has inspired resistance and change, however momentary. The cases of the Workers' Council arising spontaneously and simultaneously with the Hungarian revolution of 1956, the formation of the Worker's Defense League (KOR) in Poland in 1976, and the formation of Charter 77 in Czechoslovakia are examples of people experiencing politics.[21] In embryo, the Gdansk Agreement, as do these other cases, embodies the conception and enactment of power and authentic public life as rhetorical accomplishments. Such performances—political episodes that fuse theory and praxis—are what those living under post-totalitarian conditions referred to as "living in truth."

Rhetorical Contours of Society's Self-Production

An active society distinguishes itself by its ongoing activity of self-production. Solidarity's emergence fell along Poland's historical trajectory as a 1,000-year-old resistance community. During the communist era, resistance was forced underground where, except for labor unrest or an occasional rising, discontent manifested itself in the dark mood of cynicism, and also in the more constructive, active intellectual and practical engagement among dissidents in their struggle for some semblance of a civil society. Although an expanded analysis of Solidarity's emergence from the counter-public sphere of underground activity is not the purpose of this chapter, it is worth noting its immediate effect.[22] Solidarity aroused the larger mass of Polish society from a languor in which the vast majority of citizens were engaged in the labor of making ends meet while reserving their acts of protest to attending Sunday mass. Their arousal points us toward the theoretical relationship between rhetoric and society's self-production.

In this section, I wish to flesh out this relationship. I will draw on social theorists who maintain that an active society is marked by conflictive relations to argue that rhetoric serves as such a society's inventional resource for establishing relations by which it continually produces itself. Uncoupling this union confuses rhetoric's meaning and significance as a social practice and undermines the very concept of an active society as engaged in self-production.

Social theory commonly holds that social will is formed through discourse. However, the character of discourse often is theorized in ideal and counter-factual terms. Most notable among such formations is Jürgen Habermas's theory of communicative action.[23] Iris Marion Young claims that Habermas is not alone in this regard.[24] She points to leading deliberative-democracy theorists, such as Seyla Benhabib and Amy Gutmann, who share an equally strong insistence that discourse adhere to norms of rationality.[25] Young continues in a vein familiar to rhetoricians by observing that rationality is seldom the hallmark of social and political discourse as it actually occurs in a democracy. Moreover, as feminist and culture critics concerned with subaltern publics have argued, there are good reasons to be wary of rationality as the normative basis for understanding how democracy functions, much less functions well.[26]

I have argued in previous work for a rhetorically nuanced understanding of political exchange as essential for interpreting and assessing how actual discourse shapes social and political will.[27] Discursive phenomena are more than a society's defining expressions of knowledge and power; they manifest a society's ongoing activity of asserting its identity. These assertions are necessarily partisan expressions by citizens attempting to establish the core values and meanings that constitute them as a society—that is, as groups and classes set in relationships necessarily producing disequilibria of power, alienation, and counter-assertions aimed at reallocating society's resources. In this sense, as Alain Touraine teaches, societies are active, and their activity is to produce themselves.[28]

Although economic, historical, and institutional factors play important roles in a given society's shape and direction, the case of Solidarity's formation suggests that these elements lack sufficient power to determine a priori a society's specific contours. Rather, such factors are part of the overall set of conditions that engage citizen struggles to transform or sustain society and its institutions. Discourse has elastic agency to enable and constrain social transformation. The most fundamental resource for penetrating social consciousness of what is and what might be is society's symbols. Their capacity to expand and contract the field of relations outside the human subject—historicity, sociality, and ideology primary among them—provide rhetorical elasticity, or the varying capacity to appropriate this field of relations and tie rhetoric intrinsically to society's self-production.

A conception of society as active is equally essential to rhetoric studies. Since the 1960s, a significant body of scholarship has developed around rhetoric as a social practice.[29] These lines of research contribute to our understanding of how the symbolic means by which we establish identification, forge a sense of identity, influence choice, and propagate arbitrary practices under the appearance of being natural also drive wedges by which arbitrary practices are separated from their naturalizing representations.[30] These wedges induce social coordination and cooperation, and constitute social will. In addition, this work has expanded our understanding of how the manner of communication bears on the shape and functionality of the public spheres in which we perform acts of citizenship.

Rhetoric's agonistic quality facilitates initiatives that question social relations and sometimes transform them. In an active society, the efforts of institutional and class interest to dominate social will are not historically, economically, or socially determined; that would make rhetoric an idle practice. Neither, alternatively, do they reduce rhetoric to irrational manipulation. An active society is always producing symbolic representations of experience in which we are able to decipher rhetoric's vital role. The Lenin shipyard strikers illustrated this point when they made entreaty not to settle, on grounds that their gain would put workers elsewhere at a disadvantage. This claim emerged from long memory of the state's tactics of power and control, and equally long memory of past strikes that ended in futility when workers self-destructed by not acting responsibly and in solidarity.

Society accumulates these rhetorical residues, investing them with cultural legitimacy as self-generating activities of self-production. They are the living memory of citizen attempts to appropriate and reappropriate their own historicity, to control values and norms, and to overcome subjugation from dominant groups or institutions.[31] Turning the strike at the Lenin shipyard into a solidarity strike linked these Poles to the trajectory of opposition that runs across Poland's 1,000-year history, and framed the communist state as no different from other foreign powers that had occupied Poland's territory.

Orienting toward society's self-producing character avoids romantic or imperial portrayals of rhetoric's role in the complex process of social production. At its best, rhetoric expresses alternative relations that challenge and even disrupt community and enable society to imagine dissensus as a means for instigating social change.[32] Understanding society as active, with its principle business being its own self-production, provides a social theory that can ground rhetoric's claim to being an essential practice for social-will formation. It makes apparent why the social practice of rhetoric is more than an expression of knowledge. It also is constitutive of power.

The concept of power is used in social theory as an analytic category. Its meaning shifts with the terms that are understood to chart and alter the course of society.[33] My use here follows the lead of Hanna Arendt, who distinguishes power from strength, force, authority, and violence. Arendt argues that "power" is a special property of social community, namely, its capacity for common action. In this, she differs from other theorists who hold power to be the capacity of an individual to impose her will on the weak, through the use of force if necessary, or the unquestioned recognition of a person to command subordinates who are ordered to obey.[34] By contrast, Arendt theorizes power as a group phenomenon. Whereas violence is instrumental, which means it always stands in need of justification, power needs no justification since it is inherent in political communities.[35] Arendt elaborates on her communication-based theory of power as springing up "whenever people get together and act in concert, but it derives its legitimacy from the initial getting together rather than from any action that may follow." In this regard, power is related to a capacity to deal with conflictive relationships that typify the conditions from which publics emerge and in which societies produce themselves. Conflictive relationships are equally the wellspring from which rhetorical practices flow. Interestingly, Arendt continues to argue that when legitimacy is challenged, power bases itself on the trajectory of the past—on a group's historicity. On the other hand, violence can never legitimate itself; it can only justify itself in means-ends terms. It looks to the future, and the further its supposed end stretches into the future, its justification loses plausibility.[36]

Arendt's theory of power as a group phenomenon that derives inherent legitimacy from forming political community contrasts with the use of violence when power is being lost. The history of colonized states bears testimony to her formulation. Solidarity would never have arisen had the collective ideology of the Polish United Worker's Party (PZPR) retained legitimacy in the eyes of Polish workers. The history of Polish worker resistance prior to Solidarity's formation was one of futility, as strikes degenerated into disorganized protests that eventuated in violent melees with the police. Solidarity's success in 1980, by contrast, was a model of organization that thwarted the state's predisposition to impose its will by violence. Its power was inspired in large measure by the rhetorical experience of community during John Paul II's visit the preceding year and the dry-run opportunity it provided for KOR's communication network, which worked effectively the following year to keep workers informed of events during MKS's negotiations with the state.[37]

This discussion leads to the confluence of civil society, publics, public spheres, democracy, power, and rhetoric. They are joined by the same essential condition for their appearance in the world. Admittedly, this may say no more than Aristotle's observation that rhetoric is a branch of politics. Nonetheless, it asserts just as clearly that civil society, publics, public spheres, and democracy are more than political phenomena; they are definitively rhetorical.

Theorizing rhetoric within an active society leads to radical consequences. First, it requires a union between rhetoric and society's self-production. Uncoupling this union confuses rhetoric's meaning and significance as a social practice because it reduces rhetoric to an instrumentality for massive lawlike forces determining social development, and because it projects rhetorical practices resulting from anterior circumstances beyond its bounds and shaping its character.

Theorizing rhetoric as coupled to society's self-production focuses on the currents of competing discourses laying claim to a historicity that lies at the core of social movements. Competing rhetorics are not historically, socially, or economically determined; they are manifestations of the ongoing conflict through which society produces itself. This is society's principal activity.[38]

Furthermore, the embrace of rhetoric with an active society problematizes the orthodoxy that situation is the defining condition of rhetoric.[39] Situation is but an element, albeit an important one, in the larger concern with rhetoric's centrality to social will formation. Situations do not define rhetoric with the positivity of objective situational features calling for the actors' responses, nor is social will the product of individuals marching to the beat of necessity. Rhetorical practices and social will are the outcomes of groups and classes that share a social field attempting to define that field's nature and meaning.

Deciphering attempts to define historicity is complicated by the rhetorical practices of the dominant order. They typically are geared toward articulating principles of unity that mask disparate visions of desire. However, behind official visions of reality lies the fact of relationship. It is the defining condition of those who share a social field, and on which their power rests and is legitimated.[40] Individual discourses may be addressed to the exigencies of the given case, but in the larger frame, historical actors are not responding to the situation, but to their relationship. These relationships are necessarily unstable when understood as consisting of conflicting movements. Resolving a labor strike may have provided the exigence for the PZPR to enter into negotiations with the MKS, but the stakes of their negotiations were imbedded in pervasive power relationships within the communist Polish state. Transforming the terms by which labor was organized, which rested on the party's structural construction of authority, with a new degree of autonomy that rested on a rhetorical constitution of power, reframed political relations that eventually led to the fall of the communist state. Conflicts among groups and classes define society by the transitory conditions that mark relationship at the moment of inspection. In significant ways, these relationships are constituted by, experienced in, and sustained through society's rhetoric.

Democracy and the Vocabulary of Participation

The foregoing argument positioned rhetoric at the core of an active society. I argued that an active society is marked by conflictive relations, and that rhetoric serves as society's inventional resource for establishing relations by which it continually produces itself. I now wish to consider the intersection of this perspective with a rhetoric-based understanding of democracy. Here I am particularly interested in decoupling idealized rational norms for assessing how citizens deliberate from the actual practices of citizens. I will argue that deliberation within a democracy is less formal and less tied to institutional norms than to practices of participation, that these practices occur most evidently in civil society, that they are marked by vernacular more than formal rhetoric, and that they suggest democracy requires bottom-up political relations based more on compromise than rational consensus.

The move to reconceptualize democracy in terms of discourse makes an important shift in theorizing political relations. Instead of an exclusively interest-based politics modeled after economic relations, in which the end is personal gain,[41] it projects a politics of participation, in which the outcome is envisioned as a shared political reality. As will become apparent below, this poses its own tricky problems. For now, however, I wish to underscore that a polity marked by political pluralism requires a different vocabulary than "interests." Rhetoricians, among others, who have argued that a polity of political pluralism holds out the possibility of escaping a win-lose model, have found this vocabulary in a deliberative model of democracy.[42] A deliberative model construes democracy in terms of participation in the ongoing conversation about how we shall act and interact, or our political relations. A vocabulary of participation brings certain types of activity into focus. For one thing, it looks for the ways citizens engage one another on matters of mutual concern. Participation replaces the pursuit of private interests as the central political behavior. Participation emphasizes acts of citizenship that reflect political choice based on consensus among the community's membership.

Democratic participation is, in one form or another, deliberative, which implies that citizens have differences growing out of a plurality of perspectives and interests. Although such interactions may begin with self-interest, pluralism precludes the possibility of personal preferences carrying much weight with partners whose interests and assumptions are not necessarily the same. At this point, we move into the realm of rhetoric where concerns focus rather quickly on finding arguments that will make sense to those who do not share one another's perspectives and interests. They are accomplishments of rhetorical invention born from what Arendt refers to as "representative thinking."[43]

However, a democracy is not a debating society. It does not arrive at formal judgments of who made the better argument. People with differences often continue to disagree despite the rational or dialectical force of opposing arguments. They make headway toward common action when a rationally secured position intersects with their experience. Political action is motivated less by force of reason than by satisfaction of desire. The intersection of reason and experience can open minds to new ways of understanding and thinking beyond ideologically inscribed and routinized solutions for resolving common problems. Intersecting sound and defensible ideas with the other's experience is the basis for forging relationships of shared desires from opposing sets of assumptions, even if these relationships have no more than the coalitional strength that allows disparate perspectives to work together toward mutual goal satisfaction, and even if their agreements are ephemeral. Relationships that transcend disparate interests require inventing arguments with resonance in other frames of reference than one's own; it is a rhetorical achievement.

Beyond citizenly concern for participation, a rich theory of deliberative democracy must move from a procedural model to an inclusion model and from a philosophical reasoning model to a practical reasoning model of deliberation. The procedural model's virtue resides in affording all interested parties the same opportunity to participate in public deliberation and rationalizing decisions by aderence to norms of equal opportunities to present and have views considered, to respond, to access relevant information and media of dissemination, and to forge consensus on the basis of warranted assent without privileging any point of view.[44]

Despite its rational appeal, the procedural model's ideals do not necessarily conform to democracy as it is actually practiced in arenas of pluralistic politics. Not all beliefs are up for grabs; not all beliefs are open to deliberation. Modern democracies share ancient Greek liberties of free speech, the right to assemble, the right to participate, the right to publicize, and the like, as constitutive procedures. But modern democracies also grant other liberties, such as religious liberty, liberty of conscience, liberty of thought and expression, and rights of person and personal property.[45] These rights constrain democratic procedures. We may not share our partner's religious convictions and may even consider them as utterly irrational, but we cannot expect our partner to feel the force of denouncing her religion-based argument as irrational; it has an epistemic status independent of our own.[46] Political pluralism, as Joshua Cohen observes, entails "'the fact of reasonable pluralism'—the fact that there are distinct, incompatible understandings of value, each reasonable, to which people are drawn under favorable conditions for the exercise of their practical reason."[47] The fact that reasonable citizens who hold irreconcilable views make good-faith efforts to live with one another on mutually acceptable terms does not mean that there will be convergence on a single rationally grounded consensus, as the criterion of warranted assent implies.

Consensus alone as a deliberative ideal poses problems of its own. There is no gainsaying that at some point, consensus of some sort is necessary for deliberation to have practical consequences. However, agreements on desired outcomes may result in different degrees of satisfaction; sometimes there are winners and losers. Diametrically opposed commitments may call into question the orthodoxy of common ground and leave consensus as the basis for rationalizing action beyond reach. At the same time, deliberation minimally requires shared commitment to norms of accountability that allow agreement on the terms of engagement. As much as deliberating parties may abhor each others views— they may agree, for example, to refrain from acts that will tear the fabric of shared public values, such as their desire to preserve the network of ties that sustain ongoing practices of mutual dependency, or to protect shared personal values, such as friendship bonds among their children; they may agree to refrain from pushing their ideological differences to extremes. When they do, they affirm that in a context of expanding interdependencies, deliberation among partners with differing ideological and identity commitments goes beyond consensus alone as rationalizing the process of negotiating differences, and focuses more on the outcome of building a commonwealth of public good.[48]

For example, the MKS's demands were a performance of solidarity that linked 500,000 workers from the Baltic coast to the coal-mining center of Silesia representing 388 enterprises. The strikers clearly held views quite the opposite of the state's about their right to negotiate on their own terms. Although the state's concession on the right to form independent trade unions might be seen as a one-sided victory for the workers, the state was not without its own gains. The MKS enacted a rhetoric in keeping with Arendt's conception of power as the capacity of the community to engage in collective action. The MKS's negotiation with the PZPR was a rhetorical performance of equality. The power of collective action presented the state with options that bore serious consequences. It could let the strike continue at the risk of Soviet invasion, quash the strike with military force at the risk of significant social upheaval and, again, Soviet invasion, or agree to the twenty-one postulates, which included religious and political demands along with the option for workers to form independent trade unions. Although these propositions were outside the PZPR's ideology, the efficacy of whatever it chose rested on its capacity to build commonwealth among the PZPR and Polish workers. In return for agreeing to MKS demands, the party was able to retain power without social unrest. While foreign intervention remained a distinct possibility, it was not a certainty, as would have been the case had the PZPR not signed the accords.

Contrary to the philosopher's standard of rational consent, which is prone to reduce deliberation to exchanges among an epistemic elite credentialed to engage in critical rational deliberation, the Gdansk negotiations suggest the impact of desire whereby citizens are motivated to become involved in political issues and partake in deliberative processes. Political issues and decisions are, as Aristotle observed, in the realm of the contingent, and contingencies are not entirely explicable in rationalistic terms. Sometimes we may forge agreements based on reasons that are not mutually held. Sometimes we may come to agreements that serve different ends. Sometimes we may come to agreements that require compromises, which satisfy criteria neither of rationality nor of narrow goal satisfaction.

Rather than focusing on a procedural model to validate deliberative outcomes, a model that emphasizes, as rhetoric does, that democracy is grounded in discursive engagement places greater stock in deliberative inclusion. Inclusion means more than giving voice to a point of view. It also treats reasons acceptable to that point of view as legitimate contributions to the deliberative process, even if they fall outside the mainstream. Otherwise, as Cohen argues, these views and those who hold them are not being treated with equity. Equity is essential to maintaining horizontal relations among citizens participating in a deliberative process that is more than nominally democratic.[49]

Deliberative inclusion also acknowledges a group's vernacular rhetoric, such as formal observances that bear witness, group efforts to organize community action, and informal exchanges among citizens who lack skill or comfort in public speaking, as contributions to the deliberative process. It also stresses norms of practical reasoning that involve public reasons for prudent conduct that go beyond personal or group interest. Practical reasoning is a political faculty. It is exercised through the rhetorical practices of discussion and debate in order to find the common good that underwrites building the commonwealth. It accommodates political pluralism as part of the process of arriving at civil judgment.[50]

The lingering question remains, however, whether this is any less an ideal vision of deliberation than one that adheres to norms of rational consent but is detached from how existing democracies actually function. Were we to stop here, the argument for a revised understanding of deliberative democracy would fail to take into account, as observed above, that democracies are not debating societies, or political ensembles of equally empowered individuals and groups. More needs to be said about how we can account for these differences in a rhetorically based understanding of democracy—one that permits us to interpret political relations on their own terms of performance.

In the case of Solidarity and similar political movements that occurred in Central and Eastern European countries during the period of communist rule, an emphasis on the right to participate in free and open communication eventually was assimilated into a call for civil society. Although civil society was not the state, it was seen as the arena in which citizen exchange could utilize the publicity principle to produce a discourse with power to influence the state.[51] This was bottom-up influence that moved beyond a narrowly institutional construction of democracy to posit a vast associational network in which a broad cross section of citizens might experience democratic participation and deliberation. There is no denying the significance of institutional forums for enacting the business of a democracy, as the anti-totalitarian struggle in Poland and elsewhere for a truly representative democratic state demonstrates. However, limiting deliberative democracy to institutional actors and actions misses the most significant cultural resource on which a deliberative democracy depends: its associational network of civil society.[52]

Civil society is important for a rich conception of deliberative democracy because it is the locus for interaction with difference among citizens who are influenced by often conflicting cultural values and social relations. The primary condition for democracy is an arena for individuals and groups to understand and negotiate differences autonomous from the state. The autonomy of civil society from the state permits a political society to emerge. In it, information and arguments can circulate without state regulation of their form or content. Their circulation may employ the publicity principle to challenge the assumption that representatives, on average, are wiser, or more committed to the common good than the ordinary citizen. Civil society permits the ordinary citizen to negotiate the inevitable agonistic relations among and between groups within a democracy without subordinating difference to unity. That is the role of political parties; they function as an intermediary structure that both intervenes in these differences within civil society, and between civil society and the state. As Touraine argues, democracy requires a political system autonomous from the state, but also a political society able to establish relations with the state and civil society in a way that, in the last analysis, positions civil society to legitimate the state.[53]

The capacity of civil society to circulate information, provide a public sphere for deliberation, and utilize the publicity principle to challege the superior wisdom of state officials is reflected in the decision of KOR's members to live their lives as if an open civil society were a reality.[54] One cannot help but hear Hannah Arendt's position on reality as in the world in KOR's commitment to talk and act with openness, truthfulness, autonomy of action, and trust.[55] The absence of these conditions, coupled with these relational commitments to one another and in society generally, interrogated official "realities." Performances of open communication signaled an alternative political reality to the state's. Of course, the conditions of the post-totalitarian state—the state's monopoly on power, its capacity to impose its will with violence, and representation by only one political party—limited KOR's pre-1980 activities to civil society. On the other hand, Solidarity's secular allegiance of 10 million members in a nation of 35 million overwhelmed the party. It now functioned as a de facto political party, capable of mediating differences within Polish civil society and negotiating with the PZPR and the communist state.

Civil society's normative force resonates with the ideals of deliberative democracy that I have been discussing. The public spheres of civil society bridge the ongoing conversation on issues and interests within society and the arenas of decision making within the community and beyond. As Benjamin Barber observes, "Civil society is not an alternative to democratic government. It is the free space in which democratic attitudes are cultivated and democratic behavior is conditioned. It is not a synonym for the private market but an antidote to commercial selfishness and market incivility. It treats democratic government as civil association's highest form of expression—the association of associations: that is, common action in the name of liberty raised to its most general level."[56] Common actions, including shared discussion and deliberation on questions of shared public interest among citizens organized outside the state, are themselves, in theory, the authorizing base for action by the state.

Civil society's public spheres are, when considered from a rhetorical perspective toward their communicative activity, the discursive loci for public opinion to form.[57] Moreover and importantly, unlike the *vox populi* of an authoritarian regime, they are loci outside authority in which citizens form opinion that is regulative of authority. However, civil society frames the concept of the public sphere in a way that is not always apparent in the literature.[58] Because civil society itself is a network of associations, each bonded internally and externally in a web of mutual dependencies, it supports conceptualizing the public sphere as a plurality of publics that bear a reticulate relation to one another.[59] Whereas traditional rhetoric encourages us to think of a public realm as important for informing displays of virtuosity that may lead the community to rectitudinous action, civil society italicizes the public sphere's function to authorize action through public opinion. Public opinion is more than a nose count and more than the expressed views of its leaders. It is the civil judgments we reach through the convergence of formal and vernacular interactions dispersed across society, occurring in different media, and emanating from voices representative of different viewpoints. Civil society redirects our attention to the language of social dialogue circulating through society, and on which our understanding of political interests and possibilities rests.

This rhetoric-based understanding of democracy is not a call for people power, which is open to multiple interpretations, some of which are openly and demonstratively treacherous. It replaces the trickle-down logic of political power, which seeps from the state to the political system to civil society, with a logic that moves upward from below. Rather than focusing on democracy as based in the equality of individuals, this rhetoric-emphasizing construction focuses on groups as involved in relations that are always ones of inequality or control. The deliberative practices of national resistance groups that affiliate with a desire for civil society are instructive. Hungary's worker's councils formed after the short-lived revolution of 1956,[60] the leadership and rank and file of Solidarity during its fifteen-month history of open activity, and the various political and ethnic councils of South Africa's people of color during the period of apartheid each engaged in the deliberative practices that Vaclav Havel projected for what would transpire when citizens are free to form their own political relations. Certainly they adhered to the ethos of inclusion, but their embrace of deliberation understood it as inevitably given to the partisan wrangling that will ensue when people join in freely formed representative forums.

The goal of collective action in a democracy, itself a performance of power, is not to give everyone their due, but to advance the group's goals. The dominant will try to solidify their position of domination, while the dominated will appeal in the name of equality for support in its struggle against inequality. Justice always struggles against social hierarchy in the name of ethical principles, and the rhetoric of democracy always invokes a moral vernacular capable of ethical traction. What distinguishes this understanding of democracy from rule by an authoritarian state or rule by adherence to normative ideals is that it is based on neither repression nor consensus. Rather, it is rule based on compromise, which is always being challenged by the shifting of power vectors that get translated into laws. Although this may seem to portend a Hobbesian nightmare of each against all, there is evidence that suggests the opposite. Here we come to the tricky aspect of deliberative democracy I noted earlier: the problem of trust.

Trust: *Building the Social Capital Necessary for Deliberative Democracy*

Thus far I have argued that the inescapability of power differentials is mitigated by cascading relations of mutual dependency. Citizens used to think of democracy as a mode of governance that could keep power differentials from imposing the interests of the stronger on the weaker. Citizens realize this is no longer a viable hope, if it ever was; lobby politics reigns, and the animus of lobby politics is interest-based victory. However, democracy is an organic concept that adapts ordinary citizens' aspirations for participation in decisions that have consequences for their lives to the conditions that permit participation. I have contended that those conditions exist in civil society. Today democracy is better thought of as a mode of relationship found outside the state in the mutual dependencies of civil society. These relations are not predicated on an exclusively interest-based politics modeled after economic relations that seek personal gain, but a participatory politics in which the outcome is a shared political reality. Its telos is not consensus, but building commonwealth. In place of consensus, I have suggested that partisanship within democratic relationships is mediated by rhetorical practices that seek and perform conjoint actions of compromise. Admittedly, a rhetoric of compromise forges agreements that rely on future conduct to redeem the partners' sincerity. Equally, democratic arrangements based on compromise are always subject to challenge when the direction and magnitude of power shifts and commonwealth are jeopardized or evaporate. In this section, I will argue that the problem of radical instability that seems inherent to a participatory politics of compromise may be ameliorated, if not overcome, when the rhetorical practices of civil society are performances of trust.

Alexis de Tocqueville observed that the United States is a nation marked by the associative spirit.[61] Although some, such as Robert Putnam, have argued that this spirit is in decline, the evidence still indicates that associative bonds remain a significant national, defining feature.[62] These networks provide ongoing sites and opportunities for citizens to encounter the diversity of fellow citizens with whom they share bonds of interdependency, mutual concerns, and a common need to cooperate for building commonwealth. These relations of mutual dependency are expanded beyond the local and national scene as conditions of globalization and interconnectivity associate individuals and groups with strangers on whom they must depend for their economic, political, and social well-being. As conditions that bind us to partners whose diversity increases in scope and complexity, the idea of dialogue is eclipsed by the reality of multilogue.[63] In multilogue we lose our capacity to understand the basis for our partners' actions or their level of commitment to common goals. This diminished capacity raises trust as a paramount problem for civil society.[64]

The problem of trust arises from the risk that our partners will not honor their commitments. We need confidence that we share a reference world, and look to our partners' habits for reliable experiential background on whether to confer trust. Niklas Luhmann has argued, however, that even bonds of familiarity do not neutralize risk: "Rather than being just an inference from the past, trust goes beyond the information it receives and risks defining the future. The complexity of the future world is reduced by the act of trust. In trusting, one engages in action as though there were only certain possibilities in the future."[65] Luhmann demystifies the act of trust by not depicting it as an ungrounded leap of faith, but as a process that relies on the familiar in order to anticipate the unfamiliar. Importantly, this invaluable and necessary experience for removing the threat of difference grows from the mass of information we gather about others through inherent relations of mutual dependency experienced in the secondary associations of civil society.

Participation in civil society affords an opportunity to encounter the range of difference and acquire a sense for accommodating difference from ideas and practices circulating among interdependent partners. These experiences with difference make it possible to discover the mediating grounds of similarity that support a civic community based on relations of collaboration and the inventive possibilities of compromise. For example, the impulse for KOR's formation was not an interest in exchanges among true believers who spoke as if they were wholly knowing. Its members were agitating for a space where ideas could be exchanged openly and differences could be explored and possibly resolved, without fear of being sent to prison for expressing deeply felt ideas—especially between workers and intellectuals who theretofore had not been mutually supportive during their respective conflicts with the state (see note 17).

Civic community does not require that citizens think alike, or even that they subscribe to views that underwrite consensus. Consensus, in fact, is not to be expected when issues inflame partisan biases and alternative historicities.[66] However, civic community does require citizens who are capable of participating in the deliberative interactions of civic conversation, and who trust this conversation to prove consequential for policies eventually enacted in response to public problems.

Civic conversation contains empirical evidence of the political learning process inherent to a democracy, and thereby redeems the epistemological relevance of public life. More than eighty years ago, John Dewey argued that the means for political learning lay in communication, which required something other than technical presentation. "The essential need," he wrote, "is the improvement of the methods and conditions of debate, discussion and persuasion. That is the problem of the public."[67]

Before we can have the productive civic conversation with difference that Dewey envisioned, we first must overcome the menace of difference that provokes distrust and the antidemocratic rhetoric of intolerance or moral superiority that co-opt the political process, or cynicism and withdrawal from it. For democracy to be a functional form of governance in a society of strangers, citizens must learn how to engage difference in a way that recognizes the individual and the group as a subject.[68]

James Coleman has suggested that the success of such engagements rests on the acquisition of social capital, or the functions within a social structure that "facilitate certain actions of actors." He locates it as a quality inhering "in the structure of relations between actors and among actors."[69] Social capital is not a quality a person has; it exists in relationships. Much as the health of an economy and the prosperity of its individual members are reciprocally related, with each enriching the other, social capital serves to vitalize civil society and its members; it is the currency of trust among them. The iterative relationships of civil society carry an obligation to honor the trust one party places in the other. Trust acquires normative force, making it difficult for the trusted to violate the expectations expressed by being trusted, if only to save face. The bond of placing trust in someone, in this respect, can function as self-fulfilling. In iterative relations of mutual dependency, honoring trust is both a matter of saving face—betrayal can cost one her reputation and, if visible enough, further imperil political relations—and, more self-interestedly, an important source of social capital, making it easier to establish future political relations. As Claus Offe observes, "Trust relationships and their robustness are as much a matter of the receiving side, the trusted, as of the providing side, the truster. Trust is a phenomenon of social reciprocity."[70]

More than this, the arenas of civil society form the locales for building the sort of social capital on which a deliberative democracy depends: their internal and emergent public spheres.[71] Members enact horizontal relations of equality in these spheres. They develop deliberative competencies through consideration of issues that have internal and external significance for their association and the networks in which it is involved. These arenas emerge from ensemble performances, the rhetoric of which develops not only the voice necessary to participate in deliberative democracy, but the social capital necessary to participate in such deliberations with a trustworthy voice. This was the ideal KOR's founders had in mind when they established openness, truthfulness, autonomy of action, and trust as the four principles by which they would treat each other.

The give-and-take of civic conversation requires more than an understanding of social structures. In addition to skill at interpreting formal rhetoric, it requires skill at engaging in the vernacular rhetoric by which we conduct our public transactions with strangers: the everyday micro-practices that reflect values, aspirations, concerns, affiliations, boundaries of acceptance, levels of tolerance, and the like, that indicate shared attachments to the community and shared experiences that make ideas relevant to our lives and shape our civil judgments. Their utter mundaneness notwithstanding, these quotidian exchanges provide an understanding of those with whom we are dealing, and where our interests coincide or diverge. Their vernacular quality involves an ongoing exchange of social capital. It offers strangers assurance that they share a common world to the degree necessary to engage in the ongoing negotiation over how they shall act and interact.[72] Participating in the secondary associations that constitute the web of civil society aids our capacity to assess risk and form expectations about others that can guide our actions and contribute to a civil society in which trust becomes a public good. They represent the primary cultural resource for deliberative democracy to flourish in a nation of strangers.

Conclusion

I initiated this discussion by introducing Solidarity's struggle against oppression as a heuristic for rethinking what it means to live in an active society. Solidarity's challenge to the PZPR's monopoly on worker representation exposed the impossiblity of hermetically sealing conflicting perspectives from one another, even in totalitarian societies, and situated rhetoric as society's inventional resource for producing itself by reordering old relations and establishing new ones. Of course, conditions today in Western liberal democracies are remarkably different from those that gave rise to Solidarity. During the intervening quarter century, national and international relationships have been altered by globalization, Internet connectivity, the fall of the Soviet empire, the rise of paramilitary forces and terrorist networks, and moral elites that have gained political power in the United States and many confessional states in the Middle East. Together they may make Solidarity's rise seem a romantic story of collective action. However, conditions defining the contemporary political milieu have parallels with the deliberative circumstances prevailing at Solidarity's formation. The striking workers and the party were mutually dependent, the strike leaders required social capital to organize workers with sometimes differing agendas, the negotiators on both sides had to cope with problems of trust, and at stake in the negotiations was the role of civil society in creating a viable social order. Each of these remains a central consideration for the transformation of democracy's meaning in the early 2000s.

Democracy means more than a form of governance. It refers to a mode of locating and resolving the concerns of intertwined relationship marked by difference. Tyranny of the majority is no less a problem now than the founders of the republic feared in late eighteenth-century America. Intolerance of difference is no less a problem now than in seventeenth-century England. Willingness to exclude those who hold different beliefs is no less true today than at the time of Salem's witch trials. The reign of elites is no less a threat in the world of interconnectivity than in the client states of the Soviet Union. The argument I have advanced cannot undo these threats, but it does point to the conditions under which a democracy that places a premium on genuine public deliberation as its defining condition can at least retard, if not stem, their control.The ideal of public deliberation is in trouble because buffers between citizens and decision makers are so layered that ordinary citizens are unable to penetrate those circles in which policies are set. The experience of ordinary citizens that they and their elected officals are hermetically sealed from one another is, in part, a function of the way lobby politics is practiced. Their sense of isolation from their officals is exacerbated by conceptions of democratic deliberation that are remote from their experience and only serve to heighten a sense of futility in political participation. On one hand, idealized conceptions of deliberative democracy that portray it in the romaticized terms of equal and open participation where a citizen's views matter in determining the better argument and in shaping policy conclusions seem detached from how deliberation is actually practiced. On the other, concpetions of representative democracy that frame participation in terms of representatives who are political performers rather than the political performances of the represented seem detached from their experience of democratic life. The prevailing realities that condition the common citizen's experience of democratic life are messier and more threatening than public deliberation among partisan leaders. Fragmentation, mutual dependency among partners with ideological and cultural differences, lobby politics that seems to thwart civil society's function as the domain in which these differences are negotiated, and their own affiliations with interest-based structures that propagate distrust of what and who stands outside their power breeds a sense of distance from participatory practices and vulnerability to representatives who prey on difference to protect their political base. Both versions—that participation matters or that their representatives reflect how citizens experience politics—place too little emphasis on the priority of relationship in contemporary democratic life, which must include those whose commitments may differ from our own but whose cooperation we continue to need, if not value in order to resolve issues.

An understanding of democracy as a mode of governance expressed in structural forms projects the citizen as a governed object while ignoring that the loss of citizen agency undermines the core of democracy. A democracy presupposes an active society in which citizens have differences over resources, contest their control, and include structures that encourage and have the capacity to achieve and perform negotiated resolutions. By the same token, deliberation alone is insufficient as a recuperative practice to ameliorate differences without it being understood as a rhetorical practice for negotiating their resolution. Partisan wrangling is a natural development in negotiating power differentials that often involve presuppositions of belief, identity, and tradition. However, how we wrangle to ameliorate differences in twenty-first century democracies must be modified from persuasive practices whose telos is to achieve either majority victory or interest-based consensus.

Networks of affiliation and mutual dependency, which are defining conditions all the way down from globalization to local politics, have altered the meaning of democracy. Civil society's pervasive networks of mutual dependencies have made a politics that prioritizes state institutions, rational and even interest-based consensus, or commitment to leveraging resource advantages into partisan victory either idle or counterproductive. Democracy today is increasingly a mode of relationship found in participatory practices that seek to mediate differences through conjoint actions of compromise that are legitimated by building commonwealth. Rhetoric is essential to situating these relationships at the center of democratic deliberation and as the method for inventing compromise through the ongoing give-and-take of formal and informal, official and vernacular social conversation, wherever it may occur.

This broadened sense of democracy—a rhetorical democracy—thrives where there are civil-society structures and informal networks of association in which citizens can encounter and engage difference and, thereby, participate in a process of political learning. By the very act of participating, they are asked to reexamine their claims, develop respect for the opinions of others, and recognize the overlap of shared values that can reframe issues, or at least constrain acts of intolerance. In addition, they foster the rhetorical skills of constructing arguments and engaging in argumentation, critical listening, and adapting to audience and circumstances. Finally, participation encourages representative thinking, adherence to norms of propriety, recognition of kairotic moments as inventional opportunities to reshape sustainable relations, and openness to the possibility of change. Without these capacities, deliberation is meaningless. These acts of political learning are the basis for arriving at productive solutions with partners who are bound to us.

Finally, the realities of networks of mutual dependency, from local to global, have placed trust among the central problems that viable practices of democratic deliberation must address. Democratic values of inclusion and procedural norms are necessary conditions for meaningful delibera-tion, but they are insufficient to sustain deliberative practices. The prac-tices themselves can only be sustained if they are trusted as a means, if not the preferred and most productive means, for addressing public prob-lems. The value Polish workers placed on negotiating with officials of the Communist Party, representatives of local groups on deliberating issues in Hungary's workers' councils, and Italians on participating in partisan wrangles of political parties suggests that acts of participation led to trust of the deliberative process; it yielded productive outcomes and induced shared commitment to values and norms of engagement that legitimated these outcomes. Trust is necessary to connect people who are otherwise disconnected, to make collective political choices, and to believe that inclusion in the process, even if the outcome is less than completely satis-factory, is fair and consequential in sustaining relationships of mutuality on which the worlds they share depend.

The contemporary problems that thwart democratic practices and deliberative democracy's promise of returning democracy to its inclusive possibilities make the presence or absence of a bottom-up performance of democracy a defining concern. Performing democracy certainly requires stirring discourse that makes public moral arguments in the name of rep-resentative groups. However, at ground level it is enacted ensemble in the vernacular rhetoric of civil society that accommodates difference, en-courages trust among partners with differences, and urges compromise of rigidly held positions through the inventive possibilities of collaboration. Fusing politics and rhetoric to make common concerns and differences visible and legible, while discovering the possibilities for a new, more desirable social order, is the politics and rhetoric not only of the official forum and the empowered official; it also is the politics and rhetoric of citizens capacitated to negotiate with difference. Democracy depends on this capacity for inclusion to be meaningful, for citizens to move from being governed to having agency, and for deliberation to be consequential in addressing the discontents of today.[73]

NOTES

1. Sheldon S. Wolin, "Fugitive Democracy," in *Democracy and Difference: Contesting the Boundaries of the Political,* ed. Seyla Benhabib (Princeton, N.J.: Princeton University Press, 1996), 31–45.

2. Wolin, "Fugitive Democracy."

3. Lawrence C. Dodd, "Political Learning and Political Change: Understanding Development across Time," in *The Dynamics of American Politics,* ed. Lawrence C. Dodd and Calvin Jillson (Boulder, Colo.: Westview Press, 1994), 331–64.

4. Wolin, "Fugitive Democracy," 38.

5. Jürgen Habermas, *The Theory of Communicative Action,* 2 vols., trans. Thomas McCarthy (Boston: Beacon Press, 1984–1987).

6. See Benedito Fontana, Cary J. Nederman, and Gary Remer, eds., *Talking Democracy: Historical Perspectives on Rhetoric and Democracy* (University Park: Pennsylvania State University Press, 2004); Iris Marion Young, *Inclusion and Democracy* (Oxford: Oxford University Press, 2000).

7. Gerard A. Hauser, "Rhetorical Democracy and Civic Engagement," in *Rhetorical Democracy: Discursive Practices of Civic Engagement,* ed. Gerard Hauser and Amy Grim (Mahwah, N.J.: Erlbaum, 2004), 1–14.

8. My argument in this section is drawn extensively from my article coauthored with Chantal Benoit-Barné, "Reflections on Rhetoric, Deliberative Democracy, Civil Society, and Trust," *Rhetoric & Public Affairs* 5 (2002): 261–75. Material from this essay is used by permission of *Rhetoric & Public Affairs.*

9. Solidarity was the name of the free trade union formed in Poland during 1980. The union emerged from a solidarity strike during August of that year. It received legal status the following November. Solidarity was independent of the Polish Communist Party and represented the vast majority of Polish workers during its fifteen-month existence. The government suspended Solidarity's operation in December 1981, when a state of war was declared on the Polish people and martial law was imposed. Subsequently the union was outlawed, though its leaders appear to have maintained the aspirations of its members through underground activities.

10. See Neal Ascherson, *The Polish August: The Self-Limiting Revolution* (New York: Viking Press, 1982); Timothy Garton Ash, *The Polish Revolution: Solidarity* (New York: Charles Scribner's Sons, 1983); Jack Bielasiak and Maurice D. Simon, eds., *Polish Politics: Edge of the Abyss* (New York: Praeger, 1984); Abraham Brumberg, ed., *Poland: Genesis of a Revolution* (New York: Random House, 1983); Michael Dobbs et al., *Poland: Solidarity: Walesa* (New York: McGraw-Hill, 1981); Lawrence

Goodwyn, *Breaking the Barrier: The Rise of Solidarity in Poland* (New York: Oxford University Press, 1991); Jean Yves Potel, *The Summer before the Frost: Solidarity in Poland,* trans. Phil Markham (London: Pluto Press, 1982); Daniel Singer, *The Road to Gdansk: Poland and the U.S.S.R.* (New York: Monthly Review Press, 1982); Alain Touraine et al., *Solidarity: The Analysis of a Social Movement: Poland 1980–1981,* trans. David Denby (Cambridge: Cambridge University Press, 1983); Lawrence Weschler, *The Passion of Poland: From Solidarity through the State of War* (New York: Pantheon Books, 1982).

11. A convenient summary of the problems encountered by Gierek's economic policies may be found in Paul G. Lewis, "Legitimacy and the Polish Communist State," in *States and Societies,* ed. David Held et al. (New York: New York University Press, 1983), 445–50.

12. Quoted in Alain Touraine et al., *Solidarity,* 37.

13. The Gdansk Agreement, listing the workers' demands and the protocols for their operationalization, may be found as an appendix in Brumberg et al., *Poland: Genesis of a Revolution,* 284–95.

14. For example, repression of strikers in Poznan in 1956, and at Ursus and Radom in 1976 ended in violence, while militia action against strikers in Gdansk in 1970 ended in death.

15. Alex Pravda, "Poland 1980: From 'Premature Consumerism to Labour Solidarity," *Soviet Studies* 34 (1982): 167–99. The situation in Poland was quite different from that in free societies such as the United States, which has a tradition of open dissent stretching from its days as a British colony, often organized as social movements. For a sampling of the literature related to the rhetoric of social movements, see Thomas W. Benson and Bonnie Johnson, "The Rhetoric of Resistance: Confrontation with the Warmakers, Washington, D.C., October, 1967," *Communication Quarterly* 16 (1968): 35–42; James Darsey, *The Prophetic Tradition and Radical Rhetoric in America* (New York: New York University Press, 1997); Richard B. Gregg, "The Ego-Function of the Rhetoric of Protest," *Philosophy & Rhetoric* 4 (1971): 71–91; Leland M. Griffin, "The Rhetoric of Historical Movements," *Quarterly Journal of Speech* 38 (1952): 184–88; Griffin, "The Rhetorical Structure of the Antimasonic Movement," in *The Rhetorical Idiom,* ed. Donald C. Bryant (New York: Russell and Russell, 1958), 145–60; Griffin, *Quarterly Journal of Speech* 50 (1964): 113–35; Joseph R. Gusfield, *The Culture of Public Problems: Drinking-Driving and the Symbolic Order* (Chicago: University of Chicago Press, 1981), 1–27; Doug McAdam, "Movement Strategy and Dramaturgic Framing in Democratic States: The Case of the American Civil Rights Movement," in *Deliberation, Democracy, and the Media,* ed. Simone Chambers and Anne Costain

(New York: Rowman and Littlefield, 2000), 117–34; Robert L. Scott, "The Conservative Voice in Radical Rhetoric: A Common Response to Division," *Speech Monographs* 40 (1973): 123–35; Scott and Donald K. Smith, "The Rhetoric of Confrontation," *Quarterly Journal of Speech* 55 (1969): 1–8.

16. See Hanna Arendt, *On Violence* (New York: Harcourt, Brace & World, 1969).

17. On the significance of the public realm for meaningful politics, see Hannah Arendt, *Between Past and Future* (Baltimore: Penguin Books, 1968), 143–71. These demands echo those that evolved independently among Polish intellectuals between 1976 and 1980. See Jane Leftwich Curry, "Polish Dissent and Establishment Criticism: The New Evolutionism," in *Dissent in Eastern Europe*, ed. Curry (New York: Praeger, 1983), 153–72.

18. Vaclav Havel, "The Power of the Powerless," trans. P. Wilson, in *Václav Havel: Living in Truth*, ed. Jan Vladislav (Boston: Faber and Faber, 1989).

19. Timothy Garton Ash, "Eastern Europe: The Year of Truth," *New York Review of Books*, February 15, 1990, 17–22.

20. Ash, "Eastern Europe: The Year of Truth," 20.

21. Workers' councils were established in Hungary during its brief attempt in 1956 to break from the Soviet Union. As the political struggle continued, these councils began to organize a nationwide political system in which revocable delegates from each one undertook a program of democratic socialism based on direct rule by the producers of goods and services. The Worker's Defense League (KOR) was formed by Polish dissidents Jacek Kuron and Adam Michnick in 1976. It was an illegal committee whose purpose was to defend militant workers who were being persecuted following the riots in Radom and Ursus. Its work soon was transformed as it began to expose and publicize atrocities of Poland's apparatchiks. It developed rapprochement between labor, which had been disaffected from the Polish state since 1970 when it responded to a strike with violence, killing a dozen strikers, and intellectuals, who had been disaffected from the state since 1966, when increasingly repressive measures of the Gomulka regime became more and more patent, leading to a clash between Church and State during Poland's millennium celebrations. Together, KOR and Poland's intellectuals established the "flying university" (mobile sites, mainly churches and classrooms, in which political and intellectual exchanges prohibited by the state took place) and an extensive underground communication network. KOR's political activity was the precursor of Solidarity. Charter 77 was a petition drawn up by a group of Czechoslovakian writers and intellectuals, including Vaclav Havel. It demanded that the communist government of Czechoslovakia recognize the

basic human rights already guaranteed by the Czechoslovakian constitution and the Helsinki Accords, which the Czechoslovakian government had signed.

22. I have discussed the emergence of Solidarity in *Vernacular Voices: The Rhetoric of Publics and Public Spheres* (Columbia: University of South Carolina Press, 1999), chap. 5.

23. Habermas, *The Theory of Communicative Action.*

24. Young, *Inclusion and Democracy,* 10–11.

25. See, for example, Seyla Benhabib, "Toward a Deliberative Model of Democratic Legitimacy," in Benhabib, ed., *Democracy and Difference,* 67–94; Amy Gutmann and Dennis Thompson, *Democracy and Disagreement* (Cambridge, Mass.: Harvard University Press, 1996). For a further sampling of essays drawing in whole or in part on these strands, see James Bohman and William Rehg, eds., *Deliberative Democracy* (Cambridge, Mass: MIT Press, 1997); George E. Marcus and Russell L. Hanson, eds., *Reconsidering the Democratic Public* (University Park: Pennsylvania State University Press, 1993); Mark Warren, ed., *Democracy and Trust* (New York: Cambridge University Press, 1999).

26. Geoff Ely, "Nations, Publics, and Political Cultures: Placing Habermas in the Nineteenth Century," in *Habermas and the Public Sphere,* ed. Craig Calhoun (Cambridge, Mass.: MIT Press, 1992), 289–339; Nancy Fraser, "Rethinking the Public Sphere: A Contribution to the Critique of Actually Existing Democracy," *Social Text* 25/26 (1990): 56–80; Joan Landes, "Jürgen Habermas: The Structural Transformation of the Public Sphere: A Feminist Inquiry," *Praxis International* 12 (1992): 106–27; Hudson Meadwell, "Post-Marxism: No Friend of Civility," in *Civil Society: Theory, History, Comparison,* ed. John A. Hall (Cambridge: Polity, 1995), 183–99; Mary Ryan, "Gender and Public Access: Women's Politics in Nineteenth-Century America," in Craig Calhoun, ed., *Habermas and the Public Sphere* (Cambridge: MIT Press, 1992), 259–88.

27. Hauser, *Vernacular Voices: The Rhetoric of Publics and Public Spheres* (Columbia: University of South Carolina Press, 1999).

28. The following discussion draws extensively on Touraine's discussion of social action as self-producing. See Alain Touraine, *The Self-Production of Society,* trans. Derek Coltman. (Chicago: University of Chicago Press, 1977); Touraine, *The Voice and the Eye: An Analysis of Social Movements,* trans. Alan Duff (Cambridge: Cambridge University Press, 1981).

29. Celeste Condit, *Decoding Abortion Rhetoric: Communicating Social Change* (Urbana: University of Illinois Press, 1990; Thomas Farrell, *Norms of Rhetorical Culture* (New Haven: Yale University Press, 1993); G. Thomas Goodnight, "The Personal, Technical, and Public Spheres of Argument: A Speculative Inquiry into the Art

of Public Deliberation, *"Journal of the American Forensic Association* 18 (1982): 214–27; Robert Hariman, *Political Style: The Rhetoric of Power* (Chicago: University of Chicago Press, 1995); Hauser, *Vernacular Voices*; Michael Calvin McGee, "In Search of 'The People': A Rhetorical Alternative," *Quarterly Journal of Speech* 65 (1975): 235–49; Kent Ono and John M. Sloop, "The Critique of Vernacular Discourse," *Communication Monographs* 62 (1995): 19–47; Scott and Smith, "The Rhetoric of Confrontation," *Quarterly Journal of Speech* 55 (1969): 1–8; Philip Wander, "The Rhetoric of American Foreign Policy," *Quarterly Journal of Speech* 70 (1984): 339–62.

30. See Henry W. Johnstone Jr., "From Philosophy to Rhetoric and Back," in *Rhetoric, Philosophy, and Literature: An Exploration*, ed. Don M. Burks (West Lafayette, Ind.: Purdue University Press, 1978), 49–66; "Rhetoric as a Wedge: A Reformulation," *Rhetoric Society Quarterly* 20 (1990): 333–38 for a formulation of how rhetoric performs a "wedging" function.

31. 'Historicity' refers to a society's capacity to produce a model of itself based on its own actions. These include the actions of its cultural and social practices as they combine three components: knowledge, accumulation, and culture. Knowledge models society's image of itself and nature, accumulation models society's disposition of its excess resources, and culture models society's apprehension and interpretation of its capacity to act upon itself. See Touraine, *Self-Production*, 15–64.

32. G. Thomas Goodnight, "Opening up 'The Spaces of Public Discussion,'" *Communication Monographs* 64 (1997): 270–75; Gerard A. Hauser, "On Publics and Public Spheres: A Response to Phillips," *Communication Monographs* 64 (1997): 275–79; Ono and Sloop, "The Critique of Vernacular Discourse"; Kendall R. Phillips, "The Spaces of Public Discussion: Reconsidering the Public Sphere," *Communication Monographs* 63 (1996): 231–48.

33. For contrasts between views of power, see Arendt, *On Violence*, 35–56; Anthony Giddens, *Central Problems in Social Theory* (Berkeley: University of California Press, 1979); Max Weber, *Economy and Society*, trans. Ephraim Fishoff et al. (New York: Bedminster Press, 1968).

34. Arendt, *On Violence*, 36–47.

35. Ibid., 51–52.

36. Ibid., 52.

37. Hauser, *Vernacular Voices*, chap. 5.

38. Touraine et al., *Solidarity*, 1–29.

39. The positioning of situation as the grounding principle for rhetoric stretches from Aristotle's *Rhetoric* to Lloyd F. Bitzer's influential essay "The Rhetorical Situation," *Philosophy & Rhetoric* 1 (1968): 1–14.

40. See James Scott, *Domination and the Arts of Resistance: Hidden Transcripts* (New Haven, Conn.: Yale University Press, 1990) for an extended treatment of the power of the oppressed to resist domination through everyday acts whose mundane appearance disguises opposition performed through vernacular rhetoric.

41. Jon Elster, "The Market and the Forum: Three Varieties of Political Theory," in *Deliberative Democracy*, ed. James Bohman and William Rehg (Cambridge, Mass.: MIT Press, 1997), 67–92.

42. See Robert Asen, "A Discourse Theory of Citizenship," *Quarterly Journal of Speech* 90 (2004): 189–211; Benjamin Barber, *Strong Democracy: Participatory Politics for a New Age* (Berkeley: University of California Press, 1984); Joshua Cohen, "Deliberation and Democratic Legitimacy," in *Deliberative Democracy*, ed. James Bohman and William Rehg, 67–92; John Dryzek, *Discursive Democracy: Politics, Policy, and Political Science* (New York: Cambridge University Press, 1990); Farrell, *Norms of Rhetorical Culture*; Benjamin Ginsberg, *The Captive Public* (New York: Basic Books, 1986); Hariman, *Political Style*; Hauser, *Vernacular Voices*.

43. Arendt, *Between Past and Future*, 241.

44. Habermas, *The Theory of Communicative Action*.

45. Cohen, "Deliberation and Democratic Legitimacy."

46. Cohen, "Deliberation and Democratic Legitimacy"; Stephen Toulmin, *The Uses of Argument* (New York: Cambridge University Press, 1958).

47. Cohen, "Deliberation and Democratic Legitimacy," 408.

48. Harry Boyte, "Building the Commonwealth: Citizenship as Public Work," in *Citizen Competence and Democratic Institutions*, ed. Stephen L. Elkin and Karol Edward Soltan (University Park: Pennsylvania State University Press, 1999), 259–78.

49. Cohen, "Deliberation and Democratic Legitimacy"; Iris Marion Young, "Difference as a Resource for Democratic Communication," in *Deliberative Democracy*, ed. James Bohman and William Rehg, 383–406.

50. Hauser, *Vernacular Voices*, 82–110.

51. The publicity principle holds that there are reasons to doubt that representatives, on average, are wiser or more committed to the common good than the ordinary citizen. Luban explains as follows: "The empirical validity of the publicity principle turns not on whether the Many are ignorant or wrong-headed, but on whether their leaders are less ignorant or less wrong-headed. No doubt the Wise are few; and the leaders are few; but it hardly follows that the leaders are wise. Before we reject the publicity principle because the leaders know best, we must have reason to believe that the leaders know better. And to find that out, we must look carefully at the variety of mechanisms by which decision-making elites are actually selected. If actual selection mechanisms choose randomly

between the Many and the Wise, or affirmatively disfavor the Wise, then the foolishness of the many is irrelevant: the Few in official positions have no reason to suppose that their policy brainstorms are any less foolish." David Luban, "The Principle of Publicity," in *The Theory of Institutional Design*, ed. Robert E. Goodin (Cambridge: Cambridge University Press, 1996), 193.

52. The bonds of civil society are complex, involving three distinct but interrelated domains: economics, politics, and morals. In theory, economics-based accounts have tended to emphasize the self-regulation of free market relations; politics-based discussions have tended to emphasize the regulatory force of public opinion on the actions of the state, while morals-based inquiries have tended to emphasize the individual's role in judging conduct in concert with an internalized sense of socially negotiated norms. Despite their differing emphases, these discussions share an understanding of civil society as "a network of associations independent of the state whose members, through discursive exchanges that balance conflict and consensus, seek to regulate themselves in ways consistent with a valuation of difference" (Hauser, *Vernacular Voices*, 21). For discussion of these dimensions of civil society, see Benjamin Barber, *A Place for Us: How to Make Society Civil and Democracy Strong* (New York: Hill & Wang, 1998); Gerard A. Hauser, "Civil Society and the Principle of the Public Sphere," *Philosophy and Rhetoric* 31 (1998): 19–40; Francis Fukuyama, *Trust: The Social Virtues and the Creation of Prosperity* (New York: Free Press, 1995); A. O. Hirschman, *The Passions and the Interests: Political Arguments for Capitalism before Its Triumph* (Princeton, N.J.: Princeton University Press, 1977); Robert D. Putnam, *Making Democracy Work* (Princeton, N.J.: Princeton University Press, 1993); Adam Seligman, *The Idea of Civil Society* (New York: Free Press, 1992); Seligman, *The Problem of Trust* (Princeton, N.J.: Princeton University Press, 1997).

53. Alain Touraine, *What is Democracy*, trans. David Macey (Boulder, Colo.: Westview Press, 1997), 41–42.

54. Jonathan Schell, "Introduction," in *Adam Michnik, Letters from Prison and Other Essays*, trans. Maya Latynski (Berkeley: University of California Press, 1985), xvii–xxx.

55. Hannah Arendt, *The Origins of Totalitarianism*, 2nd enl. ed. (New York: Meridian, 1958).

56. Barber, *A Place for Us*, 6.

57. Hauser, "Civil Society and the Principle of the Public Sphere."

58. See Nancy Fraser, *Unruly Practices: Power, Discourse and Gender in Contemporary Social Theory* (Minneapolis: University of Minnesota Press, 1989); Fraser, "Re-

thinking the Public Sphere," in *The Phantom Public Sphere*, ed. Bruce Robbins (Minneapolis: University of Minnesota Press, 1993), 1–32.

59. Hauser, *Vernacular Voices*.

60. The workers' councils formed concurrently with the Hungarian uprising. Arendt's account is interesting on a number of levels, but especially in her observation that the practices of a free egalitarian political society were marked by the discord of different political interests, but avoided the stalemate of interminable political debate through discursive modes of resolution that permitted action in the world. Her account was mirrored two decades later when Vaclav Havel wrote of his expectations of a political society that both was united in its aspiration to be freed of the repression of post-totalitarian conditions, and that, once freed, would find citizens spontaneously forming political unions in which they would then do what free people always do: return to arguing with one another over matters of common concern on which they held differing opinions. See Arendt, *The Origins of Totalitarianism*, 492–502; Vaclav Havel, "Six Asides about Culture," trans. E. Kohák, in *Václav Havel: Living in Truth*, ed. Jan Vladislav (Boston: Faber and Faber, 1989), 123–35.

61. Alexis de Tocqueville, *Democracy in America*, 2 vols. (1835; New York: Vintage, 1990).

62. Robert D. Putnam, *Bowling Alone: The Collapse and Revival of American Community* (New York: Simon and Schuster, 2000).

63. Dodd, "Political Learning and Political Change."

64. Hauser and Benoit-Barné, "Reflections on Rhetoric, Deliberative Democracy, Civil Society, and Trust."

65. Niklas Luhmann, *Trust and Power* (New York: John Wiley and Sons, 1993), 10.

66. Charles Taylor, "Interpretation and the Sciences of Man," *Review of Metaphysics* 25 (1971): 3–51; Alain Touraine, *The Voice and the Eye*.

67. John Dewey, *The Public and Its Problems* (1927; Chicago: Swallow Press, 1954), 208.

68. Touraine, *What is Democracy.*

69. James Coleman, "Social Capital in the Creation of Human Capital," *American Journal of Sociology* 94 (1988): S98.

70. Claus Offe, "How Can We Trust Our Fellow Citizens?" in *Democracy and Trust*, ed. Mark Warren (New York: Cambridge University Press, 1999), 52. The reciprocity norm is interesting in that it depicts trust as a social resource as much as an individual one. If trust relationships create an obligation on the part of the trustee to keep her word, then one may opt to trust as a way to influence, at least tentatively, the outcome of a relationship. Furthermore, while the reciprocity

condition does not specifically address relationships of distrust, Benoit-Barné and I speculate that distrust is also a phenomenon of social reciprocity; that is, distrust generates more distrust. From this perspective, the benefits of trust and the cost of distrust are made obvious. Giving trust becomes a self-interested act with the positive social ramification of a win-win choice. Hauser and Benoit-Barné, "Reflections on Rhetoric, Deliberative Democracy, Civil Society, and Trust."

71. Putnam's (1993) study of regional governments in Italy, *Making Democracy Work,* is illustrative of how the vernacular rhetorical practices of citizens who participate in civil-society structures differ from those who do not. Putnam studied Italy's eighteen regional governments from their inception in 1970. His data spanned twenty years. Putnam found that participation in democratic processes could not be explained by socioeconomic indicators. Although levels of participation in civic life and the levels of trust in its processes correlated with a region's economic modernity, modernity could not explain civic performance. He did find a positive correlation between participation in associations and civic involvement. If people belonged to sports clubs, singing societies, literary guilds, philanthropic groups, commercial associations, or clubs of any sort, they also showed a greater tendency to participate in the civic affairs of the region. Importantly, the relationship had nothing to do with membership in a political party or participation in a political organization. Rather, the positive correlation was with participation in a community activity that gathers citizens who otherwise would have no reason to congregate. The lone exception to this pattern was membership in Catholic Church organizations, which, given the institutional authority the Church has traditionally held in Italy, carries ideological meaning that tends to encourage a political stance with strong allegiance to the Church's. His findings reinforce the conclusion that a person who participates in secondary associations is more likely to develop skills of cooperation and a sense of responsibility for collective enterprises.

72. Pierre Bordieu, *The Logic of Practice,* trans. Richard Nice (Stanford, Calif.: Stanford University Press, 1990); John Dryzek, *Discursive Democracy: Politics, Policy, and Political Science* (New York: Cambridge University Press, 1990); Hauser, *Vernacular Voices.*

73. I am indebted to the members of the University of Colorado at Boulder's Rhetoric Workshop, whose helpful criticisms and suggestions have been of enormous help in wrestling with the conceptual issues and forming the argument of this chapter. I alone am responsible for its contents.

Speaking Democratically in the Backwash of War: Lessons from Brigance on Rhetoric and Human Relations

Robert L. Ivie

William Norwood Brigance was a great speech teacher from whom we can take instruction and draw inspiration for the purpose of enriching democracy today. His contribution to the study of speech at Wabash College and to the field of rhetorical studies in the United States is large and enduring. Many communication educators of my generation were inspired by his teaching and scholarship; many of the next generation can benefit from his foresight and clarity of purpose.

Brigance's groundbreaking scholarship on Jeremiah Sullivan Black's surcharged logic in defense of the Bill of Rights and under the shadow of civil war fired my young imagination when I wrote an undergraduate honors paper many years ago for the annual rhetorical criticism conference at California State University, Hayward (now East Bay).[1] That inaugural paper launched a career of teaching and writing about rhetorical criticism on issues of war and peace. It led twenty-five years later to joining the rhetorical studies faculty at Indiana University, where Brigance's picture still hung prominently on the wall of the departmental library named in his honor. His palpable impact on J. Jeffery Auer's founding vision of graduate studies in public address was legendary at Indiana. Brigance's formative influence remains a true legacy to inspire new explorations of democracy's uncharted rhetorical terrain.

Indeed, it was this pioneering spirit of rhetorically engaging public affairs that brought me home, in a sense, to southern Indiana, where I discovered my Scots-Irish ancestors had settled in 1810. It was there that my great-great-great grandfather had served in the state legislature and had designed and built his family home to serve as a station on the Underground Railroad—a home that still stands occupied in Washington County. Coming home to Indiana, it turns out, was returning to the land of my great-great grandfather Frank Strain, who served the duration of the Civil War as a frontline foot soldier fighting, by his own account, to free his country forever from "the blight of human slavery."[2]

Hoosiers know a good deal about tornadoes, and something even about living in the vortex of politics—fighting for emancipation by day and harboring the Klan by night, raising Eugene Debs to campaign for labor and social justice while sending Albert Beveridge to the U.S. Senate to advocate for imperialism, or later, Senator William Ezra Jenner to serve as Joseph McCarthy's intemperate henchman during the darkest days of Cold War intolerance and paranoia. This was politically charged ground on which Professor Brigance spent a career teaching students to appreciate the role of persuasion and its importance to a democratic society.

Brigance was a patriot and a veteran of World War I who harbored a hatred for the catastrophe and senselessness of war.[3] He was also, and not coincidentally, a firm believer that a rhetorical education in the liberal arts was, in David Burns's words, "the best training for leadership in a democratic society."[4] From the 1920s through the 1950s, he wrote and spoke at the intersection of rhetoric, democracy, and war under titles such as the "Character of a Good Citizen," "Speech and War," "Speech Training in a Democracy," "Public Discussion in the Backwash of War," "Demagogues, 'Good' People, and Teachers of Speech," "Speech in the Liberal Arts Curriculum," and *Speech: Its Techniques and Discipline in a Free Society.*

Useful lessons might be drawn from Brigance's influential career of scholarly writing, undergraduate teaching, and public speaking about citizenship and rhetoric in a free society, particularly about speaking democratically in the backwash of war. The "single most important problem of democracy," Brigance believed, "on which its very life depends . . .

is that conflicting groups learn to live together."[5] Speech in a free and democratic society was to him first and foremost a discipline for improving bad human relations.[6] This was a worthy notion in its own time and remains an idea worth pondering. Revisiting Brigance's telling point about rhetoric's construction of healthy democratic relations as an alternative to chronic warfare is both timely and stimulating. This, I believe, is the heart of the matter and the kernel of a crucial insight that contemporary rhetorical scholarship should develop further into a peace-building pedagogy for a more democratic society.

Rhetoric, Democracy, and War

The most important lesson to draw from Brigance's teaching, the lesson of lessons, is how to cut to the heart of the matter when it concerns rhetoric and democracy. He understood democracy to be government by talk, and specifically a matter of settling our differences by talking them out rather than resorting to force.[7] Thus, rhetoric served democracy by producing public discourse that enhanced human relations. Unlike America's founders, who distrusted democracy and its ancient Athenian legacy and who wished to contain democracy within a republic ruled by elites speaking to one another, Brigance drew inspiration from a Greek pedagogy of educating people for citizenship.[8]

This was the kind of speech education, he argued in 1950, needed to enrich democratic culture and practice by the year 2000. Speech as a substantive curriculum in democratic relations was crucial now that film, radio, and television routinely carried human speech around the world, making it "the most powerful force that exists for mass education and thought stimulation."[9] The revolution of consequence in our political era, so far as Brigance was concerned, was that the common citizen was now empowered by the right to vote and by access to the mass media. Elites could no longer rule simply by addressing one another; leaders now had to speak to the mass of people as their primary audience. How they chose to meet that challenge would make all the difference in the life of modern democracy and would determine whether conflicting groups could learn to live peacefully together.[10]

Indeed, Brigance believed that the rise of the common citizen, not just in the United States but throughout the world, was a fact to which we must accommodate ourselves if democracy is to thrive as a system of government and if human differences are to be resolved by talk. The rise of communism, he suggested, was merely a surface manifestation of the real revolution of the mid-twentieth century. The real revolution was "the rise of the little man all over the world": "The little man, after the silence of the centuries, has come to power. To him leaders must report. From him leaders must gain consent. The creative minority of America, always outnumbered, is now outvoted. Henceforth, it must 'persuade or perish.'"[11]

Moreover, Brigance believed not only that radio and television were agents of this revolution, which transferred political power to the consent of the people, but also that these same mass media had "profoundly influence[d] the operating nature of democracy."[12] The mass public, he observed, was never "print-minded"; most people did not read much or read critically. They were instead an "ear-minded majority," and the revolution in telecommunications therefore not only had empowered the public but also, in his view, could give "impetus to the communication of serious ideas" and "make possible an alert, informed citizenry."[13]

Just as the power of the mass public was a contemporary fact of self-governance to which political leaders must adjust, the emergence of radio and television shaped the new reality of popular rule in a way that made possible the cultivation of ideas, the enrichment of public deliberation, and the enhancement of human relations, rather than a degradation of politics. Radio and television privileged an "ear-minded public" and required leaders to become skilled in public persuasion. Speechmaking, now more than ever, was inherent to a free society and to democratic governance, because radio and television had overcome the limitations of space and time to recreate an oral culture that enlarged the power of the mass public and transferred the balance of power from an elite minority to the voice of the people. Skilled rhetors could now speak directly to the masses through the electronic media. They would have to learn how to adapt their political speech to popular media and popular audiences, but the opportunity existed for enriching democratic practice through peaceful persuasion.

Indeed, speech was a substantive field of democratic endeavor, in Brigance's view. He called it "an intellectual discipline" that develops *"the ability to produce and manage ideas."*[14] Effective speaking was more than mere technique. For speakers to be popular meant that they must be

"understood by the people," not that speakers should be "careless in reasoning, weak in judgment, or irresponsible in talk."[15] Their job was to "alter
and promote thought. To water and cultivate ideas, hopes, sentiments and
enthusiasms in a way and to a degree that cannot be done while we are
separated one from another."[16] Brigance believed that the masses could
be persuaded, that they could be persuaded ethically to make decisions
reasonably, and that any failure to achieve such an outcome was a failure
of leadership, not a fault of the people; that is, it was a failure of leaders
to learn how to persuade.[17]

In taking this position, Brigance did not presume that the masses
were brilliant or intellectual, or that they were well informed or even
capable of adding ideas to the mix of public deliberation. He did, however,
credit the public—the mass of people, the ordinary citizenry—with "a
high degree of common sense," and declared them to be "excellent judges
of public policy, *if the leaders are equal to the task of persuasion that is implicit
in leadership.*"[18] Brigance understood that the people operate within a
limited frame of reference, that their thinking and intelligence develops
within "their way of life," and that they therefore can listen intelligently
to leaders who make sense of complex national and world affairs in the
ordinary terms of the public's experience, instead of in "the language of
the professional economist or specialist in management" or some other
discourse of expertise.[19] "The voice of the people is not the voice of God.
It is not infallible," Brigance insisted, but the people are competent, even
excellent, judges of public policy and able to exercise a remarkable degree
of common sense when public questions are "stripped of jargon and put
in plain language."[20]

By this measure, the ethos of democracy entails the prevalence of a
certain kind of speechmaking—speechmaking that helps people talk out
their differences, that is intellectually honest, that advances honest information and renders significant ideas in ordinary language, that arouses
listeners to reflect on public issues, and that lifts "the tone of discussion
above the level of name calling."[21] Yet it is also the case, as Brigance acknowledged, that speech is a dangerous form of power that can become
"an instrument of *tyranny*" when it assumes the forms of *"double-talk
and deception"* and resorts to "the techniques of the repeated 'Big Lie,'
character assassination, name-calling, the hysterical approach, and the
seductive slogan"—that is, when speech becomes warlike, propagandistic, and a weapon of "political assault" and hate.[22] Speech is inherent to

human society in general and to free society in particular, but it must be disciplined to the aim of improving human relations if it is to serve democratic purposes.

Here is where we confront what Brigance considered to be the greatest danger, the critical weakness, and the compelling challenge of our time: what he called "the universality of bad human relations." We are "illiterate" in "the realm of understanding people," he observed. The "relations among peoples of the world are marked by dangerous animosities, hatreds, suspicions, bigotries, and intolerances."[23] Peaceful persuasion is the only viable alternative to forceful domination, bribes, and threats if we are to have democratic relations and learn to solve human problems.[24] Yet, fear and hate and injustice persist in our time as the unwelcome "backwash of war."[25]

We live undemocratically to the extent that we live in the backwash of war, where speechmaking has become dangerous and totalitarian instead of peaceful and persuasive. Rhetoric constructs democratic relations, by Brigance's standard, only when it transcends the culture of war. "When a war is over," he warned in 1945, "a people do not stop hating. They merely transfer their hatred from the late enemy to someone else" at home or abroad, whether that someone else is, in his words, "the Negro" or "the Jew" or "Russia."[26] *"In the backwash of war,"* he observed, *"there is always the danger that you will become like the thing you fight against."*[27] When a nation fights a war against militarism, the backwash of such a war tends to make that nation militaristic, and "a free nation fighting totalitarianism tends to become totalitarian."[28] It suppresses freedom of thought out of fear for national security and tramples on the Constitution in an effort to establish a system of propaganda and thought control. Thus, the "critical danger . . . that we face in this backwash of war," Brigance warned, "is whether we can save ourselves from embarking upon a course that threatens to destroy the democracy that we fought . . . to preserve."[29] "We must take care," he insisted, "not to destroy democracy in our struggle to defend democracy."[30]

Brigance knew that "war only destroys . . . [and] never creates," that it increases misery and enlarges the enemy, and that it loses the struggle for minds because one can only win over people by peaceful persuasion.[31] War has been the choice of "white Christian people of Western democracies, with their arrogant sense of racial superiority," who must now learn to speak to the aspirations and ideas of others if they wish to prosper and survive.[32] They—that is, we—must shed "outworn concepts" such as "colonialism in foreign policy and exploitation of labor in domestic policy" that leave the masses "hungry, frustrated, desperate" and that put free societies in a state of "anxiety"—diminished, decaying, and tending toward demagoguery and totalitarianism.[33]

In a nutshell, Brigance advanced rhetoric as a substantive liberal art for producing and managing discourse that enhances human relations, which is the essence of democracy as he saw it. Toward that end, rhetoric should be made to construct discourses counter to hatred and fear of others so that conflicting groups might learn to live together in plural societies by talking through their differences rather than contesting them by force. In a healthy democracy, the creative minority must learn to provide leadership by means of ethical persuasion that respects the power and the judgment of the "ear-minded majority" of the people who have been politically empowered in an age of telecommunications. Ethical persuasion can enrich public deliberation under these circumstances by addressing complex issues honestly, and by rendering them accessible in ordinary language that is responsive to a competent public's frame of reference without devolving into the dangerous speech practices of name-calling, double-talk, and deception. Democracy exists in a discourse of peaceful persuasion; tyranny reduces rhetoric to a warlike form of political assault in which we become what we fight against: a frightened, hateful, intolerant, arrogant, racist, militaristic empire of tyranny, instead of a free and diverse people existing in democratic relations.

No wonder Brigance insisted that public persuasion, understood as speaking democratically to avoid the backwash of war, "is difficult, very difficult," but that a free people cannot govern themselves without such a discipline of speechmaking or system of public address.[34] The problem was that our schools "have failed to qualify citizens in this essential of democracy and we are paying the price for that failure." In a rhetorical pedagogy "that disciplines people in how to talk-it-out" and "discourages the demagogue technique of shooting-it-out with a war of words," we might foster effective public persuasion.[35] Ethical persuasion addressed to a popular audience is a difficult art to master, but a necessary discipline of free people who would govern themselves. If the masses cannot be persuaded, it is because their leaders have failed to persuade them and thereby proved themselves unequal to *"the task of persuasion that is implicit in leadership."*[36]

Renewing the Democratic Project

So how does this volume fare by Brigance's standard for rhetoric and democracy? Is it fair to say that it recovers the spirit of his project but also complicates his conception? That, I believe, is precisely the collective contribution of this volume to a revitalized study of democratic relations.

The value of returning our teaching and scholarship to a focus on rhetoric and democracy is made explicit in some chapters, and is at least implicit in others. Denise Bostdorff, for instance, explicitly calls on us to uphold the legacy of W. Norwood Brigance by returning rhetorical and communication education to a project of educating students for citizenship, instead of training them primarily for professional and commercial success. Bostdorff not only would have us revitalize the speech curriculum by making it politically relevant and engaged but also would have us serve as models ourselves by increasing our own involvement in the civic realm. In an age of highly polarized politics, she suggests, we should show students how to be politically engaged without becoming mean-spirited.

J. Michael Hogan would revive the tradition of constructive civic engagement and public deliberation through a return to the rhetorical pedagogy inspired by Brigance's basic notion that speech should exist in a free society to serve listeners, not speakers. However, this is not the reality of today, Hogan observes, in either political practice or rhetorical pedagogy. The responsibilities of citizenship are not currently the core concern of our public-speaking textbooks. Rhetorical scholarship and pedagogy could help revive public deliberation, for example, by rhetorical critics exploring the deceptions of demagogues as well as extracting from the history of public address useful models of constructive public deliberation. Hogan notes that this aim, consistent with the standard articulated by Brigance, must be pursued in a manner that takes into account certain changes reflecting our own time, such as growing diversity and new media techniques, but that the basic aim itself should guide our scholarship and teaching.

James Herrick calls on us to think anew about a rhetorical worldview that makes public rationality possible through deliberation, considers the public competent, and deems ethical standards appropriate to regulating public discourse. Importantly, he describes the Lithuanian critique of Western patterns of rhetoric as characterized by a radical individualism and inflated egoism that makes speechmaking and rhetoric a less venerable skill and a less appealing practice. We must learn, in short, that the successful emergence of new democracies requires a culturally appropriate education in rhetorical theory and practice.

Yes, we do seem inclined to recover a focus on rhetoric as a study and practice of democratic citizenship, with an emphasis on educating our students for constructive civic engagement, but also with an awareness that we need to update and refine our understanding of what that entails under present circumstances. We may even be willing in some cases to consider making a personal example of civic engagement in our own teaching and scholarship. This is the course of public scholarship, according to Martin Medhurst's account of formative intellectual influences on the field of rhetorical studies, that Brigance is largely responsible for pioneering. Indeed, as Medhurst observes, Brigance was himself a public intellectual who wrote for popular forums and interdisciplinary audiences, and from whom the field's contemporary engagement of the public sphere derives legitimacy as well as inspiration. Brigance's abiding commitment as a teacher-scholar-citizen was foremost to democracy, which he believed rested on a substantive practice of public discussion and a liberal art of peaceful persuasion.

Besides rededicating rhetorical studies to democratic citizenship in the spirit of enriching the practice of public deliberation under changing circumstances, contributors to this volume also are inclined to expand and complicate Brigance's take on key notions of deliberation, rhetoric, and media. Gerard Hauser, in particular, encourages us to rethink the notion of deliberative democracy as a fusion of theory and practice, a conception and enactment of power, a rhetorical performance and agonistic practice that deploys inventional resources in conflictive relationships. Hauser would direct our attention to the vernacular, quotidian, and micropractices of rhetoric that operate from the bottom up to construct a more participatory politics. These practices encompass a plurality of perspectives and can produce arguments that achieve deliberative inclusion without insisting on a consensus. He would theorize a speaking public that is rhetorically more active than Brigance's image of a public that is competent enough to judge the persuasive appeals of political leaders, but not capable of adding their own ideas to the mix of public deliberations.

Other contributors would further complicate Brigance's notion of rhetorical practice and political power. Stephen Hartnett and Greg Goodale's study of the Defense Science Board as a powerful engine of U.S. propaganda and corrosive influence on deliberative democracy underscores the importance of taking more fully into account institutional frameworks that structure presidential rhetoric specifically and political discourse generally. Speakers should be considered more like nodal points than points of origin, they conclude, and rhetorical critics should drop naive assumptions of heroic agency in order to attend to the institutional forces that drive regimes of imperial propaganda in the deliberately misleading name of freedom and democracy.

Shawn Parry-Giles complicates matters as well by raising a question of whether contemporary campaign rhetoric can serve the ends of democratic deliberation, given its propensity to target primarily undecided voters in battleground states, and to do so in a manner that constitutes a hypermasculinized citizenry with limited political power in a wartime context. Noting that nationalism operates divisively in this context as a form of white identity politics, Parry-Giles recognizes the need for a rhetoric of inclusion and diversity. She leaves us with a powerful example of such a thoroughly corrupted rhetorical culture that one must at least wonder whether we can hope to approach Brigance's democratic standard of speaking to improve bad human relations.

Finally, David Zarefsky warns that we must learn to reconcile the two faces of democratic rhetoric if we are to enhance public deliberation by making rhetoric its instrument rather than its threat. Just as politics exists because of human fallibility, and democracy is the political system that acknowledges the necessity of error, rhetoric is the civic discourse for making decisions collectively without the benefit of certainty. Healthy deliberative rhetoric, though, can degrade into a tool of polarizing demagoguery and question-begging propaganda, Zarefsky warns, becoming a technique of manipulation rather than an invitation to deliberation, especially in a prolonged period of crisis and during an open-ended war on terrorism. A rhetorical education for enhancing democratic communication requires, therefore, a pedagogy that addresses significant public issues substantively and prepares students to become deliberative members of a decision-making public.

Clearly, these authors have recognized and accepted the added challenge of carrying forward Brigance's project of peaceful democratic persuasion in today's increasingly corrupted political culture. A war culture that is even more resistant to democracy than before has evolved in an

age of globalization and imperialism. It is marked by renewed demagoguery that operates within institutional frameworks of political power
and deploys new media types and refined technologies to distort public
discourse. Present circumstances require the articulation of a rhetorically
more active public, a more participatory citizenry, a bottom-up democratic practice that is more inclusive and respectful of diversity and less
dependent on elites, and a public ethic that acknowledges differences of
perspective, is less ethnocentric, and resists the conflation of rationality
with consensus and quiescence.

The Heart of the Matter

In affirming Brigance's conception of rhetoric as a substantive discipline
of democratic governance, we are confronted with a serious agenda for
research and teaching at a critical moment in which the American polity
risks succumbing to the backwash of war and thus becoming the very
image of its enemy. How does a nation transcend a culture of war and
avoid constituting verbally and visually a politics of hate and fear, an at-
titude of coercion, and a practice of deception? How do we make democracy into more than a hollow rationalization of wars of empire? What do
our critiques and conceptualizations of democratic rhetoric reveal about
adapting to and transforming the public's frame of reference? About
bridging differences without effacing identities? About improving human
relations? Or, in Brigance's terms, about becoming literate in understanding people?

I do not believe we have lost sight of, or that we no longer are in
touch with, the question of improving human relations, but I do think we
have yet to make it the focus and framework—the heart and soul—of our
democratic endeavors, if Brigance is to be the measure and inspiration of
our scholarship and teaching.

I agree that rhetoric operates in a more complex political culture
than Brigance knew, but he did underscore the continuing, indeed increased, relevance of peace-building rhetoric to democracy and collective
self-rule under such conditions, and warned us against the ever-present
danger of succumbing to a rhetoric of assault. I agree that rhetorical critics
should expose the deceptions of demagogues and seek historical models
of healthy public deliberation—as, for example, in the Progressive forum

movement. I agree that our courses in public speaking—and throughout the rhetorical curriculum, for that matter—should make education for democratic citizenship the core concern. I agree that rhetorical studies should effect a fusion of theory and praxis on matters of democratic agonistics in vernacular as well as formal discourses, in civil society as well as state politics, in participatory and deliberative modes, and with an added capacity for accommodating a plurality of perspectives. I agree that we are challenged to adapt to a changing mediascape and increased diversity.

But I wonder if we have yet to look the beast directly in the eye. It is difficult to imagine how to address and respect the democratic Other within a political culture that is as demophobic as ours.[37] The myth of the distempered demos is deeply ingrained in our political history and Constitution. If rhetoric is a substantive discipline of democratic governance—that is, governance by talk, as Brigance insisted, and a discipline of producing and managing discourses for dealing constructively with our differences—then it must confront the engrained metaphor of disease that makes us so distrustful of the people and so unwilling to trust in their common sense and potential for exercising good judgment. If we assume that politics is rhetoric of one kind or another, and that there is no alternative to rhetoric, per se—no politics sans (above or beyond) rhetoric—then we must concern ourselves directly, immediately, and primarily with the compelling and recurring challenge of rhetorical invention: What ways of speaking can we develop and deploy to overcome our fear of the Other within and without, to transform enemy relations into constructive relations among contesting parties, to enact a democratic rhetoric of consubstantial rivalry that bridges differences without effacing identities in a pluralistic society and diverse-but-interconnected world?

Democracy at its best is an ongoing politics of contestation that aspires, as Chantal Mouffe has argued, to transform antagonistic into agonistic relations—a politics of agonistic pluralism that requires the agency of rhetoric to reach agreements and to fashion solutions through persuasion, short of seeking a full consensus or complete reconciliation that would eliminate or suppress continuing conflict over competing interests. This is the importance, she suggests, "of re-creating, in politics, the connection with the great tradition of rhetoric."[38]

Peace-building persuasion, from this perspective, cannot be viewed as the elimination of conflict, but instead, consistent with Kenneth Burke's take on a democratically inclined rhetoric, it must function as a continuous process of constructing strategies of identification to bridge the human divide. Rather than "deny the presence of strife, enmity, faction" in human relations or ignore the partisanship of rhetoric, Burke sees war as a disease of cooperation and communion, and thus a perversion of peace.[39] In peace-building rhetoric, "identification is compensatory to division," so that the two work "ambiguously together" rather than one supplanting the other.[40]

Working within the rhetorical tradition of democratic agonistics, Michel de Certeau adds an important emphasis on tactics, which are especially relevant to managing partisan relations from the vantage point of the weak.[41] In an era of continuing warfare in which elites strategically occupy positions of power and a deficit of participatory politics prevails among common citizens,[42] the tactics of dissent just may be the quintessentially democratic practice to which rhetorical scholarship and teaching should direct special attention.[43] The primary task of peace-building, democratic tactics of dissent—tactics that would resist the orthodoxy of war—is not simply to debunk war, but to advance strategically, piece by piece, a rehumanizing image of enemies, thereby enunciating an alternative framework of meaning.[44]

The tactical metaphorical migrations involved in strategically reconceptualizing sheer enemies into consubstantial rivals must also retrieve the inner enemy, which is readily projected onto outer enemies. The rhetorical critique and transformation of this troubled cultural formation—which tropes democracy as a dangerous disease of the masses and attempts to contain it as the symbolic equivalent of quelling an external enemy's savagery—is a necessary constituent of any peace-building turn from war. Although democracy continues to make a strong claim on national identity, it remains, in Sheldon Wolin's word, a "fugitive" rather than a vibrant and strongly embraced political practice; something to be managed when necessary and ignored where possible; a weak, eviscerated conception and mythic construction that "legitimates the very formations of power which have enfeebled it."[45]

Brigance insisted that democratic rhetoric and ethical persuasion are difficult, very difficult, to produce. Dangerous, demagogic rhetoric seems to operate as the political equivalent of gravity, that is, as the default condition of hateful, coercive, undemocratic politics.[46] To meet the challenge Brigance has set out for us, then, we need to turn our refinements of his rhetorical model into a productive practice that resists the backwash of war and aims to keep us from becoming our own demophobic enemy. As Zarefsky writes, "Reconciling the two faces of democratic rhetoric, making rhetoric democracy's instrument rather than its threat, demands no less of us."[47]

Thus, we have arrived where a half century earlier Brigance might well have had us begin, suggesting that the rhetorical heart of the democratic matter can be addressed directly only when we overtly transform our scholarship and teaching into an art of peace-building persuasion and constructive cultural critique, when we ourselves become practitioners of rhetorical invention for the purpose of talking rather than fighting through our serious differences. That is a genuinely difficult challenge that puts to the test Brigance's basic premise that rhetoric is a worthy subject to teach and a basic requirement of democracy.

NOTES

1. The notion of surcharged logic was Brigance's way of summing up Black's distinguishing style of speaking in which "he never appealed to mere passions, yet there was always a powerful emotional drive behind his arguments. Indeed, one of his great sources of power sprang from a rare ability to unite argument with the springs of action in human beings. He could premise logic upon impelling motives. . . . When he had finished, not only had he impelled the mind to accept his logic as true but he had aroused emotions to *want* what the mind proclaimed as true. But this was not *argumentum ad populum*. It was logic surcharged." William Norwood Brigance, "Jeremiah S. Black," in *A History and Criticism of American Public Address*, vol. 1, ed. William Norwood Brigance (New York: McGraw-Hill, 1943), 475. See also William Norwood Brigance, *Jeremiah Sullivan Black: Defender of the Constitution and the Ten Commandments* (Philadelphia: University of Pennsylvania Press, 1934).

2. Franklin Strain, *A Family Matter: A Brief Story of the Strain Family and Incidents in the Life of Frank Strain* (Phillipsburg, Kans.: Privately printed and undated).

3. David George Burns, "The Contributions of William Norwood Brigance to the Field of Speech," Ph.D. diss., Indiana University, 1970, 369.

4. Ibid., 378.

5. William Norwood Brigance, *Speech: Its Techniques and Disciplines in a Free Society* (New York: Appleton-Century-Crofts, 1952), 536.

6. Ibid., 180.

7. William Norwood Brigance, "Speech as a Democratic Educational System," *School Executive* 64 (April 1950): 47.

8. William Norwood Brigance, "General Education in an Industrial Free Society," *Quarterly Journal of Speech* 38 (April 1952): 178.

9. Brigance, "Speech as a Democratic Educational System," 47.

10. Brigance, *Speech*, 536.

11. Brigance, "General Education," 179, 181.

12. Ibid., 182; Brigance, *Speech*, 458.

13. Brigance, "General Education," 182–83.

14. Brigance, *Speech*, 19. Emphasis in original.

15. Ibid., xiii. Emphasis in original.

16. Ibid., xvi.

17. Ibid., 531.

18. Ibid., 531. Emphasis in original.

19. Ibid., 532.

20. Ibid., 460–61.

21. William Norwood Brigance, "Demagogues, 'Good' People, and Teachers of Speech," *The Speech Teacher* 1 (September 1952): 160; also see 162.

22. Brigance, *Speech*, ix, 432–33. Emphasis in original.

23. Brigance, "General Education," 180.

24. W. Norwood Brigance, "Security Is an Illusion," *Vital Speeches* 17 (15 July 1951): 528, 595.

25. W. Norwood Brigance, "The Backwash of War," *Vital Speeches* 12 (1 December 1945): 107.

26. Ibid.

27. Ibid. Emphasis in original.

28. Brigance, "Backwash," 107; Brigance, "Security," 596.

29. Brigance, "Backwash," 107.

30. Brigance, "Security," 596.

31. Ibid., 595.

32. Ibid., 595–96.

33. Ibid., 594.

34. Brigance, "General Education," 181; see also Brigance, "Demagogues," 158.

35. Brigance, "Demagogues," 160, 161.

36. Brigance, *Speech*, 531. Emphasis in original.

37. On this point, see Robert L. Ivie, *Democracy and America's War on Terror* (Tuscaloosa: University of Alabama Press, 2005).

38. Chantal Mouffe, *The Return of the Political* (London: Verso, 1993), 130; Chantal Mouffe, *The Democratic Paradox* (London: Verso, 2000), 94–105; Chantal Mouffe, *On the Political* (New York: Routledge, 2005), 2–4.

39. Kenneth Burke, *A Rhetoric of Motives* (1950; Berkeley: University of California Press, 1969), 20–23, 43–44.

40. Ibid., 25.

41. Michel de Certeau, *The Practice of Everyday Life*, trans. Steven Rendall (Berkeley: University of California Press, 1984), 34–42.

42. See, for example, Jeffery C. Isaac, *Democracy in Dark Times* (Ithaca, N.Y.: Cornell University Press, 1998), and Robert D. Putnam, *Bowling Alone: The Collapse and Revival of American Community* (New York: Simon & Schuster, 2000).

43. Robert L. Ivie, "Democratic Dissent and the Trick of Rhetorical Critique," *Cultural Studies <=> Critical Methodologies* 5 (2005): 276–93.

44. Robert L. Ivie, "Academic Freedom and Antiwar Dissent in a Democratic Idiom," *College Literature* 33 (2006): 80.

45. Sheldon S. Wolin, *Politics and Vision: Continuity and Innovation in Western Political Thought*, expanded ed. (Princeton, N.J.: Princeton University Press, 2004), 601.

46. On this point, see Tom De Luca and John Buell, *Liars! Cheaters! Evildoers! Demonization and the End of Civil Debate in American Politics* (New York: New York University Press, 2005). They look toward achieving a democracy without demons, one that is more inclusive, respectful, egalitarian, and participatory.

47. David Zarefsky, "Two Faces of Democratic Rhetoric" (this volume), 134.

Contributors

Denise M. Bostdorff is professor of communication and associate dean for the Class of 2012 at The College of Wooster in Wooster, Ohio. She is the author of *The Presidency and the Rhetoric of Foreign Crisis* (1994) and *Proclaiming the Truman Doctrine: The Cold War Call to Arms* (2008), along with scholarly and pedagogical essays related to political rhetoric. Among her passions in life is teaching undergraduates in the small liberal arts college setting.

Greg Goodale is an assistant professor in the communication studies department at Northeastern University and was formerly an attorney, congressional aide, and lobbyist in Washington, D.C. He employs his political and legal experience to research American citizenship, government, and the manipulation of images and sounds in the twentieth century.

Stephen John Hartnett is associate professor and chair of the department of communication at the University of Colorado at Denver. His most recent books are *Globalization and Empire: The U.S. Invasion of Iraq,*

Free Markets, and The Twilight of Democracy (2006) and *Incarceration Nation: Investigative Prison Poems of Hope and Terror* (2004). His *Democratic Dissent & The Cultural Fictions of Antebellum America* (2002) won the National Communication Association's Winans and Wichelns Memorial Award for Distinguished Scholarship in Rhetoric and Public Address.

Gerard A. Hauser is College Professor of Distinction at the University of Colorado at Boulder. He is editor of *Philosophy and Rhetoric.* His publications include *Introduction to Rhetorical Theory,* 2nd ed. (2002) and *Vernacular Voices: The Rhetoric of Publics and Public Spheres* (1999). He is past president of the Rhetoric Society of America and recipient of its George Yoos Distinguished Service Award. He is an RSA Fellow and an NCA Distinguished Scholar. His current research focuses on vernacular rhetorics of resistance.

James A. Herrick is the Guy Vander Jagt Professor of Communication at Hope College in Holland, Michigan. He is the author of six books and a number of scholarly articles and reviews. His research interests include the history of rhetoric, new religious movements, the rhetoric of popular culture, and the ethics of rhetoric. He is a founding member of the Baylor University Press series in rhetoric and religion. During the spring semester of 2004 he lived and taught in Lithuania, and has since traveled extensively in the Baltic region.

J. Michael Hogan is professor of rhetoric and co-director of the Center for Democratic Deliberation at the Pennsylvania State University. He is the author, coauthor, or editor of six books and some fifty articles, book chapters, and reviews. He has won a number of scholarly awards, including the Winans-Wichelns Award for Distinguished Scholarship in Rhetoric and Public Address and the Penn State Alumni Association's Distinction in the Humanities Award. He has served on the editorial boards of the *Quarterly Journal of Speech* and *Rhetoric & Public Affairs,* and he is co-director of an undergraduate educational initiative funded by the National Endowment for the Humanities, "Voices of America: The U.S. Oratory Project."

Robert L. Ivie is professor of rhetoric and public culture in the department of communication and culture at Indiana University, Bloomington, where he is also a member of the faculties of American studies, cultural studies, and myth studies and the steering committee of the Indiana Democracy Consortium. His teaching and research focus on rhetoric as a mode of political critique and cultural production, with particular emphasis on democracy, the problem of war, and peace-building communication. His most recent books are *Dissent from War* (2007) and *Democracy and America's War on Terror* (2005). He has served as department chair at Indiana University and as editor of *Communication and Critical/Cultural Studies* and *Quarterly Journal of Speech*.

Todd F. McDorman is associate professor and chair of the department of rhetoric at Wabash College in Crawfordsville, Indiana. His primary research interest is the study of legal discourse and the ways various discourse communities engage the law with respect to social and political change. His work has appeared in outlets including the *Quarterly Journal of Speech, Southern Communication Journal, Communication and Critical/Cultural Studies, Women's Studies in Communication, Journal of Sport and Social Issues,* and *Council for Undergraduate Research Quarterly*.

Martin J. Medhurst is Distinguished Professor of Rhetoric and Communication and professor of political science at Baylor University in Waco, Texas. He is the author or editor of thirteen books, including *Before the Rhetorical Presidency, The Rhetorical Presidency of George H. W. Bush,* and *Presidential Speechwriting* (with Kurt Ritter). In 2005 Professor Medhurst was named a Distinguished Scholar of the National Communication Association.

Shawn J. Parry-Giles is a professor in the department of communication and director of the Center for Political Communication and Civic Leadership at the University of Maryland. She is the author or co-author of three books: *The Prime-Time Presidency: The West Wing and U.S. Nationalism, Constructing Clinton,* and *The Rhetorical Presidency, Propaganda, and the Cold War, 1945–1955*.

David M. Timmerman is associate professor of rhetoric and chair of the Division of Humanities and Fine Arts at Wabash College in Crawfordsville, Indiana. His scholarship has focused primarily on the development of rhetoric in Greece in the fourth century B.C.E. His work has appeared in *Philosophy and Rhetoric, Rhetoric Society Quarterly, Advances in the History of Rhetoric, Argumentation and Advocacy, Presidential Studies Quarterly,* and *Political Communication.*

David Zarefsky is Owen L. Coon Professor of Communication Studies at Northwestern University. He is the author of *President Johnson's War on Poverty: Rhetoric and History* and *Lincoln, Douglas, and Slavery: In the Crucible of Public Debate,* both of which received the National Communication Association's Winans-Wichelns Award for Distinguished Scholarship in Rhetoric and Public Address. He is the author or editor of an additional six books and over 75 articles and book chapters. He is a former president of both the National Communication Association and the Rhetoric Society of America and has received the NCA's Distinguished Scholar Award.

Index